THE GERMAN-AMERICAN ENCOUNTER

THE GERMAN-AMERICAN ENCOUNTER

Conflict and Cooperation between Two Cultures, 1800–2000

Edited by

Frank Trommler

and

Elliott Shore

Berghahn Books

NEW YORK • OXFORD

Published in 2001 by

Berghahn Books

www.berghahnbooks.com

Library of Congress Cataloging-in-Publication Data

The German-American encounter: conflict and cooperation between two
cultures, 1800–2000 / edited by Frank Trommler, Elliott Shore
    p. cm.
Includes bibliographical references and index.
ISBN 1-57181-240-7
    1. United States–Relations–Germany. 2. Germany–Relations–United
States. 3. German Americans–History. 4. German Americans–Social
conditions. 5. United States–Ethnic relations. 6. Germany–Civilization–
American influences. 7. United States–Civilization–German influences.
I. Trommler, Frank, 1939–   II. Shore, Elliott, 1951–

E183.8.G3 G472 2001
303.48'273043—dc21   00-045547

British Library Cataloguing in Publication Data

A catalogue record for this book is available from
the British Library.

Printed in the United States on acid-free paper

CONTENTS

ILLUSTRATIONS

PREFACE

This volume is based on papers and discussions that were part of the conference "The Future of German-American History," which re-examined important phases of the German-American encounter in view of their significance for a common future. The culminating event of a five-year project of restoring and cataloguing the largest private German-American library in the United States, the conference was held April 15–17, 1999 in the landmark building of the oldest German-American society, the German Society of Pennsylvania in Philadelphia. The conference brought together participants from Germany and the United States and from other lands interested in helping to document, at an important historical moment, the state of this encounter.

The editors found that there is no such thing as a useful monolithic interpretation of German-American relations. The conference participants and the papers that make up this volume constitute an acknowledged and even invited set of contradictions. We see this volume as a contribution to an on-going conversation, or perhaps better, an ongoing cultural translation. We have tried to provide an edge along which the reader can follow the contours of the discussion, both in the general introduction and in the section introductions. But each piece remains at a different angle, and all contribute to the larger discussion.

Throughout the volume, we have attempted a certain consistency in the use of the term "German American." When it refers to people, we use it without a hyphen, as in "German Americans" or "German American workers." It only appears as "German-American" when used as an adjective, or when the original source that we are quoting used a hyphen. All of the translations in the individual chapters are by the chapter authors unless otherwise indicated.

The editors wish to thank the Fritz Thyssen Stiftung, Cologne, the Max Kade Foundation, New York, the University of Pennsylvania, and the German Society of Pennsylvania for their generous support of the conference; Bryn Mawr College for its assistance with the conference and the volume; Bettina Hess at the German Society Library and Kelly McCullough of Bryn Mawr College for help in providing illustrative material; and Maria Sturm for her translations and editorial comments. Above all, the editors thank Srijana Chettri whose editorial assistance made this volume a reality.

INTRODUCTION

The relationship of the United States with Germany has undergone tremendous change since the nineteenth century. At the threshold to the twenty-first century, integration of unified Germany in post–Cold War Europe and the new globalization trends radically transform transatlantic dynamics in ways that make the re-evaluation of the transatlantic relationship necessary. Although the weight of common history on these developments is often invoked, it is rarely analyzed beyond the immediate past, let alone since the nineteenth century. While Germans, the largest immigrant group in the United States, contributed to the shaping of American society and left their mark on many areas from religion and education to food, farming, and political and intellectual life, Americans have been instrumental in shaping German democracy after World War II. Each side can claim to be part of the other country's history, and yet the question arises whether this claim indicates more than a historical interlude in the forming of the Atlantic civilization.

This book takes its cue from the spirit of reevaluation of history that has accompanied the transition from the twentieth to the twenty-first century.[1] Part of a wave of unconventional reflections about how to come to terms with a century of both unparalleled progress and barbarism and what to expect from the new millennium, *The German-American Encounter: Conflict and Cooperation Between Two Cultures, 1800–2000* uses the opportunity to reframe the parameters of the German-American encounter, extending them beyond the last fifty years. It includes the experience in the nineteenth century, when mass immigration from German-speaking countries became the basis for an unusually broad influx of German ideas and cultural practices into American daily life.

While Germans looked for a better life in the New World, young Americans pursued the encounter with the Old World by enrolling in German universities. Almost ten thousand American students studied in Germany when their own institutions could not yet compete. They returned with doctorates and diplomas in many disciplines, particularly in medicine and the sciences but also in history and other humanities. A considerable number became professors themselves, like George Bancroft, who applied his apprenticeship as a young historian at Göttingen University to writing the first comprehensive history of the United States.

These transatlantic crossings of people and ideas are at the core of the German-American encounter. Until the early twentieth century, there was much less political give and take between American and German governments than between those of the United States and Britain or France. Even after the German unification of 1871 official contacts were sparse. Neither the German middle classes nor the political elites pursued an active exchange with the United States. Agents of the American connection were mainly the lower classes, for whom emigration represented a much-debated alternative to their present life, or opposition groups like the socialists, especially during their harsh treatment under Bismarck, or the liberals and democrats of the Revolution of 1848/49. The revolutionary parliament of Frankfurt took inspiration from the American model of democracy. After the failure of their attempts to create a German democracy, thousands of political refugees from Germany and Austria, the forty-eighters, engaged in the progressive politics before, during, and after the Civil War.

Given the lack of interest in the United States on the part of German middle classes and the sparse attention on the part of governments except for the question of emigration, the relationship with the United States appears to have been a rather marginal affair in nineteenth-century Germany, in contrast to the considerable engagement with Germans and German thought in the United States. Alexander von Humboldt's positive understanding of the United States remained an exception among German intellectuals who followed Hegel's negative views about the country.[2] This attitude began to change after 1900 when industrialists, businessmen, engineers, and segments of the younger generation rode the wave of enthusiasm for the United States that crossed Europe and led to the perception that the industrial future was already taking shape in the New World. Yet despite many contacts in the realm of technological and industrial cultures, it took another half century before the cultural and political elites overcame their reservations, even condescension, vis-à-vis the United States, which had been in part responsible for the left-handed military confrontation in two wars. From the other side of the Atlantic, Germany gained a peculiar status as a competitor and enemy in this period which obliterated many of the earlier bonds and communalities. This status quickly faded from view when the political antagonism abated.

A profile of the German-American relationship that does not reflect upon the discontinuities and the strange dialectic of cultural, economic, and political engagement of these two societies seems to miss the essence of this relationship. While the assumption of a coherent mutual history is beneficial for current relations, the understanding of its inconsistencies might be more helpful in asserting the points of broadly based contacts between the societies and their interests. It might even inspire historians of the United States to reverse their neglect of the German connection in their studies of the emergence of an American identity in the nineteenth and early twentieth centuries.

This volume addresses the discontinuities with a new look at those periods in which the presence of the people of one country in the other shaped politics and identities, establishing a sense of interconnectedness that has served both countries well. Instead of reconsidering the historic sequence of mutual images and stereotypes that legitimizes much current research, the authors engage with actual contributions, discussing the weight and accessibility of positive histories for yet another century.

Great inspiration comes from Kathleen Conzen's bold reconsideration of contributionism. Conzen, who, at the Tricentennial Conference in 1983, a comprehensive assessment of German-American relations since 1683, provided a key to a new understanding of the German Americans with the concept of "invention of ethnicity,"[3] proposes to do away with the old practice of placing contributionism beside filiopietism, by which the complex interference of the largest ethnic group in the social and cultural integration of the United States could not be understood. She seizes this moment of renewed interest in the contributions that immigrants make to their host societies, something that has become an international concern with the new migration waves since the end of the Cold War. Conzen's redefinition is also motivated by the concern about the current multicultural challenge to the concept of American identity that developed under a unifying paradigm in the nineteenth century, taking inspiration from the homogenizing cultural agenda of the Germans.

Continuities and Discontinuities

As much as this volume reflects on the discontinuities in the contacts between Americans and Germans, it recognizes the aura with which Alexis de Tocqueville endowed the continuous comparison of Europe and America. To the pleasure of historians who consider the creation of grand narratives their discipline's most important mission, the Tocquevillian juxtaposition of the two continents has always found a receptive audience, although the distribution of positive and negative characteristics varied widely.[4] Though fully invested in the knowledge that no society stays the same in the course of one or two centuries, historians have seldom challenged the European-American antithesis as a consistent element of Western identity. In fact, Tocqueville's sense for the ironic has made recognition of the continuities attractive since it also leaves space for the tragic.[5] It takes much history to allow the sense of irony to unfold. Only after World War II, after America's full commitment to the rebuilding of Western Europe and German democracy, could a statement like this by Ralf Dahrendorf be made and understood: "In a different form, Europe today gets back the enlightenment which it sent across the Atlantic two centuries ago; and it doesn't like it."[6] A few decades later, the antithesis is again put to use, though in reverse direction toward America, by Europeans who try to construct an identity for a unified Europe.

Again, it is carried less by governments which guard their arrangements with the last remaining superpower but rather by popular perception, the media, and social groups.

Though part of the traditional Old World-New World antagonism, the German-American encounter has its special history of discontinuities. Having supplied the largest immigrant group in nineteenth-century America, which contributed widely to the emergence of a self-sufficient, yet culturally challenged society, Germany came to represent a great adversarial potential at a particular point in America's rise to power. Daniel Boorstin, who gave the classical description of the usefulness of the European-American antagonism for the development of American identity, typically overlooked the specific role of Germans and German Americans in the process of America's turn to full participation in international politics.[7] It was the step from stressing the distance to Europe in order to build a national identity to engaging in confrontations with a European nation with the same purpose.

This event occurred at the very moment in the beginning of the twentieth century when both countries encountered each other politically and militarily during their ambitious drive to become world powers. It eradicated the German Americans as a distinct cultural and ethnic group. It also radically diminished the high standing of the German language in the educational agenda, especially in high schools and colleges, during the course of World War I. Once the loyalty of this ethnic group—which, to a large extent, had integrated into American society—was officially challenged, their political awakening could only lead to disaster, namely to the accusation of having become a fifth column for the German Reich. Squeezed between the Reich's preposterous claims of its worldwide use of Germans to propagate its course and Wilson's interest in entering the war on the allied side, the German Americans, in 1917, were pushed and pulled into a political, ethnic, and cultural limbo from which they were able to emerge only by reneging their traditions and identities.

The case has rested in the larger frame of American and German historiography, which was much more concerned with Wilson's foreign policy decisions as a reflection of American ambitions to internationalize its political role. In turn, German-American historiography, focused on the ethnic demise, rarely reconnected the case with the fundamental shifts in the conduct of international politics in the early twentieth century. Little attention was paid to the ways in which the engagement of the United States in its self-declared international mission was still predicated on a confirmation of its insularity. While the Germans initiated war provocations with unrestricted submarine warfare, the sinking of the *Lusitania*, and several acts of military sabotage, the Americans initiated their first part of the war with Germany by advancing the German Americans as the enemy within their coastlines. This emotional and widely supported move, while playing up the insularity in its expressions of both strength and vulnerability, became an unusual rite of passage into the military

FIGURE 1. Visit of German Warships to New York Harbor in 1912

Liberty greets Germania, Germania greets Liberty. At the occasion of a visit of German warships to New York on 9–13 June 1912, the allegorical meeting of the two nations, complete with their respective eagles and the rising sun of hope, foreshadowed less peaceful encounters in the twentieth century. (German Society of Pennsylvania)

conflict with a European nation that was to be fought, different from the confrontation with Spain in 1898, on the European battlefield. In other words, the confrontation was reflected as an undermining of the insular position, a scenario that played itself out again with the Japanese and the Japanese Americans in World War II, and yet again in the ideological suspicions of the McCarthy era and the Cold War.

Randolph Bourne's often quoted dispute with his teacher John Dewey illuminates the intellectual birthing pains of American exceptionalist self-empowerment. When Bourne, in "War and the Intellectuals" and "Twilight of Idols," criticized Dewey for his decision to embrace Wilson's pro-war policy, he expressed his misgivings about mixing pragmatist ideas with the aims of nationalists and militarists. Bourne wrote against using the war against Germany for a confirmation of democratic principles without distinguishing this practice from the policy of the Right. "If the war is too strong for you to prevent," he asked Dewey in 1917, "how is it going to be weak enough for you to control and mould to your liberal purposes?"[8] Bourne distanced himself from war-mongering Germans but pointed to the usefulness of German ideals, which Dewey denounced in *German Philosophy and Politics*. At this time Dewey had made his decision. It was as much a decision about intellectual self-empowerment as about the flaws of German thinking. He confirmed that the hostile engagement with things German in World War I publicly reproduced the steps toward self-recognition as a new and exceptional society.

Bourne found successors in exposing the contradictions of American moral self-empowerment, especially during and after World War II. Nothing, however, did more to renew and intensify the adversarial projection of the Germans than the images of horror and inhumanity that came out of the encounter of American soldiers with the concentration camps in 1945. Although the war against Nazi Germany was fought in the name of liberty and democracy—a decisive confirmation of the mission of the earlier war—these images renewed and perpetuated the outrage over Germans as the ultimate challengers of humanity that the sinking of the *Lusitania* in 1915 had provoked. As the history of the Holocaust awareness in the United States shows, the outrage has been institutionalized almost independently from American Cold War politics, which soon integrated West Germany in the defense and economy of the West. When in recent decades, as Peter Novick summarized, "ethical and ideological divergence and disarray in the United States advanced to the point where Americans could agree on nothing else, all could join together in deploring the Holocaust— a low moral consensus, but perhaps better than none at all."[9] Novick even detected in the much-debated Americanization of the Holocaust an attempt "to demonstrate the difference between the Old World and the New, and to celebrate, by showing its negation, the American way of life."[10] Others have found a connection between the demise of the longstanding adversary in the Cold War, communism, and the renewed interest in using the Holocaust as the ultimate moral negation of American values.

In both wars, Germany's self-empowerment as Europe's crucial nation was enhanced by the military conflict with the United States. The European-American antagonism was accentuated in order to provide legitimacy; authors like Oswald Spengler and Martin Heidegger contributed a heavy load of philosophy to the story of the defense of culture against American materialism. In keeping with much of the European anti-Americanism of the first half of the twentieth century, the confrontation with America barely concealed the fight against modernity and mechanization which was at least as much an internal as an external ideological battle. The specific German approach was shaped by the war propaganda against France and England as the reigning powers of Western capitalism and materialism, in which the United States initially filled only the background of an increasingly dark and threatening picture. Upon its entry into the war with masses of soldiers and material support, it confirmed the stereotypes about the material onslaught of the West.

There is, of course, also the sense of competition with the "other" modern nation that took root among technological and economic elites in Germany. In retrospect it has become the basis of an intriguing narrative of different paths toward modernity in contradistinction to the unified concept of modernization—created and preferred by Americans—in which Germany plays the role of the competitor who derailed in mid-course. Here the discontinuities have manifested themselves in the abrupt and disconcerting uprooting of cultural and scientific elites and their exodus from Nazi Germany to the United States. American observers did not hesitate to interpret the enrichment through the legacy of Weimar culture in the 1930s and 1940s as a continuity in the course of modernism. This view gained resonance when Americans, after the defeat of the Nazi regime, reintroduced many of these works and ideas as part of the remodernization of Germany.

Spanning one of the most dramatic acts of cultural and moral self-destruction in history, this scenario holds a painful clue to the fortunes of the deeply anchored antagonism against the West with which Germans have bolstered their identity for generations. The antagonism did not subside with the end of the war and, subsequently, entailed a differentiation between "the West" and "America." As Michael Geyer demonstrates in his examination of West German opinion polls in the 1950s and 1960s, the real turnabout did not occur until the Berlin crisis at the end of the 1950s. Little irony was lost on the realization that the Germans of the Federal Republic now embraced those democratic values and practices that had been vilified by German elites as the downfall of culture ever since World War I. Even Thomas Mann, always eager to show irony as a constitutive condition of human endeavors, had lost little time in seeing his own reversal in these terms, in particular his transformation from the harsh critic of the democratic West in his writing during World War I to the admirer of Roosevelt and American democracy during World War II. Unsurprisingly, Mann himself had been vilified for his betrayal of his Germanness after the war—until a new generation of Germans followed in his footsteps by drawing on the American model of a broadly practiced democracy.

The strong German support for the unification of Europe is not unrelated to the desire to leave the ruptures of its national and international history behind. Indeed, the American side gives every indication that after decades of a ruptured and finally normalized relationship, the ties to Germans are strongly determined by Germany's place value for Europe. In the meantime, American self-perception is shifting in regard to Europe. The demise of the Soviet Union in 1991 gave reason to renew the Americans' self-admiration as the leading nation in the world, something that may have found its most poignant expression in the economic boom in the United States in the 1990s. And yet, a recent review of American historiography stated the reluctance of historians to renew the established claims of exceptionalism. "American exceptionalism is losing much of its earlier resonance," the editors assert, pointing to the increasing multicultural diversity that is diluting the traditional unified sense of American identity. They hasten to add, "and thus Europe no longer has the same meaning for Americans as it once did."[11] In fact, many have come to understand globalization as the final blow to the privileged position of Europe in American thinking, which is reflected in the decreased attention to Europe's languages and cultures in American colleges. The 1996 president of the American Historical Association, Caroline Walker Bynum, wondered whether she was a member of the "last Eurocentric generation."[12] While Bynum added that the new frame of reference was to be the world, other historians responded critically, focusing on the fact that the "encoding" of European topics had only shifted toward different categories.

The Biographical Hinge

Having participated in the great reversal of Germany's political and cultural challenge to the West, the postwar generation of Germans and Americans is leaving the stage with strong concerns about the durability of the German-American partnership. On the German side, these concerns reflect less a particular affection for the United States than an affection for the long period of physical and spiritual security in the Federal Republic that was brought about by the American presence in the country. Geyer's conclusion leaves little doubt: whatever follows this period will be measured against this sense of security. Or will it? Does the end of the "German-American security bargain" mean a time of political uncertainty for the Germans? Of course it does. Given the German obsession with the concept of normalcy—first after World War I and then after the fall of Nazism and during the Cold War—much public readjustment will be needed in order to develop a new sense of normalcy without a protector, but also without an enemy. The latter is not much easier, and the United States is not the best model to follow. The Europeanization of the worries is the much-preferred option.

Many factors have contributed to the increasing diffusion of intellectual, economic, and moral power, among them the communications revolution and the Internet as well as the globalization of companies and markets. This predicament is addressed most critically by the historian Konrad Jarausch and most optimistically by the German Coordinator for German-American Cooperation, Karsten Voigt. The message of both contributors is paradigmatic insofar as it points to the division of concerns that a period of peaceful cooperation between countries and continents permits the contemporaries to practice. Since the overall situation can no longer be summarized by a few life-or-death maxims as it used to be in the ideological battles of the twentieth century, the division of concerns becomes a functional part of politics, projecting a new kind of public role-playing in an ever-changing, ever-provoking, and ever-entertaining re-arrangement of transatlantic opposites. The role of the pessimist is no less part of the political process than that of the optimist.

Most significant for the German-American encounter, however, seems the demise of the biographical involvement in confrontation, shock, and liberation through which twentieth-century history gained its shape for millions of Germans and Americans. So many emotional markers appear between victory and defeat, condemnation and redemption, that the feeling of having participated in a particularly intense part of history is constantly overlaying the rationalizations of historians, something that makes the younger generations suspicious about the priorities in defining German-American relations. For the younger generation of Germans, used to integrating the United States just as *primus inter pares* in a world-wide system of economic and cultural communication, the Eurocentricity and Americacentricity in the current historiography seem a rather idiosyncratic antithetical setup upon which the concept of an Atlantic civilization was able to captivate Western nations in the second half of the twentieth century. While the charms and sparks of this antithetical constellation are still cherished by the cultural elites on both sides because they provide access to the assumed dialectic of modernity, they have long begun to slide from representing a determining presence to constituting a increasingly distant legacy. There is reason to believe that if the German-American encounter is to retain its catalytic quality for future sparks across the Atlantic and to captivate coming generations of Germans and Americans, it needs to be placed within a broader and less harmonized perception of its history.

— *Frank Trommler*

Notes

1. Anthony Molho and Gordon S. Wood, eds., *Imagined Histories: American Historians Interpret the Past* (Princeton, 1998); *German Histories: Challenges in Theory, Practice, Technique,* special issue of *Central European History* 22, no. 3/4 (1989): 227–460.
2. Antonelli Gerbi, *The Dispute of the New World: The History of a Polemic, 1750–1900,* trans. Jeremy Moyle (New York, 1973), 359–72; Manfred Henningsen, *Der Fall Amerika: Zur Sozial- und Bewußtseinsgeschichte einer Verdrängung* (Munich, 1974).
3. Kathleen Neils Conzen, "German-Americans and the Invention of Ethnicity," in *America and the Germans: An Assessment of a Three-Hundred-Year History,* ed. Frank Trommler and Joseph McVeigh, vol. 1 (Philadelphia, 1985), 131–47.
4. C. Vann Woodward, *The Old World's New World* (New York/Oxford, 1991).
5. Hayden White, *Metahistory: The Historical Imagination in Nineteenth-Century Europe* (Baltimore/London, 1973), 199.
6. Ralf Dahrendorf, *Die angewandte Aufklärung: Gesellschaft und Soziologie in Amerika* (Munich, 1963), 224.
7. Daniel J. Boorstin, *America and the Image of Europe: Reflections on American Thought* (Gloucester, MA, 1960).
8. Randolph Bourne, "Twilight of Idols," in *War and the Intellectuals: Essays by Randolph S. Bourne, 1915–1919,* ed. Carl Resek (New York/Evanston, 1964), 57.
9. Peter Novick, *The Holocaust in American Life* (Boston/New York, 1999), 13.
10. Ibid.
11. Molho and Wood, eds., *Imagined Histories,* 14.
12. Caroline Walker Bynum, "The Last Eurocentric Generation," *Perspectives* 34, no. 2 (February 1996): 3–4, quoted by Volker Berghahn and Charles Maier, "Modern Europe in American Historical Writing," ibid., 408.

PART ONE

THE GERMAN PART OF AMERICAN HISTORY

INTRODUCTION
A New Look at the Nineteenth Century

Elliott Shore

Defining the world's only superpower, its composition, and its influence, presents compelling tasks for the twenty-first century. Talk of globalization of culture, of the colonization of the whole world within the compass of an American value system, makes the discovery of what "America" is and what Americans are of key importance to those who celebrate and those who fear the United States. Effective emulation of or resistance to Americanization begins with a sense of the people and the ethos that informs them, the cultural values that they treasure, the goals that move them.

The problem that immediately arises from defining America is one of frame of reference. The person or nation doing the analysis brings unexamined assumptions that mirror one another: those who offer definitions assume both that the target group can be identified in a coherent way and that the position of the one defining does not need to be examined. Even more problematic is the assumption that the two cultures are clearly distinct from one another, especially given that the United States is composed almost entirely of people whose origins can be traced to other lands.

No people has more readily posed the question of what America is and how it acts in the world, nor had a more difficult time finding a workable answer, than Germans. Certain that their own culture afforded them a standard against which to measure other cultures, other peoples, elite German thinkers (who often had little or no direct experience in the United States) developed ways of processing the idea of the America that they imagined into categories that they could mobilize for their own cultural and political purposes.

The actual people who came and settled in America, especially in the nineteenth century, brought some of these preconceived categories with them and used them in forming their own communities, their own colonies, often, as Kathleen Conzen tells us, on the frontier. These communities were to be the realization of what could have, what should have been in Germany, had the political and natural landscape been more cooperative. Those notions of an ideal Germany in the United States helped to maintain the early coherence of the new colonies that the new settlers established; the process of interaction between those communities and their neighbors, who had other ideas about life and culture and politics, helped to produce what is now America. This process, according to Conzen, which changed both the German Americans and their neighbors, was not without conflict and not without consequences. And it complicates enormously the categories of what American and German American might mean.

Conzen, following Friedrich Kapp, calls the continuing existence of German American pasts "phantom landscapes" in American life. Three central tenets of what it is to be an American, and perhaps exactly those key notions that inform the concern of those who lament and those whose celebrate Americanization, may have sprung from the interaction that became (German) America: "heartland values" from the Midwest, which move seamlessly into anti-abortion and other Christian politics; political interest in community issues and disinterest in larger ones in urban America; and the strong ideology of personal liberty that concurrently inspired or promoted progressive politics and its concomitant pluralism while abetting racial thinking, and, most importantly for the globalization argument, the development of American mass culture.

The German part of American history is more than a part; it is woven into the fabric of America. The essays in this section all follow that contention as they build a picture of phantom landscapes that undergird what counts as American. They help to make America clearer and at the same time more baffling to critics who think they stand outside of the frame, just as the interactions between German immigrants and their descendants with the larger population that surrounded them made the ideal notions that Germans brought with them less recognizable. James M. Bergquist's essay on the forty-eighters makes this clear: the radical reformers brought with them an ideal notion of what was possible in the United States and became part of mainstream political ideology. Third-party politics, the ascendancy of local issues, and the inertia of German American voters all would move in the direction of appealing to ethnic identity and cultural preservation: "conflicting interests, shifting goals, and practical possibilities," what Bergquist sees as the "real world of American politics."

Hartmut Keil sees a real continuum between the liberal forty-eighters and German working-class radicalism and describes a process of integration that moved through all of the "phantom landscapes" that Kapp and Conzen enumerate, while Patricia Herminghouse describes a similarly fraught relationship that developed between German American feminists and the larger American feminist movement. She makes a particularly striking observation in contrasting the American and German feminist movements at the end of the nineteenth century, noting that the American women demanded full citizenship rights based on "Enlightenment notions of individual freedom and natural rights," while their German sisters were "arguing for improvement in education, marriage and the professions." The most radical German feminists had already emigrated to the United States in the earlier part of the century, adding to the divide across the Atlantic.

Examining both religion and education yields further glimpses of the German American shoals that lurk not far beneath the surface of American life. A. G. Roeber finds that it was especially in the religious sphere that German Americans developed the conservative cultural cast that characterizes the American Midwest, and tantalizingly suggests that the American mystical religious strain, exemplified by Mormons and by "New Age" religions, may owe some of its power to the early German settlers on the Wissahickon Creek outside of Philadelphia. He links the power of non-traditional religion to the weaknesses of the mainstream churches in both Germany and the United States and their alliances to university life.

Daniel Fallon recounts for us the critical importance of the nineteenth-century German university ideal as a goal for American educational reformers, and alludes to the elusiveness of tracing specific German practice in United States. Here we have an excellent example of the translation of practice and theory in two countries into something much different from the two "originals." Similarly, the evolution of the Kindergarten, brought to the United States after 1848, merging with various strains of American educational thought, has emerged as another foundational piece of America.

The realm of German America that has been most closed off, most sealed away from the rest of American life is the world of German-American literature. Here the notion of a phantom landscape is at its most blurry: how could these inaccessible texts, hidden away in research libraries and written in a "foreign" language, have anything to add to our understanding of the German part of American history? Are these works antiquarian curiosities that can only be of interest as relics of a forgotten past? Both Werner Sollors and Brent Peterson vigorously contend that not only is there a rich field for research in this most voluminous of all non-English-language literatures of the territory now known as the United States, but that a sensitive reading of this body of work, a source almost completely disregarded by historians of the United States and by German scholars, would get us closer to what this nation looked like to recent immigrants and their succeeding generations. Peterson speaks of a "tangled conceptual web" that informs the short story he unpacks about the Fourth of July—a web that reveals to us in the twenty-first century a world that historians of the United States have missed. And as Sollors instructs us at the end of this section, the reading of this literature could dissolve for us those categories that we have inherited about "assimilation" and "resistance" in immigrant literature, "forging a new language that has its German as well as its American components."

— *Chapter 1* —

PHANTOM LANDSCAPES OF COLONIZATION
Germans in the Making of a Pluralist America

Kathleen Neils Conzen

There are few more evocative testimonies to the power of the immigrant urge to memorialize group contributions to American life than the magnificent library building constructed by the German Society of Pennsylvania in Philadelphia in 1888. Yet "contribution" has long been a suspect word among historians of American immigration, its simultaneously filiopietistic and assimilationist overtones too strong for most academic tastes. The initial stimulus to the research and writing of any immigrant group's history was often the desire to document the group's "contributions," justifying its presence and initial ethnic distinctiveness by stressing the value of the particular gifts it brought to its new homeland. But the resulting obsession with "firsts," the inflated claims of credit for every glorious moment in American history, the racial theorizing on which such claims often rested, all undercut the scholarly pretensions of filiopietistic "contributionist" historiography, and discredited the issue of group impact as a legitimate object of historical inquiry.[1] Today, the ongoing restoration of the German Society's treasured monument, at a moment when issues of immigrant integration have returned to public and scholarly debate, challenges us also to renovate the notion of "contributions," and to assess anew the consequences for American society of the dreams, thoughts, and actions of the German Americans whose collective heritage is harbored within its walls.[2] This essay accepts that challenge, arguing for the timeliness and necessity of again posing explicitly the issue of immigrant contributions-defined expansively as the influence of group presence upon American development—and laying out in broad, perhaps outrageous strokes an argument for interpreting German America as a colonizing venture whose consequences for the land it colonized reverberate even today.

In 1978, the German Association for American Studies under the chairmanship of Günter Moltmann organized a pathbreaking conference in

Stuttgart on "The German-Speaking Emigration to the United States," whose proceedings were subsequently edited by Willi Paul Adams.[3] That conference can stand as a benchmark against which to measure the achievements of a rich generation of transatlantic scholarship on German emigration and immigration that followed. In his presentation in Stuttgart, Moltmann could note with little exaggeration postwar German disinterest in the history of emigration, nor did he find American scholarship on the German immigrant experience much more voluminous or theoretically sophisticated. Questions of motivation and catalogs of push-pull factors structured emigration studies, while the older descriptive and contributionist interpretations of German immigrant adaptation in America were only slowly yielding to analyses of social processes and structural context. Little in the German migration scholarship on either side of the ocean, he noted, yet reflected the new currents of transatlantic migration history set in motion by Frank Thistlethwaite's landmark 1960 lifting of the "saltwater curtain." To remedy this, Moltmann proposed a daunting research agenda focusing on the interrelations among causes of emigration, migration processes, processes of alienation in the homeland and acculturation in the receiving country, reactions to the migrants in both countries, and links to broader processes of migration within both countries.[4]

Looking back at Moltmann's subsequently published wish list in the 1990s, it becomes clear that the scholarship on German migration to America has truly reached its majority in the intervening twenty-odd years. The German system of organizing individual research within the context of larger projects has proven particularly hospitable to the production of a coherent body of work addressing one item after another on Moltmann's agenda: local and regional studies of the contexts, motivations, and processes of emigration; the relationship between emigration and protest; the organization of emigration, including the roles of advertising, emigration agents, and transport routes and firms; the connections between emigration from Germany, migration within Germany, and immigration into Germany; the relationships between migration and economic development on both sides of the Atlantic; the logic of German settlement patterns in the United States and their relationship with frontier expansion; acculturation and assimilation processes, as well as cultural maintenance within the receiving society; and the use of immigrant letters to explore the subjective dimension.[5] The more individualistic organization of research in American academia has resulted in more scattershot attention, but the sum total of work here is equally impressive. The early focus on major urban communities has extended to smaller concentrations and rural settlement areas; the ranks of examined historical actors have broadened from freethinking forty-eighters to workers and farmers, women, even religious believers; German-American culture—material, popular, literary—has received serious attention.[6] Indeed, this maturing historiography is best regarded as a fully bicontinental project, with scholars from both sides of the Atlantic addressing the full range of topics, a cooperation nowhere more evident than in the sophisticated scholarship that has brought the seventeenth and eighteenth century migrations into the center of any interpretation of German activity in America.[7]

This productive generation of scholarship shares at least one general characteristic: its emphatically non-contributionist quality, its disengagement from explicit questions of immigrant impact upon the receiving nation. Some of the earlier studies, still framed by older national debates over wartime loyalties and immigration restriction, remained concerned to demonstrate that the group had not made a negative contribution, that its values had always been congruent with those of the national mainstream and that, despite fears to the contrary, its assimilation had been complete.[8] But most of the scholarship on German-American migration has been framed within a different context altogether. Like other international migration historiographies of the period, it has reflected both a theoretically driven interest in migration as among the social correlates of modern economic development, and a principled engagement with contemporary issues of international migration and minority rights.[9] Within that context, the framing questions of immigration historians have often had more to do with understanding the processes of migration and ethnic community formation and maintenance than with assessing specific consequences of those processes for the host society. The main immigrant "contribution" to American society by this logic was the multiculturalism immigrants insured by their very resistance to any deeper involvement with their new homeland.

With America during this period busily redefining itself as a multicultural society and ethnicity as an enduring form of identity, with Germany debating greater rights for the minorities in its midst, there is little wonder that German-American historiography, like other immigration historiographies, has tended to focus more on internal group dynamics than on external relations with the broader society, more on expressions of ethnic culture than on the exits from it.[10] But, no matter how it frames its questions, German-American historiography has never really been able to avoid issues of influence upon the broader society, nor to fit group history easily within an enduring multicultural model. For one thing, there is the inescapable fact of the almost total disintegration of what was once America's most visible and complex immigrant subculture, a process hastened, perhaps, by World War I, but already well underway, scholars agree, before war clouds ever loomed on the horizon.[11] The distinctive arc of the German ethnic storyline thus inevitably forces attention to the consequences of generational change, cultural modulation, and gradual integration of a once distinguishable group into the broader society. Equally inescapable, and equally forceful in binding Germans into core issues of the national experience, is a second *Leitmotiv* of their American trajectory, their own insistence on their collective right to influence the broader society, whether as forty-eighters agitating against slavery, workers demanding altered relations with capital, bourgeois parents insisting on school reform, critics striving to elevate American musical taste, or sociable drinkers preserving their access to beer.[12] Their own efforts to change America challenge us to take them at their word and measure their achievements.

But this inherently contributionist subtext to a resolutely non-contributionist German-American historiography is only one reason for accepting the challenge to rethink the question of "contributions." The framing questions of immigration history are themselves turning in a neo-contributionist direction. We are a society again concerned with the dynamics of integration in an era of mass immigration, a society concerned about the texture of our public culture, a racially divided society preoccupied with issues of identity. And so we find ourselves demanding of our history a renewed focus on the central values of the society, on the societal construction of spheres of commonality amid difference, on assessing responsibility for the failings within that public sphere.[13] To do so, assuming we take seriously the oft-proclaimed agency of non-elite as well as elite Americans, requires, as John Higham has insisted, a new narrative centered on "the relations between national identity and group identities," and hence also a renewed interest not only in the terms of admission offered to ethnic minorities, but in the varying forms of assimilation and integration they exhibited, the ethnic and racialized identities they adopted or had thrust upon them, their worldviews and the actions rooted in them, including acts of repression as well as resistance.[14] This is a recipe for a respectable, indeed even a necessary contributionism, one that still presumes separate group histories insofar as groups are products of their own migration histories, and sustain their own cultures and institutions, but views those groups neither as passive victims nor innocent bystanders but more or less empowered contributors to a constantly self-constructing nation.

Where then would the Germans fit into such a recentered, "contributionist" history? What difference has it made to America that these people were here, and that they constructed for themselves the kinds of lives and ethnic cultures that they did? American historians have done a surprisingly poor job of integrating Germans into their broader interpretations, despite the wealth of historiography on the group. Whatever their specific subject, historians can hardly avoid encountering members of a group whose first and second generations by the turn of the twentieth century accounted for more than 10 percent of the American population, and that at the end of the twentieth century claims more Americans among its descendants than any other European origin group.[15] But the very size of the German immigration, its great internal diversity and geographical diffusion, and above all its resistance to easy inclusion within the modal white working-class ethnic category, have tended to discourage careful interpretive integration. As in recent inquiries into the changing "whiteness" of European immigrants, a common solution is to simply note the German "exception" and move on.[16]

What we seem to require is a way to conceptualize the totality of the German ethnic experience, one that captures the distinctive quality of the German role in the American past and the underlying logic of its composite impact upon American development. Matthew Jacobson has written compellingly of the "diasporic imagination" of some European immigrant groups, that sense of exile and homeland obligation that explains so much in their adaptive experience, including the focus of group identities around old world nationalisms.[17] There is little sign of such an imagination among Germans, I would argue, barring a few exiled revolutionaries, despite the reams of newsprint consumed in sentimental verse to the homeland. Most were not longing to return; they were praising the essence of the homeland that they carried with them, and thus themselves. Their letters spoke less of homeland concerns and the bitterness of homeland loss than of new world opportunity, but of opportunity constructed within a largely enclosed world defined by German family, friends, and values; their identities formed through their public debates focused less on righting homeland ills than on preserving new world cultural boundaries against the temptations of "going native."[18]

Theirs, I would like to propose, was less a diasporic imagination than a colonizing vision, a vision that explains much about their interaction with American society and the distinctive quality of their contributions to it. Viewed from Germany, America until well into the nineteenth century was an empty land. Much of it was literally empty—wild land, uncultivated and therefore unclaimed, waiting to be baptized in German sweat. All of it was institutionally empty—no princes, little government, no state church, no feudal obligations, and little recognizable social hierarchy. A favorite aphorism of antebellum German Americans held that if Germany was a culture and a nation in search of a state, America was a minimalist state whose residents were still becoming a nation and seeking a culture. Nothing in America was fixed, everything was malleable, and the American's favorite motto, Germans observed, was "help yourself," with both of its meanings intentional. "Help yourself" because there is no one else whose duty it is to help you, and "help yourself" because there are riches to spare and no one to prevent you from taking whatever you want.[19]

There was enough substance to this vision of an America still ripe for cultural if not political colonization to sustain the major waves of German immigration through the middle of the nineteenth century, and to structure the expectations with which the immigrants approached the challenges of adaptation to their new homeland. This was not, of course, the literal state-sponsored colonization of resource-rich extra-European territory focused upon by today's flourishing scholarship on nineteenth and twentieth-century colonialism and its consequences.[20] It was more akin in its private sponsorship, mentalities, and structures of migration to North American settlement in the colonial era, and to settler colonialism elsewhere in the nineteenth-century world, sharing the same perceptions of emptiness and lack of indigenous civilization, the same concerns to replicate metropole society while improving one's status within it, the same obsessions with boundary maintenance and non-assimilation.[21] Nineteenth-century German Americans routinely used the term "Colonie" to refer to groups of people traveling together to establish a new settlement, usually but not always on the frontier, and to denominate such a settlement; their usage contained all the connotations of group organization, occupancy of an empty niche, and special rights to the maintenance of cultural distinctiveness that defined centuries-old German notions of colonization.[22]

While there has been valuable recent emphasis on the centrality of labor market migration to German as to other American immigrations, it remains important to recognize the dominant role of settlement migration in the formative phases of German group life in America.[23] Germany may have lacked colonizing states, but it had a colonizing population of peasants and artisans seeking room to replicate an intensely local way of life. Their allegiance was primarily to their community, not to a more abstract state, nor were they yet, in either actuality or theory, citizens of states in which hegemonic cultural uniformity was assumed. Thus more important to them than the political power controlling whatever area they decided to colonize, was the security of livelihood the new land promised, and the degree of autonomy it permitted. Whatever the realities and temptations of American society that they found upon landing, it was the essential vision of the colonizer that drew them: the assumption that they carried the essence of their homeland with them, to reestablish it by right in better and purer form in the colonized land.[24] More educated political refugees, whatever their quarrels with homeland regimes, had similar confidence in the superiority of homeland culture; later labor migrants, secure now in the possession of a powerful, culturally assertive fatherland, in this regard at least found little reason to dissent.[25]

Friedrich Kapp, that clearheaded critic of mid-nineteenth-century German-American pretensions, closed his 1867 history of Germans in early New York with a striking image. He likened the colonial German settlements of that state to fairy-tale landscapes submerged by the sea, visible now and again beneath the waves when the water is calm and the air is clear, their bells faintly echoing. The attentive observer of his day could still discern distant traces of colonial German culture beneath the uniformity of American life—the metaphorical waves parted occasionally, and an odd inherited trait or surviving material trace poked up out of the American water. But the past was truly submerged, his readers were left to infer; it was a fairy tale to imagine it would rise again, just as it would be a fairy tale to assume that the German cultural landscape of their own day would escape a similar fate.[26] I shall return shortly to his argument; at the moment, it is his vision that I would like to borrow, for the idea of a phantom landscape contains, I would like to suggest, both the essence of the German view of America, and an instructive metaphor through which to understand the America that Germans strove to mold.

We can think of eighteenth- and nineteenth-century America, viewed from the emigration areas of German-speaking Europe, as a vast phantom landscape of opportunity flung out over, or coexisting with, or superimposed upon, or hovering above, the actual national landscape that Americans were busily inhabiting. This German-American landscape had its own settlement geography, its own local and cosmopolitan cultures, its own social structure, its own institutions, its own politics and agendas, its own religious perspectives, its own intellectual life, its own sense of past and future. It was seldom possible for immigrants to solely inhabit that phantom landscape, for it could never free itself from the real American one to which it was moored. It never developed its own autonomous economy, for one thing, and the cultural appeal of the more fully developed American landscape was always very real. Numerous Germans drifted or fled into the American landscape for good; others commuted back and forth for years, even generations. There were significant conflicts with other Americans over regions that both worlds touched, in which neither emerged really victorious and both were fundamentally changed. Whole communities gradually sank nearer and nearer to the American landscape and finally disappeared, but the American landscape on occasion also rose up to absorb and incorporate into its own contours essential features of that phantom world. Finally, as the gusts of continuing immigration that held it aloft were stilled, and the winds of war blew it down, the last commuters abandoned their holds on this phantom world, and it sank slowly beneath the American waves. But as in Kapp's fairy tale, hidden shoals remain to disturb the flow of the national current, and occasional islands still poke above the sea.

Overly fanciful, perhaps, but the image of a phantom landscape helps capture how the colonizing vision of localistic, land-seeking peasants meshed with the cultural theories, prejudices, and predilections of later-arriving intellectuals and workers to create a particularly self-conscious and assertive, even if ultimately fleeting, ethnic world that had lasting consequences for American development. Let me focus on three areas of contribution in particular. Most obviously, the colonizing vision shaped the selectivity of migration and the geography of settlement, creating significant internal differentiation among German-American communities. From the beginning, those most committed to the reproduction of self-contained fragments of the homeland sought the isolation of the countryside. Here, without the formal compacts of Catherine the Great's Russia, they used the American institutions of local self-government and religious freedom to achieve a similar degree of autonomy in church-centered commercial farming communities. Theirs was as inherently expansive a culture in America as it had been in Germany, resting as it did on the family for farm labor, the farm for family sustenance, and the church to enforce the bonds of one to the other. Each new generation required new land, and new colonies were flung out further west, or onto the land of non-German neighbors, while new colonists from Germany moved

FIGURE 2. Germania, Pennsylvania in 1856

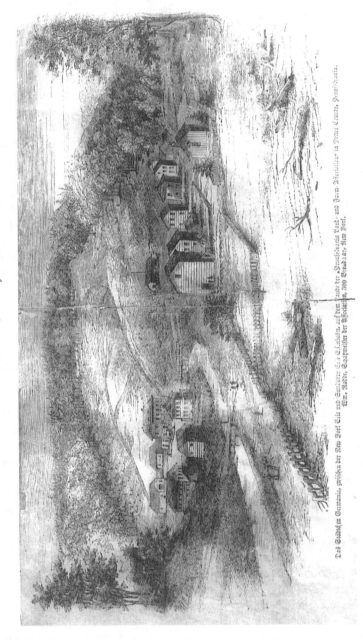

Das Städtchen Germania, zwischen der New York Seite und dem Gebiete, auf dem Lande der Pennsylvania Farm- und Land-Association in Potter County, Pennsylvania. Wm. Radde, Agent, 300 Broadway, New York.

Views of two colonies on the U.S. east coast: Germania (above), in Potter County in Central Pennsylvania, as pictured in a brochure issued from the New York office of the Pennsylvania Farm and Land Association in 1856 and Egg Harbor City (below), a town near Atlantic City, New Jersey. The latter was established as a refuge in 1855 for German immigrants who found the City of Philadelphia too worldly. (German Society of Pennsylvania)

FIGURE 3. Egg Harbor City, New Jersey in 1865

through the steppingstone communities of their predecessors. There was always leakage of sons and daughters out of the system, and its commercial orientation meant that it was never hermetically sealed off from outside influences. German farming areas developed dense systems of smaller and larger towns to handle trading needs, and the German artisans and merchants in those towns provided links to the wider world of German America, and channels for the penetration of non-ethnic ideas and practices. But the intermeshed cultural defenses of farm, family, religion, and local political control insured more enduring cultural continuity in these rural archipelagos scattered across the Northeast and much of the mid-continent than anywhere else in German America, and they represent one of the most significant and least recognized German contributions to American development. Germans remained disproportionately in farming when others left, so that American "heartland values" today are largely German-derived. They provide much of the passion behind "save the family farm" movements, they have often moved into anti-abortion and Christian politics, and they can exhibit a generations-old anti-statism rooted in European experience and reinforced during battles over the Civil War draft, school language legislation, World War I repression, Prohibition, and countless other issues. With their distinctive niche in American economic, religious, and political life, these communities, and the regional cultures influenced by them, must be counted among the few German-derived islands still visible in the American stream.[27]

But it was in the cities of the Midwest and the Northeast that German-American culture was most visible, and here its lasting contributions are perhaps better likened to subsurface shoals, still occasionally causing a ripple, perhaps, but far more influential several generations ago. These were ethnic communities that coalesced first around adventurers and transients who sniffed new opportunities, then attracted colonizers deflected by need or greed, artisans seeking a different kind of colonial opportunity, soon the shopkeepers and professionals to service them, and laborers migrating for urban jobs. Here, in the 1820s and 30s, Germans really invented the institutionalized ethnic community, built upon an amalgam of the emerging *Vereinsleben* of petit-bourgeois Germany and the American habits of association that so impressed de Tocqueville, an invention they taught to subsequent groups. But where American associations were preeminently oriented toward reform and mutual benefit, Germans in their parallel colonial world added a concern for culture, sociability, and festivity that became one of their most significant contributions to American public life. At the same time, German Catholics invented the institutionalized ethnic parish with its parochial school, their colonial vision demanding a far more enclosed ethnic world than their Irish fellow religionists ever insisted upon. German workers similarly reworked older guild assumptions into newer labor unions, channeling into the American labor movement the latest German currents while leavening American individualist tendencies with the colonizer's corporatist concern for community. The pervasiveness of the colonizing vision also clarifies one of the Germans' notorious non-contributions to American urban life, their reputed political disinterest and ineffectiveness: they could be politically skilled in defending the interests of their own community; it was broader politics which were often irrelevant to them. The forty-eighters were the exception that proved the rule; they came as exiles rather than colonists, intent upon politically mobilizing Germans and non-Germans alike in the cause of universal liberty. One of their most lasting contributions, aside from their stimulus to cultural and intellectual life, was to move a portion of the German electorate from the Democratic into the Republican Party. Thenceforth the divided German vote further militated against a specifically German electoral contribution, though the more corporatist orientation of the German colonial world helped mold distinctive political values that found particularly congenial homes in Progressivism and "sewer Socialism."[28]

Finally, discernable today beneath the American waves only as faint shimmering reflections and elusive echoes of bells, is what was perhaps the most significant contribution of the German colonizers to American development, the hundred-year culture war that they waged in defense of their shadow landscape. For, of course, their assumptions of emptiness were wrong. Rural settlers may have found sufficient space for their purposes, but America in general was never an unclaimed land culturally or ideologically, nor was its culture as primitive as Germans imagined. Its dominant political economy at the onset of mass German immigration in the Jacksonian era coincidentally held out ideal terms of integration from the perspective of German colonizers, stressing as it did minimal central governance, local self-determination, and containment of cultural difference through geographical separation. But modernizing segments of the American population were not completely coincidentally mounting an alternate nationalizing project at this same moment, evangelical, reformist, centrist, with fewer resources for tolerating difference and values often sharply at odds with the core cultural assumptions that united the disparate elements of the German community. The German shadow landscape was in reality embedded firmly within the American nation, and efforts to unify that nation under a common set of religious beliefs, values, and practices quickly ran afoul of German difference. Sometimes trivial-seeming skirmishes over alcohol, Sunday closing hours, and public celebrations readily overflowed into the nation's larger battles about slavery, state centralization, monetary policy, and foreign involvement, influencing the course of public decisions. In defense of their positions, Germans developed an ideology of "personal liberty" whose echoes remain audible today. They were forced to develop a principled defense of the legitimacy of ethnic cultural difference within the American republic, a defense whose terms, on the one hand, added significant fuel to the racial habits of thought then gaining sway in America, but on the other hand also laid the groundwork for Progressive-era conceptualizations of pluralism.[29] And their tenacious defense of an alternate public sociability helped shape the mass culture of twentieth-century American cities. Prohibition became possible only when their influence was vitiated by World War I; its ultimate defeat signified their own Pyrrhic victory. With their vision now embedded in public culture, the last wisps of their shadow landscape could drift away.[30]

* * * *

To insist upon the colonizing vision of German America is, of course, to vastly oversimplify the complex goals and mentalities of a particularly diverse and protracted immigration. But in underlining what at least was a central theme of the group's formally constructed ethnic culture, it may have the virtue also of calling attention to the variety of experience that has characterized America's immigrant peoples, helping us expand standard descriptive dichotomies of exiles or opportunity-seekers, alienation or adaptation.[31] It may suggest the interpretive potential of reintegrating into a single spectrum of analysis the categories of colonist and immigrant that, by the time Alexander Schem published his popular encyclopedia for German Americans in 1871, were already becoming explicitly separated.[32] And to assess the consequences of "colonization" for a "colonized" America, "contributionism" indeed moves to the center of our German-American history agenda.

Notes

1. For the early writing of ethnic group histories, see John J. Appel, *Immigrant Historical Societies in the United States, 1880–1950* (New York, 1980); John Higham, "The Ethnic Historical Society in Changing Times," *Journal of American Ethnic History* 13 (1994): 30–44. For Germans, see Kathleen Neils Conzen, "The Writing of German-American History," *Immigration History Newsletter* 12 (November, 1980): 1–14; Frank Trommler, "The Use of History in German-American Politics," in *The German Forty-Eighters in the United States*, ed. Charlotte L. Brancaforte (New York, 1989), 279–95.
2. See David Hollinger, *Postethnic America: Beyond Multiculturalism* (New York, 1995); Gary Gerstle, "Liberty, Coercion, and the Making of Americans," *Journal of American History* 84 (1997): 524–58.
3. Willi Paul Adams, ed., *Die deutschsprachige Auswanderung in die Vereinigten Staaten: Berichte über Forschungsstand und Quellenbestände* (Berlin, 1980).
4. Günter Moltmann, "Die deutsche Auswanderung in überseeische Gebiete: Forschungsstand und Forschungsprobleme," in Adams, ed., *Die deutschsprachige Auswanderung*, 10–27; Frank Thistlethwaite, "Migration from Europe Overseas in the Nineteenth and Twentieth Centuries, in *Rapports, 5: Histoire Contemporaine*, XIe Congrès International des Sciences Historiques (Stockholm, 1960), 32–60.
5. These are the specific headings in Moltmann's wish list. For a concise recent historiographic survey underlining the success of this generation of German scholarship in

fulfilling Moltmann's agenda, see Dirk Hoerder, "Research on the German Migrations, 1820s to 1930s: A Report on the State of German Scholarship," in *People in Transit: German Migrations in Comparative Perspective, 1820–1930*, ed. Dirk Hoerder and Jörg Nagler (Cambridge, 1995), 413–21. For a brief interpretive synthesis, see Klaus J. Bade, "German Transatlantic Emigration in the Nineteenth and Twentieth Centuries," in *European Expansion and Migration: Essays on the Intercontinental Migration from Africa, Asia, and Europe*, ed. P. C. Emmer and M. Mörner (New York, 1992), 121–55. See also Hans Fenske and Hermann Hiery, "Neue Literatur zur Geschichte der deutschen Auswanderung," *Historisches Jahrbuch* 116 (1996): 155–71.

6. Frederick C. Luebke, "Three Centuries of Germans in America," in *Germans in the New World: Essays in the History of Immigration* (Urbana, 1990), 157–89, serves as an excellent orientation to much of this scholarship from the American perspective; for examples, refer to works cited below.

7. Mark Häberlein, "German Immigrants in Colonial Pennsylvania: Resources, Opportunities, and Experience," *William and Mary Quarterly* 50 (1993): 555–74; e.g., Marianne S. Wokeck, *Trade in Strangers: The Beginnings of Mass Migration to North America* (University Park, 1999); Aaron Spencer Fogleman, *Hopeful Journeys: German Immigration, Settlement, and Political Culture in Colonial America, 1717–1775* (Philadelphia, 1996); A. G. Roeber, *Palatines, Liberty, and Property: German Lutherans in Colonial British America* (Baltimore, 1993); Hans-Jürgen Grabbe, "Before the Great Tidal Waves: Patterns of Transatlantic Migration at the Beginning of the Nineteenth Century," *Amerikastudien/American Studies* 42 (1997): 377–89. The German Historical Institute in Washington, D.C., has played a vital role in encouraging such transatlantic scholarly cross-fertilization through fellowships and support for a series of major conferences.

8. E.g., Frederick C. Luebke, *Bonds of Loyalty: German Americans and World War I* (DeKalb, 1974); Guido A. Dobbert, *The Disintegration of an Immigrant Community: The Cincinnati Germans, 1870–1920* (New York, 1980).

9. For interpretive overviews of American immigration historiography, see Olivier Zunz, "American Historians and the Changing Meaning of Assimilation," *Journal of American Ethnic History* 4 (1985): 53–72; Rudolph J. Vecoli, "From *The Uprooted* to *The Transplanted*: The Writing of American Immigration History, 1951–1989," in *From 'Melting Pot' to Multiculturalism: The Evolution of Ethnic Relations in the United States and Canada*, ed. Valeria Gennaro Lerda (Rome, 1990), 22–53; Peter Kivisto, "The Transplanted Then and Now: The Reorientation of Immigration Studies from the Chicago School to the New Social History," *Ethnic and Racial Studies* 13 (1990): 455–81.

10. For the link between German debates and emigration history, see, e.g., Klaus J. Bade, ed., *Deutsche im Ausland–Fremde in Deutschland: Migration in Geschichte in Gegenwart* (Munich, 1992).

11. Luebke, *Bonds of Loyalty;* Charles Thomas Johnson, *Culture at Twilight: The National German-American Alliance, 1901–1918* (New York, 1999); Brent O. Peterson, *Popular Narratives and Ethnic Identity: Literature and Community in Die Abendschule* (Ithaca, 1991); Russell A. Kazal, "Becoming 'Old Stock': The Waning of German-American Identity in Philadelphia, 1900–1930" (Ph.D. dissertation, University of Pennsylvania, 1998; Ann Arbor, MI: UMI, 1998) which takes up the important question of the new forms of identity adopted by those for whom a German ethnic culture no longer sufficed.

12. Brancaforte, ed., *German Forty-Eighters;* Bruce Levine, *The Spirit of 1848: German Immigrants, Labor Conflict, and the Coming of the Civil War* (Urbana, 1992); Hartmut Keil, "An Ambivalent Identity: The Attitude of German Socialist Immigrants toward American Political Institutions and American Citizenship," in *In the Shadow of the Statue of Liberty: Immigrants, Workers, and Citizens in the American Republic, 1880–1920*, ed. Marianne Debouzy (Urbana, 1992), 257–73; Henry Geitz, Jürgen Heideking, and Jurgen Herbst, eds., *German Influences on Education in the United States to 1917* (Cambridge, MA, 1995); Kathleen Neils Conzen, "Ethnicity and Musical Culture among the German Catholics of the Sauk, 1854–1920," forthcoming in *Land without Nightingales: The Musical Culture of German Americans*, ed. Phillip Bohlman and Otto Holzapfel (Madison, 2000); Ulrike

Skorsetz, "Der Franzose wechselt die Mode, wir Deutschen dagegen wechseln die Wirtshäuser: Wirtshäuser und Bierkonsum aus der Sicht deutscher Einwanderer im neunzehnten Jahrhundert," *Yearbook of German-American Studies* 31 (1996): 37–44; James Clyde Sellman, "Social Movements and the Symbolism of Public Demonstrations: The 1874 Women's Crusade and German Resistance in Richmond, Indiana," *Journal of Social History* 32 (1999): 557–88.

13. Ewa Morawska, "In Defense of the Assimilation Model," *Journal of American Ethnic History* 13 (1994): 76–87; Russell A. Kazal, "Revisiting Assimilation: The Rise, Fall, and Reappraisal of a Concept in American Ethnic History," *American Historical Review* 100 (1995): 437–71; Gerstle, "Liberty, Coercion."

14. The Higham quotation is from his contribution to "History Forum: Teaching American History," *The American Scholar* 67 (Winter 1998): 96.

15. See Kathleen Neils Conzen, "Germans," in *Harvard Encyclopedia of American Ethnic Groups*, ed. Stephan Thernstrom (Cambridge, MA, 1980), 405–25.

16. David R. Roediger, *The Wages of Whiteness: Race and the Making of the American Working Class* (London, 1991); Matthew Frye Jacobson, *Whiteness of a Different Color: European Immigrants and the Alchemy of Race* (Cambridge, MA, 1998).

17. Matthew Frye Jacobson, *Special Sorrows: The Diasporic Imagination of Irish, Polish, and Jewish Immigrants in the United States* (Cambridge, MA, 1995).

18. Wolfgang Helbich, "Immigrant Adaptation at the Individual Level: The Evidence of Nineteenth-Century German-American Letters," *Amerikastudien/American Studies* 42 (1997): 407–18; Walter D. Kamphoefner, Wolfgang Helbich, and Ulrike Sommer, eds., *News from the Land of Freedom: German Immigrants Write Home*, trans. Susan Carter Vogel (Ithaca, 1991); Peterson, *Popular Narratives*; Kathleen Neils Conzen, "German Americans and the Invention of Ethnicity," in *America and the Germans: An Assessment of a Three-Hundred-Year History*, ed. Frank Trommler and Joseph McVeigh (Philadelphia, 1985), vol. 1: 131–47.

19. See Conzen, "German Americans and the Invention of Ethnicity"; Conzen, "Ethnicity as Festive Culture: German-America on Parade," in *The Invention of Ethnicity*, ed. Werner Sollors (New York, 1989), 44–76; Trommler, "Use of History."

20. But there are connections; see Ann Laura Stoler and Frederick Cooper, "Between Metropole and Colony: Rethinking a Research Agenda," in *Tensions of Empire: Colonial Cultures in a Bourgeois World*, ed. Cooper and Stoler (Berkeley, 1997), 1–56.

21. Kenneth Good, "Settler Colonialism: Economic Development and Class Formation," *Journal of Modern African Studies* 14 (1976): 597–620; Donald Denoon, *Settler Capitalism: The Dynamics of Dependent Development in the Southern Hemisphere* (New York, 1983); Ann Laura Stoler, "Rethinking Colonial Categories: European Communities and the Boundaries of Rule," *Comparative Studies in Society and History* 31 (1989): 134–61; Robert Bickers, *Britain in China: Community, Culture, and Colonialism 1900–1949* (Manchester, 1999); Pamela Clayton, *Enemies and Passing Friends: Settler Ideologies in Twentieth Century Ulster* (London, 1996).

22. See the definitions of "Colonie" in Johann Heinrich Zedler, *Grosses Vollständiges Universal-Lexikon*, Bd. 6, Ci-Cz (Graz, 1961; reprint of Halle und Leipzig: Johann Heinrich Zedler, 1733 edition), 726.

23. Dirk Hoerder, ed., *Labor Migration in the Atlantic Economies: The European and North American Working Classes during the Period of Industrialization* (Westport, CT, 1985); Dirk Hoerder and Leslie Page Moch, *European Migrants: Global and Local Perspectives* (Boston, 1996); Hartmut Keil and John B. Jentz, eds., *German Workers in Chicago: A Documentary History of Working-Class Culture from 1850 to World War I* (Urbana, 1988).

24. Kathleen Neils Conzen, *Making Their Own America: Assimilation Theory and the German Peasant Pioneer*, German Historical Institute, Washington, D.C., Annual Lecture Series No. 3 (New York, 1990); on rural German settlements, see, e.g., Conzen, "Peasant Pioneers: Generational Succession among German Immigrants in Frontier Minnesota," in *The Countryside in the Age of Capitalist Transformation: Essays in the Social History of Rural America*, ed. Steven Hahn and Jonathan Prude (Chapel Hill, 1985), 259–92; Stephen J.

Gross, "Handing Down the Farm: Values, Strategies, and Outcomes in Inheritance Practices among Rural German Americans," *Journal of Family History* 21 (1998): 192–217; Linda S. Pickle, *Contented among Strangers: Rural German-Speaking Women and their Families in the Nineteenth-Century Midwest* (Urbana, 1996); Robert W. Frizzell, "The Low German Settlements of Western Missouri: Examples of Ethnic Cocoons," *Yearbook of German-American Studies* 33 (1998): 103–25; Walter Kamphoefner, *The Westfalians: From Germany to Missouri* (Princeton, 1987); Jon Gjerde, *The Minds of the West: Ethnocultural Evolution in the Rural Middle West, 1830–1917* (Chapel Hill, 1997).

25. Conzen, "German Americans and the Invention of Ethnicity"; Keil and Jentz, *German Workers.*

26. Friedrich Kapp, *Geschichte der Deutschen im Staate New York bis zum Anfange des neunzehnten Jahrhunderts* (New York, third edition, 1869), 367–8.

27. For just how visible, see, e.g., a recent article in the *New York Times*, 12 November, 1998, p. A-16, Jo Thomas, "Behind a Seamless Facade, The Fractures of Discontent: Small Kansas Town Known for Right-Wing Links." For examples of scholarship on these rural settlement islands, see endnote 24 above.

28. Studies of these urban communities include Kathleen Neils Conzen, *Immigrant Milwaukee, 1836–1860: Accommodation and Community in a Frontier City* (Cambridge, MA, 1976); Christiane Harzig, *Familie, Arbeit und weibliche Öffentlichkeit in einer Einwanderungsstadt: Deutschamerikanerinnen in Chicago um die Jahrhundertwende* (St. Katharinen, 1991); Irene Häderle, *Deutsche kirchliche Frauenvereine in Ann Arbor, Michigan, 1870–1930: Eine Studie über die Bedingungen und Formen der Akkulturation deutscher Einwanderinnen und ihrer Töchter in den USA* (Stuttgart, 1997); Stanley Nadel, *Little Germany: Ethnicity, Religion and Class in New York City, 1845–80* (Urbana, 1990); David A. Gerber, *The Making of an American Pluralism: Buffalo, New York, 1825–60* (Urbana, 1989).

29. Gjerde, *Minds of the West,* offers a compelling interpretation of such "culture wars" in the Midwest; see also Conzen, "German Americans and the Invention of Ethnicity."

30. Kazal, "Becoming 'Old Stock.'" The drift, however, was slower than once thought; see Don Heinrich Tolzmann, *The Cincinnati Germans after the Great War* (New York, 1987); Barbara Wiedemann-Citera, "The Role of the German-American *Vereine* in the Revitalization of German-American Ethnic Life in New York City in the 1920s," *Yearbook of German-American Studies* 29 (94): 107–16; Charles M. Barber, "The Nordamerikanischer Sängerbund versus the U.S. Treasury Department, 1944–46," *Yearbook of German-American Studies* 30 (1995): 73–116.

31. Jacobson, *Special Sorrows,* 9–10.

32. Alexander J. Schem, *Deutsch-amerikanisches Conversations-Lexicon* (New York, 1871), vol. 3: 337–38.

— *Chapter 2* —

THE FORTY-EIGHTERS
Catalysts of German-American Politics

James M. Bergquist

Early in 1999 Oxford University Press published an exhaustive and scholarly biographical encyclopedia, the *American National Biography* (*ANB*), which presents itself as the new authoritative reference work on American lives.[1] As I was pondering the question of the lasting effect of the forty-eighters on the American memory, I undertook to see how many of the German refugees of 1848 still lived in the pages of this biographical compendium of over 17,000 individuals. As a basic list of forty-eighters I used the 310 names that appeared in the compilation by Adolf Zucker in his 1950 book on the forty-eighters.[2] From this list, I found eighteen names in the new *American National Biography*. If one attempts some rough categorization of those listed, the largest number (five) would be scientists and engineers, most of whom remained outside the world of politics in their American careers.[3] Another three were prominent in American life primarily as generals fighting for the Union in the Civil War.[4] Four developed their careers primarily as journalists, although those careers certainly made them active in politics as well.[5] The cartoonist Thomas Nast might be added to the list of journalists. The printer and publisher Louis Prang stuck mostly to the business world. The one person listed who became most noted as a politician was, of course, Carl Schurz.[6] Then there were three others whom we might call "radicals without portfolio": Wilhelm Weitling, Friedrich Sorge, and the idiosyncratic Friedrich Hecker. Karl Heinzen, among others, did not make it into the *ANB*.

The purpose of this exercise is not to start a campaign against the selection standards of the *ANB*. In fact, German Americans seem to be generally well represented throughout the work, in all eras from John Peter Zenger and the Muhlenbergs in colonial days down to Wernher von Braun in post–World War II affairs.[7] Assuming that the editors relied on consultants to choose names from different aspects of American life, I would conclude that those generally concerned with the history of science and technology readily chose a number of German forty-eighters as having made significant contributions. Likewise, those charged with Civil War military history recognized a number of Germans; and those who compiled names of journalists found many in the German-language press. Those who reviewed nineteenth century American political history, however, did not find a great number of the forty-eighters to be significant movers in the very fluid world of politics at the time.

If one were to evaluate the forty-eighters in terms of their impact on the direction of American politics in general, one might have to agree that they did not make a great difference in the politics of their time. Historians have long since ceased to claim that the forty-eighters rallied the Germans under the banner of the Republican party in the crusade to abolish slavery, and thus made possible the election of Abraham Lincoln. This might have been the goal of some, but in that objective they failed.

Perhaps the more significant question is: How did the forty-eighters change the structure and direction of German-American politics? The impact they had on the German-American community and its political life was far-reaching, for they broke traditional loyalties and patterns, raised new issues, and created a more active but more controversial political life within the community.

Trying to generalize about the forty-eighters is a risky enterprise; their careers in Germany before the revolutions were as varied as the careers they followed afterward in America. Their political ideologies also varied widely; only a few reflected working class or socially radical viewpoints. But their political searching after coming to America kept them in active political discourse. They debated, first, whether and how to continue to pursue the cause of revolution in Europe. After they became resigned to the fact that renewing the revolutionary movement was impossible, they debated the course that they and other German Americans should follow in the complex American political situation of the time. When we consider the question of the impact they made on German-American politics, we must visualize the result of the continuing divisions and dialogues among the forty-eighters.

Entering the Maelstrom of American Politics

The political ideologies of these refugees as they emerged from their revolutionary past ran along a fairly broad continuum. Perhaps the most prevalent outlook that characterized them was that of liberal constitutionalism or "republicanism," to which was often added a belief in national unity as the strongest vehicle through which to achieve a liberal constitutional state. Many had been steeped in a European utopian view of the United States as a sort of ideal republic.[8] This conception seemed to accept at face value the common American self-conception that the nation's "manifest destiny" was to lead the rest of the world in the onward march toward liberal republicanism. Thus the instincts of the forty-eighters toward reform and revolution, while envisioning radical change in Europe, conformed to mainstream political ideology in the United States.

When the forty-eighters turned their attention to American politics, their first reactions were often ones of disillusion. The American party system and its heated and brawling partisanship hardly seemed to fit the model of the ideal republic.[9] The pursuit of office, advantage, and patronage seemed far more important to American political parties than did principle. German Americans generally remained tied to the Democratic party as they had been since the days of Andrew Jackson, even though that party was now increasingly influenced by slave-owning southerners. Considerations of local power and patronage kept many of the German Democrats, especially in the cities, in an uneasy combination with Irish immigrants, despite the frequent tensions between those two groups.

The alternative, however, was the now-declining Whig party, itself divided between North and South. While some anti-slavery types found a new home among the northern Whigs, the party also harbored nativists, temperance advocates, and Sabbatarians, and thus was not a welcoming place for Germans.[10] During the increasing political disarray of the mid-1850s, there also arose the new "American" or "Know-Nothing" party, whose nativism was also abhorrent to all immigrants. Confronted with these unpleasant choices, many of the forty-eighters had in the early 1850s begun to advocate that the Germans organize themselves into a power bloc to act independently of the American party system. Heinrich Boernstein of St. Louis had proposed such an idea in 1851.[11] Others tried to create a separate German political organization out of the *Freimännervereine*. Karl Heinzen was among those who favored this idea, and tried to realize it by forming a national union of the Free Men's Societies in Louisville in 1854. However, the "Louisville Platform" that was drawn up largely under his leadership served mostly to alienate Germans rather than attract them, since it contained all of Heinzen's favorite radical ideas and had something in it to frustrate almost everyone. The general advocacy of a German separatism developed more among forty-eighters in the eastern states, where there was less opportunity for Germans in the established political parties, and was not found so much in the western states, where the parties increasingly vied for the German vote.[12]

The greatest influence of the forty-eighters upon the politics of German Americans was exerted in the mid-1850s, when they were still relative newcomers to the American political environment. After 1854, the issue of the extension of slavery exerted increasing pressure upon political alignments. The Jacksonian party system was obviously in disarray, and the upsurge of nativism seemed to be achieving stronger political organization. German America itself was being transformed at the time,

FIGURE 4. Gustav Adolph Roesler

The forty-eighter Gustav Adolph Roesler, helping to bring about a short truce in the fight-ing at the barricades in Frankfurt, arrived in New York after a daring escape from Germany in 1850 with his wife Anna and their infant son. They settled in Milwaukee where Roesler published and edited a weekly political journal with a strong anti-slavery platform that supported the Whig Party. They then moved to Quincy, Illinois, in 1853, establishing a local paper. Roesler died in 1855. (German Society of Pennsylvania)

with the tides of new immigration reaching record levels in the early 1850s; many recently arrived Germans without established political loy-alties were now entering the ranks of voters. Many newcomers, then, were open to the question of what direction they should take in the polit-ical turmoil. It was the forty-eighters themselves, without long-standing political ties of their own, who particularly raised the question.[13]

Perhaps the most crucial period in this process lasted from 1854 to 1856—a crucial time for American political life in general. With the intro-duction of the Kansas-Nebraska bill, the future of slavery became the most pressing political issue, and there began what political historians have since identified as one of the major periods of political realignment in American history. Yet at the same time, the fiery controversy over the future of slavery in the West competed with the greatest increase so far of political nativism in American life. Some saw the possibility that a new nativist party might replace the nearly extinct Whig party as the second major party in the two-party system.

Confronting the Political Loyalties of German Americans

Efforts to change the direction of German-American politics had to face the fact that a great majority of Germans in America held deep and long-standing attachments to the Democratic party, and that previous leaders among the Germans had long been welcome within that party. Many forty-eighters saw that relationship as a corrupt one—selling the political support of "voting cattle" for the benefit of party patronage and minor offices. To them the Democratic party seemed increasingly to be a Southern-controlled instrument for the defense of slavery. But to the Democratic loyalists, more concerned with the rising wave of nativism, the party was their principal defense against those who sought to restrict their political rights and personal freedom. The forty-eighter Daniel Hertle observed: "Should there be here and there a spirit of opposition, the specter of nativism would be conjured up, and its terrors quickly reduced all dissidents to dead silence."[14]

Those new German refugees who entered the field of journalism often found opportunities for political activism in new German-language papers just springing up to support the anti-Nebraska or free-soil cause. When the anti-Nebraska movement began to find organizational structure within the new Republican party, particularly in the West, their leaders sought out the forty-eighter journalists, who, they hoped, might attract their fellow Germans to the new party. Journals such as the *New Yorker Demokrat* and the St. Louis *Anzeiger des Westens* began to reflect more critical views of the Germans' traditional Democratic allegiance.

Republican organizers hoped that the German immigrants generally would respond to the emerging ideology of the party, best expressed in the slogan "Free Soil, Free Labor, Free Men." Eric Foner has pointed out that this Republican vision of "free labor" embodied a very broad definition of labor, which included independent farmers, wage laborers, artisans, mechanics, and small businessmen. "Free labor," then, was not the same as the latter-day concept of the "working class"; many in the category of free labor envisioned upward social mobility, and saw little division between laboring class and middle class. "The aspirations of the free labor ideology were thus thoroughly middle-class; for the successful laborer was one who achieved self-employment, and owned his own capital—a business, farm, or shop."[15] "Free soil" was therefore closely tied to "free labor" as another kind of opportunity for upward social mobility. Land in the West should not be open to the extension of the slave system, which was a prime obstacle to extension of the land of opportunity. The land of the West should be available only to "free men."

Potentially, then, the ideology of the Republican party could attract the many Germans, particularly in the West, who held similar middle-class conceptions of "opportunity." The large immigration of the early 1850s provided many newly arrived Germans whose ties to the Democratic party were weaker. The forty-eighters, eyeing potential leadership roles in the new party, could easily take up the ideology as a natural reflection of their transferred spirit of republicanism of 1848.[16] Yet their efforts to transfer the allegiances of other Germans met the obstacle of nativism. The previous attempts of nativist elements north and south to form an American party were now leading to intraparty conflict, and many northern nativists began to seek a new home for their political aspirations.

In 1854 many Germans had reacted to Stephen A. Douglas's Kansas-Nebraska Act, showing their willingness to desert their traditional Democratic allegiances when that issue was central. In the year 1855, the leaders of embryonic free-soil parties in some states saw that the strength of the nativists was still stirring in many local elections, and began to try to win over the nativists to the free-soil cause. But the prospect of catering to nativists and temperance reformers only estranged potential German supporters, who feared a nationwide alliance between freesoilers on one hand and temperance and nativist elements on the other.[17]

The temperance issue loomed large in state elections in 1855. In Illinois, New York, and Wisconsin, the free-soil elements had become identified with efforts to pass a prohibition law, and the alienation of Germans was obvious. Those forty-eighters who had attempted to marshal German support for the movement were dispirited. The Wisconsin Republicans sought to placate the Germans by nominating the forty-eighter Karl Roeser as state treasurer. But he was defeated, because, he thought, the nativist element had refused to support him.[18] George Schneider, the forty-eighter editor of the *Illinois Staats-Zeitung*, warned that the Republican movement must change direction or be lost. The predictions seemed to be coming true when the Republicans continued to support a nativist mayor in Chicago and the municipal elections of 1856 were lost to the Democrats.[19]

The confused and sometimes contradictory movements of the Republican party in various states now became a challenge for both German leaders and party leaders in general as the country entered the presidential election year of 1856. When the Republicans held a national organizational meeting in Pittsburgh in February, westerners in the party argued that it should be more accommodating to the Germans. Charles Reemelin of Cincinnati (a German refugee of the 1830s) made a dramatic speech affirming the free-soil sentiments of the Germans and calling on the party to reach out to them. But others were conscious that the breakup of the American party offered the opportunity for the Republicans to gain nativists' votes. Thus the dilemma of party policy was avoided by making general promises to the Germans.[20] The result was intense activity in state party organizations as the Republicans prepared for their first presidential nominating convention in Philadelphia in June 1856. In Illinois, the forty-eighter George Schneider argued at two state Republican meetings for the necessity of renouncing nativist positions and winning over German support. Other party leaders agreed, and the result was a state platform with a mildly anti-nativist statement, and also the appointment of two Germans to serve as delegates to the national convention.[21] In Ohio, the party meeting also called for the equality of all citizens, regardless of birth; the drift away from nativism committed forty-eighter Friedrich Hassaurek and other German leaders to the Republican cause. But in Iowa and Indiana, where the party's position was complicated by its previous support of temperance laws, the Germans came away from the state meetings dissatisfied.[22]

Uncertainty about the ultimate position of the national party raised great concern among those elements of western Republicans who wanted to see a national platform that would not repel German support. The problem was that in eastern states the nativists within the party were often seen as more important to the party's success. Resolving this dilemma was without doubt the greatest threat to the fusion of state anti-Nebraska movements into a national party at this crucial time.

The outcome of the Philadelphia convention of 1856 (which would nominate John C. Fremont as the first Republican presidential candidate) was determined in large part by careful strategies in the organization of the meeting. The westerners succeeded in electing Henry Lane of Indiana president of the convention. Lane, who had been convinced by a group of western Republicans of the necessity of clearly stating the party's receptiveness to the foreign-born, appointed a platform committee that was conciliatory toward the Germans. That committee produced a mild and innocuous statement, calling for "cooperation of all parties, however differing from us in other respects." The platform guaranteed "liberty of conscience and equality of rights among citizens" and opposed "all legislation impairing their security." Although there were strenuous arguments from those in the party who wanted a more receptive attitude toward the nativists, the platform was adopted and delegations from the now-disintegrating American party seeking organizational ties were rejected.[23] The forty-eighters and other German leaders who had fought to free the Republican party from the taint of nativism went away from the convention ready to sell the message of "Free Soil, Free Labor, Free Men and Fremont" to those Germans who had been reluctant to leave the Democratic party.

The newspapers that had become the promoters of the anti-Nebraska cause among the Germans now rallied more German followers and more Republican party support. Forty-eighters who had been standing on the political sidelines because of the dilemma of the parties now declared themselves to be Republicans. Carl Schurz, most notably, entered the political realm in Wisconsin and allowed his name to be put forth on the Republican ticket for a legislative seat (although the district offered him no hope of being elected).[24] Perhaps more important, when the Democratic party in the election year reaffirmed its commitment to the Kansas-Nebraska Act, established German Democratic leaders like Gustav Körner of Illinois finally cut their ties to the Democrats, inducing other Germans to follow their leaders into the new party. In many areas of the

Midwest, Germans found the majority of their old political leaders now moving to the Republican party, and in following them they lost their fears of the forty-eighters' influence. But the switch was by no means universal; in areas where the fear of nativism among Republicans was greater, inherent conservatism prevailed. After the election, Carl Schurz observed privately that the German American seemed unduly conservative about both political and social change, and "through the weight of inertia, sticks anchored fast by stupid prejudices."[25] Democratic campaigners constantly warned German audiences that the nativists still lurked within the Republican camp, and many held back from the movement toward Republicanism.

The election returns of 1856 demonstrated that the hold of the Democratic party upon the German vote had been seriously weakened, and that a conciliatory stand by the Republican party could gain Germans. Overall, however, the Republicans did not win anything like a majority of German votes in the election. Perhaps the one state where they did was Illinois, where the most strenuous efforts had been made to free the party from nativist involvement. The results in Illinois showed Republican Germans to be found mostly in urban areas, among the more recently arrived immigrants, and among Protestants and freethinkers. Results in Michigan, Pittsburgh, and Missouri also showed urban and Protestant Germans' tendency to defect from the Democrats, but the Democratic party still held a majority of the Germans.[26]

However, when one considers the history of German-American politics, the election was a crucial turning point in the political life of the Germans. The near unanimity among Germans that the Democratic party had relied upon since the age of Jackson was broken, and would never be restored. The forty-eighters now were nearly all committed to the Republican party (the principal exception being the influential editor Oswald Ottendorfer of the *New Yorker Staatszeitung*).[27] But the Germans overall would continue to be divided between the major parties, and could no longer provide the predictable "bloc" of votes that politicians often hoped for. Contentions in future elections would be mostly over persuading Germans in the political middle to move from one party to another. The German vote fluctuated, particularly when issues such as temperance or nativism entered into politics, but the days of unity were over.

Even among the forty-eighters themselves there remained the constant threat of further divisions. Most forty-eighters, and especially those who had found a home within the Republican party structures in the Midwestern states, saw the party organizations as the only practical means of bringing about the changes they sought. Other forty-eighters, more often from the eastern states, were less pragmatic and still feared the presence of nativists within the party. Since 1854 they had tended to argue that neither party fully represented German-American ideals, and therefore often advocated a separatist movement among the Germans, which would organize them as a solid voting bloc. The leaders of this movement (men such as Adolf Douai of the *New Yorker Demokrat* and Karl Heinzen of the *Boston Pioneer*) ignored the fact that such an effort, fostered by the more radical element of the forty-eighters, would only further divide the Germans and strengthen the resistance of Germans still within the Democratic fold to leaving it. The calls for a German third-party movement had abated after the 1856 campaign, but they began to rise again in the years before the 1860 election, when new stirrings of nativism began to show themselves in the Republican party organizations in some eastern states, particularly Massachusetts and Pennsylvania. When some Republicans began to mention the names of politicians allegedly associated with nativism (such as Edward Bates of Missouri and Nathaniel Banks of Massachusetts), the advocates of separatism called for a meeting of Germans in Chicago before the opening of the 1860 Republican national convention. The German House meeting was to organize a pressure bloc, prepare demands and resolutions for the Republicans, and threaten to persuade the party by withholding German support. This tactic created tensions between those Germans who sought to change the party from within (including most of the forty-eighter leaders) and those who wished to threaten from without. But the result (which included party platform statements of an anti-nativist nature) was clearly achieved by the insiders, most notably the thirteen German Americans who were actual delegates to the Republican convention (including forty-eighters Carl Schurz, George Schneider, Carl Bernays, Michael Plessner, and Friedrich Hassaurek).[28] In the presidential election of 1860 the German Republicans did manage to unite in favor of Lincoln, but the great numbers of Germans who remained in the Democratic party did not change significantly in the election.[29]

The Challenges of the Civil War

Although most of the German forty-eighters supported Lincoln in 1860, a more serious division developed among them during the early years of the Civil War, and a new separatist movement now emerged. For a number of reasons, those who were disenchanted with Abraham Lincoln's prosecution of the war began to rally around General John C. Fremont as a potential candidate for the presidential election of 1864. Fremont, who had been appointed to command the army's Department of the West in 1861, had led many Germans there in the successful effort to keep Missouri within the Union. However, when he issued an edict in August 1861 emancipating all the slaves within the department, his order was revoked by Lincoln and he was removed from his post. This aroused a protest that was particularly strong among German leaders in Missouri. Forty-eighters from elsewhere joined in, because Fremont's dismissal symbolized Lincoln's hesitancy about making emancipation a major goal of the

FIGURE 5. Baxter's *Handbuch*, 1861

This translation of De Witt Cinton Baxter's *The Volunteer's Manual: Containing Full Instructions for the Recruit, in the Schools of the Soldier and Squad...*, was published simultaneously in English and in German, as were many other pamphlets and brochures hoping to attract German Americans to the Union cause. (German Society of Pennsylvania)

war. Others joined the protest when forty-eighter General Franz Sigel, highly popular with his fellow Germans, was relieved of his command after a humiliating defeat in May 1864.

But the Fremont movement had not unified all the forty-eighters. A significant element, more firmly placed within the Republican party structures, refused to join the protest. They included many appointed by the Lincoln administration to military leadership, diplomatic and consular posts, and other patronage positions. The press dominated by the forty-eighters tended also to be divided, with important papers on both sides. George Schneider had to be brought back from his consular post in Denmark to take control of the *Illinois Staatszeitung* and keep it out of the Fremont camp, and Heinrich Boernstein returned from the consulate at Bremen to lead the St. Louis *Anzeiger des Westens* against its pro-Fremont rival, the *Westliche Post*. Eventually, when the election year 1864 arrived, Lincoln had defused much of his opposition by issuing the Emancipation Proclamation, and Fremont himself eventually declined to stand for any nomination by a third-party movement.[30] The whole episode reiterated the lesson for the forty-eighters that if they were divided on their own political goals, they could never expect to gain the unified power of the German voters they hoped for. The election itself saw many of the German masses remaining on the Democratic side.

The ultimate victory of the Union tended to strengthen many Germans' attachments to the Republican party. Forty-eighters could see it as a reflection of both the constitutional republicanism and the unifying nationalism they had brought with them from Germany. Both the forty-eighters who had led military campaigns and the German masses who had served in the Union army could now glorify their sacrifices to the great cause of the Union and freedom.[31] Many of the forty-eighters were now reconciled to the party and saw the futility of separatist movements, however principled they might be.

The Tensions of Post–Civil War Politics

In subsequent years, however, the Republican party itself began to move away from Civil War issues and toward other issues that might potentially alienate German voters. Within the party, divisions began to emerge between those who saw the party's mission as fighting for civil liberties and national union, and those who saw it as working toward moral reform and cultural "Americanization." On issues such as civil-service reform, attacks upon urban corruption, and hard money, the forty-eighters might find other Germans standing with them as reforming Republicans.[32] But there were other elements of the party who now proposed measures that smacked of nativism to the German population. As early as 1867 Carl Schurz noted that the revival of temperance forces among some Republicans was putting strain on the party: "it begins once more to crack in every joint."[33] In various states Republicans espoused prohibition measures in the 1870s, which tended to drive Germans in those areas back toward the Democratic party. Protests by forty-eighters and other Republican leaders within the national party were not very successful in healing the losses.[34] New immigrants in the post–Civil War migrations were less likely to respond to appeals to support the Republican party for its defense of freedom and the Union. In 1889 and 1890, Republicans in Wisconsin and Illinois passed legislation that outlawed instruction in the German language in the schools. This drew considerable attention across the country, since it was seen by many Germans as a sign of a resurgence of nativism and an attack upon their ethnic culture. The result was a considerable movement of Germans toward the Democratic party, which had a significant effect in the congressional elections of 1890.[35] In the urban areas, the increasing identification of the Republican party with industrial capitalism had little appeal to the working-class immigrants who were becoming more numerous in the post–Civil War years; some rejected both major parties and moved in the direction of socialist and radical affiliations.[36]

By 1890, the ranks of the forty-eighters still active in politics were thinning considerably, and they were being rapidly replaced by a newer element of German political leaders, many of whom had immigrated after the Civil War. As they moved into prominence in both politics and journalism, they based their appeals on issues of German ethnic identity and cultural preservation, which seemed much more potent than the principled appeals of the forty-eighters. In elections over cultural issues, like the 1890 election, and in other anti-prohibition battles to follow, they came closer to uniting the Germans under one banner, usually Democratic, than the forty-eighters had succeeded in doing since 1856.[37]

Yet the political successes of these new leaders rested on the considerable change in the nature of German-American political life brought about by the forty-eighters in the 1850s. When they arrived, they began to question the political party system and the traditional political loyalties of the Germans. The forty-eighter journalists, in particular, provided new instruments of dissent as they transformed the world of German-American newspapers and began to present new issues and alternatives to their readers. The forty-eighters began to argue that the cause of "freedom"— that is, free soil—should outweigh the fear of nativism, and Germans should follow the Republican banner. Having cast their lot with the Republicans, the forty-eighters had to exert pressure from within the party to persuade the Republicans to disavow nativism. Though they were only partially successful, they managed to bring about the reform of the party in the West, and thus began the movement of many Germans into the Republican camp. From this point forward, the German vote could never be regarded as the exclusive property of either party, and politicians could ignore the Germans only at their own risk. While divided German America was a less powerful force in politics than it had been when united within one party, these changes did not lead to a complete nullification of German political power. The awareness of possible German defections from either party meant that political leaders had to be aware of German sentiments on issues and willing to place Germans in positions of influence. Thus the Germans did gain some power over the political process, but it was the political power of Germans in the middle, whose votes might be changed during an era when most held invariably to party allegiances. This was not the result the forty-eighters had intended, for they had envisioned uniting German Americans on a basis of ideological principle. Instead, they led German Americans away from a politics of loyalty based on ethnic defense, and toward a politics of conflicting interests, shifting goals, and practical possibilities. And that, more often than not, is the real world of American politics.

Notes

1. *American National Biography*, 24 vols. (New York, 1999).
2. Adolf E. Zucker, ed., *The Forty-Eighters: Political Refugees of the German Revolution of 1848* (New York, 1950), 269–357.
3. Rudolf Eichemeyer, Albert Fink, John M. Maisch, Christian H. F. Peters, and Charles Schott.
4. Peter J. Osterhaus, Franz Sigel, and August Willich.
5. These include Mathilde Anneke (a feminist advocate and the only woman among the forty-eighters in the *ANB*), Lorenz Brentano, Oswald Ottendorfer, and Wilhelm Rapp.
6. The lengthy biography of Schurz in the *ANB* is by Hans Trefousse.
7. Lists of German-born persons are in the *ANB*, vol. 24, 668–71; of Austrian-born, 659; of Swiss-born, 680.
8. For general discussions of the liberal-intellectual ideal of America, see Hildegard Meyer, *Nord-Amerika im Urteil des deutschen Schriftums bis zur Mitte des 19. Jahrhunderts* (Hamburg, 1929), esp. 25–68; Eckhart G. Franz, *Das Amerikabild der deutschen Revolution von 1848/49: Zum Problem der Übertragung gewachsener Verfassungsformen* (Heidelberg, 1958); T. S. Baker, "America as the Political Utopia of Young Germany," *Americana Germanica* 1 (1897): 62–102; George R. Brooks, "The American Frontier in German Fiction," in *The Frontier Re-examined*, ed. John Francis McDermott (Urbana, 1967), 155–67.
9. Franz, *Das Amerikabild der deutschen Revolution*, 57–61.
10. Michael F. Holt, *The Rise and Fall of the American Whig Party: Jacksonian Politics and the Onset of the Civil War* (New York, 1999), 190–91, 689–97, 742–46.
11. St. Louis *Anzeiger des Westens*, 15 October 1851.
12. Carl Wittke, *Refugees of Revolution: The German-Forty-Eighters in America* (Philadelphia, 1952), 161–66; Christian Essellen, "Osten und Westen," *Atlantis*, N.S. I (1854), 168.
13. James M. Bergquist, "The Forty-Eighters and the Politics of the 1850s," in *Germany and America: Essays on Problems of International Relations and Immigration*, ed. Hans Trefousse (New York, 1980), 111–21.
14. Daniel Hertle, *Die Deutschen in Nordamerika und der Freiheitskampf in Missouri* (Chicago, 1865), 17 [author's translation].
15. Eric Foner, *Free Soil, Free Labor, Free Men: The Ideology of the Republican Party before the Civil War* (New York, 1970), 15–17, quotation on 17.

16. For an interesting and thorough example of how one forty-eighter's middle-class European "republicanism" could be transformed into middle-class free-soil "Republicanism" in America, see Sabine Freitag, "A *Republikaner* Becomes a Republican: Friedrich Hecker and the Emergence of the Republican Party," *Yearbook of German-American Studies* 33 (1998): 5–17.

17. This difficult transitional stage in the Republican party is summarized in Foner, *Free Soil, Free Labor, Free Men*, 237–50.

18. Mark L. Berger, *The Revolution in the New York Party System, 1840–1860* (Port Washington, NY, 1973), 70–101; Louis D. Scisco, *Political Nativism in New York State* (New York, 1901), 153–67; Thos. J. Curran, "Seward and the Know-Nothings," New York Historical Society *Quarterly* 51(1961): 140–59; William A. Barghin, "Bullets and Ballots: The Election Day Riots of 1855," Historical and Philosophical Society of Ohio *Bulletin* 21 (1963): 267–72; Alfred G. Stritch, "Political Nativism in Cincinnati, 1830–1860," American Catholic Historical Society *Records* 48 (1937): 270–76; Frank L. Byrne, "Maine Law versus Lager Beer: A Dilemma of Wisconsin's Young Republican Party," *Wisconsin Magazine of History* 42 (1959): 115–20.

19. James M. Bergquist, "The Political Attitudes of the German Immigrant in Illinois, 1848–1860" (Ph.D. dissertation, Northwestern University, 1966), 167–92; George Fort Milton, *The Eve of Conflict: Stephen A. Douglas and the Needless War* (Boston, 1934), 206–10; *Chicago Daily Tribune*, 11, 18 February, 5, 6, 8, 14 March 1856.

20. Pittsburgh *Freiheits Freund*, quoted in St. Louis *Anzeiger des Westens* (weekly ed.), 6 March 1856; George W. Julian, "The First Republican National Convention," *American Historical Review* 4 (1898): 313–22; Andrew W. Crandall, *The Early History of the Republican Party, 1854–1856* (Boston, 1930), 28–40.

21. Bergquist, "Political Attitudes of the German Immigrant," 199–211; Paul Selby, "The Editorial Convention, February 22, 1856," McLean County [Illinois] Historical Society *Transactions* 3 (1900): 30–43; "Address by Honorable George Schneider," in ibid., 90; newspaper reports and other accounts of the Bloomington Republican convention, ibid., 148–77.

22. Stephen E. Maizlish, *The Triumph of Sectionalism: The Transformation of Ohio Politics, 1844–1856* (Kent, OH, 1983), 223–28; Morton M. Rosenberg, *Iowa on the Eve of the Civil War* (Norman, OK, 1977), 128–31; Louis Pelzer, "The Origin and Organization of the Republican Party in Iowa," *Iowa Journal of History and Politics* 4 (1906): 504–25; Roger H. Van Bolt, "The Rise of the Republican Party in Indiana, 1855–1856," *Indiana Magazine of History* 51 (1955): 205–6.

23. *Proceedings of the First Three Republican National Conventions of 1856, 1860 and 1864* (Minneapolis, 1893), 44–75. Memoirs by George Schneider are the apparent basis for accounts of efforts to organize the convention in A. T. Andreas, *History of Chicago from the Earliest Period to the Present Time*, 2 vols. (Chicago, 1884–86), 1:390; *Illinois Staats-Zeitung*, jubilee edition, 21 April 1898; and McLean County [Illinois] Historical Society *Transactions* 3 (1900): 90.

24. Hans L. Trefousse, *Carl Schurz: A Biography* (Knoxville, TN, 1982), 60–61.

25. Schurz to Heinrich Meyer, 20 November 1856, quoted in Chester V. Easum, *The Americanization of Carl Schurz* (Chicago, 1929), 117.

26. For reports on Germans in the election, see William E. Gienapp, *The Origins of the Republican Party, 1852–1856* (New York, 1987), 425–28; Bergquist, "Political Attitudes of the German Immigrant in Illinois," 234–39; Michael F. Holt, *Forging a Majority: The Formation of the Republican Party in Pittsburgh, 1848–1860* (New Haven, 1969), 215–16, 367–68; Ronald P. Formisano, *The Birth of Mass Political Parties: Michigan, 1827–1861* (Princeton, 1971), 298–300; Joseph Schafer, *Four Wisconsin Counties: Prairie and Forest* (Madison, 1927), 140–56, 388–99; Joseph Schafer, *The Winnebago-Horicon Basin* (Madison, 1937), 307–14; Eugene H. Roseboom, *The Civil War Era, 1850–1873* (Columbus, OH, 1944), 313–23; Morton M. Rosenberg, *Iowa on the Eve of the Civil War*, 142–44; Mildred Stoler, "The Democratic Element in the New Republican Party in Indiana," *Indiana Magazine of History* 36 (1940) 185–94; Emma L. Thornbrough, *Indiana in the Civil War Era, 1850–1880* (Indianapolis, 1965), 69–70.

27. For a detailed discussion of the forty-eighters who campaigned for the Republican party in 1856, see Carl Wittke, *Refugees of Revolution: The German-Forty-Eighters in America* (Philadelphia, 1952), 206–9.

28. James M. Bergquist, "The Forty-Eighters and the Republican Convention of 1860," in *The German Forty-Eighters in the United States*, ed. Charlotte L. Brancaforte (New York, 1989), 141–56.

29. For the voluminous material on the Germans in the 1860 election, see Frederick C. Luebke, ed., *Ethnic Voters and the Election of Lincoln* (Lincoln, 1971); and the information summarized in Bruce Levine, *The Spirit of 1848: German Immigrants, Labor Conflict, and the Coming of the Civil War* (Urbana, 1992), 249–53.

30. Jörg Nagler, "The Lincoln-Fremont Debate and the Forty-Eighters," in *German Forty-Eighters*, ed. Brancaforte, 157–78.

31. Wittke, *Refugees of Revolution*, chap. 16.

32. Ibid., chap. 17.

33. Joseph Schafer, ed., *Intimate Letters of Carl Schurz* (Madison, 1928), 389–90.

34. Paul Kleppner, *The Cross of Culture: A Social Analysis of Midwestern Politics, 1850–1900* (New York, 1970); Richard Jensen, *The Winning of the Midwest: Social and Political Conflict, 1888–1896* (Chicago, 1971); Samuel T. McSeveney, *The Politics of Depression* (New York, 1971); Herman Deutsch, "Yankee-Teuton Rivalries in Wisconsin Politics of the Seventies," *Wisconsin Magazine of History* 14 (1931): 262–82, 403–18; Charles E. Camp, "Temperance Movements and Legislation in Indiana," *Indiana Magazine of History* 16 (1920): 112–26.

35. Robert J. Ulrich, "The Bennett Law of 1889: Education and Politics in Wisconsin" (Ph.D. dissertation, University of Wisconsin, 1965); Jensen, *The Winning of the Midwest*, 122–60.

36. Stanley Nadel, "The Forty-Eighters and the Politics of Class in New York City," in *German Forty-Eighters*, ed. Brancaforte, 51–66; Hartmut Keil and John B. Jentz, eds., *German Workers in Industrial Chicago, 1850–1910: A Comparative Perspective* (DeKalb, IL, 1983); Hartmut Keil, "German Immigrant Workers in Nineteenth-Century America: Working-Class Culture and Everyday Life in an Urban Industrial Setting," in *America and the Germans: An Assessment of a Three-Hundred-Year History*, ed. Frank Trommler and Joseph McVeigh (Philadelphia, 1985) vol. 1: 189–207. See also Keil's article in this volume.

37. James M. Bergquist, "German-America in the 1890s: Illusions and Realities," in *Germans in America: Aspects of German-American Relations in the Nineteenth Century*, ed. E. Allen McCormick (New York, 1983), 4–6.

Chapter 3

GERMAN WORKING-CLASS RADICALISM AFTER THE CIVIL WAR

Hartmut Keil

In the last thirty years of the twentieth century an impressive body of research, in both the United States and Germany, on the traditions of German radicalism in the United States during the second half of the nineteenth century has broadened our understanding of its ideological, demographic, cultural, social, and economic components, which contributed significantly to the emergence of the American labor movement, as well as to a stream of alternative intellectual ideas.[1] In conjunction with other radical currents, for a generation or more, German radical thought offered alternative models of social development and even seemed to provide the potential for translating some aspects of these visions into practical reality. From our present perspective it is easy, perhaps even fashionable, to discard past developments and failures as inevitable results of illusionary goals. I do not agree with this view. Instead I see my task as trying to focus on what I believe are some of the central issues, partly in light of recently emerging research concerns, that had an impact upon German working-class radicalism in this country. Thus I will point to some of the characteristics of German working-class radicalism, to the obstacles and liabilities, even dilemmas, that radical organizations faced when they encountered societal pressures and when they had to come to terms with the issues of personal and group identity, cultural orientation, and social integration.

Traditions of Radicalism

German immigrants contributed to American radical beliefs and organizations that were partly indigenous in origin and partly "imported" and supported by other immigrant groups. German working-class radicalism itself, however, far from being a homogeneous school of thought or a group defined by clear distinctions and boundaries from other radicalisms, was a rather complex phenomenon. The social composition of German lower-class immigrants offers some clues as to its composite and changing nature, and it also raises a host of pertinent questions concerning the prospects of the impact of German working-class radicalism in the United States. Since German mass immigration extended over a period of roughly fifty years, beginning in the late 1830s and continuing until the depression of the 1890s, these immigrants, though of similar ethnic backgrounds, often brought quite distinct social, political, cultural, and work experiences.[2] They entered the United States at various stages of that nation's industrialization and settled in areas differently affected by the Industrial Revolution. Thus socialist immigrants in the German-American labor movement—many of whom were skilled workers who had come from Germany's early industrial states, like Saxony and some parts of Prussia—had to reckon with the many unskilled laborers who had emigrated from rural areas, had no industrial work experience, and had not been exposed to the German labor movement. The result of this extended migration was a multiplicity of class and cultural experiences that defies easy categorization.[3]

How did various groups of German working-class immigrants fare in the American context? This question raises the issue of their ability to adapt their strategies, if not their goals, to American conditions. This was not simply an institutional and ideological problem; it had far-reaching social and cultural ramifications. The development and integration of a radical movement depended upon the people supporting it, upon their social and cultural position in American society. Was German-American labor radicalism grounded in an artisan community threatened by mechanization, or in an industrial proletariat matured under the new system of mass production? At what periods were German immigrant workers at the center of production, and when did their position erode? What was the numerical impact of German workers in certain cities, industries, and occupations at specific periods? Was there a generational succession within occupations from the immigrant to the second generation? What changes did these relationships undergo, and how did the gradual erosion of the ethnic heritage affect the visibility of German American workers as well as the degree of their involvement in the American labor movement?[4]

A look at the ideological implications of the demographic, social, and cultural diversity of German working-class immigration reveals an equally complex landscape. Thus it would be incorrect to mark a clear ideological and temporal distinction between liberals of the forty-eighter persuasion and socialist immigrants, whose intellectual home was German Social Democracy. German socialists partook of a long liberal-republican tradition that was gradually incorporated into the emerging Social-Democratic movement in Germany. Republicanism thus became the historical antecedent of the socialist movement. Wilhelm Liebknecht, one of the principal founders of the German labor movement, shared this heritage of European Jacobinism and radical republicanism. Unlike many participants of the failed Revolution of 1848/49 who emigrated to the United States, Liebknecht abandoned his emigration plans but continued to show considerable interest in "the great Atlantic republic."[5] When he eventually visited the United States in 1886, he observed the results of liberal-republican convictions among the American populace, namely "an enthusiasm for justice, freedom, progress, the common good that I have not discovered to any approximate degree in the countries of the old world."[6]

Radical republicanism did not disappear overnight at the end of the Civil War but continued to exert an ideological and institutional influence well beyond the 1860s. Socialist ideas, in turn, entered the American labor movement well before the late 1870s and the 1880s. Even before the Civil War the utopian communist Wilhelm Weitling and the Marxian socialist Joseph Weydemeyer, among others, published labor papers and organized workers in the East and the Midwest.[7] Throughout the formative period of German Social Democracy, from the mid-1860s until its suppression by law in 1878, many German workers and intellectuals active in the movement emigrated to the United States, propagating political principles that were being discussed in Germany at the time of their departure.[8] Especially during this early period German socialism was not a homogeneous movement, not even after the Gotha Congress in 1875 united its major factions, i.e., the Lassalleans and Marxists.[9] The rising tide of immigrant workers strengthened the ties between the emerging socialist movements of the two countries. As it continued to sweep ideological currents across the Atlantic,[10] the German radical culture trying to gain a foothold in America had many faces, and it was reflected in a diversity of traditions and groups, such as freethinkers and radical republicans, communitarians and land reformers, Lassallean and Marxian socialists, social democrats and anarchists.[11] In this period of ideological ferment, the emerging German-American working-class movement was characterized by rivalry and factious disputes, as well as by defections of individuals and groups vying for a dominant position.

Solidarity and Fragmentation, Class and Ethnicity

The German working-class immigrant community encountered a world that was unfamiliar in many respects. Perhaps the cultural divide posed the greatest challenge. In Germany, in the absence of significant cultural differences, the emerging labor movement was able to focus on class as its overriding concern. Even if, during their itinerant work years, journeymen crossed national boundaries and sometimes worked in an international environment in urban centers like Paris, Zurich, and London, they could rely on a common artisan tradition of work and values that encouraged solidarity rather than disunity. In the United States, by contrast, in the absence of a firmly established artisan tradition common experiences quickly eroded under the pressure of mechanization, which undermined whatever work rules and regulations artisans and skilled workers tried to maintain.[12] In addition, immigrants increasingly arrived from agrarian societies. These were people who had no previous industrial background and who first entered the alien world of mines and mills after their arrival in America's emerging industrial centers. Herbert Gutman has analyzed these successive waves of new immigrant workers entering the American working class from a broader perspective, pointing to the difficulty of establishing a working-class tradition of class solidarity. Contrast this to the situation in Germany, where an intergenerational tradition often developed, as in the commercial and industrial city of Leipzig.[13] In this situation, German working-class radicals were torn between relying on their fellow countrymen and familiar institutions, and confronting the challenge of the new society; over time, they tried to do both with varying degrees of enthusiasm and success.

The German-American labor movement leaned heavily on the German example for the process of institution-building, imitating both organizational structures and functions. In order to become accepted, new associations could not operate in a vacuum but had to be responsive to the needs of immigrant workers. Immigrant neighborhoods provided their social context, so in addition to the usual lower-class social setting they had known in Germany, workers were now part of an alien ethnic culture as well. Ethnic-cultural overtones tended to have considerably more weight within the German immigrant working class than in the home country, especially during conflicts with other immigrant groups and with the dominant culture. When socialist institutions had to contend with issues of class and culture at the same time, principles were sometimes neglected for concerns that touched upon everyday life. Thus, the associational life flourishing in these immigrant working-class neighborhoods should be considered for its social functions and not just understood from an ideological perspective. As a consequence, immigrants adopted not only the organizational structures of central institutions, such as parties, trade unions, and the press, but also a variety of other secondary associations, as well as specific forms, contents, and enactments of German working-class culture. These included lodges, insurance and benefit societies, educational clubs and schools, singing and theater societies, typical forms of celebration and leisure, and a viable radical literary tradition used in a communal context to cultivate common ideological identification and class solidarity.[14] Even after this had provided for the initial stimulus, the continued vitality of working-class institutions and culture depended largely on uninterrupted migration of skilled workers and socialists from Germany, and on the intimate interrelationship with German Social Democracy. Organizational, ideological, and cultural traditions were thus maintained by an intricate network of migration, personal communication, and institutional imitation.

But German working-class radicals still clearly saw the need to reach out to immigrant workers of other backgrounds, unless they wanted to remain isolated in their ethnic cocoon. Overcoming the language barrier was the most significant practical—and symbolic—step toward interethnic cooperation. This was not exclusively a problem of German working-class radical organizations but one that other ethnic groups had to tackle as well. However, in the German-American case it resulted in serious leadership problems, since trade unions and parties led by individuals conversant only in the German language could not represent their constituents effectively in local or state assemblies, or at the national level—this at a time when German immigrant workers often provided the backbone of organization. German-language labor papers repeatedly reminded their readers of the need to learn English. Workers could not content themselves with the claim of middle-class papers that it was "the mission of German Americans" to preserve German traditions and the German language, wrote the *New Yorker Volkszeitung*. Learning English thoroughly was not the betrayal of one's mother tongue but rather an opening of the way to more effective agitation. There was no sharper weapon than colloquial English. The paper admonished its readers to attend one of the language courses offered in the numerous evening schools.[15] Wilhelm Liebknecht also addressed this burning issue during his American journey. In a speech in Brooklyn he exhorted his listeners to learn the language of their adopted country: "I tell you, study, and learn English above all else. It's a mistake that my fellow countrymen learn so little English. They must know the ways of Americans and therefore I tell you learn."[16]

English-language socialist papers were sorely lacking, and German socialists repeatedly made efforts to take remedial actions. Thus the *Chicago Socialist* was financed by the overwhelmingly German membership of the Socialist Labor Party, as were the *Leader*, the *Workmen's Advocate*, and the *People* in later years. Likewise, Albert Parsons published his *Alarm* in the offices of the *Chicagoer Arbeiter-Zeitung*. From early on, German socialists also tried to reach workers through leaflets and pamphlets written in English—an undertaking impeded by the lack of native speakers. German-Americans who were relatively fluent in English, like Friedrich A. Sorge, Alexander Jonas, Adolf Douai, Adolph Hepner, and later Gustav A. Hoehn, filled the gap.[17] Since these pamphlets explicitly referred to American conditions, they were preferred for agitational purposes over translations of German tracts reflecting German conditions.

Ethnic versus American Identity

German American socialists knew that they faced a dilemma when they tried to overcome their ethnic heritage in order to reach out to other groups of workers. They depended substantially upon the cultural embeddedness of ideological convictions but recognized that this close nexus reinforced already-existing resentments and prejudices against what was considered an "un-American" ideology anyway. Thus the burden of being alien weighed doubly heavily upon their shoulders. Henry George, who had run for mayor of New York in 1886 as the candidate of the United Labor Party, expressed his uneasiness with that party's left wing. Addressing the Syracuse party convention in 1887, he claimed that individualism was so "strongly rooted in all the habits of thought of the peoples of the English language" that "socialism of the German school can never make the headway here that it has on the continent of Europe."[18] And in an editorial he complained: "German socialism is so confused and confusing in its terminology, so illogical in its methods; it contains such a mixture of important truths with superficial generalizations and unwarranted assumptions, that it is difficult—at least for people of English speech—to readily understand its real meaning and purpose."[19] For him, "state socialism" was "an exotic born of European conditions that cannot take root and flourish in American soil."[20]

In response to such accusations, German socialist immigrant organizations consciously identified with the liberal-republican tradition of citizens' rights and obligations while trying to adapt their strategy of organizing workers to what they saw as typical American conditions. Although they sometimes doubted the effectiveness of the right to vote, they supported the suffrage that in the German Reich was used by the Social Democratic Party with such obvious success. The German labor press in the United States never tired of reminding its readers, especially before elections, to request their citizenship papers in order to be allowed to vote.[21] When socialist immigration increased in the late 1870s as a result of the anti-socialist law in Germany, a discussion occurred in the Socialist Labor Party of New York about members' rights and duties. Exiled socialists arriving from Berlin and Hamburg were asked to both join the party and apply for citizenship. In January 1880 the German branch made it "obligatory for new members to be citizens or at least to take out their papers before their temporary American card is exchanged for a regular membership card."[22] Most of the exiled socialists did indeed comply with this request. Strategy issues were more difficult to resolve because two different traditions competed for recognition.[23] Since the days of the International Workingmen's Association, Marxian socialists had unwaveringly supported trade unions as the necessary foundation of the American labor movement. They were met with opposition from several quarters, especially from Lassalleans and American socialists who, wanting to take advantage of the American political system, counted on the ballot. Neglecting the organizing of trade unions among German immigrant workers, however, would have meant isolating the radical movement from the very membership base on whose support it was primarily dependent. Political socialists fell into precisely this trap when

FIGURE 6. Police Confront Rioters in Chicago in 1877

Police confront rioters at Chicago's Turner Hall. During the national railroad strike of 1877, the altercations in this stronghold of German workers, which involved rioters of many nationalities, drew the interest of the national press. On the morning of July 26, 1877, police "cleared" Turner Hall and inflicted casualties on the demonstrators in surrounding streets. Illustration in *Harper's Weekly*, vol. 21, of 18 August 1877. (Free Library of Philadelphia)

they refused to cooperate with organizations including workers not up to their own theoretical level, whose primary concern was to improve their own economic condition. Thus Conrad Conzett, a printer from Switzerland who owned and edited the German-language labor papers in Chicago in the 1870s, concluded from his negative efforts at political organization that trade unions had a clear edge over parties, since they touched workers' immediate, practical interests:

> Workers can be more easily organized in unions, which ... offer immediate material advantages.... If we help unions in their material and ideal goals, they will help us in our ideal and political aims. Unions will soon be forced by conditions to centralize, to unite nationally and internationally, and to enter the political arena beside the economic fight in order to get laws passed that are indispensable for the working class. The fight for wages, etc., without the fight in the political field is foolish, as would be the exclusively political struggle.[24]

Eventually the Marxist approach—i.e., reaching America's working masses by identifying with immediate and practical problems while gradually educating them to become a class conscious of its condition and potential—scored significant successes in the trade union movement, which was especially strong and resilient when led by socialists. This is not to say that the ultimate goal was accomplished; rather, the course of events proved that it was difficult, if not impossible, to steer free of the enticements of co-optation and to develop the labor movement beyond a pragmatic bread-and-butter unionism. The search for alternatives to an American Federation of Labor believed to be increasingly hostile to socialist principles—be it by founding rival organizations like the Socialist Trade and Labor Alliance, or by joining the Knights of Labor, which, for a while at least, seemed to be more receptive to radical ideas—also ended in organizational failure. Efforts at the "Americanization" of the movement—beyond rescinding the language barrier referred to above— owed their partial successes perhaps more to demographic changes, i.e., the ascendancy of the American-born second immigrant generation of various ethnic backgrounds, rather than to recruiting Anglo-American workers. When the Socialist Unity Congress assembled at Indianapolis in 1901, German socialists rejoiced over the fact that this was no longer a "German" convention. Julius Vahlteich, Ferdinand Lassalle's former secretary, former member of the German Reichstag, now a Chicago resident and active labor journalist, found it highly significant that young Americans had dominated the discussions and proved their organizational skills.[25] And the editor Alexander Jonas urged Morris Hillquit to emphasize the new membership base of the Socialist Party in his report to the International Socialist Congress at Amsterdam in 1904.[26]

Other influences at work before the onset of the new century had an important impact on the mellowing of German working-class radicalism. These have been increasingly addressed by new research in recent years. First, German radicals fit neatly into the social structure of American society despite their sometimes different rhetoric in this regard. Alternatives to the bourgeois family or to accepted gender roles were rarely discussed; on the contrary, if they were suggested, it was by members of circles closer to the tradition of anarchy and communal living. It was no coincidence that the Woodhull and Claflin sisters caused an uproar in socialist circles, where the nuclear and extended family was questioned but steadfastly reaffirmed. In the ideal German working-class family, too, only the husband and sons were supposed to work for wages. Women were to take up a job only until they married, at which time when they were supposed to assume their preordained roles as housewives and mothers. These were perfect preconditions that mirrored American middle class values.[27]

Social mobility was another way of accommodating to American society. This is far from blaming working-class families for trying to improve their economic and social situation. Substantial numbers of German immigrant workers were able to take advantage of opportunities that had been absent in Germany, and although such advancement most often was modest and unspectacular, it did entail decisions that had consequences for their lifestyles and outlook. Thus working-class families tried to escape dense, crowded, unsanitary neighborhoods as soon as they had saved some money or earned enough to be able to afford one of the small frame houses that developers offered on the fringes of rapidly expanding Midwestern cities. This separation of work and neighborhood, and of home and communal leisure time activities, dealt a severe blow to a sense of working-class community and solidarity.

Finally, German immigrant workers gradually succumbed to the increasing virulence of racism in American society. It seems that around the middle of the century this had not necessarily been the case, since skilled workers and artisans often did not compete for the same jobs with blacks. Where they did, however, premonitions of what was to come on a more extended scale were visible, like in Cincinnati in the 1840s, where a cabinetmakers union excluded African American workers because of their race.[28] After the Civil War, trade unions, including those led by German socialists, systematically continued this practice. In this respect the labor movement was not different from American society at large.[29] For German immigrants—as for the German immigrant group at large—it seems that racism as practiced in the United States was not automatically adopted when they stepped ashore but was a gradual learning process and an integral part of, or even precondition to, becoming integrated into American society. Research examining this aspect of how German immigrants "became white" must include the German-American labor movement.

Notes

1. It is impossible to mention here all the relevant works that contain significant contributions while not necessarily focusing on the subject. But see the following selection: Bruce Levine, *The Spirit of 1848: German Immigrants, Labor Conflict, and the Coming of the Civil War* (Urbana, 1992); R. Laurence Moore, *European Socialists and the American Promised Land* (New York, 1970); Bruce C. Nelson, *Beyond the Martyrs: A Social History of Chicago's Anarchists, 1870–1900* (New Brunswick, NJ, 1988); Richard Oestreicher, *Solidarity and Fragmentation: Working People and Class Consciousness in Detroit, 1875–1900* (Urbana, 1986); Carol Poore, *German-American Socialist Literature, 1865–1900* (Bern, 1982); Steven J. Ross, *Workers on the Edge: Work, Leisure, and Politics in Industrializing Cincinnati, 1788–1890* (New York, 1985). Numerous essay collections include studies of German working-class radicalism, e.g., Frank Trommler and Joseph McVeigh, eds., *America and the Germans: An Assessment of a Three-Hundred Year History*, 2 vols. (Philadelphia, 1985); John H. M. Laslett and Seymour Martin Lipset, eds., *Failure of a Dream? Essays in the History of American Socialism* (Berkeley, 1974); Jean Heffer and Jeanine Rovet, eds., *Why Is There No Socialism in the United States? Pourquoi n'y a-t-il pas de Socialisme aux États-Unis?* (Paris, 1988); Dirk Hoerder, ed., *"Struggle a Hard Battle": Essays on Working-Class Immigrants* (DeKalb, IL, 1986); Dirk Hoerder and Jörg Nagler, eds., *People in Transit: German Migrations in Comparative Perspective, 1820–1930* (New York, 1995); Dirk Hoerder, ed., *American Labor and Immigration History, 1877–1920s: Recent European Research* (Urbana, 1983); Theodore Hershberg, ed., *Philadelphia: Work, Space, Family, and Group Experience in the Nineteenth Century* (New York, 1981); Hartmut

Keil and John B. Jentz, eds., *German Workers in Industrial Chicago, 1850–1910: A Comparative Perspective* (DeKalb, 1983); Hartmut Keil, ed., *German Workers' Culture in the United States 1850 to 1920* (Washington, D.C./London, 1988).

2. For histories of German emigration see Mack Walker, *Germany and the Emigration, 1816–1885* (Cambridge, MA, 1964); Peter Marschalck, *Deutsche Überseewanderung im 19. Jahrhundert: Ein Beitrag zur soziologischen Theorie der Bevölkerung* (Stuttgart, 1973); Wolfgang Köllmann and Peter Marschalck, "German Emigration to the United States," trans. Thomas C. Childers, *Perspectives in American History* 7 (1973): 449–554. For a brief review of the history of, and research on, German Americans, see Kathleen Neils Conzen, "Germans," in *Harvard Encyclopedia of American Ethnic Groups*, ed. Stephan Thernstrom (Cambridge, MA, 1980), 405–25.

3. See F. A. Sorge, "Die Arbeiterbewegung in den Vereinigten Staaten," *Neue Zeit* 9–14 (1890–1895); Hermann Schlüter, *Die Anfänge der deutschen Arbeiterbewegung in Amerika* (Stuttgart, 1907); Hermann Schlüter, *Die Internationale in Amerika: Ein Beitrag zur Geschichte der Arbeiterbewegung in den Vereinigten Staaten* (Chicago, 1918). For the period after the Revolution of 1848 see Levine, *The Spirit of 1848*; Bruce Levine, "In the Heat of Two Revolutions: The Forging of German-American Radicalism," in *"Struggle a Hard Battle,"* ed. Hoerder, 19–45.

4. For previous work on such issues see James M. Bergquist, "German Communities in American Cities: An Interpretation of the Nineteenth-Century Experience," *Journal of American Ethnic History* 4 (Fall 1984): 9–30; *People in Transit*, ed. Hoerder and Nagler; Ross, *Workers on the Edge*; *The German-American Radical Press: The Shaping of a Left Political Culture, 1850–1940*, ed. Elliott Shore, Ken Fones-Wolf, and James P. Danky (Urbana and Chicago, 1992); *German Workers in Industrial Chicago*, ed. Keil and Jentz; *German Workers' Culture*, ed. Keil.

5. "Die Botschaft des amerikanischen Präsidenten," *Osnabrücker Zeitung* no. 189, 24 December 1864, in *Wilhelm Liebknecht: Leitartikel und Beiträge in der Osnabrücker Zeitung 1864–1866* (Hildesheim, 1975), 257. Liebknecht almost emigrated to Wisconsin in 1847, and in later years he repeatedly toyed with the idea of emigrating to America; see Wilhelm Liebknecht, *Erinnerungen eines Soldaten der Revolution* (Berlin, 1976), 16 and 82; Wilhelm Liebknecht, *Ein Blick in die Neue Welt* (Stuttgart, 1887), vi.

6. Liebknecht, *Blick in die Neue Welt*, 271; quoted as translated by Moore, *European Socialists*, 29.

7. Carl Wittke, *Refugees of Revolution: The German Forty-Eighters in America* (Philadelphia, 1952); Carl Wittke, *The German Language Press in America* (Lexington, 1957); Carl Wittke, *The Utopian Communist: A Biography of Wilhelm Weitling, Nineteenth-Century Reformer* (Baton Rouge, 1950); Karl Obermann, *Joseph Weydemeyer: Ein Lebensbild, 1818–1866* (Berlin, 1968); Schlüter, *Anfänge der deutschen Arbeiterbewegung*, 8–12; *The Immigrant Labor Press in North America*, ed. Dirk Hoerder and Christiane Harzig, 3 vols. (Westport, CT, 1987); Hans-Arthur Marsiske, *Eine Republik der Arbeiter ist möglich. Der Beitrag Wilhelm Weitlings zur Arbeiterbewegung in den Vereinigten Staaten von Amerika 1846–1856* (Hamburg, 1990).

8. For a more detailed analysis see Hartmut Keil, "Socialist Immigrants from Germany and the Transfer of Socialist Ideology and Workers' Culture," in *A Century of European Migrations, 1830–1930*, ed. Rudolph J. Vecoli and Suzanne M. Sinke (Urbana and Chicago, 1991): 315–38.

9. See Guenther Roth, *The Social Democrats in Imperial Germany: A Study in Working-Class Isolation and National Integration* (Totowa, NJ, 1963); Franz Mehring, *Geschichte der deutschen Sozialdemokratie II: Von Lassalles "Offenem Antwortschreiben" bis zum Erfurter Programm 1863 bis 1891* (Berlin, 1960); Werner Ettelt and Hans-Dieter Krause, *Der Kampf um eine marxistische Gewerkschaftspolitik in der deutschen Arbeiterbewegung 1868 bis 1878* (Berlin, 1975).

10. Dirk Hoerder and Hartmut Keil, "The American Case and German Social Democracy at the Turn of the 20th Century, 1878–1907," in *Why Is There No Socialism in the United States?* ed. Heffer and Rovet, 141–65.

11. See Schlüter, *Anfänge*, and Sorge, "Arbeiterbewegung."

12. Hartmut Keil, "Das Chicago-Projekt als sozial- und kulturgeschichtlicher Forschungsansatz," *Amerikastudien/American Studies* 29 (1982): 113–32.

13. Herbert Gutman, "Work, Culture and Society in Industrializing America, 1815–1918," *American Historical Review* 78 (1973): 531–87; reproduced in *Work, Culture and Society in Industrializing America: Essays in American Working-Class and Social History*, ed. Herbert Gutman (New York, 1977). For a brilliant analysis of the formation of the working class in Leipzig see both Hartmut Zwahr, *Zur Konstituierung des Proletariats als Klasse: Strukturuntersuchungen über das Leipziger Proletariat während der industriellen Revolution* (Munich, 1981) and Hartmut Zwahr, ed., *Die Konstituierung der deutschen Arbeiterklasse von den dreißiger bis zu den siebziger Jahren des 19. Jahrhunderts* (Berlin, 1981).

14. For analyses see Hartmut Keil and Heinz Ickstadt, "Elements of German Working-Class Culture in Chicago, 1880 to 1890," in *German Workers' Culture*, ed. Keil, 81–105; Heinz Ickstadt and Klaus Ensslen, "German Working-Class Culture in Chicago: Continuity and Change in the Decade from 1900 to 1910," in *German Workers in Industrial Chicago*, ed. Keil and Jentz, 236–52. For examples of the local and communal context in which German-American working-class culture flourished, see the collection of documents in *German Workers in Chicago: A Documentary History of Working-Class Culture from 1850 to World War I*, ed. Hartmut Keil and John B. Jentz (Urbana, 1988), and Hartmut Keil, "Immigrant Neighborhoods and American Society: German Immigrants on Chicago's Northwest Side in the Late Nineteenth Century," in *German Workers' Culture*, ed. Keil, 25–58. For an analysis of the development of the German working class and of German working-class culture see Gerhard A. Ritter, *Arbeiter, Arbeiterbewegung und soziale Ideen in Deutschland: Beiträge zur Geschichte des 19. und 20. Jahrhunderts* (Munich, 1996); Gerhard A. Ritter and Klaus Tenfelde, *Arbeiter im Deutschen Kaiserreich 1871–1914* (Bonn, 1992); Gerhard A. Ritter, *Die Sozialdemokratie im Deutschen Kaiserreich in sozialgeschichtlicher Perspektive* (Munich, 1989); Vernon L. Lidtke, *The Alternative Culture: Socialist Labor in Imperial Germany* (New York, 1985).

15. Edward Thimme, "Die deutschen Arbeiter und die englische Sprache," *New Yorker Volkszeitung* (tenth anniversary issue), 28 January 1888.

16. "Wilhelm Liebknecht in Brooklyn," *New Yorker Volkszeitung*, 24 September 1886.

17. E.g., Sorge, "Socialism and the Worker," Jonas, "Reporter and Socialist," Douai, "Better Times," Hepner, "Immoral and Unconstitutional: Our Accessory Laws. A Postscription to the Chicago Anarchists' Case," Hoehn, "Labor and Capital."

18. "The New Party," *Standard*, 30 July 1887.

19. "Socialism and the New Party," *Standard*, 6 August 1887.

20. "The United Labor Party and Socialism," *Standard*, 13 August 1887.

21. See, e.g., *New Yorker Volkszeitung*, 13 October 1881.

22. *New Yorker Volkszeitung*, 18 and 20 September, 10 October, and 21 November 1881; Minutes, Central Committee, SLP New York, Socialist Party Collection, Tamiment Institute, New York University. See also Hartmut Keil, "An Ambivalent Identity: The Attitude of German Socialist Immigrants Toward American Political Institutions and American Citizenship," in *In the Shadow of the Statue of Liberty: Immigrants, Workers and Citizens in the American Republic, 1880–1920 / A l'ombre de la statue de la Liberté: Immigrants et ouvriers dans la République américaine 1880–1920* (Saint-Denis, 1988), 247–63.

23. For a more detailed discussion of these issues see Hartmut Keil, "German Working-Class Radicalism in the United States from the 1870s to World War I," in *"Struggle a Hard Battle,"* ed. Hoerder, 71–94, especially pages 76–86.

24. Chicago *Vorbote*, 13 May 1876.

25. Julius Vahlteich, "Der Einigungskongreß der amerikanischen Sozialisten in Indianapolis," *Neue Zeit* 19, no. 2 (1900–1901): 663–66.

26. Alexander Jonas to Morris Hillquit, 23 June 1904, Morris Hillquit Papers, Correspondence, Box 1, State Historical Society of Wisconsin, Madison.

27. Research on gender roles is so voluminous that only a few references are given here. See, e.g., Mary Jo Buhle, *Women and American Socialism* (Urbana, 1982); Donna Gabaccia,

From the Other Side: Women, Gender, and Immigrant Life in the U.S., 1820–1990 (Blooming-ton, 1994); Dorothee Schneider, "For Whom Are All the Good Things in Life? German-American Housewives Discuss Their Budgets," in *German Workers in Industrial Chicago*, ed. Keil and Jentz, 145–60; Ruth Seifert, "The Portrayal of Women in the German-Amer-ican Labor Movement," in *German Workers' Culture*, ed. Keil, 109–36; parts III and IV of *People in Transit*, ed. Hoerder and Nagler, 227–397; *Peasant Maids—City Women: From the European Countryside to Urban America*, ed. Christiane Harzig (Ithaca, 1997).

28. Nancy Berteaux, "Structural Economic Change and Occupational Decline among Black Workers in Nineteenth-Century Cincinnati," in *Race and the City: Work, Community, and Protest in Cincinnati, 1820–1970*, ed. Henry Louis Taylor, Jr. (Urbana, 1993), 126–55.

29. So far no specific studies have been made on German immigrant workers and their attitude toward race and identity. However, see David Roediger, *The Wages of White-ness: Race and the Making of the American Working Class* (London, 1991); David Roediger, *Towards the Abolition of Whiteness: Essays on Race, Politics, and Working-Class History* (London, 1994); Noel Ignatiev, *How the Irish Became White* (New York, 1995); James Bar-rett and David Roediger, "In Between Peoples: Race, Nationality and the New Immi-grant Working Class," *Journal of American Ethnic History* (Spring, 1997); Matthew Frye Jacobson, *Whiteness of a Different Color: European Immigrants and the Alchemy of Race* (Cambridge, MA, 1998); and Russell A. Kazal, "Becoming 'Old Stock': The Waning of German-American Identity in Philadelphia, 1900–1930" (Ph.D. dissertation, University of Pennsylvania, Ann Arbor, MI: UMI, 1998).

Chapter 4

"Sisters, Arise!"

The Intersections of Nineteenth-Century
German and American Feminist Movements

Patricia Herminghouse

In 1915, just nine years after the death of the American feminist Susan B. Anthony, Katharine S. Anthony* set out to rectify what she recognized as the widespread misconception that the German woman "still sleeps silently in a home-spun cocoon … that the German women are a leaderless and hopelessly domesticated group and are content to remain so." The images that had gained currency on this side of the ocean, she asserted, were "obviously misrepresentative; such as, what the German Emperor regards as a woman's sphere [*Kinder, Küche, Kirche*], what the German Empress thinks of woman suffrage, and what Schopenhauer has written against the sex."[1] Remarking that for many years, German women had given their sisters on the other side of the Atlantic more praise than they deserved, the younger Anthony offered the first English-language account of feminism in the Germanic countries of Europe. While one might dispute the details of her interpretation, it is indeed true that although there were some cross-national dialogues between groups of women working on particular forms of social activism,[2] the conversation, as I will attempt to show, was both intermittent and somewhat one-sided. Nineteenth-century German feminists watched and reported on the struggle for emancipation in the New World to a far greater extent than did their American sisters—including the well-traveled Susan B. Anthony, whose commentaries on her travels to Germany reflect scant understanding of theoretical or social developments in that country. In a remark that itself reveals a rather naive assessment of developments in Germany after the momentous 1904 meeting of the International Council

---

*Katharine Susan Anthony, 1877–1965, a writer, biographer, and women's rights advocate, was not related to Susan B. Anthony.

of Women (ICW) in Berlin, Katherine Anthony reports on one of the ways in which the American delegates were surprised:

> They were accustomed to think of themselves as superior orators—which they were. The discovery that the German women, in their language, measured up to them and sometimes surpassed them seemed incredible.... Susan could only deduce that a strong and powerful woman's movement lay behind this. She was partially right. The German women were already well organized. They received further impetus through the International Council, and they prospered and grew stronger with the years, until, at the impact of World War I, their organizations were all wiped out.[3]

Remarks by the 85–year-old Susan B. Anthony, for whom the Berlin meeting was the high point of her illustrious career, do imply a somewhat ethnocentric view. Her impertinent exhortation to the Empress Auguste Victoria at a reception for the visiting feminists also suggests that Anthony saw German women through the lens of the old saw "Kinder, Küche, Kirche." Anthony admonished the Empress, who had praised her lifelong work, to urge her husband to "vie with the United States in endeavoring to place German women on an equality with ours, and that he will devote his attention to this as well as to augmenting the commercial greatness of his country." To which the Empress is reported to have replied, "The gentlemen are very slow to comprehend this movement."[4]

Anthony's biographer also reports that "much amusement was created by Miss Anthony's naive remark in one of her speeches that she now appreciated more than ever the need that there should be one language for all the world, and this should be English!"[5] Among the small group of American social justice feminists in attendance, including Jane Addams, Mary Church Terrell, and Florence Kelley, there were, however, some women with solid knowledge of German who were able to engage in intellectual dialog with their German counterparts. Terrell, an African American who had been invited to speak in Berlin, noted the German women's chagrin at Anglo-Americans' insistence on the use of English and decided to deliver her address, entitled "Die Fortschritte der Farbigen Frauen," in German.[6] While the Berlin meetings in 1904—there were actually two, since a suffrage convention preceded the grander ICW meeting—marked, by all measures, the culmination of both German and American nineteenth-century feminist endeavors, it is also possible to see in this event the intersections of discourses that were more fundamentally different than the languages in which they were articulated, and to question popular notions of a unified international feminism. To grasp the sometimes complex interrelationship of nineteenth-century American and German feminisms, one might consider as exemplary some historical events of the year 1848 on opposite sides of the Atlantic.

On 19 July 1848, sixty-eight women and twenty-eight men, among them husbands of the organizers and the black abolitionist Frederick Douglass, gathered in the Wesleyan Chapel of the village of Seneca Falls,

New York, at the invitation of Elizabeth Cady Stanton and the Quaker Lucretia Mott. They met to consider an audacious "Declaration of Sentiments," which appropriated the language of the American Declaration of Independence in order to show how the situation of women and people of color was at irreconcilable odds with the most cherished values of the founding American document. "We hold these truths to be self-evident," their declaration asserted, "that all men *and women* are created equal" [my emphasis]. They argued that suffrage must be granted to all in order to remedy the abuses of fundamental rights of the disenfranchised. Douglass's support of the women's movement remained strong until the end of the Civil War, when racist elements began to pervade the discourse of American feminists who believed that constitutional amendments giving rights to freed Negro males degraded white women and deprived them of their rights.

Across the ocean in Germany, on 27 September 1848, only two months after the Seneca Falls meeting, Mathilde Franziska Anneke took over the Cologne office of her imprisoned husband, who had been editor of the *Neue Kölnische Zeitung*, and began publishing a new journal, the *Frauen-Zeitung*. Rather than the "feminist" text that one might expect from a woman who had already gained notoriety with her pamphlet, *Das Weib im Conflict mit den socialen Verhältnissen* (1847), the first issue of the paper opened with a tirade advocating absolute separation of church and school, asserting that there was no such thing as a "Christian" alphabet or a pious form of spelling, reading, writing, and arithmetic. (The second issue has been lost to history and the third was confiscated before it could be distributed.) Imposing religion on children, she asserted, merely produces "an unfortunate division and hatred between Catholics and Protestants, Lutherans, Jews, German-Catholics, and whatever else they are all called."[7] Anneke's primary concern with education and the absence of any demand for suffrage in her *Frauen-Zeitung* stand clearly in the tradition of nineteenth-century German feminism, which tended to seek remedies for social discrimination against women through amelioration of their educational deprivation rather than through access to the ballot box.

Upon Fritz Anneke's release from prison, the couple fled in 1850 to the United States, where Mathilde Franziska Anneke became, in her own way, a supporter of the American feminist cause. She quickly moved to establish the radical but short-lived *Deutsche Frauen-Zeitung* as the first feminist newspaper in the United States and later founded a Milwaukee school for German American girls. As a German woman of 1848, it was not only her lack of fluency in the English language, but her rather typical background in the anti-religion, free-thinker rebellion against the Metternichean state that initially complicated Anneke's integration into the American women's movement. By 1869, however, she enjoyed the status of vice-president of the Wisconsin chapter of the National Woman Suffrage Association.

Although some American feminists, such as Elizabeth Cady Stanton and Matilda Joslyn Gage, had emerged as anti-church freethinkers by the late nineteenth century, mid-nineteenth century American feminists came almost without exception from evangelical, church-affiliated moral reform movements. They dedicated themselves to charitable causes, such as the protection of children, care of the indigent, and especially to the temperance crusade and the abolition of slavery. Women in the movement soon realized the parallels between their own situation, particularly their lack of property and marriage rights, and the oppression of slaves. The connection was made between the enfranchisement of women and the need to purify the nation. As a result of their activities on behalf of the abolition movement in the 1840s, which included gathering signatures for petitions to Congress, organizing fund-raising fairs, and speaking out within their congregations, these women developed their self-confidence as well as a network of like-minded citizens. Thus, they were able to mobilize as they began to extend the campaign for rights to persons of both genders.[8] This was true of Lucretia Mott and Elizabeth Cady Stanton, whose feminist awakening followed the humiliation they had experienced upon their exclusion, as women, from participation in an international abolition conference held in London in 1840. Susan B. Anthony experienced similar discrimination at the 1853 World Temperance Convention in New York.

Although no formal organization existed until the establishment of the Woman's National Loyal League under Stanton and Anthony during the Civil War, the hardy band of reformers who got their start at Seneca Falls in 1848 soon began holding women's rights meetings in various cities almost every year until 1860, including national conventions (often presided over by their husbands or other male supporters). At the September 1853 convention in New York, Mathilde Franziska Anneke, who had addressed groups of German women throughout the eastern United States on what she described as an *Agitationsreise* in 1852, spoke for the first time to an American audience, despite the handicap posed by her lack of fluency in the English language. Of this appearance, Anthony and Stanton report that, "after many attempts, and with great difficulty owing to the tumult and interruption by impertinent noises, she spoke ... in German, with Mrs. [Ernestine] Rose translating her remarks into English." In her speech, she reminded those in attendance of the importance of honoring the American principle of free speech, even when people disagree among themselves, as these women's rights pioneers surely did: "There is no republic without freedom of speech."[9] Unfortunately, American activists had no access to translations of any of Anneke's German-language fiction, with its stirring depictions of the treatment of slave women at the hands of white masters.[10] In the course of the years, she appears to be the only German American woman to develop a cordial relationship with Stanton and Anthony, both of whom relied upon her in the post–Civil War period to rally Germans in various states to the cause of female suffrage. One could not assume such support, even among the liberal German element, as can be seen, for example, in a comment by Emil Mallinckrodt in the St. Louis *Westliche Post*:

The unqualified, general right to vote has turned out poorly in the United States. That not being enough, during the war some 700,000 colored votes also suddenly tumbled into the voting boxes; all that is now missing to carry out the greatest of all farces at the polls are enfranchised women, black and white, among them the genderless who do not want to be women and cannot be men.[11]

Most German women in the New World were not particularly active in the feminist cause, in part because the domestic role in maintaining the traditional culture of their ethnic communities weighed more heavily upon women than men.[12] In writing about the scant participation of German American women in the literary and journalistic sphere, Dorothea Stuecher asserts that, unlike many women writers in Germany and American women in the United States, immigrant women were seldom childless or even unmarried.[13] This pattern of non-involvement in the American women's movement was true of women who lived in urban ethnic German neighborhoods as well as those in more isolated rural areas. Their organizational activity was generally limited to their own (usually conservative) immigrant religious community, at least until after the Civil War, when more radical, political organizations, such as the Deutsche Frauen-Stimmrechtsverein of New York (1872) or the Radikaler Deutscher Frauenverein of Sauk City, Wisconsin (1871) emerged. An examination of the women's pages of urban German-language newspapers such as the *Illinois Staats-Zeitung* and the *Chicagoer Freie Presse* reveals that, insofar as the women's movement was concerned, German-language readers were informed about international developments, including the German women's movement in Germany, and about achievements of American women in education and professional life. However, almost nothing was reported about the American women's movement. The balance of coverage was devoted to the domestic sphere and to the activities of the various German women's clubs and circles.[14] The few German émigré women who attempted to break out of traditional roles in the new country, such as Anneke, had typically already done so in Germany.

This was certainly true of the fiercely independent Ottilie Assing, whose assiduous reading before her 1852 emigration had already shaped her perceptions of the contradictions between the American dream and the persistence of American slavery. Among the texts that moved her were Harriet Beecher Stowe's *Uncle Tom's Cabin*, Heinrich von Kleist's novella *Die Verlobung in St. Domingo* (1811), and Clara Mundt's *Aphra Behn* (1849), a love story whose title figure was the author of a seventeenth-century novel about a slave rebellion.[15] Within a year of her arrival in New York, Assing traveled to Rochester, New York, to meet with Frederick Douglass, a former slave who had assumed leadership in the abolition movement. Having obtained permission from Douglass to translate his autobiography into German, in 1857 she spent the first of what would be more than two decades of summers living in the Douglass household.

Only very recently has Maria Diedrich documented the extent of her years of collaboration with Douglass, including the intimate nature of a relationship that most chroniclers have preferred not to see.

Assing's attitude toward the American women's movement was ambiguous at best. Writing from New York as a correspondent for the *Augsburger Allgemeine Zeitung* in 1857, she described with considerable acumen the differences between European and American *Emancipations-Propagandisten*. In Europe, she explained, the cause of emancipation was taken less seriously because it was "promoted almost exclusively by intelligent, although quite young and impractical men and women." A second significant difference that, at least initially, minimized factionalism in the American movement, was the ability of these American "Emancipationists" to count on support from "followers of the most diverse religious creeds, whereas the issue there [in Germany] is only raised by the adherents of the most extreme freethinker persuasion and thus is opposed from the very beginning by the general masses of the population. Here [in the United States], on the other hand, orthodox believers and atheists, Quakers and Methodists ... and clergy of all faiths peacefully join hands. No one is deterred from standing up for the rights of women for fear of looking like a heretic."[16]

In the United States, she reported one year later, "many important, experienced, and generally respected men have set themselves up as defenders of women's emancipation." These included the likes of Wendell Phillips, Horace Greeley, and Horace Mann—to say nothing of Frederick Douglass and William Lloyd Garrison, whom she did not mention.[17] Assing repeatedly expressed concern, however, that not all women were sufficiently educated to be able to form well-founded independent opinions in political matters. In her reports from the 1850s, one can also find traces of nativist suffrage arguments. She asserted that it would be a scandal to have educated, informed women excluded from the vote that was available to the stupidest men, such as Germans who know hardly a word of English or illiterate Irishmen, who enjoyed suffrage as citizens just because they had lived in the United States for five years. It may be that her own lifestyle and personal beliefs, including her atheism, led her to maintain her distance from the spirited women's movement that was also centered in Rochester. Diedrich, in fact, credits Douglass with influencing Assing to be more supportive of his friend Susan B. Anthony and her circle.[18] Whatever sympathies she may have mustered for the movement turned to deep hostility when the question of who shall and who shall not have the vote surfaced with particular virulence at the end of the Civil War. Unlike Douglass, who overcame the rift that developed between the feminists and the rest of the anti-slavery coalition over the so-called Reconstruction amendments to the Constitution, Assing remained permanently antagonistic.

The American women's movement split over the conflicts regarding the rights of citizenship and enfranchisement given to blacks in the Fourteenth and Fifteenth amendments, losing some of the impetus it might otherwise have regained in the post–Civil War era. In 1868, to the dismay of their long-time supporter Frederick Douglass, many women withdrew from the recently established American Equal Rights Association to protest the inclusion of the word "male" in the Fourteenth amendment. Angered by this first attempt to restrict constitutional rights by gender, the more radical New York-based National Woman Suffrage Association (Anthony and Stanton's anti-clerical, pro-working class group) called on voters to place "Woman first, and the Negro last."[19] The more moderate Boston group, the American Woman Suffrage Association, persisted unsuccessfully in its attempt to link the cause for enfranchisement for women with that for blacks. It was not until 1890 that the two factions were finally able to reunite as the National American Woman Suffrage Association (NAWSA). However, by the late 1890s NAWSA had become "a self-consciously elite movement,"[20] as reflected somewhat comically in the glowing reports that its members sent back detailing the elegant manners of imperial Berlin in 1904. After the lessons learned in the unfortunate split during the 1870s and 1880s, the structure of the movement had also become much tighter—uptight, in fact—as its leadership strove for "perfect coordination and discipline of its ranks ... a disciplined political organization."[21] In this respect it evinced some similarities to the increasingly well-organized German movement, for which great admiration was expressed.

While the enfranchisement of women gained momentum in the western states during the last decades of the century, the influx of new immigrants in eastern cities included many men who were resistant to the idea of woman suffrage. In response to the development and enfranchisement of freedmen, feminist arguments for suffrage became tinged with nativist and racist claims. An example of such claims was that white women's votes would help to control the Negro population. The assertion was less that women needed the vote for their own self-protection, but rather for the preservation of existing institutions. The guiding belief in individual equality coupled with concern for protection of vulnerable classes that had characterized the mid-century American women's movement now shifted toward a greater emphasis on sex-role differences and the need for social control. While this tendency was benignly manifest in the work of social reformers such as Jane Addams and Florence Kelley, who in the years between 1885 and 1933 developed a network of contacts with middle-class German social welfare reformers,[22] there were also more insidious developments. The Women's Christian Temperance Union, organized in 1874, was able to forge alliances with the suffragists based on its position that women needed the vote in order to end the evils of liquor. This group too became increasingly nativist as the influx of new immigrants peaked in the latter part of the century, and xenophobia reached its height in the post–World War I era. These developments held little potential for engaging German women.

On German soil, there was little talk of votes for women in the decades after 1848, which is not particularly surprising in view of the denial of even universal manhood suffrage. More importantly, however, women's freedom of speech—here understood in terms of their right to participate in the public sphere—was effectively curtailed by the *Vereinsgesetz* (Prussian anti-association laws) of 1850, prohibiting participation in public meetings or political associations to persons who were minors, dependents, mentally defective, or female. The option that remained available to German women was the establishment of private organizations, open only to registered members. In 1865, the General German Women's Association (Allgemeiner deutscher Frauenverein) was founded by Louise Otto-Peters and Auguste Schmidt as an umbrella organization for the many private women's associations that had been formed, most of which were focused on the domestic sphere of family and the education of girls, or, increasingly, on better training and increased professional and educational opportunities for women, especially those who were not wives and mothers. The voice of Hedwig Dohm, who had called for female suffrage in 1876, long remained without resonance, whereas in the United States, Susan B. Anthony had already been arrested in 1873 for her attempt to vote in Rochester, New York, a development that elicited a passionate defense from her friend Mathilde Anneke.[23]

As Catherine Prelinger has shown, the roots of nineteenth-century German feminism can also be traced to religious origins, such as the radical free (German-Catholic) congregations. The agenda of these feminists through most of the century remained primarily philanthropic and meliorative: care for the sick and the poor, education of young girls. Unlike their American sisters, whose demands for admission to the full prerogatives of citizenship were based on Enlightenment notions of individual freedom and natural rights, German middle-class feminists were less interested in suffrage, arguing instead for improvement in education, marriage, and the professions as rights that they had *earned* on the basis of fulfilling their gender-specific duties to society. Increasingly, maternalist arguments regarding the dangers of childbirth and the importance of child rearing dominated their pursuit of equality in the domestic, economic, and educational realms rather than in the political sphere.[24] "Motherhood," Helene Lange was to declare in 1893, "is the most important career, because it includes the profession of educator of future generations."[25] It is critical to remember that, associated as it was with Young German notions of "emancipation of the flesh," the very word *Emanzipation* in German connoted a threat to the security of bourgeois women. As Patricia Paulsell cogently pointed out, the "emancipatory" impulses of the Young German era were, in terms of the social reality of the times, favorable only to men: "Easier divorces and relaxation of marriage laws would allow them to escape more easily from the only institution in which women found material security more easily; relaxation of women's protection of their virginity would most probably result in compromising situations that could lead to the stigma of unwanted pregnancy, illegitimate children and a possible life of prostitution."[26] Middle-class German women entered the public sphere reluctantly, and even Louise Otto, who began issuing her *Frauen-Zeitung* in 1849 with the call "Wohl auf Schwestern, vereinigt euch mit mir" (Arise, sisters, and join with me), soon modified her position to state that women's participation in the state would assume "a *different* character and [occupy] a *different* realm from that of men."[27] Women did indeed form "democratic clubs" to aid victims of the revolutions of 1848/49, and even—like Mathilde Anneke—fought at the sides of the men in their lives, but given subsequent political developments, these activities did not give them a basis for positioning themselves in civil society.

While American women were once again working toward unity, deep divisions, caused by a split along party lines between bourgeois and socialist women, emerged in the German movement. Socialist women, led by Clara Zetkin and Lily Braun, found their place in the Social Democratic Party (SPD). In the first year after the repeal of the anti-socialist laws, the SPD demanded women's suffrage in its 1891 platform; by 1895 it was focusing its social reform efforts on unionizing working women. The "moderate" middle-class faction, with its focus on individual rights, reorganized into the Bund Deutscher Frauenvereine (BDF) in 1894, and continued to concentrate on bourgeois social welfare programs—including a very public "abolition" campaign for an end to state control of prostitution in the late 1890s. For fear of contamination by "politics," however, they refused to admit socialist women's organizations. As a result, socialist women were not visible in Berlin in 1904, even at the establishment of the International Woman Suffrage Alliance, with which the German Association for Women Suffrage, founded in 1902, allied itself. Such a step would have been unthinkable had not the enforcement of the *Vereinsgesetz*, which was finally repealed in 1908, already been somewhat relaxed.

As has recently been demonstrated with the documents collected by Kathryn Kish Sklar and others in *Social Justice Feminists in the United States and Germany*, the most extensive dialog between German and American women occurred toward the end of the nineteenth century and until World War I among the social reformers of both countries. These were left-of-center, middle-class social justice feminists, who seriously attempted to learn from one another's political culture. On the American side, Jane Addams, Mary Church Terrell, and Florence Kelley traveled extensively and studied in Germany, taking particular interest in large-scale, nationally based social welfare programs. In Germany, Alice Salomon, Käthe Schirmacher, and Minna Cauer paid close attention to American women's grassroots political activism, which was less tied to political parties. German women were far better informed about American developments, especially those who traveled to events, such as the women's rights convention called by the National Council of Women (NCW) at the 1893 Columbian Exposition in Chicago. Upon their return to Germany they established the BDF in 1894, an umbrella organization explicitly modeled on the NCW.[28]

The middle-class liberalism of the BDF came to a swift end after the 1904 Berlin conference, however, when the large and extremely reactionary Deutsch-evangelischer Frauenbund joined its ranks in 1908. The election of Gertrud Bäumer as president of the organization in 1910 initiated a further move to the right and precluded admission of Helene Stöcker's radical Bund für Mutterschutz, whose ideas regarding legalized abortion, protection of unwed mothers, contraception, and the abolition of state regulation of prostitution were no longer acceptable to the newly strengthened conservative majority.[29] Furthermore, the end of the *Vereinsgesetz* encouraged women from the upper social classes in the Rhineland, North Germany, the Ruhr, and Silesia to join the movement,[30] which had long been dominated by women from Berlin and Saxony, thus pushing it further to the right. Even the opening of the German universities tended to have this effect.[31]

From 1908 to 1914 the movement also began to turn toward forms of Social Darwinism, nationalism, and particularism, distancing itself "from demands for universal suffrage, world peace, [and] cooperation with the Social Democrats…. The fight against vice was transformed from a fight for the dignity of the individual woman to a campaign against racial disloyalty to the German state."[32] By 1912, the Federation to Combat the Emancipation of Women had been founded, with considerable support from the Deutsch-evangelischer Frauenbund.[33]

Although German-Jewish women, especially after 1871, had been active in the German bourgeois women's movement, the 1904 Berlin meeting, which brought them together with Jewish women from other nations, provided the impetus for the establishment of their own organization, the Jüdischer Frauenbund. Founded by Bertha Pappenheim, who just two years earlier had established Weibliche Fürsorge as a kind of Jewish social work agency, the Jüdischer Frauenbund was a much more ambitious organization. Adapting the approaches of middle-class German feminism to the needs of women in the Jewish community in matters of women's rights, social ills, and opportunities for women and girls, it grew in less than a decade into the largest organizational member of the BDF.[34] In thus founding their own organization, Jewish women were part of a larger pattern, not only of Jewish women's societies (the National Council of Jewish Women was founded in United States in 1893), but of organizations formed along religious lines that ultimately undermined solidarity. Protestant and Catholic women's associations had also recently been established, in 1899 and 1903. Like these groups, the Jüdischer Frauenbund also participated in what Marion Kaplan calls "the rhetoric of domesticity," although with different emphases: "German women stressed educational and career interests, whereas Jewish women were concerned primarily with social work," placing a higher value on social reform than on strictly "feminist" goals.[35]

The lively, joyful stirrings of international sisterhood that appeared to characterize the 1904 Berlin meeting ended almost as suddenly as they had started with the onset of World War I, when even peace activists in Germany and America could not maintain their dialog. Ironically, at the end of that war, some seventy years after the movement that began at Seneca Falls, women of both nations received the vote, although through somewhat different mechanisms: in the United States, the granting of suffrage that had been well underway in individual states since the late nineteenth century was finally enacted as an amendment to the Constitution in 1920, whereas in Germany it came about through the need in 1919 to fashion a democratic constitution for the state that arose from the ruins of the empire. The increase in nativist sentiments in the United States and the drift toward National Socialism in Germany presented new obstacles to German-American feminist dialog in the subsequent decades.

Notes

1. Katharine S. Anthony, *Feminism in Germany and Scandinavia* (New York, 1915), iii.
2. Kathryn Kish Sklar, Anja Schüler, and Susan Strasser, eds., *Social Justice Feminists in the United States and Germany* (Ithaca, 1998), 2.
3. Anthony, *Feminism*, 481.
4. Ida Husted Harper, *The Life and Work of Susan B. Anthony*, 3 vols. (Indianapolis, 1908), 1319.
5. Ibid., 1321.
6. Mary Church Terrell, *A Colored Woman in a White World*, 1940 edition (New York, 1996), 169–208.
7. As quoted in Martin Henkel and Rolf Taubert, *Das Weib im Conflict mit den socialen Verhältnissen: Mathilde Franziska Anneke und die erste deutsche Frauenzeitung* (Bochum, 1976), 48–49.
8. Gerda Lerner, *The Creation of Feminist Consciousness* (New York, 1993) cites as exemplary the way that women began to challenge the authority of the church and traditional Biblical exegesis by extracting their own interpretations, such as the dissident Quaker Sarah Grimké's *Letters on the Equality of the Sexes*, published in 1838. Quoting approvingly Grimké's assertion "that intellect is not sexed; ... and that our views about ... the sphere of man and the sphere of woman are mere arbitrary opinion, differing in ages and countries, and dependant solely on the will and judgement of erring mortals" (*Letters*, 60), Lerner remarks: "Here, Sarah Grimké, reasoning by way of a close reading of the scriptural text and relying only on her own judgment and interpretations, defined the difference between sex and gender and stated, in terms which would not be as clearly stated again until late in the 20th century: gender is a culturally variable, arbitrary definition of behavior appropriate to each of the sexes" (163).
9. Elizabeth Cady Stanton, Susan B. Anthony, and Matilda J. Gage, eds., *History of Woman Suffrage*, 3 vols. (Rochester, NY, 1881), vol. 1: 571–72.
10. See Mathilde Franziska Anneke, *Die Gebrochenen Ketten: Erzählungen, Reportagen und Reden (1861–1873)*, ed. Maria Wagner (Stuttgart, 1983).
11. Quoted in Anita M. Mallinckrodt, *From Knights to Pioneers: One German Family in Westphalia and Missouri* (Carbondale, 1994), 383.

12. See Christiane Harzig, "Elemente einer deutschamerikanischen Frauenkultur: Deutsch-amerikanerinnen in Chicago vor der Jahrhundertwende," in *Frauen wandern aus: Deutsche Migrantinnen im 19. und 20. Jahrhundert*, ed. Monika Blaschke and Christiane Harzig (Bremen, 1990), 113–25.

13. Dorothea Stuecher, *Twice Removed: The Experience of German-American Women Writers in the 19th Century* (New York, 1990), 25–26.

14. Harzig, "Elemente einer deutschamerikanischen Frauenkultur," 115–17.

15. Maria Diedrich, *Love across Color Lines: Ottilie Assing and Frederick Douglass* (New York, 1999), 83–85.

16. "Frauenrechtsversammlung," in *Was die Deutschen aus Amerika berichteten, 1828–1865*, ed. Maria Wagner (Stuttgart, 1985), 15–16.

17. "Frauenrechte," in Wagner, ed., *Was die Deutschen aus Amerika berichteten*, 19.

18. Diedrich, *Love across Color Lines*," 209–10.

19. Mari Jo Buhle and Paul Buhle, "Introduction: Woman Suffrage and American Reform," in *The Concise History of Woman Suffrage: Selections from the Classic Work of Stanton, Anthony, Gage, and Harper*, ed. Mari Jo Buhle and Paul Buhle (Urbana, 1978), 15.

20. Ibid., 30.

21. Ibid., 33.

22. See Sklar, Schüler, and Strasser, *Social Justice Feminists*.

23. Anneke, *Die Gebrochenen Ketten*, 223–26.

24. See Ann Taylor Allen, *Feminism and Motherhood in Germany 1800–1914* (New Brunswick, 1991).

25. Helene Lange, "Was wir wollen," *Die Frau: Monatsschrift für das gesamte Frauenleben unserer Zeit*, 1:1 (October 1893), reprinted in Elke Frederiksen, ed., *Die Frauenfrage in Deutschland 1865–1915: Texte und Dokumente* (Stuttgart, 1981), 51.

26. Patricia Margaret Ryan Paulsell, "The Relationship of 'Young Germany' to Questions of Women's Rights" (Ph.D. dissertation, University of Michigan, 1976).

27. Emphasis as in original. *Vortrag* (1849), as quoted in Catherine M. Prelinger, *Charity, Challenge, and Change: Religious Dimensions of the Mid-Nineteenth-Century Women's Movement in Germany* (Westport, CT, 1987), 106–7.

28. Sklar, Schüler, and Strasser, *Social Justice Feminists*, 26.

29. In an eerie foreshadowing of historical developments still to come, Stöcker's radical notion of *Mutterschutz* included among its goals the ideal of "Hebung der Rasse" [elevation of the race]. Eugenic arguments were made by some in the American movement as well. See Helene Stöcker, "Ehe und Sexualreform" (1916), reprinted in Frederiksen, ed., *Die Frauenfrage in Deutschland*, 149–53.

30. Buhle and Buhle, "Woman Suffrage."

31. Richard J. Evans, *The Feminists: Women's Emancipation Movements in Europe, America and Australasia 1840–1920* (New York, 1977), 201.

32. Ibid., 200.

33. This development, which was not unique to Germany, is traced in fascinating detail in Amy Rae Legler, "Antifeminism and National Diffferences: The German League for the Prevention of Women's Emancipation and the U.S. National Association Opposed to Woman Suffrage, 1911–1920" (M.A. thesis, Michigan State University, 1995).

34. Marion A. Kaplan, *The Jewish Feminist Movement in Germany: The Campaigns of the Jüdischer Frauenbund, 1904–1938* (Westport, CT, 1979), 11f.

35. Ibid., 73.

Chapter 5

THE FUTURE OF GERMAN RELIGION IN NORTH AMERICA

A. Gregg Roeber

Historians of the late twentieth century may someday choose 1998 to date the end of the Reformation in North America. Despite three centuries of migration from the German-speaking part of Europe where the Reformation ostensibly began in 1517, the results of a study made public in 1998 suggest that 480 years later, major aspects of German religious life that have tied North America to Germany may have gone into eclipse.

Sponsored by the Lutheran Brotherhood fraternal insurance group, a questionnaire survey sampling 4,600 Lutheran households revealed that Reformation soil has eroded significantly in the United States. Nearly half of the respondents claimed to believe that people could be just in God's sight by loving others; most believe that the Gospel is a set of rules for ethical living; most thought that all world religions lead to the same God; a near-majority denied that children enter the world as sinners. Whatever else the survey reveals, it suggests that Dietrich Bonhoeffer, the German martyr of the Confessing Church in Germany, may have already discerned the fate of the Reformation in the United States in the 1930s.[1]

Bonhoeffer concluded that there had never really been a Reformation in America. Instead, he wrote, "In American theology, Christianity is essentially religion and ethics. But that means that the person and work of Jesus Christ have to retire into the theological background, and finally remain uncomprehended."[2]

German Speakers and Post-Protestant America

Since the seventeenth century, large migrations of German speakers to North America have been dominated by people connected in some way to organized religious groups. But as late as the 1970s a major interpretive text on religion in America had nothing to say about the German speakers at all.[3] More recently, however, assessments of North American Christianity, whether Catholic or Protestant, acknowledge the significance of German-speakers in shaping the Christian faith in the United States and Canada. Yet the most influential of these, Mark Noll's magisterial *History of Christianity in the United States and Canada*, rightly suggests that by the late twentieth century, North America had become, in a sense, a religious wilderness again. The passing of "Christian America" or "Christian Canada," Noll writes, may well turn out a blessing instead of tragedy. "Freed from the burden of American messianism, churches may find it possible to concentrate more on the Source of Life than on the American Way of Life."[4] If Bonhoeffer was right, however, perhaps German-speaking religion had already vanished even before the "burden of messianism" had been lifted.

Certainly, the old indebtedness of American Protestant theology to German liberal theology of the nineteenth century has passed from the scene. No contemporary German theologian such as Friedrich Schleiermacher or Adolf von Harnack, or pioneers of Biblical criticism such as David Friedrich Strauss or Julius Wellhausen, could exert on contemporary Americans the impact those giants worked upon Octavius Brooks Frothingham or Walter Rauschenbusch. Nor will America see a German theological migration like the one that connected Protestant neo-orthodoxy and the work of Karl Barth in the 1930s to North American universities in the persons of immigrants like Wilhelm Pauck or Paul Tillich. In addition, whatever cross-fertilizations occur, they may well happen outside of university contexts. If George Marsden's analysis of American universities is correct, schools of theology will continue a trajectory further and further away from actual communities of faith in America. In this respect, North America still resonates to religious patterns in contemporary Germany, for German university theological faculties seem to have few real connections to the largely empty German churches.[5]

In 1972, the late Sidney Ahlstrom, in his magisterial study of religion in North America, noted that American society had become decisively "post-Protestant." By this, Ahlstrom meant to alert readers to the death of two cherished myths in how Americans looked at their past: that of the "elect nation" and the "melting pot." Noll's assessment, noted above, affirms the shrewdness of Ahlstrom's observation. Yet even today, European observers of American religion find such a perspective puzzling. To them, despite the non-established character of religion in America, no other industrial and diverse nation in the world seems to debate religious matters so intensely as part of public discourse. The persistence of debate over religion, for them, seems to belie this notion of a "post-Protestant" or even "post-Christian" America. This chapter, however, argues that Ahlstrom was right, and no amount of engagement with the categories inherited from North America's past three hundred years can restore to Americans, whether or not of German heritage, the sense of confidence in a peculiar destiny thought to be bound to a Protestant Christian world-view and the infinite capacity of North America to absorb and to "assimilate" peoples from all over the world.[6] If this assertion is true, then one is bound to look beyond affinities of transferred German-speaking Judaism or Christianity to discern what the "future" of religious ties, which could bind the emerging "Berlin Republic" to the United States in the twenty-first century, might look like.

Three Strains of German-American Religious Life

In attempting to discern such a possible future, one should begin by reviewing the German speakers' relationship to the broader contours of American religious life. I suggest looking at three strands in Christianity. Each, in various degrees, perhaps points to a "future" in the transatlantic context. The first of these is Catholic/liturgical; the second comprises the Peace Churches (Amish, Mennonite, Hutterite, and Quaker movements); the third is the communitarian/mystical tradition. The German-Jewish Reform movement of the nineteenth century might have figured in an assessment of German-American religious connections. However, the near-collapse of this strain in Jewish life in the United States even prior to the Holocaust suggests that the shape of American Judaism is unlikely to rediscover the assimilationist approaches of the Jewish German Reform tradition in the future.[7]

The Catholic/Liturgical Strain

In terms of raw figures, Roman Catholic Christians now constitute the largest single non-Protestant group in the United States. Although experiencing such problems as non-attendance and seeming indifference to what its *Magisterium* teaches, Germany's Catholic churches are also more vigorous than their Protestant counterparts. In the German context, the book *Was den Deutschen heilig ist* (1979) revealed the curious persistence of religious affections and associations, even upon Germans who were otherwise non-religious. The study found that even among those who never attended church or considered religion to be unimportant as a way of life, the overwhelming majority with some kind of Protestant background consistently voted with the Social Democratic Party. Former Catholics, or those with some Catholic association in their extended family backgrounds, tended just as regularly to support the Christian Democratic Union (CDU) or Christian Social Union (CSU) in politics. Even if a tight correlation between a relatively more vigorous Catholicism and a CDU/CSU political influence cannot be demonstrated, the ongoing vitality of Catholicism in Germany should not be overlooked or dismissed too quickly.[8]

At first glance, the Roman Church in the United States seems to owe very little of its spirituality, organization, wealth, or power to German

Catholicism, always a very small minority within this branch of Christianity in America.[9] But again, first impressions are perhaps deceiving. The basic patterns of migration, which have been traced repeatedly, brought an overwhelmingly Protestant-German population to North America. Whether we look at the figures for 1727–1753, the renewed migration of the mid-1830s to 1861, the great wave of the later nineteenth century that peaked in the 1880s, or finally, the smaller renewals of post-1918 and post-1945, the long-term impact of German migration on American religious life was overwhelmingly Protestant. By the twentieth century, most German speakers had experienced a process of selective osmosis that adjusted them to dominant Protestant-American patterns of life and culture while they preserved, via denomination and family, whatever aspects of often highly localized German-speaking culture they wished to retain. That very success, however, meant that German speakers were only fully accepted after they discarded their "mother tongue," first in worship and even in family discourses in the second half of the twentieth century.[10]

Some authors have been tempted to claim that American Catholicism was inclined toward a more "republican" and less "Roman" posture before the 1830s, in no small part because of German parishioners in Philadelphia, Baltimore, and elsewhere who insisted on copying their Lutheran neighbors' control of church property. The so-called "Trustee" controversies in American Catholicism pitted determined lay leaders against episcopal demands that the property of churches be vested solely in the bishop's hands. Although of interest to legal and ethnic historians, the episodes actually revealed that the decisive majority of Catholics in the early republic (including the German speakers) were loyal followers of the Roman hierarchy's claims on their obedience.[11]

Roman Catholic German speakers did continue to share certain cultural and political commonalities with their German Lutheran counterparts in other parts of the United States. The surface appearance of an undifferentiated "Protestant" majority among German-speaking immigrants is quite deceiving. In the 1970s, scholars analyzing voting patterns on critical cultural issues in the American Midwest advanced the thesis that political behavior follows lines drawn by cultural habits that could transcend strictly confessional or doctrinal boundaries. Thus, while some German-speaking Protestants, heavily influenced by Pietism's disgust for liquor, card-playing, dancing, and other frivolous amusements, banded together with Methodist or Presbyterian neighbors in drying up Pennsylvania counties, German Lutherans in the Midwest did not. The distinction between "pietists" or "evangelicals" on the one hand, and "ritualists" or "liturgicals" on the other, may not tell us everything about the long-term impact on American culture exercised by German religious habits of mind. But it does seem that a good deal of Midwestern religious conservatism owes its vitality to a heavy mix of German Catholicism and Lutheranism. These two "ritualist" groups, both advocates of parochial

FIGURE 7. St. Vincent College, Pennsylvania in 1855

St. Vincent College in Beatty, Pennsylvania, as sketched by Boniface Wimmer, O.S.B., who arrived in 1846 from Metten, Bavaria, and founded it as the first Benedictine establishment in North America. The monastery and seminary that became a college began with the objective of providing training for German speakers, but quickly included English speakers. The abbey's monks were instrumental in founding many other Catholic churches and monasteries in the United States. (St. Vincent Archabbey and College Archives)

schooling, and both easily annoyed by moralistic scoldings against ritual in church and vigorous enjoyment of food and drink at social gatherings, rejected the behavioral model urged upon them by largely Anglo-Saxon Protestant social reformers.[12]

In the 1980s, a fascinating if impressionistic study of regional associations and behaviors in the United States noted the overwhelming influence of German-speakers in shaping the culture of the American Midwest, the "breadbasket" encompassing the huge sweep of land bordered by the Rockies in the west, going as far south as eastern Texas, and reaching to western Ohio north of the Great Lakes. Joel Garreau noted that it was easy to forget that the "model of stability we call the heartland" stemmed from one overwhelming factor: "to a bedrock of Anglo-Saxonism was added Germans, Swedes, Germans, Norwegians, Germans, Finns, Germans, Ukrainians, Germans, Poles, and Germans."[13] What some scholars have chosen to call "folkways" that surround food consumption, festivals, and voluntary clubs, perhaps extending into vernacular architecture as well, continue to reflect earlier patterns of settlement.[14] A preponderantly conservative *cultural* cast—as opposed to academic influence—colored German-speakers' relationship to religion in United States, and this coloration stemmed from "ritualist" (i.e., Catholic and Lutheran) influence.[15]

Connections with Germany are still strong and may remain so in the future in terms of religious debate. In taking up Bonhoeffer's challenge of being a presence interested in something more than just ethics and a vague "religion," various German religious intellectuals have provided a sharp critique of American culture. This suggests not just a legacy but a possibly contested future that may still bind Germany and the United States together. The German Joseph Cardinal Ratzinger's conservative influence within the Roman Church has nowhere found a more receptive response than in theological circles in the United States. No one has helped to propagate the conservative German Cardinal's defense of Roman orthodoxy more than the former Lutheran Church Missouri Synod pastor, Richard John Neuhaus. Neuhaus promotes the theological critique of both modern America and modern Germany articulated by Ratzinger in *First Things*, his journal of opinion. Moreover, the astonishing alliance between American Catholics and Protestant evangelicals surfaced from this quarter of American Catholicism, an alliance which as late as the 1960s would have been thought impossible, one that agrees on issues ranging from opposition to abortion and genetic experimentation on human embryos to a demand for restoration of the possibility of prayer in public schools to resolute opposition to gay/lesbian marriage and partnership benefits laws. Although it waxes and wanes in terms of actual legislation passed, it shows no signs of abating or dissolving soon.[16] While "liberal" Roman Catholics—for a time in the 1960s and 70s, at least—knew of the Tübingen priest-theologian Hans Küng, his removal from the Catholic faculty there seems to have left German and

American "liberal" Catholics without any significant rallying point or set of exchanges that can compare to the conservative transatlantic exchanges within the Roman Church.[17]

The Peace Church Strain

The "Peace Churches" unarguably rose to prominence among German speakers because of William Penn's recruitment journeys up the Rhine prior to Pennsylvania's settlement and the arrival in the New World of the *Concordia*, the first group of German settlers, in 1683. The early witness of the Germantown Quakers and Mennonites against the slave trade issued only a few years later is well-known, even though it did not lead to the suppression of that trade, or the abolition of racialist distinctions within German-speaking churches, graveyards, and communities. The German Moravian presence in the British colonies, especially their extraordinary success in developing communities among the Delaware Indians and at least some modest success among African American slaves, has finally begun to receive attention from scholars on both sides of the Atlantic. Scholars have recognized that Mennonites, Amish, Quakers, and Moravians contributed in major ways to what H. Richard Niebuhr called the "Christ against culture" witness both before and after the American Revolution.[18] Yet the Peace movement that was rejuvenated in the Mexican War received little of its impetus from German-speaking religious witness. Numerically small, the Peace movement that arose in the 1840s reflected the fact that German-speaking enclaves continued to operate in a somewhat parallel but separate universe from the dominant, New England-based peace movements of William Ladd, Charles Sumner, Henry Barnard, or Elihu Burritt.[19]

Ironically, it was the rise of profound anti-German sentiment in the First World War that revealed the Peace Churches' self-conscious testimony. Their plight also deepened awareness on the part of the broader public when they learned of government action against the Mennonites and Old Order Amish in Pennsylvania and Indiana communities. By the Mennonites' own estimation, they had not articulated a "peace testimony" until the First World War, and in some respects a self-conscious assessment of their international witness did not come until the appearance of a watershed study in 1944. Guy Hershberger's *War, Peace, and Nonresistance* began a serious assessment of the "peace testimony," which even with the founding of Goshen College in 1902 had not crystallized into a reflective self-identity for these largely Swiss, Russian-German, and Dutch Christian groups.[20]

The post–World War II international conferences in Switzerland and the Netherlands built upon initial conferences of the 1920s and witnessed a challenge to the traditional "defenseless," or nonresistance, theology that had been pioneered at Goshen College by Mennonite theologians. In the hands of either J. Lawrence Burkholder, who had studied at Princeton, or Theodore J. Koontz, who pondered the possible moral legitimacy of some form of formal state violence, a younger generation of Mennonites adjusted theological witness to the neo-orthodox Protestant insights of H. Richard and Reinhold Niebuhr, and the witness of Bonhoeffer. Simple nonviolence or nonresistance might not be sufficient, they argued, in confronting the radical evils unleashed in the twentieth century. These reassessments became eminently practical questions in the 1960s and 70s as Mennonite communities in Canada gave refuge to United States men fleeing the draft in the United States. Yet by 1989, even in Mennonite communities, many were willing to serve in the military instead of choosing alternative service, as the Peace Churches had overwhelmingly done in World War II. With the collapse of the Cold War, and absent the draft, a Civil Rights movement, or a clear set of issues around which to debate a Peace Witness, the 1990s have seen yet another turn in the Peace Churches' thinking.

Such assessments stand in sharp contrast to the more optimistic Peace Testimony theologians of the 1950s and early 60s, who suggested that the gradual amelioration of society could be expected as the power of God reshaped the world.[21] The general upsurge in revivalist movements, and a forthright, if nervous, expression of the American religious and economic capacity to remake the world, had shaped the Peace Churches in their immediate postwar perception of the future. And, not unlike the generally somber assessment of American religion Ahlstrom offered in his 1972 classic survey, the Peace Testimony theologians also reflected the sense of frustration many Americans felt with the intractable problems of poverty, racism, warfare, and the transformation of economic life brought on by the collapse of traditional industries and labor markets. Yet, by the late 1990s, no one would seriously question the continuing international significance of the Peace Churches and the potential for future German-speaking contacts and exchanges, especially given the ongoing nature of the crises in the Balkans and in the Middle East, as well as the fierce debates in Germany itself over the use of German troops as peacekeepers in African missions of the UN.[22]

In fact, the Peace Churches did contribute in a significant way to the events that led to the fall of the Berlin Wall in 1989. Throughout their tense and sometimes compromised relationships with the German Democratic Republic state and party, the Evangelical Lutheran churches were careful not to engage in directly confrontational criticism. Indeed, the Swords into Plowshares movement and the denunciation of deterrence as a policy still looked beyond the socialist state to more universal Christian connections and obligations. While aspects of the East German churches' theology seemed to draw explicitly upon Bonhoeffer, or other Lutheran influences, the story was actually much more complex. To have made explicit appeals to "western" peace groups whose congregations were located primarily in the United States and Canada would have delegitimized church peace efforts, and any such references were always carefully modulated, if articulated at all. The infiltration of the churches by the Stasi turned out, of course, to have been more pervasive than the self-image of the churches ever allowed for.

The East German theologian Wolf Krötke, in shaping his critique of both acquisitive individualism and liberal societies and presenting equally critical assessments of the East German state, made clear his indebtedness to the Mennonite tradition. The work of John Howard Yoder especially pushed Krötke to analyze the importance of non-withdrawal from the world, to insist upon social engagement, and to articulate ways in which the churches could stand with marginalized populations. In this way, a theme that the Evangelical churches in East Germany had come to endorse by the 1980s—providing "space" within their churches to various "alternative" groups—received an additional boost from an explicitly "Peace Church" theologian, the American Mennonite Yoder.[23]

The eventual collapse of the former East German state revealed, among other things, that cooperation among various denominations, while cautious, had been a substantive reality, with German Baptists, Moravians, Mennonites, and Lutherans producing participants in the Christian Peace Conference and its offshoot, the International Peace Pilgrimage. To a large degree, however, these groups still tended to refer largely to strains within their own European background, and participants did not reveal any deep awareness of the North American Peace Church tradition.[24]

The Mystical-Antinomian Strain

The third strain of German-language religious exchange between Europe and America is more difficult to assess. The mystical roots of various communitarian experiments that began at Wissahickon Creek with Johann Kelpius seem to have transmogrified beyond immediate recognition today. Although never the dominant strain at Ephrata, Conrad Beissel's theosophical and Gnostic speculations never completely disappeared. Reinventors of a supposed mystical tradition believed by the early 1900s that a Rosicrucianist subculture could be traced from medieval days to the shores of North America. By the time Julius F. Sachse's fanciful approach to German Pietism added to this legend, its future seemed almost secured. More plausibly, as John Brooke has recently shown, early Mormon theology may well have drawn on the mystical, theosophical, and white magic traditions of Pennsylvania as that religious movement began in upstate New York.[25]

Purely communitarian experiments, whether of the Ephrata variety or later manifestations at Economy, Pennsylvania, Zoar, Blooming Grove, and Amana in Iowa have long since vanished. But while countercultural utopian experiments have come and gone, a German mystical tradition that informed some of these nineteenth-century experiments never completely died out, and may in fact have manifested itself again in New Age religious thinking.[26]

While the original "New Thought" or "New Age" writings of the 1860s owed some of their inspiration to Swedenborgian currents that boasted ties to the theosophical tradition, the initial use of the term "New Age" religion did not specifically draw upon the German mystical tradition. Some have suggested that the term first arose as a result of the 1893 meeting of the Chicago World Parliament of Religion. Regardless of the exact pedigree of the term, Jakob Boehme and Meister Eckhardt surfaced beyond the boundaries of the strictly German-language communities of early Pennsylvania in highly selective form among later "New Age" advocates. What, for example, is one to make of the recovery of Hildegard of Bingen among both German and American Christians interested in mystical speculations? Does it reveal a similar interest in medieval Catholic sources that seem to transcend specific confessional or denominational boundaries? Twentieth-century followers of Rudolph Steiner's anthroposophy movement and the transplanting of Waldorf schools in the United States also confirm a persistent "spiritual" fascination that seems genuinely transatlantic.[27]

A basic antinomian tendency to reject institutionalized norms of religious life links some of the insights of the German mystical tradition to holiness traditions in American Methodism and the continuing upsurge in Pentecostalist churches in the late twentieth century in the United States. But one should not exaggerate these links. Most of the holiness movements, and even the rise of a feminist consciousness in some dimensions of American Methodism, seem to have occurred without any direct linkages to a German mystical past. Indeed, one might go so far as to suggest that such patterns in American religion were viewed with considerable alarm by German commentators before the 1920s.[28]

By the 1970s, German observers noted with concern the growth of "New Age" or "New Age Religious Movements" (NRM) throughout Europe. The upsurge in varieties of Scientology, Eckankar, Arica, Esalen, Synanon, EST, and Church Universal movements provoked considerable critique in Germany during the 1980s. These combinations of the Western occult, Theosophy, and Rosicrucianism, liberally sprinkled with some East Asian religious influences, seemed to confirm to critics that altogether too many ties bound America to German and European religious life. By the 1990s, such influences seemed to transmogrify in many areas of Europe into renewed concerns for peace, but they mutated more conspicuously into holistic health movements, animal rights concerns, and other forms of a somewhat vague "spirituality." In that context, a vigorous debate in Germany over whether "scientology" constituted an actual "religion" only makes sense if seen within the context of this longer debate over "American" religious influences. If Robert Wuthenow is correct, North America and German social patterns may still be similar enough to keep alive a shared metaphysical tradition. Wuthenow's analysis of American religious life since the 1950s traces the resurgence of highly individualistic and antinomian "seeker" religions in America that belie easy summary. If any common thread binds this survey of North America life to assessments of contemporary Germany, the inadequacy of institutional structure of either Protestant or Catholic Christianity for capturing the yearning for "spirituality" seems the most obvious.[29]

Conclusion

Rather than rehearse the familiar "contributions" to North American religious life by German speakers, we have instead traced at least three plausible strands of religious connection between German-speaking Europe and North America. Philosopher Stephen Turner has recently offered a sobering critique of the way in which historians often seek to account for the persistence or non-persistence of "social practices." As Turner succinctly puts it: "Habits die with individuals. If something persists in history, it cannot be habits alone. Traditions do persist. So traditions cannot consist of habits. This is a simple formulation of a problem with no simple solution."[30]

How indeed can one "explain" what appears to be the collapse of conventional Protestant convictions among German Americans and their English-speaking neighbors in the late twentieth century, and at the same time the persistence of at least some version of Christian piety? How, in other words, can one account for Bonhoeffer's insightful critique of the weak Christology of the Protestantism he encountered in the 1930s? One could, plausibly, point to the equally old mystical-antinomian tendency among German-speakers that denied the importance of "original sin." Not only has such a tendency persisted, it has apparently grown more vigorous in both Germany and North America since the 1950s as structural-institutional forms of religious and political life seem increasingly unrewarding. Indeed, one analysis of "New Age" religion focuses on just this, asserting that whatever else separates the various strands of modern spiritualism, all such movements reject the classic Western Christian concept of original sin and share the conviction that "we must save ourselves and the planet, and, perhaps, even God."[31]

For the history of German speakers and religion, we might conclude that definitions of American freedom dating from the seventeenth century centered upon individual religious freedom of conscience and a deep concern for material welfare; that migrations seldom brought coherent communities to North America as much as they did individuals or families in chain migration patterns; that German attachments to religious custom persisted throughout the various waves of migration into the twentieth century; that once in the land of unlimited freedom of choice with regard to religious belief, Germans tended toward a cultural and religious conformity. In their desire to conform and not be regarded as troublesome, the majority of Protestant and Catholic German speakers and their descendants eschewed religious experiments that challenged the dominant public order from the outset. One can always cite the occasional Ephrata experiment or the German-founded Amana Colonies, and the ongoing visible dissent of the Old Order Amish. But such unique splinter groups remained marginal and statistically insignificant signposts compared to the beliefs of the vast majority of Lutherans, Reformed, and Roman Catholics among German Americans. As long as "mainstream" America remained demonstrably Protestant-Christian and (later) grudgingly accommodated a growing Catholic presence, German speakers for the most part remained tied to a traditional theological system as well. With the collapse of "Christian America" in the 1960s, German-speaking descendants—in part, at least—adopted conservative countercultural responses (as did many of their anglophone neighbors), or joined the renewed wave of individual "seekers" after spirituality, a path also pioneered by remote German-speaking ancestors.

One could argue that what links the conservative ritualists, Peace Testimony, and more radical spiritual seekers together is a common identity as relative outsiders, in the sense that none of these traditions will easily be capable of joining an evangelical "crusade" to make America a "Christian republic." Indeed, recent reflections on the creation of an American identity suggest that globalization of the economy, coupled with renewed migration from Asian and Latin American countries, has deepened worry about the very nature of both German and American society and life. With the Cold War at an end, "one finds despair and longing for community wherever one looks ... attention has become directed at the inner life of the country and the result is despair about the condition of American society and pessimism with regard to its future."[32]

Such a gloomy prognostication may strike some as more typically German than American. Both the Peace Churches and the conservative-liturgical strands share a conviction that a common worship life stands at the center of any vital religious community. But both would also agree that worship must bring together people who share common convictions that can be discussed in a shared language where the rules of discourse are also agreed upon. The more radical antinomian strand in the three influences we have been tracing points more directly to individual access to the spiritual experience of humans. At the turn of the twenty-first century, it requires a prophet, not a historian, to suggest which of the three strains in the German-American religious past seems poised to make a vigorous and convincing entry into the next millennium.

Of the three, both Roman Catholic and Lutheran traditions share global connections to areas of the developing world, especially Africa and Asia, where these religious traditions are actually growing, not shrinking, in numbers and influence. While less impressive numerically, Mennonite and other Peace Church groups also share an institutional linkage that seems increasingly global. It is less clear whether the more radically antinomian and individualist-mystical "tradition" finds much resonance outside the Atlantic world. If the populations of both Germany and the United States become increasingly diverse and less obviously "European" in the coming years, as all projections indicate will be the case, will we witness a revival of a sober sense of limitation, a renewed "tradition" of original sin and the obligation to seek both justice and peace—or a continued aspiration toward non-institutional and highly individualized religious seeking?

Notes

1. The full text of the document can be accessed via the Internet at: http://www.luthbro.com/aboutLB/survey98.html.
2. Dietrich Bonhoeffer, *Gesammelte Schriften* (Munich, 1965–69), vol. 1: 323–54, citation at 354; see also the commentary on this unpublished essay in Eberhard Bethge, *Dietrich Bonhoeffer: Man of Vision, Man of Courage*, trans. Eric Mosbacher et al. (New York/Evanston, 1970), 562–65.
3. John M. Mulder and John F. Wilson, eds., *Religion in American History: Interpretive Essays* (Englewood Cliffs, NJ, 1978); the exception is a brief excerpt from Will Herberg's classic *Protestant, Catholic, Jew*, on the role of the German Jewish Reform and its eclipse after 1945 (379–96).
4. Mark Noll, *A History of Christianity in the United States and Canada* (Grand Rapids, MI, 1992), 552.
5. See Marsden, *The Soul of the American University: From Protestant Establishment to Established Non-belief* (New York, 1994), 173–80, 415–28; on Rauschenbusch, see, e.g., C. Howard Hopkins, *The Rise of the Social Gospel in American Protestantism, 1865–1915* (New Haven, CT, 1967), 215–32; on the later confrontation of neo-orthodoxy with the Social Gospel, Sidney Ahlstrom, *A Religious History of the American People* (New Haven/London: 1972), 933–48. On the impact of David Friedrich Strauss's *Das Leben Jesu* and other German liberals on American theology, see James Turner, *Without God, Without Creed: The Origins of Unbelief in America* (Baltimore/London, 1985), 148–50.
6. Ahlstrom, *Religious History*, 1–13, 1094–96.
7. For a survey of the German Reform and its impact on the new world via German-speaking migration, see Shelly Tenenbaum, "The Jews," in *Encyclopedia of American Social History II*, ed. Mary Kupiec Cayton, Elliott J. Gorn, and Peter W. Williams (New York, 1993), 769–81; for a fascinating case study, see Steven M. Lowenstein, *Frankfurt on the Hudson: The German-Jewish Community of Washington Heights, 1933–1983* (New York, 1989); for the postwar period, see Shlomo Shafir, *Ambiguous Relations: The American Jewish Community and Germany since 1945* (Cleveland, OH, 1999).
8. Gerhard Schmidtchen, *Was den Deutschen heilig ist: Religiöse und politische Strömungen in der Bundesrepublik Deutschland* (Munich, 1979). Despite the real problems posed by statistical summaries of church affiliation, the most recent estimates still suggest that some 1.9 billion of the world's 5,672,815,000 persons are Christians, of whom 54 percent are Roman Catholic, 9.9 percent Orthodox, and 3 percent Lutheran—approximately 58.5 million in 1993. Of the Lutherans, at least nominally Germany and the United States still represent the two main geographic centers, although Africa is experiencing far more significant growth than that reported by either German or United States churches. See David B. Barrett's *World Christian Encyclopedia* (1994 update),

accessible via http://www.lcms.org/introlcms.html; http://www.christianity.net. news/rns981/rns8120.html.

9. The classic studies remain Colman Barry, *The Catholic Church and the German Americans* (Milwaukee, 1953); and Philip Gleason, *Conservative Reformers: German-American Catholics and the Social Order* (Notre Dame, 1968); despite later synthetic overviews of American Catholicism, these essays remain the most exhaustive to date.

10. For more details on this process, A. G. Roeber, "German Speakers," in *Encyclopedia of American Social History*, vol. 2: 719–27.

11. See, e.g., Dale B. Light, *Rome and the New Republic: Conflict and Community in Philadelphia Catholicism between the Revolution and the Civil War* (Notre Dame/London, 1996), 27–39.

12. The classic study is Paul Kleppner, *The Cross of Culture: A Social Analysis of Mid-Western Politics 1850–1900* (New York, 1970). For a cautionary word on the liturgical/evangelical model and why it may not work for pre–Civil War issues such as the Know-Nothing Movement, see Richard J. Carwardine, *Evangelicals and Politics in Antebellum America* (New Haven/London, 1993), 199–227, 456–61.

13. Joel Garreau, *The Nine Nations of North America* (Boston, 1981), 328–61, quotation at 343. But more nuanced scholarly analyses also confirm the basic conservative religious influence of German-speakers in the regions. See essays in *Encyclopedia of American Social History II*: Jeremy W. Kilar, "The Great Lakes Industrial Region"; Susan E. Gray, "The Upper Midwest"; and James R. Shortridge, "The Great Plains," 973–86; 987–1000; 1001–16.

14. Perhaps the most famous, if controversial, use of this "folkways" approach remains David Hackett Fischer, *Albion's Seed: Four British Folkways in North America* (New York, 1989).

15. Considerable disagreement surrounds the question of whether German "ritualists" in Europe influenced Americans, or whether, in the United States context, Anglican "high church" ritual provided the basis for liturgical renewal. For the latter argument, see Timothy Quill, *The Impact of the Liturgical Movement on American Lutheranism* (Lanham, MD, 1997) and Frank Senn, Christian *Liturgy: Evangelical and Catholic* (Minneapolis, 1997); for a contrary view, see J. Jeffrey Zetto, "Aspects of Theology in the Liturgical Movement in the Lutheran Church Missouri Synod, 1930–1961" (Th.D. dissertation, Christ Seminary-Seminex, 1982). On the recovery of a theology of the church and liturgics among Roman Catholics, traceable to German theologians such as J. A. Moehler and Pius Parsch of Austria, see Ahlstrom, *Religious History*, 1012–13.

16. Neuhaus, upon leaving the Lutheran Church Missouri Synod in the 1970s, worked for years as co-editor of the *Lutheran Forum* and for a time directed the Rockford Institute Center on Religion and Society, editing *The Religion and Society Report*. By 1987 he and Michael Cromartie had edited the essays in *Piety and Politics: Evangelicals and Fundamentalists Confront the World* (Washington, 1987), where George Weigel's essay "Evangelicals and Catholics: A New Ecumenism" (355–62) reviewed the issues creating a coalition comprised of Catholic and Protestant, and some Lutheran, theologians. The emergence of a "religious right" since the 1980s has spawned an enormous literature; most of it, however, is more sensational than carefully analytical, and, to my knowledge, none of it pays attention to the impact of German theological or religious thought.

17. I have surveyed German Catholic colleagues and their summaries of the German *Katholikentag* programs to confirm my sense that American personalities or issues are strikingly absent from contemporary liberal German Catholic sensibilities.

18. See variously, Hermann Wellenreuther, *Glaube und Politik in Pennsylvania, 1681–1776: Die Wandlungen der Obrigkeitsdoktrin und des Peace Testimony der Quäker* (Cologne/Vienna, 1972); Richard K. McMaster, *Land, Piety, Peoplehood: The Establishment of Mennonite Communities in America, 1683–1790* (Scottdale, PA, 1985); Beulah Stauffer Hostetler, *American Mennonites and Protestant Movements: A Community Paradigm* (Scottdale, PA/Kitchener, Ontario, 1987), 317–29; Donald F. Durnbaugh, "Religion and Revolution: Options in 1776," *Pennsylvania Mennonite Heritage* 1 (1978): 2–9. Niebuhr's famous schema of possible ways for Christianity to interact—i.e., Christ against culture,

a Christ of culture, Christ above culture, a paradoxical relationship of Christ to culture, and culture transformed by Christ—appeared in *Christ and Culture* (1951); the "Christ against culture" approach was already signaled, however, in Niebuhr's manifesto, co-authored with Wilhelm Pauck and Francis Miller, in *The Church Against the World* (1935); see Noll, *History of Christianity*, 433.

19. See, e.g., the summary in Alice Felt Tyler, *Freedom's Ferment: Phases of American Social History from the Colonial Period to the Outbreak of the Civil War* (New York, 1962), 396–423.

20. See Lee Driedger and Donald B. Kraybill, *Mennonite Peacemaking: From Quietism to Activism*, with a forward by John A. Lapp (Scottdale, PA/Waterloo, Ontario, 1994), 13–25; on the issues facing Mennonites and Amish in specific communities during World War I and II, Dorothy O. Pratt, "A Study in Cultural Persistence: The Amish in LaGrange County, Indiana, 1841–1945" (Ph.D. dissertation, Notre Dame University, 1998).

21. See variously, the essays in John R. Burkholder and Barbara N. Gingerich, eds., *Mennonite Peace Theology: A Panorama of Types* (Akron, PA, 1991); Driedger and Kraybill, eds., *Mennonite Peacemaking*, 83–132, 254–56; Nathan Yoder, "Mennonite Fundamentalists, 1890–1950: A Conservative Voice in a Changing Context" (Ph.D. dissertation, Notre Dame University, 1998).

22. The Peace Churches did not encompass all antiwar religious protestors; see, e.g., Mitchell K. Hall, *Because of their Faith: CALCAV and Religious Opposition to the Vietnam War* (New York, 1998); CALCAV (Clergy and Laity Concerned About Vietnam) included, for a time, Neuhaus and Peter Berger.

23. See John P. Burgess, *The East German Churches and the End of Communism* (New York, 1997), 36–72; on Wolf Krötke's influence, 122–33; Yoder's major essays are *The Christian Witness to the State* (Newton, KS, 1964), and *The Politics of Jesus* (Grand Rapids, MI 1972).

24. See, e.g., participant reflections in these events documented in Jörg Swoboda, *Die Revolution der Kerzen: Christen in den Umwälzungen der DDR* (Wuppertal/Kassel, 1990), translated now as *The Revolution of the Candles: Christians in the Revolution of the German Democratic Republic*, ed. Richard V. Pierard, trans. Edwin P. Arnold (Macon, GA, 1996).

25. Julius Friedrich Sachse, *The German Pietists of Provincial Pennsylvania, 1694–1708* (Philadelphia, 1895); John Brooke, *The Refiner's Fire: The Making of Mormon Cosmology, 1644–1844* (Cambridge/New York, 1994); on the radical strains within Pietism, see F. Ernst Stoeffler, *The Rise of Evangelical Pietism* (Leiden, 1965) and *German Pietism in the Eighteenth Century* (Leiden, 1973), 168–216; for an assessment, Hans Schneider, "Der radikale Pietismus im 18. Jahrhundert," in Martin Brecht et al., eds., *Die Geschichte des Pietismus: Der Pietismus im achtzehnten Jahrhundert II* (Göttingen, 1995), 107–97, especially at 167–69; on Beissel's theosophism, see Wendy Everham, "Johann Konrad Beissels Leben und Theologie: Versuch eines Grundverständnisses," trans. Leo Schelbert, *Eberbacher Geschichtsblatt* 90 (1991): 55–67.

26. In addition to the categories developed in Tyler, *Freedom's Ferment*, see the contemporary observations in Charles Nordhoff, *The Communistic Societies of the United States from Personal Observations* (New York, 1966, original ed., 1875), 25–113.

27. See, e.g., Sabina Flanagan, *Hildegard of Bingen, 1098–1179: A Visionary Life* (London, New York, 1989); Heinrich Schipperjes, *Hildegard of Bingen: Healing and the Nature of the Cosmos*, trans. John A. Broadwine (Princeton, 1997); and Maud Burnett McInerney, *Hildegard of Bingen: A Book of Essays* (New York, 1998).

28. See Noll, *A History of Christianity*, 378–81; Jean Miller Schmidt, "Denominational History When Gender Is the Focus: Women in American Methodism," in *Reimagining Denominationalism: Interpretive Essays*, ed. Robert Bruce Mullin and Russell E. Richey (New York/Oxford, 1994), 203–21; on the skepticism with which German observers of American religion viewed the growing influence of women in American society before World War I, see Alexander Schmidt, *Reisen in die Moderne: Der Amerika-Diskurs des deutschen Bürgertums vor dem Ersten Weltkrieg im europäischen Vergleich* (Berlin, 1997), 170–74, 190–205.

29. For summaries of the European reaction to the "New Age" movements, I have used Elisabeth Arweck and Peter B. Clarke, *New Religious Movements in Western Europe: An*

Annotated Bibliography (Westport, CT/London, 1997); see especially Johannes Aagaard, "Modern Syncretist Movements: A General View," originally in *Update: A Quarterly Journal on New Religious Movements* 5 (2) 1981: 29–36, at 1–2 in Arweck and Clarke. For a sharp criticism of the critics, see Frank Ursarki, "Die 'New-Age'-Bewegung. Historische Bezüge, soziologische Einordnung und inhaltliche Charakterisierung einer 'neu-religiösen Strömung,'" in *Geschichte-Erziehung-Politik*, Berlin, 2 (3) (1991): 218–24; Robert Wuthenow, *After Heaven: Spirituality in America since the 1950s* (Berkeley, 1998), especially 188–98.

30. Stephen Turner, *The Social Theory of Practices: Tradition, Tacit Knowledge, and Presuppositions* (Chicago, 1994), 78.

31. Mary Farrell Bednarowski, *New Religions and the Theological Imagination in America* (Bloomington/Indianapolis, 1989), 138.

32. Herbert Dittgen, "The American Debate about Immigration in the 1990s: A New Nationalism after the End of the Cold War?" 197–232, quotation at 222, in *The American Nation-National Identity-Nationalism*, ed. Knud Krakau (Münster/New Brunswick, NJ, 1997).

Chapter 6

GERMAN INFLUENCES ON AMERICAN EDUCATION

Daniel Fallon

As a developing nation, the United States was fortunate to have acquired contributions from many sources and cultures; those from the German speaking countries of Europe have been considerable and varied. None, however, has been more significant to the civic and economic development of the United States than those brought from Germany into the sphere of education. In this arena alone, the compass is large. Although informed by the whole, the present treatment focuses principally on two critical contributions, which happen to be at the extreme ends of the educational continuum—the Kindergarten and the University.

A helpful device for understanding the German and American interaction in the nineteenth century is to consider this proposal: Americans welcomed the German ideas they recognized as embodying the ideals of the American Revolution. Like all generalizations, this can mask a much more complex reality. Nonetheless, as a starting point, it can persuasively organize the documentary record.

The German enlightenment provided a fertile seedbed for concepts transplantable to the new American republic because there was a genuine affinity of intellectual premise between German and American liberal thought in the late eighteenth and early nineteenth centuries. The Americans perceived and used German ideas even if they understood very little of the heavily class-oriented society that characterized German life. In general, the Americans formed the simplest, most direct, naive interpretation of the circumstances in which they found themselves. Two icons from the late eighteenth and early nineteenth centuries illustrate some basic commonalities of thinking: Wilhelm von Humboldt and Thomas Jefferson.

In May 1792, at the age of 24, Wilhelm von Humboldt completed an essay entitled "Ideen zu einem Versuch, die Grenzen der Wirksamkeit des Staats zu bestimmen."[1] This piece was first known in English as "The Spheres and Duties of Government," and later as "The Limits of State Action."[2] The impetus for the essay seems to have originated in his correspondence with his friend, Friedrich von Genz, about political implications of the revolution in France. Humboldt sent the essay to another friend, Johann Friedrich Biester, who published parts of it in his journal, the *Berlinische Monatsschrift*. Because censorship prevented publication of most of the essay, Humboldt sent a complete copy to Schiller, who published a short excerpt in his journal, *Neue Thalia*, returning the rest of the manuscript to Humboldt, who then set it aside. Thus, only a small fraction of it was published at the time it was written.

In 1852, more than a decade after Humboldt's death, the complete version of Humboldt's paper first appeared in print when his brother, the famous explorer Alexander von Humboldt, published a posthumous collection of his brother's works. It was translated into English in 1854 and served as an immediate inspiration to John Stuart Mill, who began his monumental essay "On Liberty" at about this time. When Mill's study was published five years later, it opened with an epigraph quoting Humboldt: "The grand leading principle, towards which every argument unfolded in these pages directly converges, is the absolute and essential importance of human development in its richest diversity."[3] This revolutionary idea, conceived by Humboldt precisely during the infancy of the United States, seems to have arisen from the same values that were inspiring the founders of the American republic. Consider, for example, the following episode.

In 1820, Thomas Jefferson, a vigorous and lively seventy-seven years old, was nearing the conclusion of a quest he had begun some forty years earlier to encourage the Commonwealth of Virginia to found a public university. The state government had just appointed a board of commissioners to lay plans for the university, and Mr. Jefferson had begun to design both the curriculum and the buildings and grounds. After Christmas, on the evening of December 27, in a letter to an English correspondent, William Roscoe, he described the enterprise that now occupied his everyday life: "This institution will be based on the illimitable freedom of the human mind. For here we are not afraid to follow truth wherever it may lead, nor to tolerate any error so long as reason is free to combat it."[4] This is an extraordinary statement, saturated with a contemporary sense of liberty and a commitment to the power of intellect. Its roots were nourished in the same soil that proved fertile for Wilhelm von Humboldt, who had also just (in 1810) founded a university, an institution that became a cornerstone of the modern era, the University of Berlin.

Jefferson, Humboldt, and others of their generation lived at a time characterized by governmental revolution and impassioned consideration of ideas about human society. It is not easy, even now, to put labels on these ideas or on this time, which some consider the consolidation of the beginning of the modern era. In Germany, it represented the culmination of the German enlightenment and the budding of Romanticism, with publication of the works of the young Goethe and Schiller. In the United States it has been called the age of reason and the manifestation of the American enlightenment. For both German and American intellectuals, the continuing force of the Renaissance, with its emphasis on the rediscovery of the ancient Greeks and Romans, provided energy for a less pious and more secular view of religion, approximating pantheism, and for the development of an idealistic philosophy. There were, of course, differences between the Germans and the Americans, most clearly seen in the pragmatic bent of the American thinkers, and in their unquestioning commitment to democracy and the collective wisdom of the citizens. Nonetheless, the similarity between the pervading American philosophy during this period and the views of liberal German reformers is striking.

It was from the Romantic ideas of the early nineteenth century that the German educational reformer Friedrich Froebel developed the idea of a school-like setting for young children, designed to prepare them for instruction and for life. His school was originally called *Anstalt für Kleinkinderpflege*, or "Institution for the nurture of small children" but he was dissatisfied with the name. Acknowledging his love of nature, he came up with the term "*Kindergarten*," or "garden of children." His *Kindergarten*, founded in 1837 in Blankenburg, near his home in Keilhau in north central Germany, became widely known and successful.[5]

After the suppression of the Revolution of 1848/49 in Germany, a number of German reformers went to England and from there to the United States. Bertha Meyer Ronge, a liberal German refugee, who had been inspired by lectures given by Friedrich Froebel, established the first kindergarten in England. Bertha's sister, Margarethe Meyer, who had also studied successfully with Froebel, came to London to help her sister during an illness. Bertha introduced Margarethe to another liberal German refugee, Carl Schurz. The couple married and then emigrated to the United States in 1856, where Margarethe Schurz opened the first kindergarten in the United States in the Schurz home in Watertown, Wisconsin.[6]

For many years the early kindergartens in the United States, like Margarethe Schurz's, were for German-speaking children; instruction was in German. This began to change after two New Englanders, Henry Barnard and Elizabeth Peabody, became inspired advocates. Henry Barnard was elected to the Connecticut legislature in 1837 and became a vigorous proponent of public schooling for young Americans, helping to create a state board of education in Connecticut. He was appointed the first commissioner of education for the state of Rhode Island, and ultimately, in 1867, became the first U.S. commissioner of education. Barnard met Margarethe Schurz's sister Bertha Ronge, on a visit to London in 1854 and was impressed with the idea of kindergarten that she had developed. What he observed was a fundamental belief in the goodness of the child, the raw material of democracy, and an orderly curriculum that helped children see their role in nature, and thus in the world, preparing them to accept the benefits of a democratic education. He championed the kindergarten of Froebel in reports to the Connecticut legislature and, most importantly, supported the development of kindergartens when he later became the commissioner of education for the United States.[7]

Elizabeth Peabody was intrigued by Barnard's description of kindergartens when she first heard him lecture in Boston. Shortly thereafter she had a chance encounter with Margarethe Schurz and came away overwhelmed by the beauty of the idea of kindergartens for American children. She founded an influential kindergarten in Boston, and through energetic and inspirational lectures she encouraged the widespread development of kindergartens throughout New England. Like her colleagues Emerson and Thoreau, she was sympathetic to transcendentalism and admired such early German philosophers and poets as Schiller, Goethe, and Hegel, who, she believed, surely saw the world in the same way as the New England intellectuals.[8]

The decisive step for the implantation of the kindergarten in the United States took place in 1873, when the superintendent of schools for the city of St. Louis, William Harris, established the kindergarten as an integral part of the city's public school system. Assisting him in this effort was Susan Blow, whom Harris asked to direct the first kindergartens. Both Harris and Blow had studied the German idealists, and were admirers of Fichte and Hegel. Harris and Blow saw the ideas of Froebel and the Romantic German philosophers as exceptionally well-suited to the development of American schoolchildren. Harris believed that the kindergarten was the means by which the extremes of society, the rich and the poor, could be reconciled to prepare for their participation in democratic life. After more than a decade as superintendent of schools for St. Louis, Harris served as commissioner of education for the United States for sixteen years, during which he promoted the kindergarten as an appropriate cornerstone of American education. Susan Blow developed the curriculum of the public school kindergarten, emphasizing the ideals of love, gratitude, and service, using songs and games to provide a common social foundation for future citizens of the American republic.[9]

The development of the kindergarten in the United States incorporated many indigenous American social and economic trends not common in Germany, including, for example, a strong philanthropic component. Thus, during the years of its founding in the United States, the kindergarten was often seen as a charitable enterprise, especially as it accommodated the children of poor immigrants and farmers. The enthusiastic proponents of the kindergarten, those founders who succeeded in establishing it, were not Germans, but Americans. They were citizens of the United States who sensed in the ideas of Friedrich Froebel a kinship with the ideals of the new American republic. They borrowed ideas selectively and implemented what they took from Germany in an American way, fashioning the kindergarten as part of the vision by which the perfectibility of humankind and society could be fostered through education.

FIGURE 8. A German Kindergarten in Brooklyn, New York, before World War I

A German kindergarten in Brooklyn, New York, before World War I. The German concept of kindergarten was introduced to the United States by Margarethe Schurz, wife of Carl Schurz, in the mid-nineteenth century and soon replicated everywhere. (From Randall Miller, ed., *Germans in America*)

The development in the United States of the elementary school, the secondary school, and the academies through which teachers were educated also owes much to German influence. The pioneering reforms of Wilhelm von Humboldt during his brief period as minister of culture for the king of Prussia in 1809 and 1810 included, in addition to the design and implementation of the University of Berlin, a complete restructuring of Prussian elementary and secondary education.[10] These products of the German enlightenment soon became models for public education in the modern era, stimulating emulation especially in France and in the United States.

In 1838, Henry Barnard devoted an entire issue of his widely read Connecticut Common School Journal to "an exposition of the Common School system of Prussia." He made clear in his presentation that the system, while admirable, could not simply be transplanted to America. He was offended by the class structure of German society and by what he saw as an authoritarian and anti-democratic government. "Our system must be adapted to our wants," he wrote, "and to our circumstances."[11] The well-known and highly respected educational pioneer Calvin E. Stowe, however, was less cautious. He wrote in the same issue of Barnard's journal, "... if it can be done in Prussia, I know it can be done in Ohio."[12]

Stowe also delivered this message in a very influential report to the legislature of Ohio in 1839. He carefully laid out six points illustrating what the democratic developers of the American schools saw as valuable in Germany: (1) teachers must be skillful and trained to their business; (2) teacher training academies are, therefore, essential; (3) the profession of teaching must be supported in such a way that teachers can do their work and earn a comfortable living; (4) attendance at school must be compulsory for children, who should be made comfortable in school; (5) pupils must be subordinate to the discipline of the school and the teacher, and parents must respect this authority; and (6) the curriculum must be orderly, gradual, and inexorable, leading step by step to full comprehension and mastery.[13]

In the adoption of elements of primary and secondary education from Germany, we see the same pattern we saw with the kindergarten. Americans, not Germans, developed the reforms; they are carefully selected in accordance with principles congenial to the democratic ideals of the American republic; and they share the values of the German enlightenment. Let us turn now to the most visible and impressive case—the birth of the American research university.

As the United States was building itself into a modern nation after a disastrous civil war, many saw higher education as a key to insuring a just society and also to developing new knowledge and understanding of the universe, for both industrial and civic purposes. In the first half of the nineteenth century, higher education in the United States was largely taught in what Kant and Humboldt called the "lower faculty." This was elementary instruction in the liberal arts. American scholars who wanted to study beyond this point had to go to Europe. Normally, because of language and cultural ties, they might have gone to Great Britain, but the Americans had just recently been fighting the British for independence, and both nations were uneasy with each other. Furthermore, in the early nineteenth century, leading British universities maintained a system of quotas for admission, effectively keeping Americans out. With the founding, under Humboldt's direction, of the University of Berlin in 1810, a more modern university began to take shape in Germany, and its reputation made it an appealing European destination. The early experience of American intellectuals with German universities was positive, and laid the foundation for an increasingly widespread American view that advanced intellectual work could be productively undertaken in Germany.[14]

The substantial American investment in German intellectual ideas did not develop significantly until the extraordinary acceleration of the American economy in the late nineteenth century. Before 1850, about 200 American students had visited German universities. By 1900, however, more than 9,000 Americans had studied there.[15] Because the German language seems to be a formidable obstacle to studying in Germany, one might assume that many of these traveling scholars were German Americans. Although no careful research has been done on this question, what we know suggests quite the contrary. The names of those who studied in Germany and were inspired by the example of the university they found there do not suggest a German heritage. The tide was begun in 1815 by Edward Everett, who was followed by an American who became a distinguished professor of Spanish at Harvard, George Ticknor. Others of that era were George Bancroft, Joseph G. Coggswell, and John Lothrop Motley.[16] In the late nineteenth century, those who had studied in Germany and led the reforms that established the American university included James Burrill Angell (Michigan), Charles W. Eliot (Harvard), Daniel Coit Gilman (Johns Hopkins), G. Stanley Hall (Clark), and Andrew Dickson White (Cornell). These leaders were American, not European, and many were born and grew up on farms in the American heartland.

What the Americans found in Germany appealed immensely to their own American ideals, which were steeped in the same philosophy of the Enlightenment that had informed Humboldt. This was the philosophy of the founders of the republic, people such as John Adams, Benjamin Franklin, Alexander Hamilton, Thomas Jefferson, and James Madison. Because American scholars were treated as honored guests by their German hosts, they had unusual access to German professors, of a kind that very few German students ever achieved. The Americans thus developed an idealized model of the German university that they felt could readily be transplanted to American soil.

It is impossible to underestimate the power of the vision American intellectuals brought from Germany in the late nineteenth century. Consider, for example, this statement by G. Stanley Hall, one of the founders of modern experimental psychology and the first president of Clark University. In 1891, Hall wrote, "The German University is today the freest spot on earth.... Never was such burning and curiosity.... Shallow, bad ideas have died and truth has always attained power.... Nowhere has the passion to push on to the frontier of human knowledge been so general. Never have so many men stood so close to nature and history or striven with such reverence to think God's thoughts after Him exactly."[17] Even making allowances for the romanticism of the era, this vision sounds more like heaven than like any human organization.

In introducing the concept of a modern research university into the United States, American intellectuals made good use of the latitude they had to work within many different kinds of higher education institutions. Whereas Humboldt had transferred the teaching of the liberal arts to secondary schools of academic preparation, the *Gymnasia*, the Americans kept this instruction within their own institutions, letting it form the heart of what is now called undergraduate education. Further, the American reformers argued that pursuit of the union of research with teaching leading to the doctoral degree, to be called graduate education, ought to be limited to a small set of institutions capable of investing sufficient resources toward this objective. This meant that many different institutions could undertake to provide high-quality education, and that the university, in the Humboldtian sense of that word, would comprise only a limited sector. Such differentiation was unknown in Germany. In the American context, it made the idealized version of the Humboldtian model much easier to implement.

Most Americans who studied in Germany attended either Göttingen or Berlin, which were the most liberal and well-developed of the German universities.[18] For example, neither required an oath of allegiance to religious authority, which was common at German universities in the south, and which was enforced even at Cambridge until 1856 and at Oxford until 1854, and for fellowships and other privileges at those English universities until 1882.[19] Three principles dominated American intellectuals' thoughts about what should constitute a modern university. These were (1) the unity of teaching and research, (2) the essential protections afforded by academic freedom, and (3) the central importance of the faculty of arts and sciences. Each of these ideas is a direct legacy of Humboldt's Enlightenment vision of the role of the university in society.

In the centennial year of the American republic, 1876, Johns Hopkins University was founded in Baltimore, and it proudly proclaimed its allegiance to the model of the German university. In a famous essay, Walter Metzger noted that of the fifty-three faculty on the roster of Hopkins in 1884, virtually all had studied in Germany, and thirteen had attained doctoral degrees there.[20] Doctoral degrees were first awarded, in an almost honorary way, by American universities in 1861, but Johns Hopkins University was the first to establish them as the central feature of the modern university.[21] In 1890, 164 doctoral degrees were awarded in the United

States; over twice as many were conferred in the following decade. In 1871 the total number of postgraduate students studying in the United States was less than two hundred, but by 1890 that number had risen to almost 3,000.[22] The traditions of the Humboldtian university were the powerful inspiration behind the rise of the American research university. The milestone "Report on Academic Freedom" of the American Association of University Professors, issued in 1915, was signed by thirteen professors; eight of them had studied in Germany.[23]

Careful scholarship counting the number of American scholars studying in Germany decade by decade from 1850 through 1930 has yet to be done. The peak was very likely in the decade of the 1870s, with the flow slowing considerably by the 1890s, and coming to a virtual halt in the early twentieth century. By the end of the nineteenth century, the American research university had essentially been established. An American scholar seeking an academic appointment in the United States in 1870 would have found a graduate credential from a German university exceptionally valuable. In 1910, a graduate credential from an excellent American university was at least as good. Although Germany was still clearly predominant in scholarly research in the early twentieth century, the United States had developed a critical mass of research scholars, libraries, and laboratories, and a self-sustaining university tradition. It was no longer necessary to go abroad to obtain a credible and sufficient graduate education.

Just as in the case of kindergartens and primary and secondary education, the German contribution to the American university was an American interpretation of certain ideas derived from German intellectuals, rather than an importation of a German product. Metzger has written persuasively to this point, noting that "America took from German sources only that which fitted her needs, only that which was in harmony with her history. In a certain sense the German academic influence, powerful as it was, reinforced rather than initiated native American tendencies toward change."[24] Indeed, the record suggests that Humboldt's rationalistic Enlightenment philosophy was more congenial to the American political economy than it was to the Prussian. On the basis of available evidence a surprising conclusion is possible: no German university ever succeeded in adhering so faithfully to Humboldt's ideals as the typical American research university.

The German influence on American education is profound, even if only in a curious inspirational way. There is little in U.S. education that directly copies German practice, nor does it seem that any specific institutions or curricula were carried over and implanted with consequence. Instead, what emerges is the sympathy of the American revolutionary spirit with the ideals of the enthusiastic exponents of liberal thought who flourished in the late eighteenth and early nineteenth centuries in German speaking territories of Europe. These were philosophers, statesmen, and poets whose conception of the modern world was highly compatible with the vision of American revolutionaries. There was even room for pragmatism in the creative idealism of German Enlightenment thought, perhaps best expressed by Humboldt's simple instruction for creating a university. He wrote, "If ultimately in institutions of higher learning the principle of seeking knowledge as such is dominant, then it is not necessary to worry individually about anything else."[25]

Notes

1. Wilhelm von Humboldt, *Ideen zu einem Versuch, die Grenzen der Wirksamkeit des Staats zu bestimmen* (Stuttgart, 1967).
2. Wilhelm von Humboldt, *The Limits of State Action*, ed. and trans., J. W. Burrow (London, 1969).
3. This is the first translation, rendered in 1854 by the English editor and translator Joseph C. Coulthard, of the words "Nach dem ganzen vorigen Räsonnement kommt schlechterdings alles auf die Ausbildung des Menschen in der höchsten Mannigfaltigkeit an," in Humboldt, *Ideen zu einem Versuch*, 69.
4. Thomas Jefferson, *The Writings of Thomas Jefferson*, ed. Andrew A. Lipscomb and Albert Ellery Bergh, vol. 15 (Washington, D.C., 1903) 303.
5. Friedrich Froebel, *Autobiography of Friedrich Froebel*, ed. and trans. Emilie Michaelis and Henry Keatley Moore (Syracuse, 1889).
6. Carl Schurz, *Intimate Letters of Carl Schurz, 1841–1869*, ed. and trans. Joseph Schafer (Madison, 1928); Barbara Beatty, *Preschool Education in America: The Culture of Young Children from the Colonial Era to the Present* (New Haven, 1995), 52–71.
7. Richard Emmons Thursfield, *Henry Barnard's American Journal of Education* (Baltimore, 1945).
8. Elizabeth Palmer Peabody, *Letters of Elizabeth Palmer Peabody, American Renaissance Woman*, 1st ed., ed. Bruce A. Ronda (Middletown, CT, 1984); Louise Hall Tharp, *The Peabody Sisters of Salem* (Boston, 1950).
9. International Kindergarten Union; Committee of Nineteen, *Pioneer of the Kindergarten in America* (New York/London, 1924), 184–203; Kurt F. Leidecker, *Yankee Teacher: The Life of William Torrey Harris* (New York, 1946).
10. Wilhelm von Humboldt, "Der Königsberger und der Litauische Schulplan," in *Wilhelm von Humboldt: Werke in fünf Bänden*, vol. 4, ed. Andreas Flitner and Klaus Giel (Stuttgart, 1964), 168–95.
11. Quoted in Daniel Hovey Calhoun, *The Educating of Americans: A Documentary History* (Boston, 1969), 196.
12. Calhoun, *The Educating of Americans*, 197.
13. Ibid., 197–99.
14. Daniel Fallon, *The German University: A Heroic Ideal in Conflict with the Modern World* (Boulder, CO, 1980).
15. Charles Franklin Thwing, *The American and the German University: One Hundred Years of History* (New York, 1928), 42.
16. John Albrecht Walz, *German Influence in American Education and Culture* (Philadelphia, 1936), 10.
17. G. Stanley Hall, "Educational Reforms," *The Pedagogical Seminary*, now *Journal of Genetic Psychology* 1 (1891): 1–12, 6–8.
18. Richard Hofstadter and Walter P. Metzger, *The Development of Academic Freedom in the United States* (New York, 1955), 392.

19. John William Adamson, *English Education, 1789–1902* (Cambridge, 1930); Goldwin Smith, *A Plea for the Abolition of Tests in the University of Oxford* (Oxford, 1864), republished as CIHM/ICHM microfiche series no. 50474 (Ottawa, Ontario: Canadian Institute for Historical Microreproductions, 1985).

20. Hofstadter and Metzger, *Academic Freedom*, 377; Thwing, *The American and the German University*, 43.

21. Frederick Rudolph, *The American College and University: A History* (New York, 1962), 335.

22. Hofstadter and Metzger, *Academic Freedom*, 378.

23. Ibid., 396.

24. Ibid., 367.

25. "Wird aber endlich in höheren wissenschaftlichen Anstalten das Prinzip herrschend: Wissenschaft als solche zu suchen, so braucht nicht mehr für irgend etwas Anderes einzeln gesorgt zu werden." Wilhelm von Humboldt, "Über die innere und äussere Organisation der höheren wissenschaftlichen Anstalten in Berlin," in *Wilhelm von Humboldt: Werke in fünf Bänden*, vol. 4, 255–66, 259.

Chapter 7

HOW (AND WHY) TO READ GERMAN-AMERICAN LITERATURE

Brent O. Peterson

In the heyday of British literature it seldom occurred to anyone to read an American text; today readers of German-American literature are even rarer.[1] Of course, "anyone" in this context refers to scholars; during the nineteenth century, ordinary Americans frequently read works by American-born writers. So too did their German-American counterparts consume a large and variable literature written in German and published in books, magazines, and newspapers. But professors of German literature have seldom stooped to that "low" level. Even when it became fashionable to consider the appeal and danger of so-called popular literature, in German more pejoratively *Trivialliteratur*, researchers preferred texts from Germany. The roots of their prejudice are long-standing and understandable, if not entirely noble. Trapped by notions of quality and bound to the civilizing mission of contact with great literature, professors preferred Goethe to Gillhoff.[2] One more theory about "the great one" represented another publishable article, whereas those who wrote about German Americans could seldom find an outlet for their musings. In large part, editors justifiably suspected the latter of filiopietism, and toilers in the field of German-American literature were often engaged in a hopeless search for some great and still undiscovered work by the German American Goethe, Heine, or Storm. Content to make ridiculous claims, not infrequently about their own ancestors, they, too, overlooked what most German Americans read. The following essay seeks to begin redressing the balance, not by surveying the textual universe but by offering a paradigmatic, close reading of a single text in an effort to show what is at stake in dealing with a literature that, for the most part, still awaits its first serious readers.

I choose, for no logically compelling reason other than its obscure richness, a short story, "Der vierte Juli: Erzählung aus dem deutsch-amerikanischen Volksleben," which appeared in 1871 in St. Louis in *Die*

Abendschule, a German-American family journal.[3] The magazine identified the story's author only as J. C. W., and not until seven years later could assiduous readers learn that the initials hid J. C. W. Lindemann (1827–1879), a Lutheran pastor and pedagogue born in Germany but residing in Illinois.[4] In its briefest outlines, the plot concerns three young men, Jürgen, Hans, and Stoffel, who worry about attending a Fourth of July celebration at a local tavern. Since they are all devout and very conservative Lutherans, the combination of drink and dance poses a threat to their creed—indeed, it threatens their very souls. If the tale were simply a pious diatribe against immorality, there would be little reason to read on, but this short story illustrates the tangled contextual web that readers need to appreciate before they can understand what was at stake in such seemingly minor publications. Only a close reading of both text and context can unpack what such works meant to contemporary readers and what they can mean to scholars and ordinary readers today.

To begin, German unification automatically frames any text published in 1871. On the one hand, Prussia's victory over France finally permitted the creation of a German national state, and Germans of almost every political, religious, economic, and cultural orientation had long awaited such an event. The events of 1871 also reverberated through the German-American community as thousands marched, sang, orated, and performed gymnastic exercises to celebrate Bismarck's achievement. The year 1871 marked a moment of ethnic pride in a community that was increasingly aware of its common heritage and sense of mission.

On the other hand, in both German-speaking areas of central Europe and German enclaves in the United States, a not inconsiderable number of Germans and German Americans dissented. Liberals hated to see a state headed by the autocratic Prussian chancellor, whose presence in the Prussian government was an affront to their hopes for an effective constitution. Moreover, Kaiser Wilhelm I had earned the title "Prince Grapeshot" for the role he played in putting down the Revolution of 1848/49, and decades would elapse before some Germans would look back fondly and want their old Emperor back. Radicals hoped for a German republic. They also longed for social change, and in 1871, Prussia seemed unlikely to introduce the social legislation that came in the 1880s. Catholics remained suspicious of the Hohenzollerns, while conservative Protestants remembered with distaste the forced merging of Prussia's Lutheran and Reformed churches in 1822. Finally, some German Austrians felt left out. They wondered about the point of a German state that failed to include them. In other words, the 1871 solution to the German question left the fundamental issue of German identity unresolved: Who was German, and what did that label imply at the level of content? German Americans participated in this outpouring of pride, and, as "Der vierte Juli" indicates, they also worried about the implications of a pan-Germanic identity. In short, both the hopes and fears of German immigrants in the United States as they related to events in their old homeland form an essential context, even intertext, to any work published in German in 1871.

Not surprisingly, therefore, a key passage in the "Der vierte Juli" refers to "Catholics and Jews, Prussian Unionists and Lutherans, church people and mockers. They all *appeared* to be brothers today" (p. 6, emphasis added). The narrator regards the appearance of brotherhood among all Germans as a dangerous fantasy. In fact, associating with such people, joining their sinful activities, and regarding them as fellow Germans imperils the central characters' prospects for eternal life. The men at the tavern might speak the same language, hail from the same area of central Europe, and share a variety of customs—not the least of which was an affinity for drink—but for the text's young heroes, as well as for its readers, membership in the larger community of Germans meant overlooking ties of faith. Catholics, Jews, and Prussian Unionists, i.e., the products of that 1822 decree, might all be Germans, but they were not Lutherans. Neither were the mockers who mixed freely with church people. Only the latter had any hope of eternal salvation, but they endangered that happy prospect by their behavior this Fourth of July. In short, the text attacks the idea of a common, German identity head on, and, in so doing locates the day's political concerns firmly within its boundaries. "Der vierte Juli" undercuts demands that we deal with literature as a separate realm above and apart from the mundane world occupied by writers and readers alike. Without taking into account the extent to which German unification saturated the consciousness of the German-American reading public, the narrator's "appeared" remains inexplicable.

Another way of making the same claim stems from an analysis of the physical context in which the story appeared. On the one hand, *Die Abendschule* functioned as a partisan, if also secular and independent, arm of the Lutheran Church Missouri Synod. Founded in the United States in 1847, the Missouri Synod remained free of ties to any mother church in Europe. At the same time, it held fiercely to the German language in an effort to foster Luther's teachings in their purest form. *Die Abendschule* numbered several pastors among its regular contributors, and there is some indication that clergymen both sold and collected for subscriptions among their congregations. On the other hand, the magazine's editors remained interested in events and conditions in their former homeland, and they assumed their readers shared that concern. Along with "Der vierte Juli," the 1871 volume contained both an extended, first-person account of the Franco-Prussian War written by a knight of the iron cross and a twenty-four-part series dedicated to "The History of the German People."[5] Note that the author or editor of the latter treats "the German people" as a singular noun; although three of the sixteen episodes were dedicated to Luther, he (or, less likely, she) uses "German" as an overall metaphor. The first installment recounts what historians at the time knew about "our" heathen forebears, so readers of "Der vierte Juli" were implicated in an ancestry that included not only

Catholics and Prussian Unionists but also the unchurched Germans of pre-Christian Europe. Thus, in a gesture that was almost schizophrenic, "The History of the German People" implicitly proclaims the very brotherhood that "Der vierte Juli" explicitly denies. Furthermore, the journal celebrates German unification and assumes its readers would like to know the details of how such political unity was achieved at the same time that it warns them against such strivings, even on a cultural level, in their new homeland. Thus, as striking as the statement about the *appearance* of brotherhood may be in the limited context of "Der vierte Juli," its larger ramifications become visible only when we take into account both the wider political and the narrower physical context in which the story was published.

Two other, less obvious features also frame the text physically. First, it appeared in a German-language journal issued in St. Louis, and, second, *Die Abendschule* bore the subtitle "a German Family Journal." Of course, the language says something about the text's intended audience. Since the story was available only in German, its primary function was to explain life in the United States to German immigrants. A different set of texts by German and other immigrants, written in or translated into English, explained immigrant life to the English-speaking majority of America. Nowadays, foreign-language texts exist almost invisibly in archives, because American historians frequently lack the linguistic competence to deal with them (especially in the multiplicity of languages that were once literary languages in the United States) while scholars of these languages remain tied to works produced in the home country. In practice, German-American texts are not legitimate objects of inquiry for American Germanists. They exist outside both the graduate and undergraduate curriculum and are read, if at all, mainly by filiopietistic amateurs in a manner lacking all rigor. The present essay argues for their inclusion in history and literature, both as a means of understanding the hopes and fears of their original readers and as an opportunity to reflect on the function of language within other ethnic groups, at other times and places. A comparative study of such texts that linked them to nineteenth and twentieth-century Italian, Finnish, and Chinese literature produced in the United States, as well as to texts written by Turkish and other "guest workers" in Europe, might well increase our understanding of all these literatures.

In addition, German-language publications produced an unconscious brotherhood as Bavarians, Saxons, Westphalians, and others learned standard German by reading them. They could "visualize," as Benedict Anderson has reminded us, "the existence of thousands and thousands like themselves through print-language."[6] Moreover, they encountered this particular text in a journal whose avowed purpose was to strengthen the German family. The story's explicit message was reinforced by masthead images picturing an ideal family seated together with the father reading aloud to his wife and children and, sometimes, to an extended

FIGURE 9. *Englisch-deutsches Anfangsbüchlein*, 1852

These two title pages (Figs. 9 and 10), from the same primer published in 1852, illustrate two suggestively different images of the way that children of two language cultures might learn to read. The text is in English and German on facing pages throughout. (German Society of Pennsylvania)

FIGURE 10. *English and German Primer*, 1852

ENGLISH AND GERMAN PRIMER.

PUBLISHED BY THE
AMERICAN TRACT SOCIETY,
150 NASSAU-STREET. NEW YORK.

family of servants, neighbors, and grandparents. Implicitly, this ideal family maintained its values by sharing German-language literature. Indeed, at some level the term "German" stood for the family, and one could interpret disagreements about inclusive versus exclusive membership in any German community as disputes within a larger family dealing with its wayward members.

That same tension about the meaning of the term "German" also appears within the text, where the narrator combines his attack on the notion of a pan-Germanic brotherhood with explicit praise of some German customs. He notes, for example, that Germans maintained their homes and farms in a manner superior to their non-German neighbors. Although it was the Fourth of July, no one thought about the celebration until they had performed their chores. "After the cattle had been fed, the stalls cleaned, and the barnyard organized according to German standards, the men and servants, women and maids, went to put on their Sunday clothes" (p. 3). Presumably, Catholics and Jews, Prussian Unionists and Lutherans, church people and mockers shared such traits, which set them apart from their neighbors and suggested, both to unknowing outsiders and to deluded insiders, that Germans were all brothers. Neatness divided them from their American neighbors and linked them together in an orderly community.

Taken together, the story's confused statement about what it meant to be German and the tension that surrounds the label's content indicate how central, how difficult, and how contentious the issue of identity had become for German Americans. Without a detailed analysis of the texts that they read and wrote, and might be fooled by outpourings of ethnic pride such as those produced so publicly in 1871, we might conclude that Germans were all brothers, united by language, custom, and origin while relatively untroubled by differences of religion, political orientation, or class. Though the latter two identity markers do not appear in "Der vierte Juli," one can easily find their incursions into what some scholars have long regarded as the strictly literary output of Germans in the United States. In fact, texts such as "Der vierte Juli" frequently center on questions of identity; they indicate that German Americans' sense of who they were—as well as who they were not—varied widely, especially over time. At any given moment, German immigrants either juggled a number of competing identities, or they occupied subject positions composed of layer upon layer of contradictory material. Literature, which invariably contains a surplus value of meaning beyond its plots and characters, provides unparalleled access to those tensions and lets us understand German Americans. It functions as a repository of recoverable values no matter what its "quality" may be. Furthermore, "Der vierte Juli" allows for this rich reading without necessarily providing any of the liberating potential some cultural studies scholars regard as the most important reason for its recovery. There is no feminism, political radicalism, or queer consciousness here, nor would there be any in most German-American literature. However, "trivial" stories for conservative Lutherans can still open a world we understand too little, once we read deeply enough to let these texts speak to us.

Part of the language of any literary text is silence, so careful readers of "Der vierte Juli" must also ask what is missing from the text. First and foremost, except for the title, the narrator fails even to mention the Fourth of July as an American holiday. The German Americans in this text do not celebrate their new homeland's national holiday. The day simply provides them with an occasion for the sort of drunken revelry their detractors probably associated with German customs all along. Although opposition to temperance had long united Germans, the majority of the celebrants in this particular story lend credence to those who argued for closing taverns and beer gardens on holidays and the Sabbath. Germans typically claimed their version of Sunday united families outdoors, particularly at a time when the urban poor had little access to fresh air.[7] However, in "Der vierte Juli," a seventeen-year-old boy upbraids his father for daring to send him home before the festivities have ended, "I'm supposed to go home while my old parents stay and dance and booze it up. You probably think I'm a greenhorn, that I don't know what the customs in this country are. I work, the farm belongs to me, too. I want my share of the money.... And the old man had to give the money, as much as he despised it" (p. 5). Yet, as much as this passage sounds like an advertisement for Sunday and holiday tavern closings, the young man identifies his behavior not with German customs but with American modes of celebration. In a strange role reversal, the negative traits that American Know-Nothings ascribed to Germans become American, while the positive treatment of abstinence from alcohol becomes, if not German, then at least German Lutheran.

What Americans, that is, the English-speaking members of the community, actually did remains a mystery to present-day readers of this text. Thus, to understand J. C. W.'s version of the holiday, one would have to contrast it with what we know about typical celebrations of the national holiday in the United States by English speakers and others. Jon Gjerde talks of various hybrid celebrations:

> Swiss Americans saw no incongruity in incorporating the history of Switzerland into their Fourth of July observance in 1876. Their centennial parade float contained representations of Helvetia and Columbia surrounded by images of the Swiss cantons with their coats-of-arms. Members of a rural German community six years later celebrated American life by reading the Declaration of Independence and listening to a speaker discuss the role of Germans in the Revolutionary War....[8]

In 1871, one would expect to find some considerable mention of not only the principle upon which the United States was founded, but also and more important, the celebration of national unity that had been concluded just six years previously. Since German Americans fought in the

Civil War, largely on the Union side and in disproportionately large numbers compared with their proportion of the civilian population, the absence of German veterans of the Grand Army of the Republic is particularly striking. These missing veterans demand attention if we are to understand both the text's implicit message and its wider implications for the position of Germans within American society. At the very least, and without mention of a specific mode of celebration, "Der vierte Juli" subjects the ideas of freedom and independence to a damaging critique. By its very nature the holiday symbolized choices immigrants had to make between German, American, and Lutheran values. Implicitly, one message has to be that freedom is a dangerous right, best exercised by rejecting it. In other words, the readers of this text were supposed to decide—of their own free will—to accept the Old World values of social and religious conformity, even at the cost of German-American unity.

Even though the text thematizes problems within what we might regard as a not-yet-defined German community in America, Americans and what they represent still figure in the text. Among other things, when the text blames various American norms and values for its protagonists' difficulties, it raises questions about the idea of assimilation on the part of the otherwise "model" immigrants. It is, after all, the town drunk who encourages a community elder to join him in a drink by saying, "Today we're all free Americans, all brothers" (p. 4). At another point one of the young men asks what advice the other would have received at home, that is, in Germany. "Ah, my parents, they advised me according to what they understood and what they were used to from the old days. If they were in America, they would think completely differently!" (p. 5). However, by adopting the values he associates with his new homeland, this character has doomed himself to a life of drunken dissipation and an afterlife in hell. In other words, based on the evidence presented in "Der vierte Juli," there is no reason to believe that acculturation would prove easy or even desirable. Other concerns have pushed the United States right off the page, except as a foil for the Germans. But only by paying attention to the absence of Americans does the reader become aware of both their implied presence and of the role Americans played in the struggle for German-American identity.

Any close reading must also devote particular attention to issues of class and gender. The three young men who comprise the text's central characters are all hired hands, and they meet at the home of the childless widow who employs Stoffel. Since the text indicates he had worked there for eight years, these men represent relations of dependency more common to Germany than America. At the very least, they are part of an older economic order in which hired men and women live as part of their employers' families; they are not free to come and go as they please. In fact, the assertion of such freedom marks the start of their downfall. The widow warns her charge and the other two against the celebration— termed "innocent" in heavy-handed irony, first by the other boys and then, repeatedly, by the narrator. Undaunted, they decide to ask another neighbor also when they invite his hired man to accompany them. He rejects the widow's advice and says, "I know what's right, dancing is a harmless activity, and everyone is allowed an innocent pleasure.... I believe that if [I] old Wenne is going with his people, you boys can be there too" (p. 4). This advice giving, coupled with the fact that Wenne refers to the workers on the farm as "his people," indicates that the relationship transcends an exchange of money for labor. Even though they pit one elder against the other, these young men live in a world characterized by deference. They expect and receive both a home and moral guidance from their employers, who sometimes stand in for missing parents or town elders.

A chief difficulty with the celebration is, therefore, that it threatens to upend the accepted order. "Old, gray-haired Wenne drank with old Sonne, whom, only a few years before, he had helped kick out of the congregation for being a drunk" (p. 4). The tavern keeper, by contrast, is everyone's friend so long as they have money, while the heroes and heroines of this tale remain part of a premodern, even antimodern organic community (*Gemeinschaft*) at a time when capitalist pressures were reshaping lives in both the old and new worlds. Indeed, it was an escape from this cash nexus that conservative immigrants sought in the United States. Their nostalgia for a past that never would be also became part of the identity of German Americans for decades to come. Among other things, this antimodern orientation helps explain the Bavarianization of German-American culture today. In a fashion that would baffle and horrify their forebears, descendants of Protestants, freethinkers, socialists, anarchists, and communists—who were all hoping to preserve a very different way of life—adopted the kitschy reference so beloved by American tourists charmed by the same antimodernist theme park in the old country. Characters' location in a complex social system thereby functions as both a historically specific marker and an indicator of longer-range concerns within and about the German-American community.

Gender plays less of a role in this text, in large part because "Der vierte Juli" accords its few female characters subordinate positions. In setting the scene, the narrator speaks of "men and servants, women and maids," thereby setting the rank order that characterized this community (p. 3). Only one woman, the childless widow, has the moral and economic wherewithal to offer independent advice. By contrast, Old Wenne's wife supports her husband's opinion once he indicated to "his people" that he would attend the celebration. Wenne's daughter Minna also puts in an appearance when her father notices that one of the two young heroes in attendance has not yet danced. Wenne orders the girl to take a turn on the dance floor with the reluctant Hans: "Minna—take this coward and twirl him around properly" (p. 5). But Minna's being more active than the cowardly young man scarcely allows her freedom. In fact, she is far more dependent on her father's whims than the boys in his family, and the text treats her as a willing temptress rather than even a minor heroine. In essence, except for the widow, women seem bereft of moral judgment; they can only participate or refrain from frivolity at the behest of the stronger males. In this sense, too, "Der vierte Juli" remains a thoroughly conservative text.

The text's only subversive moments are those endemic to morality tales: Their portrayal of evil may not look so bad, while goodness frequently comes across as less appealing than their authors intended. For example, readers of "Der vierte Juli" could easily conclude that the dance and accompanying drinking sounded fun and could be enjoyed in moderation. As the narrator is forced to admit, "many families had returned to their farms when it began to get dark" (p. 5). Their pleasure had in fact been "innocent," and not everyone who remained fared as badly as Jürgen and Hans. Moreover, the reader learns nothing of what must have been a dull evening passed by Stoffel and the widow who employed him. Although "the boys" might enjoy coffee and cake with the elderly lady on holiday afternoons, the prospect of spending an entire day and half the night in pious conversation pales in comparison with festivities at the local tavern. In addition, participation by the congregation's elders reveals them to be hypocrites; "the pastor lies sleeplessly in his bed and sighs to God," incapable of any action (p. 5). Thus, except for Stoffel, the forces of good remain powerless or worse, while evil, despite the author's intentions, remains an attractive and powerful temptation, even in this stilted tale of virtue.

Still, the narrator emphasizes that conservatism though repeated appeals to antirationalism. Recourse to reason implies mistrust in God, abandonment of faith, and the rejection of Christian morality. Among the most boisterous participants in the celebration were those who "had never been seen in church, for they belonged to the 'educated' [*gebildet*]" (p. 4). Sonne, the old drunkard, also calls his belief in living happily and then, at the last minute, dying holy, "smart," and once Wenne decides to join him, Sonne says, "I'm so glad you guys are finally getting smart" (p. 4). The text locates human intellect in this world rather than the next, which means that for God-fearing people, all of the above questions and dilemmas are mere epiphenomena, barely worth discussing except that some of their number might fall victim to temptation. However, these questions become important, first, because good Christians repeatedly try to lead their fellows on the path of righteousness, and second, because "Der vierte Juli" tends to conflate the profane, rational world with America. "Stoffel, you're a good guy, but you let priests and Pharisees lead you around by the nose. If you use your brains you will soon realize that young people need a little freedom. We are now living in America. No official, no priest has any say in what happens here" (p. 6). Except that the Lutheran Church Missouri Synod was a thoroughly American institution, one might ask why its adherents remained in the New World rather than return to the Old. Its members must have struggled with the dilemma of forging identities in a manner that sometimes kept them apart from both Germans and Americans. These fictional characters had not yet achieved hyphenation, and they remained wary of that process's homogenizing inclusivity. Here, too, the heroes were supposed to use their newfound freedom to choose deference to accepted authorities.

Thus far, I have been unpacking "Der vierte Juli" to highlight various concerns that troubled German immigrants in the United States. I claim that although this text and thousands like it provide unparalleled access to the discursive universe in which German Americans lived, one should never mistake literary representations for either reality or reflections of reality. Unless coupled with other sources from different kinds of archives, "Der vierte Juli" cannot give reliable evidence about the manner in which German Americans actually celebrated the Fourth of July in 1871. Literature operates by its own rules, and although plot, character, language, and narration sometimes contradict one another, a work's extra-literary surplus value generally supports the message one can tease out of the story using traditional literary means. Thus, any serious reader operating in the world of cultural studies must also make a more formal analysis of the text without necessarily making judgments about its literary quality. In other words, "Der vierte Juli" demands a "literary" reading as well.

For a short story, J. C. W.'s text possesses an unusually large cast of characters, which it arranges into two neat triangles. Like the heroes and heroines of romance fiction, its three young men consist of value constellations that pit one of them against the other two. Resolution comes when the character in the middle chooses sides and opts for values favored by the text. On the one hand, Stoffel listens to the widow who employs him. He accepts her renunciation of drink, dancing, and other temptations of the secular world. Stoffel favors revealed truth over intellect, the inherited social order over "American" freedom from external controls, and Lutheranism as his central identity. He is, therefore, not part of the pan-Germanic, religiously mixed horde at the Fourth of July celebration. Stoffel parts company from his two friends and stays home with the widow. On the other hand, Jürgen rejects the widow's advice and attends the dance. He not only drinks to excess, but he also rejects the religious values and the control exercised by his parents and the community's elders. As a sign of how complicated these markers can become, Jürgen simultaneously joins the "apparent" brotherhood of Germans and rejects the core German values he associates with the Old World in favor of American freedoms. "We live in America now, where no official or pastor can tell you what to do" (p. 6). By contrast, Hans lends the tale interest, because he moves between these two poles. The tale ends happily because his final position resolves the conflict in a manner that the narrator regards as positive.

When Hans and Jürgen first visit the widow who employs Stoffel, she almost convinces Hans to forgo the pleasures of the celebration. He is still unsure when they arrive at Wenne's farm, and only the elder Wenne's approval convinces him to accompany Jürgen and the others. Once he arrives at the tavern, Hans tries to remain on the sidelines. At first, he drinks moderately, and he only dances when Wenne's daughter Minna drags him onto the dance floor. Having succumbed, there is no stopping, but the following day Hans regrets his behavior. He tells Stoffel, "Oh, I'm so ashamed, I wish I could sink into the ground. In the afternoon I was still a child of God, and that night they had to carry me home drunk" (p. 6). Luckily, he has time to repent. More important, readers can identify with both his troubles and his redemption. By investing their emotional energy in a character like Hans, readers come to care about his fate, which makes them more likely to accept the text's message. "Der vierte Juli" also offers Stoffel as an object for reader identification, but since he never strays from the path of righteousness, he probably engages the audience less.

Since literary texts are almost invariably overdetermined, it is not surprising that "Der vierte Juli" contains a parallel triangle of supporting characters. The widow and Old Wenne function in the same relationship as Stoffel and Jürgen, while various members of the congregation who attend the celebration but return home early echo Hans's role. A more thorough investigation might locate additional redundancies, but from a literary standpoint the more interesting characters are Mr. Everthirsty (Herr Immerdurst) and Mr. Neversober (Herr Nienüchtern). They represent a throwback to a much earlier form of storytelling in which stock characters present a simple morality tale. Here, they only make cameo appearances, because the fundamental issue remains identity rather than temperance. Still, they merit attention, because they link this text to a larger and longer literary tradition and indicate that even the most trivial text participates in the discourse of literature, a fact that popular literature's academic detractors seldom concede.

Language, namely the richness and poetic tone associated with quality literature, remains a problem in dealing with texts like "Der vierte Juli." Although one would have to make a compelling case for why the determination would matter, one could easily conclude that J. C. W.'s work fails to rise to the level of his canonical contemporaries in Germany. He does, however, employ many of the mannerisms and methods that readers would encounter in other realist texts. For example, the story opens with a description of the weather, and since the scene does not unfold during a dark and stormy night, we expect and are rewarded by the appearance of positive characters.[9] The text also contains more than its fair share of heavy-handed irony. Either the author or the narrator must have decided that some readers would react positively to terms such as "educated" (*gebildet*) and "innocent" (*unschuldig*), so they appear in quotation marks. Good Lutherans were neither ignorant nor debauched, but someone wanted to remind them of the dangers of trusting reason rather than revealed truth, or of believing what their neighbors said about the supposedly innocent pleasure of drink and dancing. In other words, the writer was careful, if not particularly artistic, in his use of language, and like every other detail his usage contributed to the overall effect and reinforced the text's message.

By now, if not earlier, readers of the present essay might wonder why "Der vierte Juli" merits an analysis that is already more than half again as long as the original story. Would every German-American text demand as thorough an explication? Ideally, I would say yes. Whatever one might ultimately think of J. C. W.'s efforts, his facility with plot, character, and language, and of the messages he either intended to convey or revealed without thinking, there is a richness here that becomes apparent only by pulling out all the stops. More importantly, performing the same exercise on a range of other texts would reveal a great deal that we do not yet know about the discursive universe in which German Americans lived. Without reading what they read (and taking it seriously), without teasing out factors that they took for granted (and exploring connections of which they were only dimly aware), the hopes and fears of German immigrants remain closed to subsequent generations of readers. Without knowing, for example, how difficult the struggle for German-American identity actually was, how it permeated everything Germans in America did, we can never appreciate the choices these immigrants made and the lessons they offer to contemporary "others." And note again that this argument for a serious engagement with German-American literature does not rest upon the recovery of great works of literature or upon liberating accounts of resistance. We can certainly find the latter in texts produced by and for the German-American working class, but such quests limit the range of interesting texts unnecessarily.[10] Such "positive" examples probably do not represent the lion's share of German-American literature, which means that concentrating on them excludes the great bulk of German Americans.

Of course, at the moment, we know very little about either the content or amount of literature that needs such a reading, and the German Society of Pennsylvania's rich holdings present a prime example of the problem. Although we do not yet have exact data, rough estimates put the proportion of literature at 40 to 50 percent of the library's 70,000 volumes. The German-American collection comprises about 10,000 volumes, but that number does not include the wealth of poetry, short fiction, and novels serialized in the German-American press and held under the same (new) roof, to say nothing of elsewhere. As I indicated above, nonfiction provided a context that also demands inclusion if we are to understand the literary works, and as recent work on the popular press in Germany has shown, nonfiction aimed at a general audience presents a special, extraordinarily revealing category of prose.[11] But until someone surveys the textual universe and begins to assemble a bibliography of the available material, we can only speculate about what a series of readings might produce. In the meantime, I suggest that texts like "Der vierte Juli" are rich enough sources of insight into the German-American community to warrant a broadly contextual approach. They require a German-American Cultural Studies that should interest Germanists in the United States and Germany, as well as scholars of other national literatures, historians, and the extra-academic generalists we all hope to reach. For all of those potential readers, "how," when done in enough depth, ought to provide a convincing argument for "why."

Notes

1. Margaret Fuller made one of the classic statements against American literature in her *Papers on Literature and Art* (1846): "It does not follow because many books are written by persons born in America that there exists an American literature." In part, Fuller was arguing for books about America, but she deemed it unlikely that anyone in America was intelligent enough to produce them.
2. With apologies for the alliteration, the reference is to Johannes Gillhoff's *Jürnjakob Swehn der Amerikafahrer* (1917).
3. "Der vierte Juli: Erzählung as dem deutsch-amerikanischen Volksleben," *Die Abendschule* 18, 1 and 2 (September 15, 1871): 3–6. For an extended analysis of the journal, see Brent O. Peterson, *Popular Narratives and Ethnic Identity: Literature and Community in Die Abendschule* (Ithaca, 1991). I would like to thank my colleagues at Ripon College, Paul Axelrod and Russell Blake, for enriching my arguments in the course of our joint first-year seminar on immigration. In addition, A. J. Zydzik, a gifted student from my section, translated the story for his fellow students. I quote from that manuscript but use page numbers from the German original.
4. See A. C. Stellhorn, "J. C. W. Lindemann: First Director of the Evangelical Lutheran Teachers' Seminary in Addison, Illinois," *Concordia Historical Institute Quarterly* 14 (October 1941): 65–92.
5. "'Meine Erlebnisse in Frankreich,' Für die 'Abendschule' erzählt von einem Ritter des eisernen Kreuzes," 2–3, and "Die Geschichte des deutschen Volks: Nach den Quellen für die 'Abendschule' erzählt," 6–8.
6. Benedict Anderson, *Imagined Communities: Reflections on the Origin and Spread of Nationalism* (London, 1983), 74.
7. For a "literary" paean to German Sundays, see Henry (Heinrich) Boernstein, *The Mysteries of St. Louis*, trans. Friedrich Münch (Chicago, 1990), 123. The German version of the text appeared, in serial form, in the *Anzeiger des Westens*, February–June 1851.
8. Jon Gjerde, *The Minds of the West: Ethnocultural Evolution in the Rural Middle West, 1830–1917* (Chapel Hill, 1997), 61.
9. For an "appreciation" of that tactic in "German" literature, see F. C. Delius, *Der Held und sein Wetter: Ein Kunstmittel und sein ideologischer Gebrauch im Roman des bürgerlichen Realismus* (Munich, 1971).
10. The Boernstein novel cited above appears in Kerr's "Foreign-Language American Left Series," and Philip S. Foner has edited an English-language version of *The Autobiographies of the Haymarket Martyrs* (New York, 1969). In German, see Carol J. Poore, *Deutsch-amerikanische sozialistische Literatur, 1865–1900* (Berlin, 1987).
11. See Kirsten Belgum, *Popularizing the Nation: Audience, Representation, and the Production of Identity in Die Gartenlaube, 1853–1900* (Lincoln, 1998).

— *Chapter 8* —

GERMAN-LANGUAGE WRITING IN THE UNITED STATES
A Serious Challenge to American Studies?

Werner Sollors

In American literary studies, languages other than English have simply tended to disappear from view, and the presence of multilingual elements in English-language texts is largely ignored, even by multiculturalists with specialized interests in ethnic studies or by American students of "foreign languages" (such as German) interested in cultural studies. German-language texts published in the United States have come to be ignored by *Germanisten* as well as *Amerikanisten*. Though it is a stepchild of German as well as American studies, the German-American literary tradition is particularly rich. This is obviously true in quantitative terms. In the Harvard University library system alone, for example, there are more than 120,000 imprints published in the United States and written in scores of languages other than English, ranging from Amerindian texts to Spanish, French, Dutch, and Russian colonial writings, and from immigrant literature in all European, many Asian, and some African languages to French and Arabic works by African Americans. More than 25,000 of these titles are in German, making it by far the largest single language group. (How many more might the Library of Congress, the New York Public Library, and the University of Chicago Archives hold?) Five thousand newspapers and periodicals are listed in Karl Arndt and May Olson's *The German-Language Press in the Americas, 1732–1955* (1980).

We may have known for a very long time that there is a lot out there, but the question is really how to connect it and make it interesting to the work of existing disciplines. Are there any "good" texts, or at least "interesting" or otherwise "important" ones? What do they tell us that we don't already know from better sources?

In this essay I will focus on the challenges that an examination of German-American texts might present to American studies, and I shall try to suggest the beginning of an answer by touching briefly upon a variety of examples. The American studies themes range from "exceptionalism" to "whiteness studies," and from comparisons of blacks and Jews for the concept of "race," to "gender studies," to the problematic theme of lesbian representation and notions of "assimilation" and "resistance." The exemplary challenges will stem from German-American fiction and nonfiction, and I will conclude with a "Germerican" poem.

Exceptionalism: The Country without Novels of Manners and *Die Geheimnisse von Philadelphia*

Lionel Trilling remarked that the American literary tradition lacked a strong novel of manners tradition and therefore showed a predilection of romance at the expense of the fuller representation of a social world. This assertion, often repeated in American studies of the 1950s and 60s, was used to make exceptionalist claims about the American character. Yet some nineteenth-century German-American works of fiction would appear to be good examples of a Balzacian eye in the United States, engaged in an ironic investigation of manners without resorting to "romance" strategies or adopting *parti pris* positions.

Since this chapter is based on a paper read at a conference in Philadelphia in which Elliott Shore participated, it is absolutely irresistible to start with the anonymous *Die Geheimnisse von Philadelphia* (1850), of which only the beginning chapters have survived. The novel was, of course, part of the international vogue in urban *Mysteries* following the publication of Eugène Sue's *Mystères de Paris* (1842); it may have been the first German-American participant in this genre. It shows its inspiration by starting with the standard opening, "It was a stormy, cold, wet November night" (though using it only in the *second* chapter). *Die Geheimnisse von Philadelphia: Eine Tendeznovelle und zugleich ein Beitrag zur Sitten- und Cultur-Geschichte des Amerikanischen Volkes*, which was printed in Philadelphia by "Druck u. Verlag A. Gläser, J. M. Reichard, and N. Schmitt" at 61 Callowhill St., includes lively interracial scenes in a black-German bar. What I wish to highlight here is a remarkable account of the Philadelphia upstarts' efforts to create the useful illusion that they spend endless hours shopping in expensive and fashionable stores, thus appearing to be richer than they are. The details of this account are remarkable. I am quoting from Elliott Shore's not-yet-published translation of the opening chapter of the novel, entitled "Die Chesnut- und Bedford-Straße."

> We continue to stroll down Chestnut Street, seeing and enjoying all of the beauty around us. All appears lustrous, and splendid and rich, but appearances are often deceiving. The velvet mantillas and the rustling dress and the bustle all demand respect from the look of the women proudly strutting by. But none of it is yet paid for. In the overcoat pockets of the husband upon whose arms she leans as they walk is a bill from the tailor.... But that does not seem to matter so

much, for the lady stops suddenly in front of a glittering silk shop, the biggest, richest, and most famous in the city, admiring a costly cashmere shawl displayed in the shop window as expensive bait. She thinks: "One *can* go in and ask about the price. The shawl is marvelous!"… The lady has the cashmere shawl and ten others and many other beautiful wares spread out before her, asks about the prices, bargains and haggles, and, after the course of a half-hour, gets up, shakes her head disapprovingly and says that for today, nothing caught her fancy—maybe tomorrow. The polite business attendant opens the door for the lady and gentleman, they walk out slowly and deliberately. The lady first pulls on her gloves in the doorway, thereby gaining more time to show passersby that they were in the most fashionable store on Chestnut Street, proving that they know how to build up credit in the eyes of the world.

Correspondingly, the shop owners arrange to have many coaches wait outside of shops in order to suggest that they are more popular than they are.

It strikes the observer that twelve, twenty, often thirty coaches are always waiting before each of the bigger stores at this time of day. One mustn't believe that customers, male and female, came in these coaches.… No, these carriages are as good bait as the shawl in the display window. If business gets "sluggish" [*flau*] that means, if more carriages stand in front of other shops than this one, the business manager dispatches his errand-boy to those places where carriage drivers gather and orders … six, eight, or ten carriages, to drive up from various sides and wait for a half hour or even a full hour in front of the shop.

Two of the three known surviving copies of this novel are at the German Society of Philadelphia; Elliott Shore has traced the possible authors to the radical newspaper *Der Volksvertreter*. There is little German-Americanist secondary literature and virtually no reference to this book in Americanist scholarship.

Contemporary Americanists might be amused by such an example but would hardly be shocked by it, since the "romance" theory is no longer as lively as it used to be—though the examination of American novels of manners in an internationally comparative frame has not exactly flourished in recent years either.

So let us now look at three areas which have been prominent in American studies in the age of multiculturalism: whiteness studies, black-Jewish relations and comparisons of "ethnicity" and "race," and gender studies and the representation of same-sex love in literature.

Whiteness Studies and the Case of Ottilie Assing

Studies of immigrant adjustment have, in recent years, strongly emphasized the position of racial privilege that was made available to Europeans in the United States, which they happily adopted in defining themselves against black Americans: "on the backs of blacks," as Toni Morrison put it. *How the Irish Became White* is the model for this approach, which has offered many new insights. The approach could, however, be balanced by studies of how German American Missourians held out against slavery and against fears of miscegenation. One literary example of an author who is well suited to illustrate this is Ottilie Assing, much discussed since the publication of her biography (by Maria Diedrich) and the appearance of her collected German-language journalism, entitled *Radical Passion: Ottilie Assing's Reports on America and Letters to Frederick Douglass*, introduced, edited, and fabulously translated by Christoph Lohmann.

Assing (1819–1884) was the daughter of David Assur, a Jewish physician from Königsberg, and Rosa Maria Varnhagen, a member of a famous family of Romantic artists. Orphaned in her twenties and sympathetic to the radical forty-eighters, she fled for America in 1852, where she started writing the reports for German newspapers (both published and unpublished) that Chris Lohmann has now collected. She wrote about the antislavery and women's movements for Cotta's *Morgenblatt für gebildete Leser*, translated the second edition of Douglass's autobiography, and formed a twenty-eight-year long attachment as Douglass's "other woman" that ended only when Douglass remarried in 1882. Assing committed suicide in Paris in 1884, making Douglass her sole heir and leaving instructions to have all her correspondence burned. Diedrich stresses that the Assing-Douglass relationship invites us "to rethink gender and race in the nineteenth century":

> Assing and Douglass performed their interracial romance in a quasi-public realm, and they lived their liaison in the Douglasses' domestic setting, in the very space that was occupied by Douglass's wife Anna Murray and their children.... Ottilie Assing and Frederick Douglass spent a lifetime pretending that race was not an issue in their relationship. And yet race was central to the way they perceived and approached each other; it was a powerful, eroticizing magnet in their liaison; it influenced the decisions they made about their life together; it shaped their contemporaries' attitude toward them. Loving Douglass made Assing guilty by association to many of her contemporaries; she violated dominant notions of racial purity. Loving Assing made Douglass a traitor to his race, especially to black women.[1]

Unlike studies of other forty-eighters, Assing's relevance to the American scene has been established by her connections with *black* Americans, and especially with Frederick Douglass. The very title of the new biography, *Love across Color Lines*, alludes directly to the nature of that long-lasting connection.

Yet it is not only in her life, but also in her journalistic writing that Assing proves to be a fearless spirit who directed her European-made political radicalism against the grain of American race taboos. Hardly the kind of figure that whiteness studies have portrayed, Assing shows her German radical cultural baggage in the many unconventional ways in which she approaches slavery and the Civil War, John Brown, *The Octoroon*, Lincoln, and Reconstruction. I have chosen for an example here her response to the *Miscegenation* pamphlet, a hoax that was circulated in 1864 by Democratic journalists in the hopes of luring abolitionist Republicans to endorse it. Assing engaged with this publication in "Effects of War on Social Conditions and on Slavery," an essay for the *Morgenblatt* of January 1864. The context of her observations is her belief that if Southerners were ready to "put down their arms on the condition that slavery would be guaranteed within the existing boundaries, without a doubt the president, his cabinet, and a majority of the Congress and the people would gladly consent." She continues:

> The change that is occurring in public opinion is nevertheless immense. The force of events brings about what the nation's sense of morality and justice has been unable to accomplish, and no one finally can escape its effects. It is a sign of the times in this respect that a pamphlet has recently appeared with the title "Miscegenation" [which Assing consistently misspells as "miscenegation"], in which it is argued that the intermingling of the white and the black race is an unavoidable necessity and the only means by which the ongoing degeneration of the race on this continent can be prevented. The piece is obviously well-meaning and is the product of honest conviction [Assing fell for the hoax], but it is written with neither brilliance nor originality. The moral, physiological, and historical reasons adduced by the author have mostly been accepted by people of enlightened thought; some of his other reasons are either superfluous or lack a sound foundation. Its significance, however, lies in the fact that there is someone today who dares to champion a cause that hitherto has been banished by society. A woman who may have left her husband with another man has a better prospect of being again accepted into the graces of this society than she who marries the most respectable and well educated colored man out of love, respecting all legal formalities.
>
> As little as two years ago, any word in favor of mingling the races would have caused a unanimous outcry of shock and horror. It was the very issue on which even declared abolitionists, who called for complete civil equality for the Negro, could not overcome their prejudice. Many who treated the colored man socially as an equal and did not hesitate to go against public opinion by showing themselves in public with him as a friend would have revolted against the thought of darkening their pure Anglo-Saxon blood by mixing it with the African. And those who had perhaps no personal objections were loath to incur the rejection and contempt of the masses. Even Wendell Phillips, one of the most courageous leaders in the struggle for the cause of the Negro, came out only last year in favor of the intermingling of the races; and Harriet Beecher Stowe, in all her descriptions of southern life and relations between the races, did not give a single instance of true love between their representatives, and yet, though rare, they do occur in spite of all prejudice and ostracism. The author of "Miscegenation," meanwhile, has not dared to publish his work under his name, thus significantly diminishing the value of his commendable service; but now that someone has made a start, the issue will not be allowed to rest.[2]

As Lohmann puts it, these comments, given "Assing's relationship with Frederick Douglass,… are most revealing and interesting." Assing does present a challenge to certain assumptions of whiteness studies, and it is to be hoped that more careful examinations of German-African American relations will complicate the story of white immigrant privilege that has been disseminated in recent years.

"Race" and "Blacks and Jews": Du Bois in Nazi Germany, 1936

German-American texts are not necessarily texts written by German emigrants; many non-German Americans also wrote in German. One of them is W. E. B. Du Bois, who contributed an essay on the "Negro problem" to the *Zeitschrift für Sozialwissenschaften* that Max Weber edited. Long after Weber's death, however, Du Bois kept his German connection alive. Little known is the fact that he submitted a grant proposal in 1935 (preserved in the papers) that, amazingly, outlined the purpose to help update Tuskegee's system of industrial education by studying "the way in which popular education for youth and adults in Germany has been made to minister to industrial organization and advance; and how this German experience can be applied so as to help in the re-organization of the American Negro industrial school, and the establishment of other social institutions."[3] The application was funded, and Du Bois left New York on June 5 aboard the Hamburg-Amerika Line's *St. Louis*.[4] After some traveling around, he stayed in Germany for five months.

In an interview that Du Bois gave the *New York Staatszeitung und Herold* on 27 January 1937, shortly after his return to the United States on 30 December 1936, he was quoted as saying that he found the attitude of the German press toward the colored Olympic athletes "quite fair, even friendly." The anonymous journalist praises Du Bois's German pronunciation, mentions that Du Bois had studied in Germany thirty years earlier (with Treitschke, Schmoller, and Adolf Wagner), and finds his observations particularly interesting since Du Bois, as a member of a race persecuted in America, was uniquely qualified to make comparative observations on Germany. Du Bois also commented on a Nuremberg rally, and found quite terrible what was said there: it was the sort of thing that would have caused a war in the past. Rudolf Hess made a good impression on him, though Du Bois believed that his influence was waning. He praised the Nazi government's program for construction of apartments (unmatched in Europe) and highways, but found the national mood depressed, lacking *Gemütlichkeit*. He noticed food shortages and the publicized winter aid collections, but he observed an unconditional trust in national socialism and in Hitler personally, as well as much gratitude for what he had done in the few years of his rule.

Speaking directly to the issue of race, Du Bois also observed that the treatment of Negroes in Germany did not yet show any traces of racial hatred, although he "simply could not comprehend" the German attitude toward Jews. The situation of the Jews was, he said, very regrettable, but it could not be compared with that of the Negroes in the United States. What happened in Germany took place quite legally, even if it was cruel and unjust; in the United States, by contrast, the Negroes were discriminated against and persecuted in glaring violation of the law. The reactions of blacks and Jews were similar: they tried to remain unnoticed. Both races were stereotyped as lascivious, and Du Bois compared the tone and content of Streicher's violently anti-Semitic paper *Der Stürmer* with similar Negrophobe propaganda in the South. Apart from that, the situation was not comparable. The interview ended with Du Bois's declaration that he himself had been received very cordially in Germany and had not suffered any racial prejudice whatsoever.[5]

Du Bois's position may, of course, have been misrepresented by this German-language journalist from New York. We do, however, at least have a bit of correspondence surrounding the interview; an officer of the American Jewish Committee wrote the National Association for the Advancement of Colored People (NAACP) for the full text of the interview, and when Du Bois answered that he had not seen it, sent Du Bois a copy of the printed article for confirmation. Du Bois answered on 10 March 1937, with the statement that

it is extremely difficult to express an opinion about Germany today which is true in all respects without numerous modifications and explanations. In the first place what I said ... was strictly confined to my experience and to what was apparently happening while I was there. I am convinced that without doubt the mob rule and illegal aggression practiced upon Jews in the earlier days of the Nazi Movement was very grave and equaled in some cases the aggression upon Negroes in the United States. But the point I was trying to make in my interview in New York was that while I was in Germany the Nazi[s] had so changed the laws that practically anything they did to Jews was legal, and what you had was legal oppression rather than the illegal cast[e] and lynching of Negroes in the United States. On the other hand, the difference between these two methods is not essential, but it does make direct comparison between the plight of the Negroes in America and the Jews in Germany difficult and in many respects misleading. Of course I was not at all deceived by the attitude of Germany toward me and the very few Negroes who happened to be visiting there. Theoretically, their attitude toward Negroes is just as bad as toward Jews, and if there were any number of Negroes in Germany it would be expressed in the same way. But the point that interested me was that while this is the theoretical attitude, there was on the part of the populace no natural reaction of prejudice toward Negroes while there was such reaction toward Jews. This arose naturally from the frightful anti-Semitic propaganda.[6]

Nathan Huggins has pointed out that Du Bois covered his trip in articles for the *Pittsburgh Courier*, and some critics have begun to examine these most interesting essays, which were written in English. In these opinion pieces, Du Bois was unambiguous in his assessment and pessimistic in his prognosis; and he writes in the remarkable piece on "The Present Plight of the German Jew":

> There has been no tragedy in modern times equal in its awful effects to the fight on the Jew in Germany. It is an attack on civilization, comparable only to such horrors as the Spanish Inquisition and the African slave trade. It has set civilization back a hundred years, and in particular has it made the settlement and understanding of race problems more difficult and more doubtful. It is widely believed by many that the Jewish problem in Germany was episodic, and is already passing. Visitors to the Olympic Games are apt to have gotten that impression. They saw no Jewish oppression. Just as Northern visitors to Mississippi see no Negro oppression. (19 December 1936)

Du Bois reminds the optimists that Germany is now in the hands of the Nazis, of Hitler and his "coadjutors and backers," and that an integral part of their policy "just as prominent now as earlier and perhaps growing in prominence, is world war on Jews. The proof of this is incontrovertible, and must comfort all those in any part of the world who depend on race hate as the salvation of men." He continues:

> Adolf Hitler hardly ever makes a speech today—and his speeches reach every corner of Germany, by radio, newspaper, placard, movie and public announcement-without belittling, blaming or cursing Jews. From my window as I write I see a great red poster, seven feet high, asking the German people to contribute to winter relief of the poor, so that Germany will not sink to the level of the "Jewish-Bolshevist countries of the rest of the world." At Nuremberg recently he accused the "foreign Jewish element" as causing the rotting of the Aryan world. His propaganda minister was more insulting, and said that the whole oppression of Germany by the world was caused by Jewish emigrants. Every misfortune of the world is in the whole or in part blamed on Jews—the Spanish rebellion, the obstruction to world trade, etc. One finds cases in the papers: Jews jailed for sex relations with German women; a marriage disallowed because a Jewish justice of the peace witnessed it; Masons excluded from office in the National Socialist Party, because Jews are Masons; advertisements excluding Jews; the total disfranchisement of all Jews; deprivation of civil rights and inability to remain or become German citizens; limited rights of education, and narrowly limited right to work in trades, professions and the civil service; the threat of boycott, loss of work and even mob violence, for any German who trades with a Jew; and, above all, the continued circulation of Julius Streicher's [*Stürmer*], the most shameless, lying advocate of race hate in the world, not excluding Florida. It could not sell a copy without Hitler's consent. (19 December 1936)

There are many more remarkable points that Du Bois made in these columns than I can relate. Perhaps no point is as significant as the fact that he unambiguously condemned the Nazi political system while he remained distinctly fond of Germany—German culture and Wagner's operatic œuvre—and of Europe in general. Even in the middle of the serious international political crises he commented on—the Balkans and

Spain, for example (17 October 1936)—Du Bois stressed the centrality of Europe for an understanding of modern culture and pointed out that "civilization does not center in the United States or in Australia.... Despite all our boasting and national pride, we turn continually and repeatedly toward Europe to know and understand the last word of human culture in matters of vital and everyday interest to us" (26 September 1936). He was happy about the greater possibility of human contacts across the color line that Europe afforded in the 1930s. "I have not especially sought such contacts, but they have been all the more welcome and valuable because they have come naturally. Even on this trip it was a great source of knowledge and understanding to dine with Malinowsky, the great English anthropologist; to have a visit from De Cleene, the colonial expert, in Belgium; to meet in Germany, Westerma[nn], who knows more African tongues than any man, and to lunch with H. G. Wells in London." He concluded that "more is being done today in the scientific study of races and race relations in Europe than elsewhere in the world. And this is the primary reason why I am here" (26 September 1936). And even after he had left Germany and felt more at liberty to be critical of its racial politics, he reiterated that he had been "treated with uniform courtesy and consideration" in Germany and added pointedly, "It would have been impossible for me to have spent a similarly long time in any part of the United States, without some, if not frequent cases of personal insult or discrimination. I cannot record a single instance here." (5 December 1936)

W. E. B. Du Bois's visit to Nazi Germany constitutes an interesting intersection of African American and European history; it is also an undoubtedly rare case of an early examination of Nazi rule and of the nature of its anti-Semitism by a German-speaking Harvard and Berlin-trained historian and sociologist whose life-long specialty was the field of race relations. It is also an unexamined case of black-Jewish relations, for Du Bois approached the danger of the impending holocaust with remarkable insight and compassion.

"Gender" and the Apparitional Lesbian

In her marvelous study of representations of lesbian love, Terry Castle notes that her mostly French and English examples include an "apparitional," or "spectral" element that often intervenes before a full representation of a kiss or an embrace can occur. "The kiss that doesn't happen, the kiss that *can't* happen, because one of the women involved has become a ghost (or else is directly haunted by ghosts)," Castle writes,

> seems to me a crucial metaphor for the history of lesbian literary representation since the early eighteenth century. Given the threat that sexual love between women inevitably poses to the workings of patriarchal arrangement,

it has often been felt necessary to deny the carnal *bravada* of lesbian existence. The hoary misogynist challenge, "But what do lesbians do?" insinuates as much: *This cannot be. There is no place for this.* It is perhaps not so surprising that at least until around 1900 lesbianism manifests itself in the Western literary imagination primarily as an absence, as chimera or *amor impossibilia*—a kind of love that, by definition, cannot exist.... It cannot be perceived, except apparitionally.[7]

Castle's argument is a very good one, but it is challenged in the area of German-American literature. It takes us back to our first example, as it comes from another German-language novel of the *Mysteries* tradition, Ludwig von Reizenstein's *Die Geheimnisse von New-Orleans*, which, after a long serialization in the *Louisiana Staats-Zeitung* in 1854 and 1855 was set as a book, the publication of which was ultimately suppressed. The proofs have recently been found and translated by Steven Rowan. This novel contains a remarkably nonapparitional chapter entitled "Lesbische Liebe." The narrator frames the amorous dialogue between the German Creole woman Orleana, who lives on New Orleans's Toulouse Street and has just been harassed by a drunk German immigrant, and Claudine de Laussure, who has just left her husband. "An authority from ancient Greece tells us that women once lived on the isle of Lesbos who did not allow themselves to be touched by any man, since a whim of nature had given them the gift of being happy among themselves." And more explicitly,

> If any maid in Greece was blessed with this gift, she rushed to this island to seek a companion for life. When the Romans became lords of Hellas, they transported these women to the City of the Seven Hills and exploited them as slaves, compelling them to assist in the baths.
> They lived free in a few places in Magna Grecia, enjoying there the same rights they once had been conceded on their island.
> Later, when the Romans were subjected by the Germans, many went to Lombardy, Switzerland and southern Germany [Reizenstein's home turf].
> In ... Meran ... they gathered and found a place for their secretive activities....
> So much for the closer understanding of the mysterious stirrings of feeling on the part of our beautiful Orleana.

The love dialogue between Orleana and Claudine is fairly extensive, interrupted only by the narrator's explanatory comments suggesting that their relationship—even though it is like that of flower cups that will not accept *männlichen Blüthenstaub* (male pollen)—may be of a kind widespread in New Orleans (as in Meran, which the emigrant Reizenstein places in Switzerland). Here, I follow Steven Rowan's translation:

> "Do you really love me, Claudine?"
> "Oh, how the fresh warmth of your proud neck confuses me!"
> "How your breasts make my blood boil!"
> "Orleana, Orleana, how excitingly loose your clothes are!"
> "Claudine, Claudine, how tightly you are corseted!"
> "Orleana, Orleana, how easily your clothes fall away!"

"Claudine, Claudine, how hard it is for me to get these things off!"
"Orleana, how pure and white your shoulders are!"
"Claudine, where did you get these scars on yours?"
"Orleana, Orleana—Albert did that."
"And you really love me, Claudine?"[8]

The difference between Reizenstein and the anonymous author of *Die Geheimnisse von Philadelphia* makes one wonder whether W. C. Fields did not have New Orleans rather than the grave in mind when he said, "I'd rather be here than in Philadelphia." Reizenstein's chapter is certainly unlike anything I am aware of in English-language American fiction, and the binational location may also have made Reizenstein bolder than most German writers of the 1850s—and, according to Castle, exceptional altogether in the history of representations of lesbian love.

Conclusion: Negotiating "Progress" and "Der alte Weg"

Perhaps a closer study of German-American literature could not only force a rethinking of certain older and more recent tenets in American studies, but might also suggest more complicated and ironic answers to the question of whether "assimilation" or "resistance" characterized immigrant literature, whether "freedom" or "constraints" marked its parameters, and whether it is best characterized by "possibility" or by "failure." K. M. S. [i.e., Kurt Stein] rendered an answer to these gnawing questions, which take up much space in contemporary American criticism. His poem "Iss Progress Fortschritt" (1953) from the collection *Die allerschönste Lengevitch* offers us an appropriately meditative conclusion to our ruminations, as well as support for the assertion that German-American literature may have more than antiquarian significance and contain as many challenges for American studies as it does for German studies. The literature may anticipate issues of the transnational world that were perceived to be as odd, isolated, and wrong as the many examples of Germerican "gemixte pickles" that could be quoted dismissively by anglophone and German-speaking readers. I will close this essay with this poem, wishing only to call attention to the remarkable fact that it does not juxtapose the "pure" language of an old-time resister with the mixed language of an assimilationist "language traitor," but represents both grandmother Schmatz and her collegiate grandchild as equally inventive in forging a new language that has German as well as American components.

ISS PROGRESS FORTSCHRITT?
Der alter Missis Schmatz ihr Enkelkind,
A Coedgirl with horngerimmten Shpecs,
Geshtufft mit Knowledge, aber shy an Sex
Besucht die Grandma during der Vacation.

Ich lissen mit mei Ears zurückgepinned
Von der Front Shtoop zu ihrer Conversation.
"Well, Kind, was tun sie Euch denn alles teacheh
Dort auf der grossen University?"
"Oh, alles, Grandma. Xenophon and Nietzsche,
All kinds von Languages und History.
Ich hab in Sciences geshpecialized
Und major dies' Jahr in Biology
Das iss a Field! So vast! Du wärst supprized
Was für Improvements die Professors mache'.
Why, es iss nowadays a simple Sache
Life artificially zu reproduceh!"
"Is dat so! Golly, das iss wunderbar!"
Sagt Grandma, "Shtill, mich tät's net so enthuseh.
Of course, 's iss upzudate, das iss ja wahr.
But, after all (sie heaved a couple Sighs).
Der alte Weg, ach, der war doch so nice."

Notes

1. Maria Diedrich, *Love across Color Lines: Ottilie Assing and Frederick Douglass* (New York, 1999), xxviii.
2. Ottilie Assing, "Effects of War on Social Conditions and on Slavery," in *Radical Passion: Ottilie Assing's Reports from America and Letters to Frederick Douglass*, ed. and trans. Christoph Lohmann (New York, 1999), 277–78.
3. Memorandum to the Board of Directors of the Oberländer Trust, 8 February 1935, Du Bois Papers. This section is drawn from my more detailed account, "W. E. B. Du Bois in Nazi Germany, 1936," *Amerikastudien/American Studies* 44, no. 2 (1999): 207–222.
4. The very same SS *St. Louis* became infamous three years later when on 13 May 1939, under Captain Gustav Schroeder, it carried German Jewish refugees leaving Germany, who were then refused entry into Cuba and were returned on the *St. Louis* to Europe.
5. "Farbiger bereist Nazi-Deutschland," *The New York Staatszeitung und Herold* (29 January 1937), clipping in Du Bois Papers.
6. Letter to Leo Stein, American Jewish Committee, 10 March 1937; Du Bois Papers. It is not clear how the interview was given. Du Bois refers to a telephone call he received from the *Staatszeitung* after an inaccurate and misleading interview had appeared elsewhere, but the *Staatszeitung* describes Du Bois stroking his graying "Van Dyke beard" as he was contemplating the question whether the German population was happy, which creates the impression that the journalist interviewed Du Bois in person.
7. Terry Castle, *The Apparitional Lesbian: Female Homosexuality and Modern Culture* (New York, 1993), 30–31
8. *The Mysteries of New Orleans*, trans. and ed. Steven Rowan (Baltimore, 2001).

PART TWO

THE AMERICAN PART OF GERMAN HISTORY

INTRODUCTION
From World War II to the Fall of the Berlin Wall

Elliott Shore

The frame of reference we set in the first section and through which we analyzed the German part of American history now reverses its angle of vision as we turn towards the Americanization of postwar Germany. But these different angles also reflect one another. As was true for Germans in the United States, the desire for coherence, for a reality that would embody the abstract dream, eluded and defeated the German state, although the habit of the mind persisted. As Michael Geyer states, the questing Germans of the early twentieth century saw themselves as opposed to what they thought counted as American values: this was to be their century, and it was the American nation that brought them low in wars, not once, but twice.

The incontrovertible demonstration that even resorting to tenacious barbarity could not make the abstract real put Germany under the formal power of its conceptual other. Although it forced changes in everyday life, this political reconfiguration only slowly and incompletely revised the German desire for coherence. That the "America" with which Germans had to contend was a complicated culture, interwoven with notions that derived from the same sources as those upon which they themselves drew, may not have been visible to the defeated. But that these tangled derivations played a large role in the American part of recent German history is illustrated by the two larger stories told in the following six essays.

Michael Geyer, Volker Berghahn, and Rudy Koshar have used three different sets of sources to get at the notional world of the postwar German public: what opinion polls reported, how imported "Fordist" industrial culture was domesticated, and the ways that travel literature written for English-speaking tourists by popular writers in the United States and in the U.K. provided keys to understanding 1950s Germany. In one way or another, all of these sources themselves derive from the German relationship to the United States. Geyer uses the Allensbach polls as his chief source on the opinions of Germans in the postwar period. The impetus and methodology behind the instruments created by this opinion research institute, which began its existence in 1947, come from the work of the institute's leader, Elisabeth Noelle-Neumann, who had been sent to the United States just before World War II as a young scholar. With German government support, Noelle-Neumann was to study American opinion research methods and introduce them to Germany in order to support Nazi thinking. Her efforts instrumentalized for Germany an apparently effective mass mobilization tool appropriated directly from America, and it is through the lens of this tool that German public opinion was recorded.

The opinion polls showed how strong the habit of decontextualization was for the defeated nation. For at least a decade after the war, "the cognitive dissonance between what appeared feasible and what the respondent imagined as possible," was one of the chief ways of dealing with questions. Detaching themselves from the realities of life after the war, the population seemed to cling to notions of a world that they themselves had helped to shatter. Attitudes towards Americans remained hostile throughout the decade, only changing in the early 1960s after the Berlin and the Cuban missile crises proved to the German public that they were secure under American protection. "Because America was to the Germans (and had always been) a state of mind, it challenged and intimidated the German sense of self and autonomy." Even after the Americans provided security to the Germans, which Geyer calls the "single most important commodity that brought about the Americanization of Germany," America still remained "an alien country." Even to those Germans who were now more charitably inclined toward it, the United States continued to be the source of both good and bad counter examples in a rhetoric that relentlessly decontextualized.

Berghahn rightly places the business influence of America on Germany much earlier than after World War II, dating it at least from the turn of the twentieth century. Germans were intrigued by the emerging managerial revolution in the United States, with new ways of organizing information and of advertising: the German periodical literature of the new professions, such as advertising and management journals, were filled with stories of what their counterparts were doing in the United States. And as in the case of Geyer's findings, the context—of American business success in this case—was missed. "The inseparability of political democracy and industrial democracy, or of how deeply American businessmen, politicians, and academics believed that the one could not thrive without the other," has not only eluded the writers of economic history, but more importantly, the prewar and the postwar German industrialists, who picked and chose what it was about the American juggernaut that they found compelling. It took at least a generation before the West Germans recognized that industrial culture also had to change if the benefits of intersocietal transfer were to fully emerge. This is an area of understanding that also eludes American businessmen, who with similar lack of success, have attempted to "learn" from Japanese industrial methods almost entirely out of context.

Koshar finds that there may be another way to look at the intersocietal transfer between Americans and Germans: not only as two societies decontextualizing each other, but as an "interactive and negotiated" process. In the travel literature he surveys he finds attitudes about life and culture that are neither American nor German, but rather an amalgam of Northern European, English, and American notions of self, where the common "other" is neither the Germans nor the Americans, but rather the French. Koshar reminds us that the feelings of the American people towards the German people, even at the height of World War II and immediately afterwards, remained mostly positive, characterized by a "sense of cross-cultural identity and universalism." Shared feelings about personal habits, interpersonal relationships, public space, order and cleanliness, explain much about the interactions of the more than one million U.S. military personnel and the hundreds of thousands of tourists to Germany, as do what looked to Americans like the admirable (and partially shared) traits of industriousness, regional diversity, and a respect for craft and tradition.

Lily Gardner Feldman, Moshe Zuckermann, and Manfred Henningsen tell the story of another American part of German history since World War II, trying to disentangle the threads of the legacies of the German murder of European Jewry. These have been woven deeply into the relationships between and among Germany, the United States, and the state of Israel. Whereas the questions of German public opinion and industrial and tourism culture show some growth and change over half a century, the meanings of the Holocaust seem frozen in time, a moment of horror that still, more than fifty years later, does not admit to the kind of re-visionings that Koshar, Geyer, and Berghahn have accomplished for German meanings of Americanization. After the time that has passed, Germans may want to move beyond the horror. American, Israeli, and German Jews may want to remember it. And some Americans and some Germans may want to do both: turning away from their own country's past horror by focusing on others' genocides—a human activity that is almost impossible to contemplate. Each of these three essays de-emphasizes the human dimensions of Holocaust legacies by concentrating their analyses within the frames of institutions and politics. Feldman describes the institutional frameworks that promote the discussion of the policies that the nations have adopted vis-à-vis each other to deal with the Holocaust aftermath; Zuckermann describes the manipulations of the meanings of the Holocaust by all three sets of national political actors; and Henningsen tries to link two different countries, two different contexts, and two different times to remark on the changing role of national memory.

— *Chapter 9* —

AMERICA IN GERMANY
Power and the Pursuit of Americanization

Michael Geyer

I f the twentieth century did not become the German century, it is because the United States of America defeated Germany twice in the first half of the century, the second time for good; Germany neither recovered the status of a "great power" nor was it tempted to try. Although the emergent West German democracy was essentially homegrown, it only developed under American aegis.

The vast majority of West Germans came to like it that way, mostly because the condition of semi-sovereignty turned out to be an unequivocal success. West German society flourished in the second half of the twentieth century. This is somewhat ironic, since Germans had built their quest for making the century their own in opposition to, and, ultimately, in denial of quintessentially American values—"life, liberty and the pursuit of happiness"—which the German majority had now come to embrace.[1] This reversal in German fortunes and its concomitant success are stunning. How Germans came to accept this novel condition and how they made it their own is a puzzle with no easy solution. Three possible reasons have been put forward by historians of the postwar period. First, they have pointed to deliberate policies of the American victor to reorient the values of Germans, making them more compatible with those of the United States.[2] Second, they single out the extraordinary rise of an American-inflected popular culture and take this culture of mass consumption to be the main conduit for American influence in Germany.[3] Third, they stress the eagerness of the younger members of the postwar generation to embrace what they think American ideals and values to be, as a substitute for the beliefs they had lost.[4] However, the United States was neither simply the icon of commodity culture nor primarily the beacon of democracy; it was also the military force that had pounded the *Wehrmacht* and the civilian population. The United States also represented the atomic force that, in case of another war in Europe, would turn Germany into its main battlefield. Whatever else may be said about the Americanization of Germany, one might presume that German-American relations and the process of postwar German reorientation toward the West depended on the way the Germans came to grips with the role of the United States as the dominant military power in Western Europe.[5]

Russians and Americans

A postwar settlement would be brokered either by the United States and the Soviet Union or not at all, and by 1948, it was clear that there was not going to be a formal peace agreement. If there were to be anything at all it would be a piecemeal settlement, and what this arrangement would entail was uncertain. More importantly, though, it was unclear whether there would be any agreement at all or whether there would be a new war over who would control Germany. We now know that a hot war was averted, but the danger of a superpower war over the spoils of World War II was real enough—and this was not because one or the other side was a single-minded aggressor, but because the state of affairs in the heart of Europe was volatile and unstable.[6] The place and role of the United States in Europe was contingent on the way the Soviet Union arranged its presence in Germany.

It would, however, be wrong to presume that the acceptance of "America" in Germany was the mere aftereffect of a Russian threat, purported or real. It also always involved the self-perception of the Germans, which proved to be far more volatile than the hagiography of German-American friendship would have it. The opinion polls conducted by the Institut für Demoskopie in Allensbach, a conservative and pro-western center for public opinion polling, provide a useful starting point for disentangling the Germans' perception of themselves and of their relations to Americans and Russians. Allensbach undertook its first comprehensive survey of attitudes toward Russians and Americans quite late, in November 1953. It found that the West German population had a "generally positive attitude" toward America and a starkly negative one toward Russia. Unsurprisingly, German public opinion overwhelmingly opted for a western orientation over an eastern one. German respondents credited the United States with "good will" in its relationship to Germany by a huge margin (65 percent), whereas only a small minority (13 percent) granted the same "good will" to the Soviet Union.[7] In a general way, then, Germans appreciated the Americans as much as they distrusted the Russians. Allensbach confirmed what American pollsters had found before and would continue to reconfirm thereafter.[8] There was something akin to a "foundational consensus" in West German public opinion that put Germany into the Western camp and wanted to keep it there.[9]

But Allensbach instantly second-guessed its own data. The pollsters noted a "skepticism" and "bitterness" in the perception of *Amerika* and Americans underneath an "altogether amiable surface."[10] They could not quite identify the problem: notwithstanding an overall pro-Western orientation, the polling results indicated that a great many people did not care for the Americans and would rather have done without them. It takes some digging to get a firmer grip on Allensbach's hunch that German pro-Westernism was more conditional than the polls suggested. Early on it became evident that the resentment of defeat could not possibly be overestimated as a factor. The Germans hated the experience of occupation. Again, the Russians stand out as the bête noir of German attitudes. When asked, in 1951, about the quality of the four occupation regimes, 71 percent of the respondents considered their experience with Russian occupiers to be "very unpleasant" and another 24 percent characterized it as "unpleasant," whereas a mere 1 percent thought of it as positive.[11] This was an extreme reaction, but the animus against the Russians was only the far end of an altogether dismal scale. The French and the Americans fared only modestly better—the French occupiers were disliked by 65 percent of the respondents and the Americans by 49 percent of the sample. That is, while virtually all Germans showed a tremendous antagonism toward the Russians, two-thirds were inclined against the French and about half the population did not care for the Americans either. They tended to like the British, but the reasons for this are telling: nearly half the respondents indicated that they had not really noticed them, suggesting that in 1950 the Germans wanted all of their occupiers to be invisible. The less they were present, the better. The bottom line was to get rid of any and all "alien" presences in Germany, including the American one.

Hence, the fierce rejection of the Russians is best understood in the context of a more general German opposition to occupation. It reflected a general refusal to deal with the consequences of war and defeat, which left some observers, like Hannah Arendt, speechless.[12] German public opinion was quite unanimous in considering the years between 1944 and 1947 the worst years of their lives, followed by the years 1947–50—but not the war years 1939–44, and surely not the prewar years between 1933 and 1939.[13] If one adds the notorious polls about the persistence—or, in fact, the revival—of the Hitler myth deep into the 1950s, one begins to wonder what "Western orientation" was all about.[14] Denial and self-pity are generally and rightly taken as the main reason for this unreconstructed attitude, but how they could go hand in hand with pro-Western sentiments remains largely unexplored—except, of course, if one thought of fascism as a capitalist and, hence, American conspiracy.[15]

Another Allensbach poll provides us with a better sense of German edginess. When they asked, in the midst of the Korean crisis, what could possibly be done in order to prevent a war on German territory, the answers struck the Allensbach pollsters as outright "utopian speculations"—and this is not just because respondents did not say what the

Adenauer government wanted to hear. Some respondents (9 percent) held out for intra-German dialogue and neutrality. Another 10 percent thought that nothing could be done at all. An insignificant minority favored rearmament (4 percent) or active propaganda toward material and moral support for the eastern zone (2 percent). The single largest opinion block (22 percent), though, hoped to avoid war by way of creating a unified (eastern and western) German front against *Amerika* and *Russland*, with another 13 percent having similar, but less explicitly nationalist ideas in mind.[16] The cognitive dissonance between what appeared feasible and what the respondent imagined as possible suggests that in order not to think about war and defeat, a sizeable population willfully disconnected themselves from reality. Lack of realism, though, did not diminish the popularity of this option into the late 1950s.

What Germans rejected was not so much superpower rivalry but the loss of autonomy and control, whether it concerned threats and violations to personal integrity such as rape, the prosecution of Nazi perpetrators, or the fate of the German nation. They wanted to be left alone, in control of their own destiny and, perhaps even more so, of their own history. A deep and quite vicious xenophobia, a rejection of anything and everything that was not "their own," can be seen throughout the public opinion polls of the 1950s. National autonomy as the foundation for personal security was the prerequisite against which any alien presence on German territory was measured. Public opinion indicated that Germans would have preferred to keep both sides at a distance.[17] The Russians, perceived as mortal danger, fared worst in this respect. But the Americans, while generally welcome and considered necessary to fend off the Russians, were not particularly liked.

Lest we underestimate this anti-interventionist sentiment, we need to take a closer look at the German attitude toward the Russians because it provides us with the key to reading the more cryptic German sense of the Americans. The real surprise is how quickly German opinion started to favor a *rapprochement* with the Soviet Union, although the same opinion polls indicated continued fear and loathing of the Russians. While late Stalinist initiatives like the 1952 unification offer were rejected in public opinion surveys,[18] Allensbach pollsters were appalled to discover that the (Soviet) idea of "co-existence" spread rapidly in the mid-1950s and found supporters especially among the younger age cohorts.[19] While a sizeable majority held that Russia was a threat and that the Communists ultimately wanted "world revolution," a good third of the respondents now came around to thinking that, notwithstanding the ultimate ends of Soviet policy, Easterners and Westerners ("eastern communism" and "western democracies," as the poll put it) could live side by side. If it had not been for the distinctly hostile reactions by women to the pollsters' question concerning coexistence, this view would even have garnered a slight majority. Early in 1961, before the culmination of the Berlin crisis in August, Allensbach discovered (in stark contrast to the poll ten years earlier) that

FIGURE 11. The One-Millionth CARE Package

The one-millionth CARE package is donated by Ernst Reuter, Governing Mayor of West Berlin (second from left), to an East German refugee couple. At the commemorative ceremony in 1952, Reuter recognized the memorable relief operation conducted by the American people for Germans after World War II. (German Information Center)

only about one-third of the West German respondents had first-hand experience with the Russians, and a fair number of these now averred that they always had *menschlich gute Begegnungen*, good human relations, with them.[20] It is quite apparent that the West Germans entered a period in which they left behind some of the memories and accumulated fears of the 1940s and early 1950s. While the currents of anxiety and distrust never really abated, there was a window of opportunity for the Soviet Union as far as West German public opinion was concerned. The Berlin crisis in 1961 shut this window.

The thaw in German-Russian perceptions is poignant because during the same time, German public opinion of Americans went from bad to worse. The first and main problem with America was that almost every-body in West Germany thought that although the United States meant well, American presence was alien and intrusive. It comes as somewhat of a shock to realize how very critical the German public actually was. When asked in 1953 whether they were positively inclined toward Amer-icans, West Germans were evenly divided. About one-third opted for the Americans, the same number against, one-fourth declared themselves to be neutral, and the rest had no answer. With the exception of the Berlin-ers (39 percent of whom were for the Americans and 24 percent against), respondents from the American zone held a decidedly negative view (26 percent for and 36 percent against). The score was even for the rest of Ger-many, where no American troops were stationed. That is, with the excep-tion of Berlin, Americans were liked in those areas where they had no presence, but even there opinion was divided.[21]

Two conclusions emerge from this survey. The perceived lack of respect for local custom and tradition was the strongest factor for one-third of the West German opinion (and more than one-half in rural areas with American presence nearby) that disliked Americans. The fact that they were relatively rich and overwhelmingly powerful, and simply did not need to pay attention to local opinions, added insult to injury.[22] The rejection of an American presence in Germany was borne of parochialism and envy. It was the resistance of villages against the outside world.[23] Sec-ond, negative experiences with *Amerika* and the Americans were not mit-igated by class or ethnic counterimages. That is, the French *poilu* (and more so the North African ones) were outcasts, but French culture surely was not. The Russians were feared for their violence, but they were also the source of romantic compassion. There was no such variance with the American image. One group of Germans disliked Americans for perenni-ally chewing gum, playing cowboy, being oversexed and undereducated, lacking discipline and manners, being black, being arrogant, having money but no culture. Other Germans, who appreciated them for more or less the same reasons, liked a certain casualness, a looseness of manners, as well as the swing and the blues and the money.[24]

Amerika was championed by the educated classes.[25] Pro-American at-titudes, as opposed to support for a Western orientation, was a political movement primarily of aspiring high school students, intellectual elites, and professionals. Even in public opinion polls, which by their nature favor mass opinion, their fondness for America is evident. *Amerika* was "cool" and modern. Metropolitan modernity found itself localized in America. Cultural Westernization meant, to a large extent, Americanization. The new look of the Federal Republic, from education to town planning (functionalism), from music to advertising aesthetics (Madison Avenue), from modern style and taste to automobile design, from kitchen devices to educational ideas, was highly influenced by American culture.[26]

The image, as fantastic as it appears to be, does capture a prevailing sentiment. The mirror image was a more raucous youth culture that liked rock 'n' roll, but was much more tenuously linked to America.[27] Both of these *Amerikas* promised liberation from German constraint, whether caused by scarcity, customs, and traditions, or by the memory of the Third Reich.

But all of this modernity also made America a persistently intrusive presence—much more so than the French or British, or even the Russians, who were shut off in East Germany. Because the United States was invested with so much *Phantasie* and because commodity culture was everywhere, the United States proved to be a pervasive and amorphous challenge to German sensibilities. America invaded the German consciousness.[28] Whether it was coveted or rejected, the U.S. presence in Germany was magnified by the fact that America had entered the German mind. *Amerika* was impossible to quarantine, because it was always already there. If American physical presence was disliked by a good part of the population, American intrusion into the German mind was considered an affront and a conspiracy to undermine German integrity.[29] The lingering "bitterness" against Americans had much to do with the fact that the United States, while for the most part not a physical threat, was muddying German identity. Because America was to the Germans (and had always been) a state of mind, it challenged and intimidated the German sense of self and autonomy.[30]

The other problem with this notion of America was that abstract constructs do not make good protectors. Even those new professionals who desired "America" and the politicians who built their future on a Western orientation found it difficult to separate their American dream from the United States. In their minds, the qualities of *Amerika* as German object of desire made the United States a weak opponent to the Soviet Union. Because *Amerika* was perceived as a free-floating land of unconstrained energies, popular opinion was not at all convinced that the United States would actually fight a war, or whether, if and when the Americans actually did fight, they could hold their own against the vaunted Red Army. German public opinion wondered if American policy could—and, in case of danger, would—provide protection.

German negativism was relentless. Trust in the American ability to fend off a Soviet attack declined precipitously throughout the 1950s, reaching a state of crisis in 1957–58. If in March 1952 a good third (36 percent) of public opinion believed that the United States and Western Europe together could repulse a Russian attack, only 17 percent were left in November 1957. No less than 23 percent of public opinion—as opposed to 6 percent in 1952—now held that Western Europe would be conquered by Soviet forces. The group (29 percent) that believed that Western Europe would be overrun and only subsequently liberated "after a protracted war" remained unchanged, much as did the group (16 percent in 1952 and 14 percent in 1957) that expected a stalemate on German soil. Allensbach noted with a certain dry humor that before NATO and the Bundeswehr had come into existence, Germans had been much more optimistic about the effect of Western orientation than they were thereafter.[31]

The significance of this shift becomes fully evident if we add that in 1957 the Soviet Union re-entered the technological imagination of the West Germans with the launching of Sputnik into orbit. Germans registered the event with extraordinary alacrity. They came to the conclusion that the Soviet Union had drawn even, if not overtaken the United States in developing future technologies. (CDU voters did not have much more faith in the United States than did SPD voters.) The Soviet Union had become more than a match for the United States, in the minds of the German public.[32] Doubts arose, not simply about the military prowess of the United States, but also about the American ability to succeed in the technological race.

All the postwar hang-ups that had bedeviled German-American relations found a convenient outlet in the Sputnik debacle. Pollsters discovered a malicious joy, especially among men, that the Americans, despite all the bragging about their unsurpassed material wealth, had lost out in their rivalry with the Soviet Union. A full 39 percent of German opinion thought it served the Americans right. Besides, an absolute majority of Germans (71 percent) was convinced that the Russians could never have done it without the support of German engineers. Hence, the Russian advances were in fact belated German successes. This attitude caught on. While SPD voters and men with an elementary school education (the pollsters in Allensbach did not recognize a working class) had always shown a penchant for heavy industry, a different class of middle-aged, well-educated men joined the chorus. They came to think, or rediscovered the idea, that dictatorships had their advantages. Half of the respondents with gymnasium diplomas now professed "that, in the long run, technological progress would be greater under a dictatorship than in a democracy."[33] (Of course, there was another half who did not think so.) In the late 1950s, the idea of a well-ordered and, if need be, authoritarian state as a prerequisite for scientific and technological progress was on the upswing.

Of all the polls Allensbach conducted in the late 1950s, a very brief one about a purely domestic affair is most telling about this state of opinion. When asked if they preferred to live in a country where taxes were high but "the state cared for everyone" or in a country where taxes were low but "the state only helps in emergencies and people care for their own economic security and old age," 79 percent of respondents chose the former and 14 percent the latter. Only the rich—and there were very few of them—thought otherwise.[34] In the mind of the Allensbach pollsters, this said as much about America as it did about West Germany.

With the easing of East-West relations after Stalin's death, the anti-communist certainties of the early 1950s were gone and it looked like the Americans might well be the losers. There was more at stake here than the *Schadenfreude* of middle-aged men who felt that overbearing Americans might finally get what was coming to them. With the threat of war and the imminence of occupation receding, cultural memories that had been repressed and frozen resurfaced. If the 1950s in general had hearkened back to prewar, even pre-World War I ideals and sentiments, the late 1950s saw this retro-orientation take on a new direction. The sudden recovery of anti-Semitism is one of the reminders of this phenomenon. The resurfacing of strongly nationalist and left-wing sentiments in favor of neutralism is another symptom. The fact that both of these tendencies worked themselves out in the clash over atomic weapons, nuclear politics, and new technologies suggests that the retro ideals of earlier days were now tied to more future-oriented projects. Germans began to rediscover a wider horizon beyond securing daily necessities. It turned out that for a good part of German public opinion, the Americans were no longer important. Public opinion recovered a taste for a distinctly German capitalism and for the German welfare state.

The West German government hoped that the curious discrepancy between the West German profession of Western orientation and the simultaneous resilience of anti-American sentiment would decline with the transformation of the occupiers into allies, but these officials miscalculated the nature of anti-Americanism. What the Germans disliked about the Americans did not change with the end of occupation. For some, America was the dream of freewheeling capitalism and mass consumption, with all their presumed and real effects on society. But for many more, this dream was a nightmare. If Americanization had merely been a matter of Bill Haley fans trashing dance halls in Essen and Berlin, Americanism would have been good for a juicy scandal. But the threat of disorder and insecurity associated with American capitalism, and the panic over decadence and loosening morals as an effect of growing mobility and mass consumption, were far more pervasive.[35] They were also far more intimate. Mass consumption now began to remake the lives of Germans. While there can be no doubt that the German public seemed to want all of it and more, Germans did not easily accept the idea that the good life might actually be just that. As material wealth began to accumulate, they felt as if their lives were falling apart. We need not concern ourselves here with the question of whether this was actually the case.[36] What matters is that Germans believed it was the case, and knew who was at fault. They called this phenomenon "Americanization."

The combination of a crisis of American leadership with doubts about American values as signposts for order and stability came to a head in a military/strategic matter. In introducing nuclear weapons into Germany to counter the Soviet threat, the United States appeared to have opened Pandora's box. What came out this time was the fear of mass death and even extermination. In a classic act of displacement (the poll was taken in 1954!), a near majority of Germans was convinced that they would be the ones exterminated in a nuclear war.[37] With the introduction of atomic weapons, this fear gained an aura of reality. The United States was now seen as potentially exacerbating the danger of war, and was perceived to be a reckless nation.

Several things came together here. While Americans were generally perceived to be peaceable and hence solid guarantors against a threat of war, German lore also held the opposing view that Americans had a way of smashing things and people they did not like; i.e., Americans were prone to using excessive violence. The stain of "terror-bombing" persisted throughout the 1950s.[38] One did not even need to refer to Dresden, because there was a more traditional case that one "knew": the Americans had exterminated the North American Indians. The only open side to the question was whether or not this was worse than what the Germans did (as Nazi propaganda had asserted). It is poignant that in the late 1950s there was a revival of the cult of noble Indians (and their good German friends).[39] This cluster of debates and innuendoes circulating around the time of the introduction of atomic weapons in Germany resulted in the loss of the presumed benefits of Western orientation, such as avoidance of war, and the old stereotypes about America as a supremely violent nation were revived. No second thought was given to German atrocities, and no irony was intended.

The cultural panic about capitalist disorder had found a political outlet with the mobilization against the atomic threat. For a minority this led to a wholesale revision of their pro-Western outlook, but even the majority of public opinion toyed with images and ideas that came easily because they were so familiar. If the Russians and Communists had been identified as the supreme physical threat in the aftermath of the war, their kind of violence now appeared to be child's play compared to the danger of "nuclear death." Perceived as supremely fickle and unpredictable in their politics and excessively violent in war, Americans had gained control over life and death in Germany. If Americanism had always been perceived as unduly intrusive, and if Americans were disliked for their utmost disrespect for customs combined with their refusal to accept local constraints, the threat of nuclear war now fused all of this into one great American danger. The German antinuclear movement of the late 1950s mobilized and crystallized this sentiment, liberating it from the parochialism and nationalism of the 1940s. Anti-Americanism suddenly gained a future.

The late 1950s were a time of genuine crisis in German-American relations. This crisis came when, for the first time, the relentless threat of war eased and there was a genuine chance for the recovery of the good life for broader segments of the population.[40] In the end, of course, this was also the silver lining. The German public did not want this moment spoiled—not by taxation, nor by inflation, nor by atomic bombs.[41] But the same Germans who held these opinions also surely did not want to have the fun ruined by fear mongering: memories of mass death and extermination, or negative stereotyping by Americans. This was the moment when the rubble was cleaned away and people came to hope that memories would fade as well.[42] If only security could be gained without the risk of war ...

Security and the Pursuit of Happiness

Security without the risk of war is what the United States came to provide. Within four years, between 1958 and 1962, it took on a hegemonic role in Western Europe that it has not since relinquished. The key to this transformation was the Berlin crisis in 1961 and its resolution. The message of Berlin, and subsequently of Cuba, was that the Americans could be trusted after all. It was not just that they stood by the Berliners, an action that was rated very highly by the public, all the more so since Chancellor Adenauer blundered badly and miscalculated the seriousness of the event.[43] Rather, the public was also enthused about the fact that the Americans took on the Russians and won.[44] The year 1961 was the moment when, according to public opinion polls, the Soviet Union lost the cold war. It was only then that postwar life really began in Germany.

The public opinion run up to the August 1961 crisis was dramatic. German opinion remained torn between a desire to do nothing and an aggressive anti-communism. The East German "Pankow" regime provided a popular target. Being out-muscled by the Russian Bear was one thing, but being duped and bullied by Ulbricht was too much for West Germans. The shift in the perception of East Germany as the site of a detested regime rather than the home of German brothers and sisters had been underway for some time.[45] In 1959–60 some West Germans had already given up their fear of engaging in yet another war, although this change of mind was aided by the belief that it would not come to that.[46] Finally, in August 1961, a slight majority (with nearly a third of the respondents refusing to take sides) came out in favor of holding Berlin, even at the cost of war. The usually cautious and circumspect pollsters in Allensbach lived up to the occasion. They asked: *Berlin ... aufgeben oder einen Krieg ... riskieren?* Give up Berlin or risk a war? Altogether 36 percent of West German respondents spoke in favor of war over Berlin, while a mere 30 percent was opposed.[47] In terms of West German public opinion, the 36 percent who opted for war, if only a temporary aberration, amounted to a monumental change. The significance of this change becomes obvious if we recall that Chancellor Adenauer, who had always seemed to be aligned with public opinion in the 1950s, proved to be completely wrong.[48] He had stayed away from Berlin in order to minimize the fear of war, but doing what was right for the 1950s was wrong for the 1960s. In an act of poetic justice of long-term political consequence, the Social Democratic mayor of Berlin, Willy Brandt, who was lambasted by conservative propagandists for being a Socialist and whom the rumor mill had attacked for having abandoned Germany during the war (Brandt had fled to Scandinavia), emerged as the hero at the front line of the cold war.[49]

What made this choice so quintessentially "1960s," and *West* German at that, is that not only did Germans get away with risking war, but they even considered themselves to be the victor. While Adenauer was disgruntled with the United States for what he considered a defeat, i.e., the *status quo minus* that now saw Berlin divided and access to it limited, the West German public considered the outcome positive. West Berlin was "saved." What mattered more was that the United States had won the battle over Berlin without ever firing a shot. The Cuban missile crisis reinforced this sentiment: winning wars without having to fight them was a state of affairs West Germans—not all of them, but a growing majority—could get used to. Berlin and Cuba provided the solution to the problem of securing West Germany without risking war. The results were tangible. Americans now appeared to be unbeatable.[50] John F. Kennedy emerged as by far the most popular "German" politician.[51] In 1965, Allensbach reported that the alliance with the United States was "popular."[52]

Some, if not all, of the German "nuclear fears" were relieved by the settling of the Berlin crisis into a new status quo and, in the wake of the Cuban missile crisis, the Test Ban Treaty. The United States had made war disappear and guaranteed that it would stay that way. This is the single most important reason why Germans came to like Americans and accepted their presence in Germany.[53] They had achieved what appeared impossible: guaranteeing security without the risk of war. Notwithstanding protests against the Vietnam War and the anxiety over neutron bombs and Pershing missiles, this basic compact between Germans and Americans proved to be unshakable for the next thirty years.[54]

Lest the disappearance of war be considered a mere metaphor, we should note that after 1961–62, the 1950s' sense of constant danger rapidly gave way to a perception of relative security.[55] To be sure, cold war angst never quite disappeared. The number of Germans (38 percent) who felt there was no longer a real Soviet threat to speak of first surpassed those who felt threatened (37 percent) in 1966, and by only an insignificant margin (1 percent).[56] Although perceptions lingered, the cold war world picture changed. While the Soviet Union remained a threat for more than a third of the public, West Germans at large no longer feared the imminent danger of war. Typically, issues of foreign policy and military strategy that had ranked unusually high on the list of public concerns throughout the 1950s now vanished into the background.[57] The gap between a presumed general threat of war, which very few in Germany dared to discount, and a perceived, imminent danger of war widened.

FIGURE 12. Kennedy at the Brandenburg Gate in 1963

President John F. Kennedy on his historic visit at the Brandenburg Gate in Berlin in 1963. Berlin's population celebrated Kennedy's reassurance for the well-being of the city after the Wall was built. To Kennedy's left is Willy Brandt, the Governing Mayor of West Berlin. (German Information Center)

Even though there were crises, such as Prague in 1968, public fears continued to diminish.[58]

The most significant indicator for change, though, was a wholesale reversal in the composition of pro-American public opinion. Whereas previously the key support for Western orientation had come from the well-educated, urban middle and upper classes and had met a rather tepid and ambivalent response among the more rural and less educated, basic support for pro-American and pro-NATO sentiments could now be found among the latter; that is, among people with elementary school education, living in mid-sized towns, together with those living in urban industrial areas. The conversion of blue-collar opinion, which had been the backbone of the antinuclear protest, made this transformation complete. Once the war scares subsided, the majority of women—who had backed Western orientation but not the Americans—now also came to underwrite the consensus in favor of *Amerika*.[59] In this democratic and popular sense, American security came to form the foundational consensus of West Germany.

"Security" had become a mass cultural worldview—and was now increasingly advertised and sold in this fashion.[60] It was the single most important commodity that brought about the Americanization of Germany. The very notion of "security" was new and American. West German military reformers had busied themselves with redefining the military as a more civic-minded force. Although the idea slowly began to make headway against considerable resistance, it remained an uphill struggle. Old *Wehrmacht* habits died slowly.[61] But even the reformers for the most part still spoke of a need for "defense." The language of military security, with its corollary of deterrence and arms control, entered German parlance slowly. This was an American language—of deterrence as opposed to military defense, of war prevention rather than military rivalry, of crisis management rather than brinkmanship. By the 1970s, "Deterrence and Security" had become a language of military preparedness for non-war against a non-enemy, and the *Bundeswehr* may well have been the only army in the world to take this unique mission seriously.[62] In any case, the West Germans who had reacted fiercely in opposition to the introduction of nuclear weapons onto German territory in the late 1950s now came around to accepting nuclear weapons as a means of suspending the threat of war.[63] If this consensus began to fray in the late 1970s and early 1980s, this was due above all to new doctrines of nuclear and non-nuclear conflicts. A new arms race had begun to undercut the quiescence that prevailed in the 1960s and 1970s. However, even at the height of antinuclear mobilization, the popular consensus about America did not change.[64]

The hostility toward American forces on German territory also began to diminish. Germans began to get used to "their" Americans. The reverse process was altogether more limited, but the sense of two alien worlds colliding diminished distinctly. This also happened at the level of elites, where integration became a meaningful, if again one-sided, concept. A new crop of German officers was not just oriented toward the Atlantic alliance, but had quite frequently acquired a close working familiarity with American military culture. If anyone believed in this new Atlantic order, it was the German military.[65] The older ideal of Western orientation—an alliance of free world states against communism—had mutated into a network of professional and personal exchanges on both the grassroots and elite levels. These were mostly one-way engagements, Germans adapting to American hegemony as they left behind the hostile parochialism and knee-jerk xenophobia that had prevailed in the opinion polls of the 1950s.

One can debate to what extent these transformations were real, but there are two important issues at stake. First, the notion of Americanization of West Germany is inseparable from the American guarantee of German security and with it the massive presence of American forces in Germany. The Germans accommodated themselves to this new perception of the United States because of the tangible benefits they received. The United States promised a suspension of war in Germany and on the European continent, and as far as it appeared that the United States delivered, mass support for America remained unshakable in West Germany. This is also to say that, as much as some groups loved America and the Americans for the sheer idea of *Amerika*, Americanization worked only as long as there was something in it for those who were Americanized. "Empire by invitation" only partially describes this phenomenon.[66] Security was a long way from chocolates, cigarettes, and nylons, but for the most part it worked on the same principle of exchange. And lest there be any doubt, this was "Americanization" in the more analytic sense of setting a new standard of modernity. The American-German security bargain, as a tradeoff between ruler and ruled, had been inconceivable for even the most enlightened of the Western-oriented cold warriors. It was the reverse of the German military tradition.

Second, the process of accepting the new notion of security was so very successful, because it effectively set in motion a general relaxation of social and cultural boundaries, leading to benefits in mobility and in an opening toward commodity culture.[67] Security became a central value of public life, not just a military concern.[68] The two processes facilitated by security, détente and leisure, were interdependent. The newly gained sense of security facilitated a process of privatization in which the masses, for once, existed for their own enjoyment rather than for purposes of political or military mobilization. From all that one can gather, the German masses enjoyed themselves immensely and tended to forget their fear of impending doom. "Security" not as constraint and obligation, but as leisure and enjoyment—this was the "silent revolution" that was set in motion by the winding down of the cold war, a winding down which German public opinion rightly read as the American moment in Europe.[69]

The "real" America remained an alien country, even for those Germans who were more curious than censorious.[70] Overall, it proved to be livable and hospitable for the trickle of German immigrants who ventured

FIGURE 13. Carter and Schmidt at Wiesbaden-Erbenheim in 1978

President Jimmy Carter and Chancellor Helmut Schmidt (left) review American troops at the Military Air Base at Wiesbaden-Erbenheim in 1978. The review was part of an official visit of the U.S. president to West Germany. (German Information Center)

FIGURE 14. German Demonstrators, Bonn, 1981

Germans demonstrate in Bonn against the NATO policy of stationing new medium-range missiles in West Germany in 1981. The escalation of the cold war in the early 1980s put the close political and military cooperation between Washington and Bonn to a severe test. (German Information Center)

overseas, even if some intellectuals were put off by the "American" way.[71] U.S. technological feats, as well as political struggles and military disasters, were watched with utter amazement and considerable incredulity. West German intellectuals, of course, developed something of an obsession with America's overbearing reality, which they could not shoehorn into their own worldview. Yet in West Germany, this strange country was for the most part accepted as a military presence and as an image and model for largely homegrown social and cultural transformations. What Germans consistently liked about America (if they did actually like it, a position that varied over time) was the difference from their own regimented past. But above all, America was accepted in Germany because in the eyes of the mass public, it made the difference between war and peace.

The Return of the Authentic

The rejection of America did not vanish from the scene, but it had a curious career. While it morphed into a popular movement for German cultural authenticity in East Germany, it flared up in the West German antinuclear scares and the pro-environmentalist mobilization of the 1970s and 1980s. These mobilizations and actions were ultimately losing propositions, in spite of their considerable clamor and intellectual cachet on both sides of the German divide. They were unable to alter the basic political consensus in favor of the security bargain on which postwar West German society was built.[72] Just when one would have thought from a West German perspective that the power of this consensus was spent at last in the late 1980s, it still sufficed to seduce the East Germans into a mutiny against their ramshackle welfare authoritarianism. This topsy-turvy revolt may yet turn out to hold the key for America's role in Germany, for it ended the need for an American security guarantee in Europe (which had been the nightmare of the East Germans in any case). It also put the Germans on the spot to figure out for themselves how they wanted to live together.

The more boisterous of the two authenticity movements was the West German antinuclear protest movement of the 1970s and 1980s. Its origins are commonly traced to a mythic 1968, but, in fact it emerged from the 1950s divide that ran through the professional classes and higher education, setting apart the stratum that most strongly supported a Western orientation. It came into its own as the technocratic-progressive elite, filled with the "cool" crowd of the jazz and Sinatra aficionados and represented by Chancellor Helmut Schmidt, who struck more than one observer as a better American than President Jimmy Carter. The opponents of these progressive technocrats first gathered in opposition to atomic weapons, cutting loose from the right-leaning cultural critique that had dominated German anti-Americanism, to form a radical humanist wing.[73] This movement may not always have been strong, but was consistent in its wholesale critique of the German-American security consensus. It took off in the late 1970s as a mass movement against nuclear and environmental threats. The fiery German American Petra Kelly of the Greens may well be taken as its representative, if only to indicate that this opposition to America and its search for a more authentic Germany was a distinctly transatlantic enterprise.

This movement gained popular appeal when its protestations against American war and violence hit a deep-seated German angst about catastrophe. One of the curious features of West German public opinion was that even when fears about imminent war declined during the 1960s, a generalized anxiety about impending doom continued to loom large. A majority of West Germans was as certain in 1954 of their extermination in a future nuclear war as they were convinced, in 1964, that *Weltuntergang*, an apocalypse, would before long befall Germany.[74] Even in 1965, when the Russian scare had become an issue for only a minority of Germans and American sympathies ran high, "the fear of a new war or a world war … was psychically the daily meat and potatoes of public opinion," as Allensbach put it.[75] By the late 1970s, a new, younger generation was certain that the end was near.[76] This "white noise" accompanied West German affluence, oscillating between a guilt-ridden past and the uncertainties of life in a postindustrial society, and has given rise to the notion of a "damaged nation."[77] The success of this mobilization depended on linking specific American actions, such as the deployment of Pershing missiles, to the more general fear of catastrophe. The combination of the two resuscitated the idea of America as the culprit of the alienation, inhospitableness, and dangers of modernity.[78] Since both these dangers and the white noise of the German past were real enough, America was regularly exorcised in order to preserve the integrity of modern life. With the fading of the security consensus in the 1990s, and with America crowding in on Europe as an effect of globalization, the American bogeyman was increasingly invoked in a rhetoric of difference that separates an urbane and wise European slow-track modernity from a reckless American modernism that risks life (and global survival) for the pursuit of material happiness.

The persistence of anti-American sentiments in East Germany is quite a different story. In part, it is simply a consequence of "the Soviet bloc form[ing] a powerful barrier against Western ideas and influences."[79] But East Germany was less cut off than it was moving in a different direction. It is striking that East Germans (including dissenters) never developed the same infatuation with America that drove so much of Eastern European dissent. Quite to the contrary, anti-Americanism became a genuinely popular currency—so much so that it thrived despite the heavy-handed propaganda that usually produced the opposite of the intended effect.[80] The prevalent ploys of trashing America as a hell for an impoverished and suffering working class, a torture chamber for minorities, and a den of decadence did not diminish the grassroots rejection of

America. Nor could one say that East Germans did not crave the goods capitalism provided. But this hoped-for cornucopia was not at all attached to America; rather, it was part of an all-together wholesome, because non-capitalist and un-American, modern German culture. Protecting a mass culture that was authentically German may appear to be a somewhat quixotic enterprise, but it was a challenge that was taken up with considerable enthusiasm. If the intellectual high road was to create a post-fascist Germany, the mass cultural low road consisted in indigenizing, as if in a cargo cult, items of mass consumption. If a leading cultural critic can write, with or without irony intended, of the East German youth's "preference for loud, rhythmic music of western origin, produced in small collectives [*Kleinkollektiven*] such as the Beatles … Jimi Hendrix, etc." one must consider this effort a success.[81]

There is no better and surely no more salacious example of the quest for authenticity than the post-unification debates on who had more and better orgasms during the time of division: the high-strung, neurotic, and Americanized West Germans (women in particular), or the more body-conscious, free, and altogether more natural East Germans.[82] The peculiarities of post-unification sexual politics aside, what matters is that the difference from America (and an Americanized West Germany) defined the authentic in German high culture and popular culture. Maybe the popularity of this East German identity politics had to do with the fact that the media and their state-sponsored propaganda could not stop talking about larger-than-life female sexuality in and of America, while the youngish West German intellectuals tended to be engaged by more ethereal and principled things, such as the American system.[83] In any case, the popular appeal of anti-Americanism and its incorporation into everyday practices (literally so, if one trusts East German academics) makes the East German example not just historically interesting, but also politically significant. Historically, it is a variation on the old theme that defined German authenticity in contradistinction to the West, and an effeminized West at that. Politically, we find here, separated for thirty years from an Americanized West by the Wall, a populist and popular rejection of America in the name of a more genuine German identity—an authenticity that moreover promised its own distinct and tangible benefits and enjoyments.

If we look back at the perception of America during the 1950s in West Germany, we find that this kind of anti-Americanism had once been pervasive and quite self-evident. It receded in the 1960s and 1970s, because the United States provided physical and spiritual security for a war-torn country that struggled to escape the shadow of its past and remade itself in the process. It brought a semblance of stability to Germany, which is the reason that the image of America proved to be so immensely productive in shaping the postwar West German worldview. This period has come to an end, if only because the Germans must now figure out for themselves how they can live in peace—with themselves and with the rest of Europe.

Even if the Germans were to choose America as their model, which is difficult to imagine, the challenge of unification still amounts to an end to the German-American security bargain. A united Germany might well adopt America as an icon of "lifestyle," but this is distinctly not what America had been during the thirty years between 1961 and 1991. It seems that media opinion is betting on a more authentically German Germany. Germans, it is said, want to dream their own dream of modernity. In this situation it may well be appropriate to remember that, insofar as Americans have a dream (though they often forget it), it is to institute governments in order to secure certain unalienable rights among which life, liberty, and the pursuit of happiness figure most prominently. It seems that this dream describes quite appropriately what happened in the 1950s and 1960s in Germany, when the United States "constructed" a European peace and thus gained a physical and spiritual presence in Germany.[84] So, if it becomes necessary for one people to dissolve the political bands which have connected them with another, it might be useful to remember that government is the challenge—and it will be government without a German-American security consensus. It seems that after ten years of unification, this challenge has just begun to sink in.

Notes

1. Anselm Doering-Manteuffel, *Wie westlich sind die Deutschen? Amerikanisierung und Westernisierung im 20. Jahrhundert* (Göttingen, 1999).
2. Hermann-Josef Rupieper, *Der besetzte Verbündete: Die Amerikanische Deutschlandpolitik 1949–1955* (Opladen, 1991).
3. Reinhold Wagnleitner, *Coca-Colonization and the Cold War: The Cultural Mission of the United States in Austria after the Second World War* (Chapel Hill, 1994).
4. Michael Hochgeschwender, *Freiheit in der Offensive? Der Kongreß für kulturelle Freiheit und die Deutschen* (Munich, 1998).
5. Roger Morgan, *The United States and West Germany, 1945–1973: A Study in Alliance Politics* (London, 1974).
6. John Lewis Gaddis, *We Now Know: Rethinking Cold War History* (Oxford/New York, 1997).
7. Institut für Demoskopie [IfD], Stimmung im Bundesgebiet # 117: Amerikaner und Russen (November 1953); Bundesarchiv Koblenz BAK B 145/4224.
8. Anna J. Merritt and Richard L. Merritt, eds., *Public Opinion in Occupied Germany: The OMGUS Surveys, 1945–1949* (Urbana, 1970); Anna J. Merritt and Richard L. Merritt, eds., *Public Opinion in Semisovereign Germany: The HICOG Surveys, 1949–1955* (Urbana/Chicago, 1980).
9. Gottfried Niedhart, "Locarno, Ostpolitik und die Rückkehr Deutschlands in die internationale Politik nach den beiden Weltkriegen," in *Deutschland in Europa: Nationale Interessen und internationale Ordnung im 20. Jahrhundert*, ed. Gottfried Niedhart, Detlef Junker, and Michael W. Richter (Mannheim, 1997), 17.
10. IfD, Stimmung # 117, 4.
11. IfD, Das politische Klima: Ein Bericht über die Stimmung im Bundesgebiet 1951; BAK B 145/4221.
12. Hannah Arendt, *Besuch in Deutschland*, trans. Eike Geisel (Berlin, 1993).

13. Michael Geyer, "Cold War Angst: The Case of West-German Opposition to Rearmament and Nuclear Weapons," in *The Miracle Years: A Cultural History of West Germany, 1949–1968*, ed. Hanna Schissler (Princeton/Oxford, 2000), 376–408.

14. Norbert Freit, *Vergangenheitspolitik: Die Anfänge der Bundesrepublik und die NS-Vergangenheit* (Munich, 1996).

15. Jürgen Danyel, "Die Opfer- und Verfolgungsperspektive als Gründungskonsens? Zum Umgang mit der Widerstandstradition und Schuldfrage in der DDR," in *Die geteilte Vergangenheit: Zum Umgang mit Nationalsozialismus und Widerstand in beiden deutschen Staaten*, ed. Jürgen Danyel (Berlin, 1995), 31–46.

16. IfD, Appendix to Stimmung # 8, Adenauer und die Wiederbewaffnung (February 1951); BAK B 145/4220.

17. EMNID Informationen Nr. 26/1958 (28 June 1958); BAK B 145/5481. While 1–3 percent of respondents favored Russia, 36–48 percent chose America; however, 48–58 percent preferred neutrality. The year 1958 is the high point of this development.

18. However, the IfD notes "with surprise" that one-third of the respondents considered unification to be the primary goal of German politics; in IfD, Stimmung # 56, Einheit oder Sicherheit? (August 1952); BAK B 145/4222.

19. IfD, Stimmung # 210, Die russische Einladung (Nachtrag) (October 1955); BAK B 145/4226.

20. IfD, Die Ablehnung des Militärs: eine psychologische Studie (1961), tables 26–29; courtesy of Detlev Bald, Munich.

21. IfD, Stimmung # 117.

22. Ibid., with some rather forthright comments.

23. Typically, military training in the United States was inconceivable for the majority of Germans, especially for German men. IfD, Stimmung # 35, Sollen künftig deutsche Offiziere und Unteroffiziere in den U.S.A. ausgebildet werden? BAK B 145/4222.

24. IfD, Stimmung # 117 and IfD, Amerikaner in Deutschland: Eine Leitstudie über die Urteile der Bevölkerung im Heidelberger Raum und in Bayern (1961); BAK Zsg. 132/916.

25. E.g., Paul Betts, "Die Bauhaus-Legende: Amerikanisch-Deutsches Joint Venture des Kalten Krieges," in *Amerikanisierung: Traum und Alptraum im Deutschland des 20. Jahrhunderts*, ed. Alf Lüdtke, Inge Marßolek, and Adelheid von Saldern (Stuttgart, 1996), 270–90.

26. Hermann Glaser, "Daily Life and Social Patterns," in *The American Impact on Postwar Germany*, ed. Reiner Pommerin (Providence/Oxford, 1995), 91.

27. Kaspar Maase, *BRAVO Amerika: Erkundungen zur Jugendkultur der Bundesrepublik in den fünfziger Jahren* (Hamburg, 1992).

28. See *Amerikanisierung: Traum und Alptraum*, especially the essays by Miriam Hansen and Alf Lüdtke.

29. Dan Diner, *America in the Eyes of the Germans: An Essay on Anti-Americanism* (Princeton, 1996).

30. Ibid.

31. IfD, Stimmung # 336, Das Vertrauen in die westliche Allianz hat abgenommen (January 1958); BAK B 145/4230.

32. IfD, Stimmung # 328, Der technische Wettlauf zwischen den USA und der SU (January 1958); BAK B 145/4230.

33. IfD, Stimmung # 328, p. 8.

34. IfD, Stimmung # 298, Für den Wohlfahrtsstaat (May 1957); BAK B 145/4229.

35. Uta Poiger, *Jazz, Rock, and Rebels: Cold War Politics and American Culture in a Divided Germany* (Berkeley/Los Angeles, 2000).

36. IfD, Stimmung # 359, Was die Bevölkerung wünscht (November 1958); BAK B 145/4230.

37. IfD, Stimmung # 157, Furcht vor dem Atomkrieg – Die Wasserstoffbombe (August 1954); BAK B 145/4225.

38. IfD, Stimmung # 72, Ramcke – Das Verbot der SRP (December 1952); BAK B 145/4223.

39. Gabriele Wilczek, "Volkskultur aus fremder Hand: Indianer- und Westernhobby in Deutschland zwischen Amerikanisierung, Anti-Imperialismus und popularisierter Ethnologie" (Ph.D. dissertation, Universität Freiburg, 1997).

40. Nuclear panic and fear of war did not go together in the late 1950s. IfD, Stimmung # 375, Kriegsfurcht nicht aktuell (May 1959); BAK B 145/4231.
41. IfD, Das Zentrum der Krise: Eine Studie (March 1957); BAK Zsg. 132/552.
42. Robert G. Moeller, "War Stories: The Search for a Usable Past in the Federal Republic of Germany," *American Historical Review* 101 (1996): 1008–48.
43. IfD, Blitzumfrage über die Reaktion der Öffentlichkeit auf die Vorgänge in Berlin im August 1961 (1 September 1961) (telegram); BAK B 145/4235.
44. IfD, Stimmung # 516, Das Bündnis mit den USA (April 1962); BAK B 145/4235. IfD, Stimmung # 550, Nach Kuba: Wachsende Zuversicht in die Stärke des Westens (November 1962); BAK B 145/4236.
45. To my knowledge, there is no good study on this topic. However, the decline of "national consciousness" (*nationale Gesinnung*) may be taken as one indicator. The declining interest in neutrality is another. IfD, Stimmung # 458, Material zum Thema "nationale Gesinnung" (August 1960) and IfD, Stimmung # 463, Für den Westen—der Neutralismus verliert Anhänger—Die SPD Wähler zögern (October 1960); BAK B 145/4234.
46. IfD, Stimmung # 365, Berlin (January 1959); BAK B 145/4231. IfD, Stimmung # 375, Kriegsfurcht nicht aktuell (May 1959); BAK B 145/4231.
47. IfD, Stimmung # 501, Die Verteidigung Berlins (23 August 1961); BAK B 145/4235.
48. IfD, Blitzumfrage.
49. Ibid.
50. IfD, Stimmung # 593, Der Westen ist militärisch stärker geworden (November 1963); BAK B 145/4239.
51. IfD, Stimmung # 568, Kennedy (June 1963); BAK B 145/4237.
52. IfD, Stimmung # 686, Das Bündnis mit den USA wird populär—Nachlassende Sympathie für Neutralität der Bundesrepublik BAK B 145/4246.
53. As a result, the De Gaulle initiative never stood a chance in public opinion. France was considered a "minor military power." IfD, Stimmung # 587, De Gaulle, Kennedy oder die Amerikaner (October 1963); BAK B 145/4238.
54. Hans Rattinger, "The Federal Republic of Germany: Much Ado about (almost) Nothing," in *The Public and Atlantic Defense*, ed. Gregory Flynn and Hans Rattinger (Totowa, NJ, 1995), 101–74.
55. IfD, Stimmung # 617, Kriegserwartung läßt nach (April 1964); BAK B 145/4240.
56. IfD, Weniger Angst (August 1966) (press release); courtesy of Detlev Bald.
57. This is the result of EMNID's survey of "public concerns" (öffentliches Interesse) in the 1950s and 60s. The turning point came between 1958 and 1961 with a precipitous decline of interest in military issues after 1961–62. BAK B 145/4261/176.
58. IfD, Dreißig Jahre NATO (September 1979); courtesy of Archiv des Instituts für Demoskopie, Allensbach.
59. First indications are in IfD, Stimmung # 463 (October 1960). Consolidation of this profile in Stimmung # 593 (November 1963).
60. Rainer Gries, Volker Ilgen, and Dirk Schindelbeck, "*Ins Gehirn der Masse Kriechen!*" *Werbung und Mentaliätsgeschichte* (Darmstadt, 1995), 125–51.
61. Donald Abenheim, *Reforging the Iron Cross: The Search for Tradition in the West German Armed Forces* (Princeton, 1988).
62. Jost Delbrück, Knut Ipsen, Wilhelm A. Kewenig, and Georg R. Bluhm, eds., *Abschreckung und Entspannung: Fünfundzwanzig Jahre Sicherheitspolitik zwischen bipolarer Konfrontation und begrenzter Kooperation* (Berlin, 1977).
63. Dieter Senghaas, *Abschreckung und Frieden: Studien zur Kritik organisierter Friedlosigkeit* (Frankfurt am Main, 1969).
64. Emil-Peter Müller, *Antiamerikanismus in Deutschland: Zwischen Care-Paket und Cruise Missile* (Cologne, 1986).
65. The other case, of course, is German business. See Volker Berghahn, *The Americanisation of West German Industry, 1945–1973* (Cambridge, 1986).
66. Geir Lundestad, "Empire by Invitation? The United States and Western Europe, 1945–1962," *Journal of Peace Research* 23 (1986): 263–77.

67. Hans Braun, "Das Streben nach 'Sicherheit' in den 50er Jahren: Soziale und politische Ursachen und Erscheinungsweisen," *Archiv für Sozialgeschichte* 18 (1978): 279–306.

68. Franz Xaver Kaufmann, *Sicherheit als soziologisches und sozialpolitisches Problem: Untersuchungen zu einer Wertidee hochdifferenzierter Gesellschaften* (Stuttgart, 1970).

69. Ronald Inglehart, *The Silent Revolution: Changing Values and Political Styles among Western Publics* (Princeton, 1977).

70. For a broader discussion of this phenomenon, see Frank Trommler, "The Rise and Fall of Americanism in Germany," in *America and the Germans: An Assessment of a Three-Hundred-Year History*, ed. Frank Trommler and Joseph McVeigh, vol. 2 (Philadelphia, 1985), 332–42.

71. E.g., Hans Magnus Enzensberger, *Politik und Verbrechen* (Frankfurt, 1964).

72. IfD, Dreißig Jahre NATO, suggests that the mobilization against the neutron bomb had the opposite effect. American forces were more welcome in 1979 than at any time in West German history.

73. Michael Ermarth, "Amerikanisierung und deutsche Kulturkritik, 1945–1965: Metastasen der Moderne und hermeneutische Hybris," in *Amerikanisierung und Sowjetisierung in Deutschland 1945–1970*, ed. Konrad Jarausch and Hannes Siegrist (Frankfurt/New York, 1997), 315–34; Ilona Stölken-Fitschen, *Atombombe und Geistesgeschichte : Eine Studie der fünfziger Jahre aus deutscher Sicht* (Baden-Baden, 1995).

74. IfD, Stimmung # 609, Skala der Befürchtungen (March 1964); BAK B 145/4240.

75. IfD, Stimmung # 657, Fast jeder zweite Bürger der Bundesrepublik hält einen neuen Weltkrieg für möglich (April 1965); BAK B 145/4224.

76. Klaus R. Scherpe, "Dramatisierung und Entdramatisierung des Untergangs – zum ästhetischen Bewußtsein von Moderne und Postmoderne," in *Postmoderne: Zeichen eines kulturellen Wandels*, ed. Andreas Huyssen and Klaus R. Scherpe (Reinbek, 1986), 270–301.

77. Elisabeth Noelle-Neumann and Renate Köcher, *Die verletzte Nation : Über den Versuch der Deutschen, ihren Charakter zu ändern* (Stuttgart, 1987); Thomas Blank and Peter Schmidt, "Verletzte oder verletzende Nation? Empirische Befunde zum Stolz in Deutschland," *Journal für Sozialforschung* 33 (1993): 391–415.

78. In addition to Diner, *America*, see Paul Hollander, *Anti-Americanism: Critiques at Home and Abroad, 1965–1990* (New York, 1992).

79. Anselm Doering-Manteuffel, "Turning to the Atlantic: The Federal Republic's Ideological Orientation, 1945–1970," *Bulletin of the German Historical Institute* 25 (Fall 1999): 3–21, especially 4.

80. I am indebted to Jaco de Been's extensive preliminary work for a thesis proposal on "The Resilience of Anti-Americanism in Communist Germany" (Department of History, University of Chicago, spring term 2000).

81. Wolfgang Engler, *Die Ostdeutschen : Kunde von einem verlorenen Land* (Berlin, 1999), 307.

82. Dagmar Herzog (Michigan State University) pointed me to these debates. See Dietrich Mühlberg, "Sexualität und ostdeutscher Alltag," *Mitteilungen aus der kulturwissenschaftlichen Forschung* 18, no. 36 (1995): 8–39.

83. Ina Merkel, "Eine andere Welt: Vorstellungen von Nordamerika in der DDR der fünfziger Jahre," in *Amerikanisierung: Traum und Alptraum*, 245–54.

84. Marc Trachtenberg, *A Constructed Peace: The Making of the European Settlement 1945–1963* (Princeton, 1999).

Chapter 10

FORDISM AND WEST GERMAN INDUSTRIAL CULTURE, 1945–1989

Volker R. Berghahn

This chapter deals with the evolution of the powerful German industrial system in the twentieth century, now frequently called the "American Century," but which—according to the well-known French sociologist Raymond Aron—could also have been the German one.[1] It raises the question of how, over a longer period of time and with ups and downs, American business came to be present in the German system.

However, the light that this contribution is trying to throw upon this particular subject differs from traditional economic history in two important respects. To begin with, it contains no statistical analyses of the kind that one would usually find in treatments of modern business. I am not concerned with plotting growth rates, production figures, human resources, inflation, or any other quantitative material. What follows instead revolves around the less tangible aspects of what has been called industrial culture.[2] I am interested here in attitudes, practices, and traditions of behavior of entrepreneurial and managerial elites, not at a company level—the traditional domain of business historians—but at a branch and national level. The study of the culture of particular enterprises that these historians have increasingly engaged in may be seen as an illuminating complement to the approach taken here, since such works rarely capture some of the issues of the larger national and international milieu that are at the center of the following analysis.

Furthermore, the study of a national industrial culture in its larger international setting invites comparisons with other countries. These can be made horizontally, so to speak, to bring out the differences and/or similarities between, say, German and French business traditions and patterns of behavior. Next to horizontal comparisons there is another approach, which in fact is being adopted here and signifies the second peculiarity of this article: National comparisons can equally be made by asking whether, in what ways, and to what extent another industrial system had impacted upon a particular country. To be sure, comparisons of this kind also tend to be at least implicit in quantitative economic history. Thus, those German economic historians who, after 1945, resumed the study of industrialization in nineteenth-century Central Europe usually worked with notions of late-coming and relative backwardness in relation to Britain, the "First Industrial Nation."[3] It is in this context that they examined the patterns of growth and the no doubt impressive achievements of German industry before and after the founding of the Bismarckian empire that propelled the country, within little more than a generation, into the top ranks of the industrialized world.

However, as indicated above, this is not a quantitative history of German business, but a cultural one. It pursues the second of the approaches mentioned above and asks whether and how one industrial culture may have penetrated another. More specifically, it examines the role of American business influence on Germany. What springs to mind most immediately in this connection is of course the question of technological imports from across the Atlantic. But given our perspective, it is important to be mindful of Heinz Hartmann's argument that such exports never arrive, as it were, in the "raw." Whoever takes in foreign industrial technologies must also grapple with ideas of work organization and resource management that are inseparable from the application of modern technologies in the country where they were first developed. More than that, at least in the case of the United States as an exporter of technologies in the twentieth century, just as in the case of Britain in the nineteenth, the question of influence extends to mentalities and practices beyond the workplace.[4] With the rise of America as a major industrial power, German industry also faced the problem of how much to adopt and adapt from the American ways of conducting business at all levels of economic activity.

The time when questions of adoption and adaptation in this wider sense confronted German industry most directly was, most obviously, after World War II. It was in these years that the United States itself took an unprecedentedly strong interest not merely in subtly influencing German mentalities but, more importantly, in actually recasting a system that, in the eyes of the Allies, had been badly warped by the Nazi experience. In the historical literature, this period is usually called the period of postwar reconstruction. But the word "reconstruction," like its German translation *Wiederaufbau*, does not very well capture what in fact happened.

Reconstruction conjures up images of edifices and structures, badly damaged by some catastrophe, that were subsequently put together in much the same shape and form they had existed in before. The notion of recasting seems to be a better concept to understand postwar processes. It points to a rebuilt structure whose elements are reconstituted in a somewhat, though not fundamentally, different way. This approach also seems to offer a way out of the debate on early post-1945 "restoration or revolution" that agitated German political economists in the 1960s.[5] They asserted that owing to American intervention, a fundamental, indeed revolutionary, restructuring of the German economy was forestalled, and that the old organizations and practices were simply restored. Echoes of this position can be found in Carolyn Eisenberg's book on American occupation policy in Germany or, with respect to business, in Henry Wend's recent study of the reconstitution of the shipbuilding industry.[6] Extrapolating from that industry's experience, he asserts that postwar American policy toward Germany, "rather than severing the links that German industry had with the past, actually readjusted these industries onto a developmental trajectory more in line with the traditional path of the German economy."[7] Elsewhere he writes, "the implementation of American policies helped to reconstruct German patterns of industrial organization along pre-existing" lines, adding somewhat vaguely "albeit more democratic lines."[8]

The line of argument adopted here agrees that the German economy remained capitalist in its basic shape and was certainly not revolutionized and transformed into a socialist one, as many people expected or even publicly advocated at the time. But the bricks of the edifice were nevertheless rearranged in line with the conceptions of the hegemonic occupation power and with the compromises that the hegemon struck with its French and British allies, on the one hand, and West German entrepreneurs and managers, on the other. The point to bear in mind, though, is that the American approach to the recasting of German industry was not merely concerned with industrial organization and institutional structures. From the start, Washington also realized that a purely constitutional approach might well end in failure, unless mentalities and attitudes of Germany's industrial elite, i.e., those who would run the system, were also recast.

What makes this latter aspect of American industrial policy-making so intriguing is that, in contrast to the determination to recast organizations and institutions, the idea of influencing the milieu did not make its first appearance in the 1940s. Much is to be said for the view that the turn of the century represents a better starting point for examining German-American industrial relations from this perspective, for it was around 1900, at the Paris World Exhibition, that the United States moved into the telescopes of the Europeans as an industrial power to be reckoned with in the future. By all accounts, the new technologies shown in the American pavilion at Paris attracted a great deal of attention, and soon thereafter businessmen and engineers from Western Europe could be seen traveling across the Atlantic to study not only new steel-making techniques in Pennsylvania or rationalized factory production in Michigan, but also the fresh ideas about work organization promoted by Frederick Taylor and the scientific management movement.[9] By 1914 several major European companies—the Stuttgart electrical engineering firm of Robert Bosch and the French car manufacturer Renault among them—had begun to experiment with Taylorist methods of rationalized production.[10] It should be pointed out, however, also in regard to our subsequent analysis of the German-American business relationship after 1945, that the results of this encounter were mixed.

Next to enthusiasm, there was also a good deal of resistance to the productivity drives and the infamous "Bosch tempo." This resistance culminated in 1913, when the powerful Metal Workers' Union proclaimed a full-scale strike against Bosch. However, other employers also opposed this kind of "Americanization," Daimler-Benz among them. They believed that what was coming from across the Atlantic was not suited to German industrial conditions and principles, and Bosch's troubles therefore merely caused a certain amount of *Schadenfreude* in some business circles.

This pattern of fascination on the part of some and resistance by others continued after World War I. Once again, German businessmen, engineers, and this time trade unionists as well, traveled to the industrial centers of Pennsylvania, Ohio, New York, and Michigan. They tried not to miss Henry Ford's vast assembly lines at River Rouge or other installations of rationalized production in Pittsburgh or Akron. The visitors wrote many reports, which Mary Nolan evaluated in her important *Visions of Modernity*, and invariably raised the question—as Wichard von Moellendorff put it—of the "transferability" of American ideas and practices to German industry.[11] The important point to be borne in mind here is that most of these ideas concerned methods of production and management. In this respect Weimar industry, steeped as it was in its own patriarchical traditions and with heavy industry exerting its mighty conservative power—political weight that the modernizers in the "Siemens camp" could never throw off—only introduced certain elements of Fordism, as it had by then become widely known.

The Ruhr barons liked the rationalization of production, but refused to take on board the other side of Henry Ford's vision, which he had mapped out in his quickly translated and best-selling memoirs.[12] Mass production, as the father of the "T Model" had postulated, would be illogical if it did not lead to a reduction in prices, i.e., if the productivity gains were not passed on to the consumer. To him, rationalization made sense only if it put the new products within reach of a growing number of people.

Conservative and politically anti-democratic German entrepreneurs, however, were tied into traditional structures of market organization, the cartels and syndicates that, for reasons to be dealt with in a moment, made price reductions very difficult. They had been socialized into this system and could not conceive of there being a better one. The liberal economist Moritz Bonn described the difference between American attitudes toward mass production and mass consumption and those prevalent in Germany when he wrote in 1930,

> Ford's significance does not lie in [his] assembly-line [production] and a well-thought-out division of labor which the grown-up German children who visit

America for the first time see as the *raison d'être* of American life. Rather it lies in the sober fact, which is propagated under the slogan of "social service" and hence somewhat removed from rational analysis, that American entrepreneurs like Ford know that the masses will only tolerate the accumulation of great wealth in the hands of a few, if they themselves derive a corresponding advantage from it. In a wealthy country like America one permits the entrepreneur to earn as much as he likes, provided that those through whom he makes his money also benefit from it...The authoritarian German capitalism and heavy industry in particular has never allowed others to share in their earnings. Obsessed by technically perfectly correct organizational ideas, it has tried to achieve the removal of all technically dispensable intermediate links. As a result not only the ranks of those who wish to earn a share have been thinned, but also the number of those has been reduced who in their hearts take a benevolent interest in the continuation [of capitalism].[13]

Then, in 1929, the Great Depression hit the world economy, making a mockery of the Fordist dream of a prosperous mass production and mass consumption society. Millions of unemployed were struggling to survive on both sides of the Atlantic. As the German economy recovered by the mid-1930s, it was not the patriarchs of industry but Adolf Hitler who, in his quest of creating a racist folk community of loyal Nazis and contented *Volksgenossen*, returned to the idea of a mass consumption society, supported by mavericks like Ferdinand Porsche. In this sense Porsche's *Volkswagen* was a genuinely Fordist product, even if it was to be available only to the "Aryan" citizens of the future Greater German empire.[14]

Beyond this, the German industrial system had by this time developed into something very different from the notions of capitalism espoused in the United States. As Hitler established his dictatorial rule, German industry became almost completely cartellized. Not least in order to satisfy the government's voracious demand for armaments, the free market and the principles of competition had, for all practical purposes, been abolished in the key branches of industry. Prices were fixed and regulated. Levels of production depended on the allocation of raw materials according to the military priorities of the regime. The labor market was similarly restricted. Trade unions were proscribed. Their leaders were put into concentration camps or forced into exile. The Nazi Labor Front did not allow for free collective bargaining. As far as international trade was concerned, the Nazis increasingly moved toward notions of self-sufficiency and the conquest of an autarkic empire by violent means.[15]

There is no need to elaborate on the very peculiar capitalism that developed in Germany under Hitler. While American businessmen and politicians observed the evolution of these peculiarities during the 1930s with growing alarm and alienation, they set their sights on the restoration of the multilateral world trading system and the Open Door to counter Nazi economic nationalism.[16] Secretary of State Cordell Hull was ever more firmly wedded to the idea of multilateralism as he watched not only Hitler expanding eastward, but also Mussolini conquering parts of North and East Africa and the Japanese gaining a foothold, again by force of arms, on the Chinese mainland. The outbreak of World War II and America's entry into it in December 1941 prevented, at least for the moment, the practical pursuit of Hull's internationalism, but it also sharply contrasted the differences between the German (and Japanese) ways of running a modern industrial economy, on the one hand, and the American approach, on the other. This is why some historians have taken the year 1941, rather than 1900, as the starting point of their historical analysis of the German-American economic relationship in this century.

On closer inspection we are probably dealing more with interrelated complementarities. Until 1941, as we have seen, America served as an industrial model only in a more indirect way. Those who propagated this model wanted to rely on the force of persuasion rather than compulsion. The Fordist dream, they thought, would be so attractive to all involved—producers and consumers—that German entrepreneurs and trade unionists would sooner or later emulate it with enthusiasm; always, of course, with modifications in line with indigenous business and labor traditions. It is also true that those attitudinal and mental changes that would eventually come about related primarily to the shop floor and management. They did not deal with business structures and institutions, and with market structures in particular.

In this respect 1941 was indeed a major break. The organization, not just of labor relations but of industry as a whole, required, in the American view that was now emerging in postwar planning bodies like the Committee on Economic Development (CED), a more fundamental recasting. Above all, since the organization of German industry was now made directly responsible for having facilitated the outbreak of World War II, Washington was no longer prepared to assume a passive role, hoping that the lure of Fordism would over time do the trick. Once this war was over, the victorious Americans would determinedly and decisively reshape Nazi Germany's industrial system, no matter how strong the opposition among the country's industrial elite. As the British historian Callum Macdonald put it in 1980, the United States had come to see National Socialism "as a ruthless, expansionist, autarkic system backed by the German industrial cartels which had financed the rise of the Nazi party. As a political movement fascism could not exist without an economic base which was at once closed and expansionist. Washington opposed Nazi Germany because U.S. democracy, defined as a system of political pluralism based on free economic competition at home and abroad, was threatened by the expansion of the closed Nazi economic system."[17]

This meant not only that democracy, free labor unions, and collective bargaining would once more be established; it also signified that all notions of autarky would have to be abandoned, and that the Germany that the Nazis had pushed in the direction of autarky would return to the world market. Finally and perhaps most importantly, the Washington policymakers involved in the preparation of this return to the Open Door insisted that all cartels and syndicates be destroyed and market competition in prices, products, and services be reintroduced. The old German practices of fixing prices and production quotas, as well as all other restrictive practices, would be banned once and for all. The model for this innovation was, plainly and simply, the American system of antitrust legislation through which, with various modifications, the formation of cartels and other forms of monopoly had been banned in the United States under the Sherman Act of 1890.

The year 1945 therefore brought an important change in the way in which the United States came to be present in Germany's economic system. Up to this point, and particularly in the interwar period, the impact had been in terms of ideas and practices related to production and consumption; it had been more indirect and "cultural." America served as a model to German industry, one that was happily adopted and adapted by some branches and emphatically rejected by others. Fordism as a system for the promotion of mass production and mass consumption had met— Moritz Bonn put it so well—with resistance and misunderstanding. But at no point had the Americans tried to impose their ideas on German business. Nor, in the isolationist political climate prevailing in the United States in the 1920s, was the government in Washington prepared to give explicit support to the export of Fordism.

All this changed after 1945, when the United States appeared as an occupying power in Germany endowed with extensive executive privileges to shape the vanquished country's future. Most importantly, this time the political will to intervene in German society, politics, and economy was very strong. There was a widespread feeling that the political system created by the Nazis and their military aggression in 1939 were directly linked to the country's economic system, and that fundamental change had to be effected if a repeat performance was to be avoided and Germany was to become a peaceful member of the international community again.

Many studies have been produced on how this determination on the part of the United States was translated into political change.[18] This change was initiated at two levels: structural-institutional and ideological-cultural. From the start, the Americans, in cooperation with Britain and later also France, began to revamp the political and administrative structures of their zones of occupation. This process began at the local and regional level and culminated in the decision to encourage the Germans to draft a constitution for the West German state that was to emerge in the wake of the escalating cold war with the Soviet Union and the division of the former Reich along the Iron Curtain. John F. Golay was among the first scholars to examine the creation of what came to be known as the Basic Law of the Federal Republic of Germany. He and others have also analyzed how the U.S. military governor and his adviser in constitutional matters, the Harvard political scientist Carl Joachim Friedrich, helped to shape the West German constitution.[19] From 1949 onwards, the West Germans therefore had an institutional framework in the shape of a parliamentary-democratic republic, within which they were thenceforth able to develop their domestic political agenda. Designed as a federal system, the *Grundgesetz* (Basic Law) was complemented by *Länder* constitutions approved by the Western Allies in previous years and a reformed administrative structure all the way down to the level of local government.

This structural-institutional change was accompanied by a program to transform the political culture and mentalities of the Germans who, as citizens in a parliamentary democracy, were supposed to fill the Basic Law with civic life and make it work. This development and the American input into it have likewise been studied by historians and social scientists. A large number of books and articles have been produced on Allied denazification and the program of re-education that followed it.[20] Here, the idea was to eradicate what were thought to be the authoritarian and anti-democratic traits in the "German mind," and replace them with the practices of a civic society along the lines of the Western model of democratic participation and liberal support for the new constitutional order. Ultimately, the structural-institutional and ideological-cultural duality was seen, especially by the Americans, as two sides of the same coin. The Basic Law could not work without the emergence of a democratic political culture; conversely, the old attitudes and mentalities could not be successfully transformed without a liberal-parliamentary constitution.

What has been overlooked is that these principles of structural and cultural change in the field of politics had their exact parallel in the economic sphere, a thesis about which we still have very little information. One reason for this oversight seems to be the direction that economic history took in the Federal Republic after 1945. Insofar as economic historians began to deal with the postwar period, they were, like their colleagues who worked on German industrialization in the nineteenth century, primarily concerned with the quantitative aspects of reconstruction. They compiled many useful statistics on the impact of wartime bombing and Allied dismantling. They looked at growth rates and crises, particularly in the field of transportation. They argued over whether the Marshall Plan made a difference to postwar reconstruction or whether the country pulled itself into the Erhardian "economic miracle" of the 1950s more or less by its own bootstraps. They examined the 1948 currency reform and the problems of the "dollar gap."[21]

However important this work has been for creating a sound statistical base for future research, economic historians were not very interested in the kinds of questions that are at the root of our analysis here. They were not aware, at least in the American conception of things, of the inseparability of political democracy and industrial democracy, or of how deeply American businessmen, politicians, and academics believed that the one could not thrive without the other. To quote the Yale University economist Thurmond Arnold, who headed the Anti-Trust Division in the Justice Department during the 1930s, a "vigorous industrial democracy" was a "democracy able to work at full industrial capacity, since it could distribute goods to its own people instead of piling them up in huge surpluses because prices do not respond to purchasing power."[22] No less significantly, where the power of the producers over the market amounted to monopoly, the free mechanisms of that market were destroyed, which in turn threatened to obliterate political democracy. In other words, in the American tradition, just as political democracy required checks and balances, so did "industrial democracy." A pluralist society was threatened not only by centralized and authoritarian government, but also by the concentrated power of large private corporations.

Bearing in mind this linkage that Americans had been making between politics and economics since the nineteenth century, we are already in the middle of our analysis of the structural-institutional and cultural-ideological change that the United States, as the economic hegemon of the West in the cold war era, was determined to introduce in West Germany's industrial system in parallel with the parliamentary-democratic transformations it had begun to initiate in the field of politics and constitutional government. At the core of the structural change was the creation of a competitive, liberal-capitalist Open Door market. Accordingly, cartels and syndicates, and with them the entire old German system of anticompetitive, protectionist market organization that emerged in the late nineteenth century and was perfected under Hitler in the 1930s, were abolished. Virtual monopolies, like the giant I. G. Farben and *Vereinigte Stahlwerke* trusts, were to be broken up into smaller units that would compete against each other.[23]

However, it is important to emphasize that the decartellization and deconcentration process was not to be pushed so far as to create a myriad of small enterprises. The idea was to craft an American-style *oligopolistic* system that would allow smaller companies to exist and thrive, provided they themselves remained efficient, but would also have a sufficiently large number of bigger corporations to act as engines of growth in the projected reconstruction of not only West Germany's, but also Western Europe's industries. Recognizing that Germany, and its industrial heartland, the Ruhr, continued to be the economic powerhouse of Europe, Washington's concern was to build a competitive structure free from both cartels and syndicates. They also aimed to construct enterprises that would, through their stronger capital base and large-scale Fordist production facilities, stimulate a rapid expansion to overcome wartime devastation and depression and help to create an American-style mass consumption society in the whole of Western Europe.

With the founding of the Federal Republic, which returned a large measure of legislative sovereignty to the West Germans, Allied anti-cartel decrees had to be reformulated into properly ratified laws. Accordingly, Ludwig Erhard, the neoliberal economics minister who actively promoted the structural Americanization of West German industry, introduced a bill that was patterned after the antitrust legislation of the United

States. With West German industry not only having recovered physically, but also having regained its once badly shattered self-confidence, Erhard encountered strong opposition to his plans. This opposition and the ultimate adoption of a West German *Kartellgesetz* in 1957 have been examined in detail elsewhere.[24]

What is important in our context are the conclusions to be drawn from this struggle. The resistance of the conservatives, especially in the Ruhr regions' heavy industries, demonstrated the interdependence of constitutional and mental change. The Americans were right in insisting that legislation was crucial, but the slow ratification of a West German antitrust law showed that deeply ingrained attitudes could not be changed overnight. Still, West German industry did get its *Kartellgesetz*, which, though watered down in some respects, did in the long run effectively wrench it away from its earlier anticompetitive traditions and institutions: the Federal Republic's economy did develop in an oligopolistic direction, as envisaged in the late 1940s by, for example, William Draper, the head of the economic division in the U.S. military government. And the oligopolies did leave enough room for the middle-sized and small entrepreneurs to thrive as well.

West Germany's industrial structures had been recast in such a way as to be functional within the multilateral, liberal-capitalist Western world economy that the United States was determined to shape and recast after the experience of fascism, economic nationalism, and autarkic blocs, such as the Nazis, Italians, and Japanese had been trying to create in World War II. Erhard once put this outcome very neatly into a nutshell when he referred to the *Kartellgesetz* as the Federal Republic's "Economic Basic Law."[25] Indeed, this was the industrial structural complement to the political constitution that had been promulgated, with Allied help, in 1949 to provide a framework for parliamentary politics.

If the focus of the analysis has so far been on institutional change, let me now turn to the American postwar effort at the level of ideology and industrial culture in a broader sense. Again, while we have many studies on political re-education, much work is still to be done on the "economic re-education" program that the United States began in West Germany in tandem with the recasting of industry's structures and institutions. This time, this particular effort to transform mentalities was made much more persistently and systematically than in the 1920s, when German businessmen and trade unionists had gone to visit Ford's factories and other American industrial installations on their own initiative. Paid partly out of Marshall Plan funds, Paul Hoffman, a former president of the Studebaker Corporation and the Plan's administrator in Europe, actively invited the Europeans, with many German businessmen among them, to travel to the United States to inspect American production facilities and marketing practices, to talk to the organizers of mass production and the beneficiaries of mass consumption, and to consider the adoption of American practices of factory organization and labor relations.[26]

The scheme was promoted through Hoffman's productivity councils, which also covered the costs of these visits. And for those European and West German businessmen, engineers, and trade unionists who did not participate in the American travel program, a Training Within Industry (TWI) scheme was organized to enable them to hear and read at home about the secrets of Fordist production, and mass marketing for the creation of a mass production and mass consumption society—a system that would bring "prosperity for all."[27]

Historians and even some economic historians have at last begun to study these attempts to exert an overt ideological influence on West Germany. The notion that the United States had a profound effect on the industrial culture of the Federal Republic is taken as seriously as are studies relating to the American impact on the country's political culture. Inevitably, there has been some debate over how fast or slow this process was and whether this process ought to be called "Americanization" or something else.[28] It seems generally accepted that this kind of cultural change proceeded more slowly than the institutional transformations. There is a good deal of evidence that it took the emergence of another generation of businessmen, managers, and trade unionists to accept the implications of this cultural Americanization and the transition to Fordist mass production and mass consumption. The changes mentioned above came more rapidly in some branches than in others. Some businessmen, like Otto A. Friedrich, the brother of Carl Joachim who monitored the drafting of the Basic Law, learned more quickly than others.[29] But there seems to be little doubt that by the 1960s, both the *structures* and the *culture* of West German industry were tangibly different from those of the 1940s.

Even then, to be sure, it was by no means all West German businessmen who had been converted to believe in the superiority of the American system of industrial organization and culture. Nevertheless, by the 1960s the American impact had been generally profound, even if the American "victory" was at no point total and remained subject to constant negotiation.[30] What emerged therefore was a blending of American imports with indigenous traditions. The actual "mix" of elements varied, not only in different branches of industry, but also in different areas of industrial activity. Thus, differing degrees of American influence could be seen, for example, among management styles, labor relations, and marketing practices.

Even after full account has been taken of these variations, overall it may be said that the process that has been traced at different levels in this chapter continued throughout the 1970s. West German industrial culture at the time of German reunification was not a replica of the American system, but it was probably the most Americanized among the major industrial nations of Western Europe, all of which had been intensively exposed to the hegemonic pressure of Fordism, as defined above, since World War II. Thus, our examination of Fordism in the wider sense opens up most interesting questions of comparison, not only between the industrial systems of Western Europe in the age of the postwar Pax Americana, but also between different genres of cultural history. The study of industry and its culture is not normally included in this kind of historical research. However, it should be. After all, it is difficult to see how we can fully understand the evolution of mass consumption, mass entertainment, youth culture, Americanism, and anti-Americanism in postwar Europe without including the producers and capitalism in our analysis.

Conversely, economic historians, having become more interested in the qualitative aspects of postwar industrial developments, may find it illuminating to inform themselves about what is happening across the fence in the different fields of European cultural studies, and to contemplate some of the other articles in this volume.

Notes

1. Cited in Fritz Stern, *Einstein's German World* (Princeton, 1999), 3.
2. See Jürgen Kocka, *Industrial Culture and Bourgeois Society* (Oxford/New York, 1999).
3. Peter Mathias, *The First Industrial Nation: An Economic History of Britain* (London, 1969).
4. Heinz Hartmann, *Amerikanische Firmen in Deutschland* (Cologne, 1963).
5. See Eberhard Schmidt, *Die verhinderte Neuordnung* (Frankfurt, 1981).
6. Carolyn Eisenberg, *Drawing the Line* (Cambridge/New York, 1996); Henry B. Wend, *Recovery and Reconstruction* (in press, 2000).
7. Wend, *Recovery*, 422.
8. Ibid., 1.
9. See Robert Kanigel, *One Best Way: Frederick Winslow Taylor and the Enigma of Efficiency* (New York, 1997).
10. See Patrick Fridenson, *Historie des usines Renault* (Paris, 1971); Anita Kugler, "Von der Werkstatt zum Fliessband," *Geschichte und Gesellschaft* 13 (1987): 304–39.
11. Mary Nolan, *Visions of Modernity: American Business and the Modernization of Germany* (New York/Oxford, 1994); Wichard von Moellendorff, *Volkswirtschaftliche Vergleiche zwischen Vereinigten Staaten von Amerika, Deutschland, Grossbritannien, Frankreich, Italien*, vol. 1 (Berlin, 1930), 4.
12. Henry Ford, *My Life and Work* (New York, 1922).
13. Moritz Bonn, *Das Schicksal des deutschen Kapitalismus* (Berlin, 1930), 46ff.
14. See Philipp Gassert, *Amerika im Dritten Reich* (Stuttgart, 1997).
15. See Timothy Mason, *Social Policy in the Third Reich* (Oxford, 1993); Reinhard Opitz, ed., *Europastrategien des deutschen Kapitals, 1900–1945* (Cologne, 1977); Robert E. Herzstein, *When Nazi Dreams Come True* (London, 1982).
16. See, e.g., Robert M. Collins, *The Business Response to Keynes* (New York, 1981).
17. Callum A. Macdonald, "The Politics of Intervention," *Journal of Latin American Studies* (November 1980): 394.
18. See, e.g., Hermann-Josef Rupieper et al., eds., *American Policy and the Reconstruction of West Germany* (Washington/New York, 1993).
19. John F. Golay, *The Founding of the Federal Republic of Germany* (Chicago, 1958); Friedrich K. Fromme, *Von der Weimarer Verfassung zum Bonner Grundgesetz* (Tübingen, 1962).
20. See, e.g., Edward N. Peterson, *The American Occupation of Germany: Retreat to Victory* (Detroit, 1978); James F. Tent, *Mission on the Rhine* (Chicago, 1982).

21. See, e.g., Christoph Buchheim, *Die Wiedereingliederung Westdeutschlands in die Weltwirtschaft, 1945–1958* (Munich, 1990); Werner Abelshauser, *Wirtschaft in Westdeutschland* (Stuttgart, 1975); Gerold Ambrosius, *Die Durchsetzung der sozialen Marktwirtschaft in Westdeutschland, 1945–1949* (Stuttgart, 1977).

22. Thurmond Arnold, *Bottlenecks of Business* (New York, 1940), 293, 10.

23. See Raymond G. Stokes, *Divide and Prosper: The Heirs of I. G. Farben under Allied Authority, 1945–1951* (Berkeley, 1988).

24. See, e.g., Rüdiger Robert, *Konzentrationspolitik in der Bundesrepublik* (Berlin, 1976); Volker R. Berghahn, *The Americanization of West German Industry, 1945–1973* (New York, 1986), 155.

25. Quoted in Berghahn, *Americanization*, 178.

26. See, e.g., Nick Tiratsoo and Jim Tomlinson, "Exporting the 'Gospel of Productivity,'" *Business History Review* 71 (Spring 1997): 41–81.

27. Ludwig Erhard, *Wohlstand für alle* (Düsseldorf, 1957).

28. There is some resistance to using the term "Americanization" in Germany, but this may be because it is understood to mean a kind of overrunning of German culture by that of the United States. However, as indicated above and again below, the debate on the German-American cultural encounter in this century has moved to a more differentiated interpretation that emphasizes negotiation and blending of indigenous traditions with foreign influences that may be quite variable. In light of this development it is also not quite clear how much is to be gained from the notion of the "*Amerikaorientierung*" of German businessmen that is being advocated by members of the Arbeitskreis für Kritische Unternehmens- und Industriegeschichte, headquartered at Bochum University. Still, the work of this group is to be welcomed, as it has been trying to shift German business history in a "culturalist" direction.

29. See, e.g., Volker R. Berghahn and Paul J. Friedrich, *Otto A. Friedrich: Ein politischer Unternehmer, 1902–1975* (Frankfurt, 1992).

30. See now: Heide Fehrenbach and Uta G. Poiger, eds., *Transactions, Transgressions, Transformations: American Culture in Europe and Japan* (New York, 1999).

Chapter 11

"GERMANY HAS BEEN A MELTING POT"
American and German Intercultures, 1945–1955

Rudy Koshar

Tourism and Intercultures

Americans touring Germany in the early 1950s had but one up-to-date and comprehensive English-language guidebook to help them plan their itineraries.[1] It was published by the David McKay company in New York and edited by Eugene Fodor, founder of the now famous Fodor's Modern Guide series. Reflecting the fraught political situation in Central Europe, Fodor began on a note of contention by defending the handbook's title, *Germany 1953*. Even though it would cover only a part of the country, both "West Germany" and "The German Federal Republic" would be too cumbrous as titles, and in any case, as the editor put it, "it's a fairly safe bet that there isn't a great deal of pleasure travel going on, for tourists who speak any language, in the other Germany."[2]

The guide began with the usual practical information on preparing the trip, traveling from North America to the Continent, and getting around by train and auto once in Germany. A major part of this introductory material was devoted to "the German scene," which included essays by journalists and travel writers on food and customs as well as on "national character" and history. An unsigned article entitled "The Germans: What They Think and How They Act" took a long view of national character, beginning with Tacitus's account of Germanic tribes and then plummeting ahead to Beethoven, Wilhelm II, and Hitler. But this long history, so different from that of the country from which American travelers came, suggested a degree of identification between the two cultures. "The monolithic facades of the Kaiser's and Hitler's Reichs have obscured the fact that through most of its history Germany has been diverse, disunited and unstable," read the guide. "It has accepted foreign influence, and been caught up in dynastic struggles and international storms. Germany has been a melting pot with new ingredients continually added and pressures and temperatures erratically changed."[3]

The use of the then still popular American term "melting pot" may seem extraordinary as a description of a country that less than a decade ago had been the radical "other" to Western liberal values.[4] One could, of course, dismiss the language as yet another example of touristic kitsch, an inevitable outcome of the dissolution of serious, educated travel into an ahistorical and commercialized tourism. On a more elaborate conceptual level, one could analyze how Germany was "constructed" or "invented" through such discourse. There is enough literature on the so-called "Americanization" of Germany to consider the Fodor guide as yet another instance of the imposition of American ways on a beaten and fragmented nation. Political history might insist on emphasizing how the handbook reflected a process whereby the cold war transformed German enemies into American friends. And from the point of view of imagology, one could argue that Fodor used a series of "heteroimages," not to understand another culture but to reaffirm the "autoimage" of American society as a community welded together from diverse ethnic and cultural influences.

These approaches finally obscure more than they illuminate. Using the conceptual binary of "travel" and "tourism" tells us more about social theory's anxious response to commercial culture than about the historical experience of tourism and the literature it has generated. Emphasizing the invention of Germany meanwhile skirts much too closely to older arguments stressing "false consciousness" and structural misrelationships between society and culture, to say nothing of the fact that this conceptual language has by now become something of a cliché. Studies emphasizing how Europe was "Americanized" often miss the interactive and negotiated elements of this process. As for the effects of the cold war in its earliest stages, it is not at all clear that a sudden or unprecedented change took place in the image most Americans had of Germany or that most Germans had of America, at least in the first post–World War II decade. Imagology's study of the interaction of autoimages and heteroimages can be useful, especially when, as Peter Freese argues, it uncovers the way in which perceptions of alterity serve the boundary-making goals of the observer. Yet like those who stress the invention of tradition, Freese falls into an overly "constructivist" position. Analyzing the German "other" in American fiction, he argues that "whether German characters as presented in American literature are true to life is entirely beyond the point."[5]

My goal in this chapter is to demonstrate that it is not at all beyond the point to ask whether the type of historical and social imagery one finds in tourist literature has anything to do with the lived experience and history not only of the society tourists visited but of the tourists themselves. I leave for another discussion the question of whether it is possible to speak of "the reality content of national images," a phrase used by David Barclay and Elisabeth Glaser-Schmidt in their edited volume on transatlantic images of Germany and the United States.[6] But I do maintain that it is useful to ask how touristic images worked in relation to the lived historical experience of those who employed such images and ideas. In the case of Germany after World War II, it can be argued that the Fodor guide's view of the German past did much to elucidate a historically specific intersocietal transfer between Americans and (West) Germans that characterized the first decade of the postwar era and continued to shape relations between the two cultures thereafter.[7] Such transfer did not entail relations between two bounded and homogeneous national communities—there was in this sense nothing "international" about it— but rather transnational or subnational encounters and contacts that merged elements in new syntheses, or rather in a series of layered "intercultures" neither distinctly American nor German.[8] In the following pages, I plan to use the Fodor guidebook as the point of departure for an analysis of such intercultures. My primary focus will not be on some of the standard subjects of postwar history—American military government, denazification and re-education, economic and urban reconstruction, Americanization, memory (or lack thereof) of the Holocaust, and the evolving cold war. Nor will I make an argument about yet another chapter in the "special relationship" between the two societies.[9] My focus will not be on institutions and political relations, but on the memories, representations, and experiences of soldiers, journalists, and tourists. In a brief moment of fantasy about the predictive value of historical scholarship, I also want to use this information to make a concluding remark about the possibility and direction of future intercultural contact between the two countries.

Fodor's Germany

In understanding the evolution of postwar American perceptions of Germany, it is important to emphasize that there was a continuity between World War II and its aftermath. At no time in World War II, except in November 1944, did the share of Americans who saw "the German people" as the enemy rise above 20 percent. Conversely, in Great Britain, despite a degree of sympathy for the Nazi regime earlier in the 1930s among some members of the British elite, the share of those who were hostile to the German people was as high as 50 percent. At the end of the war, and after public knowledge of the concentration camps was widespread, only 13 percent of American respondents expressed support for the controversial Morgenthau plan to "pastoralize" Germany. The majority of Americans polled, perhaps more than two out of three, did not give voice to an intense hostility toward Germany, but took a long view stressing the possibilities of education and democratic transformation in a new postwar German state.[10] The title of a 1954 editorial in a special edition of *Life* magazine featuring Germany as the "awakened giant" summed up

FIGURE 15. American Soldiers as Tourists, 1966

American soldiers as tourists. Two members of the occupation forces pose for a photograph in front of a lion of the Feldherrnhalle in Munich in 1966. (Bilderdienst Süddeutscher Verlag)

this attitude: "Furor Teutonicus: If History Can Change the Character of a Nation, Germany's Is a Better Bet."[11]

The reasons for this comparatively liberal assessment are numerous. The German background of a significant part of the American population is one factor. Moreover, unlike British populations, Americans never experienced direct attack by German military forces. American popular culture—cinema in particular—played a significant role in shaping attitudes and, even when it confronted the history of Nazi concentration camps in films such as "The Mortal Storm," did more to minimize than to encourage public criticism of the Nazi regime. More than a conscious strategy, this tendency reflected Hollywood's commitment to a kind of entertainment that avoided overly disturbing "realism" or controversial moral issues. World War II also galvanized Americans' commitment to universal values of freedom of speech and democracy, and re-emphasizing a liberal American identity created the potential for a more open and tolerant view of other societies, even those that had attacked the United States and created political systems diametrically opposed to American traditions.[12] Well before the rhetoric of globalization and the global community had taken hold of pundits and politicians, the American Nobel Prize novelist Pearl Buck was writing that "the world has become a neighborhood." This proximity to the world meant that Americans had to take a direct interest in seeing to it that "good people" prevailed in Germany. In Buck's eyes, good Germans were ultimately not Germans at all, just as Americans lost their national distinctiveness when they saw themselves in a "natural brotherhood of the good among all peoples."[13] The era of liberality in American political culture may have passed by the early 1950s, at least for the majority of Americans, but the sense of cross-cultural identity and universalism continued to persist.

The Fodor travel guide appeared at a propitious time in postwar Germany. Not only did the U.S. military occupation bring almost a million American military personnel and their dependents, government agents, writers and journalists, and business representatives to the defeated country, but government and business on both sides of the Atlantic encouraged American tourism in Europe after political relations and the beginning of economic recovery allowed for leisure travel on the Continent as well. The share of American families with incomes exceeding $3,000 grew from 16 percent in 1941 to 50 percent in 1947. Although American tourists were a varied group, they came largely from families with "middle-class incomes" at or above the $3,000 level. It was estimated that in 1950 alone some 327,000 U.S. "dollar bearers" traveled to Europe, contributing $370 million dollars to Organization for European Economic Co-operation (OEEC) countries. In 1948-49, American tourists to Germany accounted for only about 2 percent of the total number of American travelers in Europe, down from 15 percent ten years earlier.[14] But the early 1950s saw a rapid increase in Germany's attractiveness as a tourist destination for Americans. Between 1951 and 1955, the number of overnight stays registered by travelers from the United States during the West German summer tourist season nearly tripled, reaching over 800,000 and well exceeding the rate of increase for overnight stays by all foreign visitors to West Germany in the same period. Of all foreign guests in the Federal Republic in the 1955 travel season, only the Dutch registered more overnight stays than Americans did.[15]

The revival of German tourism depended on the provision and improvement of accommodations, and Germany was making great strides on this score. The Fodor guide praised the wide availability, cleanliness, and inexpensiveness of German hotels, stating that "you can put it down pretty confidently as a fact that even in frequented resorts and big cities, there are always good rooms available at six marks."[16] More than simply pointing to the convenience of West Germany as a land of leisure travel, this statement also situated tourism in a larger cultural matrix. Many observers of German culture, from novelists to anthropologists, had identified cleanliness as an enduring German trait, and some had seen an overbearing attachment to cleanliness as symptomatic of distorted emotional relations manifested in authoritarian family structures and extremist political movements.[17] Political meanings aside, the image of German cleanliness was hardly arbitrary, as it found concrete expression in postwar Germany well before Fodor tourists had set foot on the Continent. In one of the most informative early accounts of the American occupation zone, American journalist Julian Bach noted that U.S. soldiers had positive first impressions of Germany based on their bad memories of having fought first in France. Aside from Paris, which continued to capture the imagination of Americans abroad, the towns and villages of rural France appeared muddy, dirty, and run-down to U.S. soldiers. By contrast, houses and villages in Germany, where Allied bombers had not done their work, were well-built and clean, the roads were in good shape, and sanitary conditions were more like those the servicemen were accustomed to in the United States. In comparison to France, wrote Bach, the GI "smelled less manure in the countryside, and found more sidewalks in the cities. As the highest praise that most Americans feel like bestowing on anything foreign is, 'It's clean!' he was surprised and pleased with Germany's physical plant."[18]

Bach's account was based on nearly two years of experience reporting on American troops in the European theater. He was able to watch American servicemen who had fought in the European theater arrive and stay in Germany until as late as December 1945, and he was there when a new wave of soldiers without prior experience of European combat arrived by the thousands in an occupied country. No friend of Germany, Bach nonetheless strove for accuracy and fair-mindedness, and although critics saw his book as "neither very well written nor very profound," its observations on the middle and lower echelons of military government and on the attitudes of American servicemen were regarded (by no less an authority than Paul Sweezy) as "on the whole sound and useful."[19]

Bach's observation on U.S. soldiers' first impressions is noteworthy partly because it reminds us that ruin and destruction were not the only or even the dominant images many formed when they first encountered Germany in the last days of the war and the early postwar years. In addition, it suggests that such heteroimages gain a large part of their resonance not only from comparisons between one's home and a foreign country but also between other foreign countries. Germany was "not France," and that was almost as important as the character of Germany itself. Significantly, German nationalist rhetoric, from Weimar-era criticisms of French occupying troops after World War I to Nazi racist propaganda during the Saar campaign, also contrasted "dirty" France and "clean" Germany.[20]

Even more important in this context is the fact that relative cleanliness, as it was being defined, was a significant element of the bodily memory of U.S. soldiers. Sight, smell, and tactile experiences of the physical environment were as important to the intercultural negotiations that were taking place between Americans and Germans as were more programmed or directed experiences. Reflecting broader tendencies in the burgeoning postwar tourist industry, Fodor's handbook exploited this sense of cleanliness as a key switching point, a moment of significant intersocietal transfer, between Americans and Germans. Clean hotel rooms were imbricated in a larger set of memories and experiences that operated quite literally close to the skin, and that American travelers could draw on as they traversed postwar Germany. It should also be noted that the trope of cleanliness was also deeply historical in the sense that it suggested a more urban and "middle-class" sense of the term as it was used in both journalistic and tourist accounts. If Americans and Germans effectively had the same understanding of cleanliness, this may have been based on a broader cultural matrix that was not specifically national but rather transnational in character and oriented largely to Anglo-American and Northern European standards.[21] The boundaries of this particular intercultural site were not confined to America and Germany.

Bach argued that cleanliness was linked in the minds of U.S. soldiers with qualities such as modernity, orderliness, and industriousness, enduring elements of the public imagery of Germany derived from direct experience after World War II. U.S. soldiers were interested in getting things done, and they often expressed admiration for the way in which Germans quickly began rebuilding roads, schools, offices, factories, and architectural landmarks. Military personnel coming to serve a tour of duty in Germany in the early 1950s received an official pocket guide to the country that began with a short account of how Germans "picked their way through the wreckage of their cities and of their pride to the beginning of a new phase in their history."[22] One could argue that the imagery of a kind of self-made nation literally "rising from nothing," as popular German rhetoric of the time put it, appealed to Americans' autoimage as "self-made men" who with hard work and a bit of guile "made" something of themselves.[23] Germans understood "success," argued Bach, and U.S. soldiers always admired success. Again, the Franco-German comparison was important: Bach said U.S. soldiers considered the French to be lazy while Germans were seen as willing workers. The continuity with the Nazi period should not be overlooked, as postwar images of German productivity picked up on National Socialist attempts to place *Leistung* at the center of the "*Volk* community."

This American heteroimage gained additional strength in Fodor guide descriptions of partially rebuilt German cities that often expressed a degree of wonder at what had been accomplished in Berlin, Cologne, and other badly bombed towns. The technical process itself was often the source of fascination. For Frankfurt am Main, Fodor tourists were encouraged to visit the "unique spectacle" of the "ruins processing facility" (*Trümmerverwertungsanstalt*) in the eastern part of the city, where every day thousands of blocks and other building materials were efficiently manufactured from the Hessian metropolis's twelve million tons of war rubble.[24] The German propensity for work was even the subject of a satirical introductory essay in the Fodor guide by the British writer George Mikes, who mischievously noted that foreign observers, having seen the material well-being already achieved in the early 1950s in Germany, were wondering how they might get their countries to lose a war to America.[25] The sense of wonder at German reconstruction quickly became a leitmotif of tourist guidebooks; even the venerable Baedeker guide to northern Bavaria, published in a new English-language edition in 1951, wrote of Germans' "indestructible energy" in rebuilding the country.[26]

The perception of German industriousness ramified throughout the relations between Germany and America. It had an impact on both high-level industrial relations between the two countries and the politics of Allied policy toward the Germans. It enabled the "complex process of interaction between the two industrial cultures" that Volker Berghahn has analyzed.[27] It is quite possible that the symbiosis that occurred between U.S. and German firms, which Berghahn discusses from the German side, also depended on American business's regard for German colleagues and the expectation of future German productivity. One should not overlook the way in which such American attitudes toward German business mirrored those of German manufacturers, who since early in the century had admired (not always without doubt) American business methods and efficiency, and who, much more than French businessmen, regarded the U.S. economy as a positive, if not entirely transferable, model.[28] The failures of denazification in all three Allied zones may be attributed in part to the fact that, as relations between the Soviet Union and the United States deteriorated, expectations of German industriousness put a premium on using experts who could get the job done regardless of individuals' prior involvement in the Nazi party. This was, of course, a highly controversial subject, and journalists such as William Shirer, a vitriolic critic of Germans, bitterly attacked American troops' less-than-activist approach to denazification with respect to industrial managers and other key figures in German manufacturing industry.[29]

In the tourist industry, the trope of German industriousness also shaped American travelers' consumption habits and promoted shared understandings of the meaning and nature of commercial culture. German industry had been based not only on extensive mass production, but also on a reputation for manufacturing high-quality goods marked by taste and technological excellence. For many Germans, such high-quality production values had symbolized an antidote both to the alleged shoddiness of U.S.-style mass-produced goods and later, in the 1950s, to the appearance of cheap manufactured products from East German industry. Modern production values that had not lost touch with artisanal tradition represented a "third way" between the alternatives of full-scale capitalism and socialist industrialization. As Frank Trommler has argued, German national identity also derived a good part of its resonance from the status given to skilled labor and quality work.[30] The revival of the nylon stocking (Perlon) industry in West Germany was based on precisely this kind of hybridity: an acceptance of modern values of consumerism that still retained the German tradition of "quality work," a value that only one of the postwar Germanys would be allowed to call its own.[31]

But this symbolism had a similar meaning for postwar American travelers. The Fodor guidebook included an essay on shopping in Germany by the American writer Nan Robertson, who also wrote a column on fashion and shopping for the Armed Forces Edition of the *New York Herald Tribune*. She advised tourists to avoid gift shops with English-language signs, arguing they "are run by tradesmen who offer vulgar junk or souvenirs under the misconception that this is what Americans or Britons want."[32] The wise foreign traveler sought out shops where one could find high-quality antiques, Bavarian handicrafts, "clothes from the Dirndl belt," beer steins, binoculars, cameras, candles, clocks, dolls, figurines, *Lederhosen* and loden cloth, porcelain and silver, steelware, and toys. On the landscape of such artifacts and goods, Americans and Germans established a symbiotic relationship grounded simultaneously in a critique of mass production and an embrace of "elite" forms of consumption. This reflected a more general tendency of modern leisure travel in which, as Ellen Furlough has written, "mass tourism's success and appeal from the middle of the twentieth century was due to its ability both to be popularly accessible and to express social distinction and cultural difference."[33] But because American identity had become so thoroughly associated with mass production techniques and industrial discipline, this perspective possibly represented a sharper critique of American tradition for U.S. tourists and soldiers than the insistence on "quality work" and craft production did for West Germans, who returned to these values after World War II. In this regard, the postwar period, so often seen as a moment of one-way imposition of American values on Europe, also included significant movements in the other direction as Americans embraced or adapted to "European" values and representations.

German industriousness and success at rebuilding consumer culture were not equivocally regarded as positive characteristics. George Mikes's satirical Fodor guide essay expressed a degree of discomfort with the "strange mixture of ruins and luxury" one found in Munich. "Shop windows, furnished with exquisite taste and packed with alluring treasures delight your eyes," wrote Mikes, "but you know that a few corpses must be still buried under the ruins, just a few yards from the handbags, jewelry and toys."[34] Much has been written about German reconstruction as a compensatory act enabling a society to avoid full confrontation with its violent history. This was also a recurring theme in travel narratives of the postwar era.[35] Yet it can be argued that Mikes's discomfort had something to do with a realization that the juxtaposition of ruins and luxury was also the product of a kind of intercultural understanding. It was not only Germans who looked to the promises of future prosperity as a balm for the past.[36] Americans too, having experienced economic depression, the social unrest of the 1930s, and the war, viewed consumption as redemption from a past marked by austerity and want. It was not that the past should be forgotten entirely, but the quest for "normalcy" and prosperity were now more important. Thus the Fodor guidebook did not fail to mention Dachau in its section on excursions from Munich. For many Americans, Dachau, liberated by the U.S. army in 1945, had come to stand for the Holocaust, just as Belsen symbolized Nazi atrocities for English audiences much more than Auschwitz did. Dachau, according to the Fodor text, "was notorious for the concentration camp east of it, where a monument to its victims now stands, but before the Nazis provided it with an evil reputation it was a pleasant old town … much frequented by landscape painters, for the beauty of its scenery." "It is also a gayhearted place," the commentary continued, "with a mid-August festival in local costumes and races, not of horses, but of cattle."[37] Touristic value trumped historical significance in this account, just as the luxury items in Munich shop windows deflected the (not quite extinguished) public memory of nearby corpses.

Developing American-German intercultures also gained much impetus from gender relations. Without the slightest embarrassment, the Fodor guidebook duly noted that Tacitus had found women of the Germanic tribes to be unusually chaste and incorruptible. But Tacitus might have raised his eyebrows, the guide stated, at estimates that West Germany now had a 10 percent illegitimacy rate. Elsewhere the guide alluded to the problem of so-called fraternization between U.S. soldiers and German women. It noted Germans' "anger and shame at the spectacle of German women giving themselves for chocolate bars and companionship" in the first years after the war, but it also pointed out that the shame and anger had receded with improved economic conditions. And it suggested that although Germany was still very much "a man's country," German

FIGURE 16. Re-enactment in 1992 of the American Occupation of Munich at the End of World War II

Re-enactment in 1992 of the American occupation of Munich at the end of World War II. At the occasion of the departure of the last three thousand U.S. soldiers from Munich, a German student and a captain of the U.S. Army delight the onlookers on Munich's Marienplatz by acting out the scene with period uniforms and a 1945 jeep. (Bilderdienst Süddeutscher Verlag)

women were now "far removed from the braided Gretchen type, fecund and docile, which was the old ideal of the German male."[38]

Such comments should be understood against the background of an American-German conversation about sexual relations that had begun almost immediately after U.S. soldiers set foot on German soil. The American military's non-fraternization policy had been implemented in part as a reaction to the scope and intensity of contact between U.S. soldiers and the German populace. The policy was a failure with regard to heterosexual relations, as in some companies between 50 and 90 percent of male soldiers went "frattin'" with German women. By 1946 more than two thousand marriages between American soldiers and German women had taken place, and by the mid-1950s more than seven thousand West German women married occupation soldiers annually.[39] Fraternization became a well-known theme in American commercial culture, stimulated by cinematic representations such as those of Billy Wilder in *A Foreign Affair* (1948), or by illustrated magazines such as *Life*, whose sometimes shocked readers found information on how the American military fought sexually transmitted diseases by publicizing a "VD Hall of Fame" featuring only infected German women but not American soldiers.[40]

One should not underestimate the moral outrage expressed by American military elite and public opinion leaders about fraternization. Nor should one forget that for Germans, U.S. soldiers' relations with German women not only appeared to defile women but also represented the larger degradation of national culture at the hands of the occupation. In developing this narrative, Germans forgot that widespread promiscuity and short-term liaisons had become frequent in the last years of the war, not just during the occupation. Furthermore, Germans' sense of degradation, which quickly evolved into a fear of "national rape" in the earliest months of the occupation, resulted in part from the continued effect of Nazi racist propaganda, which had depicted Slavs and American blacks defiling Germany.[41]

Yet it is equally important to point out that U.S. soldiers were responding to a German female sexuality that in many ways seemed more "American" than that which they had encountered in England or France. Once again, the journalist Julian Bach is a good source for understanding the kind of intercultural identity that was being formed.[42] He argues that Americans come from an overly sexualized culture, and thus they were not only more intensely attracted to women, but women were more attracted to them. Yet American soldiers, still Puritans at heart, liked German women partly because, in comparison to French women, they seemed more respectable. French women seemed "fast," while German women would say "no." American soldiers criticized unusually promiscuous German women just as much as Germans did. American soldiers wanted little to do with talk of politics or recent history, and they found willing companions among German women, who, Bach wrote, were among the most politically immature individuals he had ever encountered. Political immaturity aside, neither American soldiers nor their German female companions were unaware that their relationships were rooted in a universal human right. "However sordid love over a chocolate bar and a box of salt water taffy may be," wrote Bach, "it does represent the right of two human beings freely to pick their own associates."[43]

To the (in Bach's mind) considerable degree that Germans understood this, they had already moved in the direction of accepting democracy. The Fodor guide had in any case hit on a particular mix of "chastity," sexuality, and growing independence in its characterization of German women. Bach's discussion suggests that this characterization was rooted in a series of intercultural encounters and sexual understandings over which elites in both national cultures had little control, and which continued to operate once the political twilight period of occupation gave way to the more settled conditions of the 1950s. The recurrent Franco-German comparison also reinforced a long tradition on the part of American journalists, tourists, and novelists that emphasized the sexual license and immorality of French society.[44] In the interwar era, American tourist literature also pinpointed German sexual excess,[45] but the themes of German morality and female respectability always seemed to be stronger.

No single idea was ultimately more important to the Fodor guide's sense of Germany than regional diversity.[46] "Anyone who moves around Western Germany is bound to be most strikingly impressed by the regional differences," read the guide. These differences could be seen not only in the landscapes and towns, but also in the physical characteristics of the people, which ranged "from the small, brown haired, brown eyed Alpine people of the south to the flaxen haired, rawboned, blue eyed northerners." Such diversity struck the guide as rather American insofar as Bavarians detested the Prussians as much as Alabamans or Georgians disliked Yankees. Geographical markers were as distinct in Germany as in America: "The Main River is a sort of Mason-Dixon line in Germany, and those who live north of it consider themselves more cosmopolitan, more liberal, and harder working." Although this passage characterized German attitudes, it nonetheless also reversed a long-standing American discourse in which southern Germany was viewed as the "good" Germany and northern Germany as the Prussianized and militarized "bad" part of the country.[47] It is not surprising to find a tour guide using the geographical and cultural vernacular of tourists to enlighten them and make foreign lands more comprehensible. But once again, there was something more going on in such passages.

Regional diversity had been a significant trope of American identity even before the founding of the nation. Ethnicity played a major role in the formulation of regional characteristics. The consideration of "racial groups" and "national character" was an important part of both scholarly and public discourse on both sides of the Atlantic in the 1930s and 1940s. It is significant that the American Guide Series to American states published in the 1940s by the Work Project Administration often included a section devoted to "racial elements" of the population in a manner that was not at all foreign to guidebook literature for continental Europe between 1919 and 1945.[48] And although Nazism had finally discredited racial thinking and racial categories, touristic literature persisted in the use of a language of racial and ethnic character well into the postwar era. Military life during the occupation was seen by some as a melting pot in miniature, and hence a key element in the continued evolution of an "American character" built out of diverse ethnicities, regions, and experiences.[49] The fundamental question of American identity, the dialogue between unity and multiplicity, could in this context be easily transposed onto German soil.

Yet it was certainly more than a simple transposition. Eric Hobsbawm noted some time ago that "Paradoxically, the most democratic and, both territorially and constitutionally, one of the most clearly defined nations faced a problem of national identity in some respects similar to imperial Germany."[50] Americans had to be "made" out of immigrants who, especially after the middle of the nineteenth century, could not be counted on to have the same customs and values held by the largely Anglo-Saxon populations who no longer constituted the majority of the population. The German nation had to be mobilized from populations with well-established territorial, linguistic, social, and religious traditions rooted in a broad though largely undefined cultural identity, and not from immigrant groups. More than Americans, Germans defined themselves existentially, a point Hobsbawm does not mention in his analysis. Yet the lack of political and territorial unity in Germany resulted in a situation in which both existential and ideological elements, both ethno-cultural and civic definitions, interacted. In either case, the intense dialogue between dispersed and focused identities, between multiplicity and unity, and between "the many" and "the one," was constitutive of nationality. This "dialogue," which at certain moments turned into bloody conflict on both sides of the Atlantic, also gave each nation a constant sense of newness, of discontinuity and malleability, that was perhaps less salient in other national traditions. This implied the corresponding idea of a great need for tradition and history, of which there was an abundant supply in Germany—and for which American tourists and soldiers searched in their travels throughout Europe.

Transatlantic Hybridities

Imagologists debate whether group images are constantly in flux or if they endure for long stretches of time, even when the conditions that produced them have changed or been eliminated. I cannot address that debate here, but it does seem worthwhile to suggest that the matter cannot be reasonably discussed without referring to certain constitutive moments in the history of national images. Such moments rarely create the possibility for a radical departure from previous understandings—a sociologist would argue they are "path-dependent"—but they do seem to lend themselves to important recastings and reformulations. The decade after World War II was certainly one of those moments in the history of intercultural exchange between Americans and Germans. American heteroimages of German cleanliness, industriousness, artisanal production values, history, female sexuality, and regional tradition were in many important ways confirmed as U.S. military government gave way to West German statehood, and as soldiers were joined by an increasing number of American tourists, exchange students, academics, and businessmen. Yet the moment was also unprecedented in the history of American-German relations. Without being able to provide full supporting evidence, one can nonetheless argue that the sheer quantity of interactions resulted in a qualitative shift. It was not only that the "binational perception process" that had characterized such relations in the past continued,[51] but rather that process also resulted in a more intense, sustained, and deliberate kind of interaction that gave rise to a hybrid form. This was not a relationship between two bounded national entities, but a series of emergent, experiential intercultures operating "to the side," as it were, of military government, business corporations, and national states. The degree of "oppositional" value these intercultures had is perhaps less crucial in this context than is the observation that they had the potential of creating new modes of understanding and new sites of intersocietal transfer that worked more like tactical maneuvers than strategic interventions for those who were involved in them. They should not be confused with (although they were undoubtedly related to) a very different and strategic "transnationality" promoted, for example, by major multinational business corporations.

Harold James argues that the Americanization of postwar Germany "was generally not a conscious process."[52] I have already expressed skepticism about the notion of Americanization, but the general point about the unplanned or even subterranean quality of the process is defensible. In addition, one should note the countermovement. It is hardly difficult to find numerous and one-sided criticisms of German society by Americans after World War II.[53] From the other side, anti-American thought in Germany, having been nurtured by twelve years of Nazi propaganda, continued well after Hitler left the scene. Many Germans regarded Americans and Russians as roughly the same: childish, barbaric, naive, and incapable of understanding the profundity of German culture.[54] The juvenile behavior of American servicemen themselves often did little to promote "the American way of life," as numerous studies have shown, and American tourists provided more than enough ammunition for anti-American sentiment.[55]

A tiny minority of intellectuals in postwar Germany hoped for a renascent Prussianism that espoused a high-cultural and universal tradition of austerity equidistant from both American consumerism and

FIGURE 17. Carl Schurz Barracks, 1983

German policemen guard the American barracks in Bremerhaven that carry the name of the most prominent German American, Carl Schurz. On October 15, 1983, German demonstrators chose this installation to express their opposition against U.S. military policies in Germany. (Bilderdienst Süddeutscher Verlag)

Soviet communism. In this view, stated most controversially by Heinrich Hauser, a new "melting pot" made up of occupation forces, displaced persons, refugees, and Germans nested in newly rediscovered and valued homelands was forming in Germany. This hybrid community of "new German thought" would sever forever the bonds that had grown between America and Europe.[56] Hauser's political metaphysics, developed in part during the author's stay in the United States during the war, was ultimately closer to the ideas of the failed conservative resistance to Hitler than to the sentiments of those who encountered Americans in daily life, as Michael Ermarth has noted. On the ground, meanwhile, the interchanges Hauser wanted to end once and for all were evolving with a force and intensity that could hardly be stopped. And Hauser himself admitted that Germans and Americans still had "many traits in common," even as he predicted the opening of an unbridgeable chasm between Europe and the United States.[57]

There are many who argue that that chasm, filled in by the cold war, has now indeed been reopened due to the fall of the Berlin Wall and the larger demise of communism in Europe. Frank Trommler predicts that although Germany has always played a constitutive role in American self-images, it is likely that the twenty-first century will bring more distance between the two cultures, partly because Germany has little to offer to the narrative of America's declining position in the world.[58] This may be true despite institutional efforts to strengthen transatlantic ties. Certainly no one could expect another era of intense intercultural exchange of the kind that existed in the postwar decade and expanded in the Federal Republic in the ensuing years of German-German division. Yet if we turn to more subterranean and everyday processes, if we move from the realm of institutional and official contacts to the messier dynamic whereby images, stereotypes, emotions, and bodily memories shape transnational relations, then perhaps there is reason to be less pessimistic, if not more optimistic.

A dystopic version of the argument for continued and intense interaction may be found in Thomas Molnar's perspective, which envisions an "Atlantic culture" dominated by America, propelled forward by the "triumph of desacralization," but also strangely unidentifiable as a moment of clear American cultural and technological hegemony.[59] More promising (and less counter-intuitive) is a line of analysis that derives new forms of transcultural interchange, if not "understanding," from the increasingly self-reflexive nature of modernity itself, a modernity with which the United States has always been closely identified. If "the American dream"—based not only on unexampled prosperity but also on a melting pot of cultural diversity—has been "dreamed out," then perhaps this is the moment to rethink the dream and adapt it to a new world.[60] A more self-reflexive American identity might quite possibly reopen a discursive space for Germany—and for other cultures as well, since Germany has always been but one of America's "others"—based on a longer history of transnational relations and a deeper emotional fundament of shared attributes as well as prejudices and memories (positive and negative). Just as the history of the Third Reich and World War II has played a big role in American identity in the second half of the twentieth century, a transatlantic memory of the Holocaust shaped in part by new generations of Americans and Germans may be one site on which such interactions will again emerge and become more intense. A self-reflexive identity would encourage broad new intercultures rooted not in the belief of differentiated national identities, but in a more indeterminate process of transsocial mixing dispersed across an array of media, from travel and education to cinema, television, and the Internet. Beneath and between the two national cultures, in the interstices formed by both official and "unofficial" encounters between Germans and Americans, new identities might re-emerge that are neither distinctly German nor American, but something else. It is doubtful that "multiculturalism" has much to offer in this context, because even when its proponents proclaim humane understanding and contact between cultures, they consistently and often unintentionally support both public policy and cultural representations that stress irreducible ethnic and national differences. Perhaps it is time to turn to a recast Eurocentric "universalism," as defined by Slovenian political theorist Slavoj Žižek, as an alternative that both politicizes intercultural contacts and finds common ground for them in a language of shared human rights (including leisure) and equality.[61]

Notes

1. Eugene Fodor, ed., *Germany 1953* (New York, 1953). There were, of course, guidebooks to specific regions and towns, such as Karl Baedeker, ed., *Munich and Its Environs: Handbook for Travellers* (Hamburg, 1950); Karl Baedeker, ed., *Northern Bavaria: Handbook for Travellers* (Hamburg, 1951); and Karl Baedeker, ed., *Southern Bavaria: With Excursions to Innsbruck and Salzburg* (Hamburg, 1953). But the Fodor guide was the first to take in all of (West) Germany. In addition, there were "tour guides" for U.S. military personnel, such as Armed Forces Information and Education Division, ed., *A Pocket Guide to Germany* (Washington, D.C., 1951).
2. Fodor, *Germany 1953*, 7.
3. "The Germans: What They Think and How They Act," in Fodor, *Germany 1953*, 42.
4. The term "melting pot" was discredited in serious discussions of American identity in the 1920s, but it persisted in journalistic and popular usage and enjoyed a revival in academic discussion in the 1950s. The ethnic revival of the 1960s and 1970s again discredited it, but the term continues to reappear in public debate. See Philip Gleason, "American Identity and Americanization," in *Harvard Encyclopedia of American Ethnic Groups*, ed. Stephan Thernstrom (Cambridge, MA, 1980), 39–40.
5. Peter Freese, "Exercises in Boundary-Making: The German as 'Other' in American Literature," in *Germany and German Thought in American Literature and Cultural Criticism*, ed. Peter Freese (Essen, 1990), 111.
6. David E. Barclay and Elisabeth Glaser-Schmidt, eds., *Transatlantic Images and Perceptions: Germany and America since 1776* (Washington, D.C., 1997), 8.

7. My analysis draws in part on recent discussions of "hybridity" and intercultural relations, as discussed most cogently in Susan Friedman, *Mappings: Feminism and the Cultural Geographies of Encounter* (Princeton, NJ, 1998), especially 82–93. See also James Clifford, *Routes: Travel and Translation in the Late Twentieth Century* (Cambridge/London, 1997).

8. I will use the plural "intercultures" because I aim to draw attention, first, to the multiplicity of sites in which Americans and Germans interacted (in military government, tourism, business, journalism, and university and cultural exchanges, for instance). Of course, it is impossible to treat any of these areas comprehensively in this short piece. Second, I want to avoid the connotation that there was a homogeneous or uniform cultural ground on which Americans met Germans. Finally, although the idea of intercultures bears some resemblance to the notions of "contact zones" and "transculturation," as used to good effect by Mary Louise Pratt, I think "intercultures" does a better job of drawing attention to the intermingling or intersection of images and values between two roughly "equivalent" or "Western" cultures than do Pratt's concepts, which are developed to address colonial encounters. For Pratt, see her *Imperial Eyes: Travel Writing and Transculturation* (London/New York, 1992).

9. Hans W. Gatzke, *Germany and the United States: A "Special Relationship"?* (Cambridge, MA/London, 1980).

10. Klaus-Dieter Henke, *Die amerikanische Besetzung Deutschlands* (Munich, 1995), 75; Richard L. Merritt, *Democracy Imposed: U.S. Occupation Policy and the German Public, 1945–1949* (New Haven/London, 1995), 47. On British attitudes in the 1930s: Angela Schwarz, *Die Reise ins Dritte Reich: Britische Augenzeugen im nationalsozialistischen Deutschland (1933–1939)* (Göttingen/Zurich, 1993); and Angela Schwarz, "Image and Reality: British Visitors to National Socialist Germany" *European History Quarterly* 23 (1993): 381–405. One should point out, however, that in an August 1945 survey only 20 percent of the American respondents thought that Germany could learn from World War II and give up its aggressive designs in world politics; see Konrad Jarausch, "Das amerikanische Deutschlandbild in drei Jahrhunderten," in *Das Deutschland- und Amerikabild: Beiträge zum gegenseitigen Verständnis beider Völker*, ed. Klaus Weigelt (Melle, 1986), 16.

11. *Life* (10 May 1954), 34.

12. On film, see Dietmar Haack, "The Mortal Storm: Stereotypical Frames," in *Mediating a Foreign Culture: The United States and Germany. Studies in Intercultural Understanding*, ed. Lothar Bredella (Tübingen, 1991), 93–107; on liberal identity, Gleason, "American Identity and Americanization," 48.

13. Pearl S. Buck, "Letter to Germany," *Common Ground* VI, 2 (Winter 1946): 3–10, here 6.

14. Foster Rhea Dulles, *Americans Abroad: Two Centuries of European Travel* (Ann Arbor, 1964), 170–73; Organization for European Economic Co-operation, ed., *Tourism and European Recovery: An OEEC Report* (Paris, 1951), 11–26.

15. Statistisches Bundesamt, ed., *Statistisches Jahrbuch für die Bundesrepublik Deutschland* (Stuttgart/Cologne, 1954), 364; Statistisches Bundesamt, ed., *Statistisches Jahrbuch für die Bundesrepublik Deutschland* (Stuttgart, 1956), 340. The high number of overnight stays was no doubt related to the fact that when U.S. tourists traveled to Europe, they tended to stay longer than European tourists did. No comparative statistics on this matter were available, but in *Tourism and European Recovery*, 21, it was reported that on average American tourists stayed 63 days in Europe, as compared with 52 days in 1937–38.

16. Fodor, *Germany 1953*, 24.

17. Freese, "Exercises in Boundary-Making," 121–22, argues that the image of German cleanliness and orderliness had its counterpoint in an equally strong image of German gluttony and drunkenness.

18. Julian Bach, Jr., *America's Germany: An Account of the Occupation* (New York, 1946), 271.

19. Paul M. Sweezy, "Germany from the Ruins," *The New Republic* 144, 16 (22 April 1946): 586. Sweezy also reviewed Saul K. Padover, *Experiment in Germany: The Story of an American Intelligence Officer* (New York, 1945). Taken together, Bach and Padover gave the most informed account of the first stages of American occupation at that time, but

Sweezy noted that while Padover's book was more analytical, Bach's was more timely and more knowledgeable in its assessment of soldiers' attitudes.

20. See Josef Bürckel, ed., *Kampf um die Saar* (Stuttgart, 1934).

21. See Paul Monaco, "Stereotypes of Germans in American Culture: Observations from an Interdisciplinary Perspective," in *Amerikanisches Deutschlandbild und deutsches Amerikabild*, ed. Frank Krampowski (Baltmannsweiler, 1990), 176, note 2.

22. Armed Forces Information and Education Division, *A Pocket Guide to Germany*, 5.

23. See the illustrated publication by Kurt Zentner, ed., *Aufstieg aus dem Nichts: Deutschland von 1945 bis 1953. Eine Soziographie in zwei Bänden*, 2 vols. (Cologne/Berlin, 1954).

24. Fodor, *Germany 1953*, 120.

25. George Mikes, "A Satirical Glance. Danger: Men at Work!" in *Germany 1953*, 53–56.

26. Baedeker, *Northern Bavaria*, 5.

27. Volker R. Berghahn, "West German Reconstruction and American Industrial Culture, 1945–1960," in *The American Impact on Postwar Germany*, ed. Reiner Pommerin (Providence/Oxford, 1995), 65–81, here 73.

28. See Mary Nolan, *Visions of Modernity: American Business and the Modernization of Germany* (New York/Oxford, 1994); Alexander Schmidt, *Reisen in die Moderne: Der Amerika-Diskurs des deutschen Bürgertums vor dem Ersten Weltkrieg im europäischen Vergleich* (Berlin, 1997), 138–53.

29. William L. Shirer, *End of a Berlin Diary* (New York, 1947), 306–07.

30. See Frank Trommler, "The Historical Invention and Modern Reinvention of Two National Identities" in *Identity and Intolerance: Nationalism, Racism, and Xenophobia in Germany and the United States*, ed. Norbert Finzsch and Dietmar Schirmer (Washington, D.C., 1998): 21–42.

31. See Erica Carter, *How German Is She? Postwar West German Reconstruction and the Consuming Woman* (Ann Arbor, 1997), 164–70.

32. Nan Robertson, "Shopping in Germany," in *Germany 1953*, 83.

33. Ellen Furlough, "Making Mass Vacations: Tourism and Consumer Culture in France, 1930s to 1970s," *Comparative Studies in Society and History* 40, 2 (April 1998): 247–86, here 248.

34. Mikes, "A Satirical Glance," *Germany 1953*, 53–54.

35. See, e.g., Carlo Levi, *The Two-fold Night: A Narrative of Travel in Germany*, trans. Joseph M. Bernstein (London, 1962).

36. Ralph Willett, *The Americanization of Germany, 1945–1949* (London/New York, 1989), 121, 127.

37. Fodor, *Germany 1953*, 253–54.

38. Ibid., 38, 48.

39. Elizabeth D. Heineman, "The Hour of the Woman: Memories of Germany's 'Crisis Years' and West German National Identity," *American Historical Review* 101 (1996): 381. See also Elizabeth D. Heineman, *What Difference Does a Husband Make? Women and Marital Status in Nazi and Postwar Germany* (Berkeley/Los Angeles/London, 1999), 95–107; and Henke, *Die amerikanische Besetzung Deutschlands*, 185–204.

40. "Occupied Germany: *Life* Presents a Progress Report on the U.S. Zone," *Life* (10 February 1947): 91, where it was stated that American soldiers were more "victims than culprits" in the matter of venereal disease. On Wilder, see Willett, *Americanization of Germany*, 28–44.

41. See Heineman, "The Hour of the Woman"; idem, *What Difference Does a Husband Make?* 96; Lutz Niethammer, "Privat-Wirtschaft: Erinnerungsfragmente einer anderen Umerziehung," in *"Hinterher merkt man, daß es richtig war, daß es schiefgegangen ist": Nachkriegs-Erfahrungen im Ruhrgebiet*, ed. Lutz Niethammer, vol. 2 of *Lebensgeschichte und Sozialkultur im Ruhrgebiet 1930 bis 1960* (Bonn, 1983), especially 22–34.

42. For the following, see Bach, *America's Germany*, 71–83, 235, 268–69.

43. Ibid., 81. Given the degree to which the U.S. military and the German police violated the civil rights of German women in their attempts to control sexually transmitted diseases, "fraternizers'" liaisons with U.S. soldiers did have a kind of "oppositional"

quality. On "vice-raids" and other methods whereby "fraternization" was regulated, see Heineman, *What Difference Does a Husband Make?* 102–3.

44. See Harvey Levenstein, *Seductive Journey: American Tourists in France from Jefferson to the Jazz Age* (Chicago/London, 1998), 198–203.
45. An example: Arthur Milton, *Berlin in Seven Days: A Guide for People in a Hurry* (New York, 1935), 65–66.
46. For the following, Fodor, *Germany 1953*, 42–43.
47. See Freese, "Exercises in Boundary-Making," 115–19. The destruction of Prussia may have made it possible to consider northern Germany independently of the heritage of Prussian militarism after World War II.
48. See, e.g., Michigan State Administrative Board, ed., *Michigan: A Guide to the Wolverine State*, American Guide Series (New York, 1941), 103–112.
49. Gleason, "American Identity and Americanization," 47–48.
50. Eric Hobsbawm, "Mass-Producing Traditions: Europe, 1870–1914," in *The Invention of Tradition*, ed. Eric Hobsbawm and Terence Ranger (Cambridge, 1983), 279.
51. The term is used by Jörg Nagler, "From Culture to *Kultur*: Changing American Perceptions of Imperial Germany, 1870–1914," in Barclay and Glaser-Schmidt, *Transatlantic Images and Perceptions*, 146.
52. Harold James, *A German Identity, 1770–1990* (New York, 1989), 188.
53. For numerous examples, see Dagmar Barnouw, *Germany 1945: Views of War and Violence* (Bloomington/Indianapolis, 1996).
54. For a well-argued but ultimately overdrawn discussion of anti-Americanism in Germany, see Dan Diner, *Verkehrte Welten: Antiamerikanismus in Deutschland. Ein historischer Essay* (Frankfurt, 1993). Diner discusses the similarities between Americans and Russians in German perceptions at page 124.
55. On U.S. troop behavior, see John Gimbel, *A German Community under American Occupation: Marburg 1945–52* (Stanford, 1961), 69–70.
56. See Heinrich Hauser, *The German Talks Back* (New York, 1945); Michael Ermarth, "*The German Talks Back*: Heinrich Hauser and German Attitudes toward Americanization after World War II," in *America and the Shaping of German Society, 1945–1955*, ed. Michael Ermarth (Providence/Oxford, 1993), especially 126–28.
57. Hauser, *The German Talks Back*, 87.
58. Frank Trommler, "Unification Policies and the German Image: Comments on the American Reaction," in Barclay and Glaser-Schmidt, *Transatlantic Images and Perceptions*, 353–61.
59. Thomas Molnar, *The Emerging Atlantic Culture* (New Brunswick/London, 1994).
60. See Alf Lüdtke, Inge Marßolek, and Adelheid von Saldern, "Einleitung," in *Amerikanisierung: Traum und Alptraum im Deutschland des 20. Jahrhunderts*, ed. Alf Lüdtke, Inge Marßolek, and Adelheid von Saldern (Stuttgart, 1996), especially 32–33.
61. See Slavoj Žižek, "A Leftist Plea for 'Eurocentrism,'" *Critical Inquiry* 24 (1998): 988–1009.

— *Chapter 12* —

THE JEWISH ROLE IN
GERMAN-AMERICAN RELATIONS

Lily Gardner Feldman

Introduction

From the early days of the American occupation of Germany until the late 1990s, there has been a constant, yet changing, Jewish role in German-American relations. "Jewish role" can be defined in three ways: a long-term, institutionalized relationship between organized American Jewry and Germany as an autonomous element of societal connections between the two countries; the attempt on the part of American Jewry to influence German-American relations at the official political level in both Germany and the United States; and the actual influence by American Jewry on the outcome of bilateral ties. These activities have involved both organizations and key individuals. Here, then, "role" does not embrace the attitudes toward Germany of American Jewry at large.[1]

Since 1945, the Jewish role has exhibited eight principal features:

1. The Jewish role in German-American relations has never been monolithic, but has incorporated a variety of perspectives from disinclination, or a non-role, to minimal involvement to active engagement.
2. The Jewish role has evolved from a reactive stance in the postwar period to an agenda-setting position in the 1990s. The quiet, unheralded efforts of the first twenty years transformed into more open efforts in the 1980s, reaching an apex of focused public affairs and lobbying in the 1990s.
3. What was often an ancillary or parallel role through the mid-1980s began to intersect directly with German-American relations in the late 1980s.
4. In the 1990s, the Jewish role has become a central dimension of the political, economic, and cultural relationship between Germany and the United States.

5. The issue of compensation for victims of Nazism has constituted a central theme of Jewish activity, but other issues have emerged over time, including positions on German domestic and foreign policy topics of significance in the official American relationship with Germany.
6. The activities of Jewish individuals and organizations have displayed two means by which nongovernmental organizations can affect official foreign policy: attempting to influence government policy in the home country, or directly building a relationship with the government of the other country.
7. Until the 1990s, the dominant activity was undertaken by American Jewish individuals and organizations, but since unification it has been accompanied by a German Jewish effort to be involved with the United States.
8. Since the 1980s, the German government has actively and publicly sought an American Jewish role in the bilateral relationship.

The following observations focus on the character and consequences of the Jewish role in German-American relations in the 1990s. They start with an assessment of the changes that took place in the 1980s, enabling the active public-shaping role in transatlantic ties a decade later. The American Jewish Committee (AJC) is the main example, since it assumed the principal Jewish role in German-American relations in the 1990s.

Building Societal and Official Ties in the 1980s

The Israeli scholar Shlomo Shafir has demonstrated the ambiguity and limits of an American Jewish dimension in German-American relations into the 1980s in the two domains of activity that constitute a role: the development of ties to German society and the influence on official American policy.[2]

After the failure of the AJC's "Operation Candle" program in the 1950s, which called for engagement and constructive cooperation with Germany (rather than ostracism) through visits to the United States by Germans, and education in Germany about Judaism, there was a pattern of relative nonengagement of American Jewish organizations with German society, although the AJC did maintain small efforts at education in Germany.[3] The Anti-Defamation League of B'nai B'rith shared a similar assumption about the potential for German democracy, with irregular contacts in the 1950s and 1960s. According to Shafir, the American Jewish Congress and the World Jewish Congress (except for Nahum Goldmann) remained steadfastly "critical and skeptical" in the first three decades.

At the level of official relations, results were mixed until the 1980s. In the late 1940s and early 1950s, Jewish opposition (albeit hardly uniform) to the American embrace of Germany as a major ally had failed, although Jewish individuals such as Jacob Blaustein and Nahum Goldmann did

FIGURE 18. The Reagans at Bergen-Belsen, 1985

President Ronald Reagan and his wife Nancy Reagan visit the concentration camp Bergen-Belsen accompanied by the prime minister of Lower Saxony, Ernst Albrecht as part of Reagan's state visit to West Germany in 1985. The stop at Bergen-Belsen was added to convey a more sensitive attitude of the president toward the Holocaust because his trip had included an ill-conceived visit to the Bitburg cemetery where members of the Waffen SS were buried. (Bilderdienst Süddeutscher Verlag)

affect American policy on Germany's reparations and restitution obligations, exemplified in the 1952 Luxembourg Reparations Agreement.[4] In the 1960s, Jewish leaders did influence the emergence of a sense-of-Congress resolution, pressing the President to pressure the German government to extend the statute of limitations on war crimes. Jewish leadership, particularly in the person of Nahum Goldmann, played a role in the official pursuit by the U.S. government of Jewish property claims in the process of establishing diplomatic relations with East Germany in the 1970s. Yet a decade later, American Jewish leaders were not able to prevent President Reagan's 1985 visit to the Bitburg cemetery, an event that for Chancellor Kohl demonstrated the reality of German-American reconciliation. Bitburg, however, became a turning point in the Jewish role in German-American relations, particularly for the American Jewish Committee, which developed a structured institutional relationship with key elements of German society in the 1980s (as did B'nai B'rith, to a lesser extent).[5]

With Bitburg, for the first time since the 1950s, organized American Jewry was forced to confront its feelings toward Germany in a comprehensive, systemwide sense. Three other factors compelled the AJC to consolidate and institutionalize the ties it had already forged with the Konrad-Adenauer-Stiftung (1981) and the Friedrich-Ebert-Stiftung (1983), and to expand them to other organizations such as the Atlantik-Brücke, and other venues, such as East Germany:[6] a marked growth in Holocaust consciousness among American Jewry, exhibited concretely in plans for a Holocaust memorial museum in Washington, D.C., and the creation of the Simon Wiesenthal Center in Los Angeles; a recognition of "Germany's growing international prominence,"[7] including its role in the European Community, an understanding already registered by David Ben-Gurion and Israel in the early 1950s; and the open effort by the German government to deepen ties with the American Jewish community, now considered the "main torchbearers of the Ashkenazic heritage," and a political force in American politics and foreign policy.[8] Until the early 1980s, in its efforts to confront the past the German government had centered most of its attention on the Israeli government and society.

The institutionalized societal ties of the 1980s, coupled with the presence in the German Embassy in Washington of a diplomat assigned to active engagement with the Jewish community, furthered intensive interactions between the American Jewish Committee and German political leaders. With German unification, the AJC essentially endorsed the American government's trust in Germany as a stable, robust democracy.

Influencing the Official Agenda of
German-American Relations in the 1990s

After unification, the AJC's connections to German political leadership expanded even further through regular visits to Germany, where Jewish leaders have encountered open access at the highest levels of the German government, and through encounters in Washington and New York, including the AJC's annual meetings, at which the German chancellor and German foreign minister have been featured regularly.[9] The broadening of ties was facilitated by the creation of a European affairs section of the AJC and, in 1992, a Center for German-Jewish Relations.[10]

Topics of discussion have ranged from German and European Union Middle East policy to Libya, Iran, and Iraq—i.e., areas of interest for American foreign policy in general—and issues of particular concern to American Jews, namely anti-Semitism and xenophobia, Holocaust remembrance and education, and compensation for forgotten Jewish victims of Nazism. The latter two areas reveal the significant role of American Jewry in contemporary German-American relations, as the Berlin Republic signals its priorities and identity to the United States and the United States recalibrates its relationship with post-unification Germany. The American Jewish Committee, then, has contributed to the salience of history in current German-American relations in its influence on both the American government and the German government.

Compensation to Forgotten Victims

After a period of unsuccessful private overtures to the German government, beginning in 1995, to provide compensation to Eastern European victims who had been excluded from Germany's compensation and restitution legislation, the American Jewish Committee launched a multipronged public campaign in spring 1997. Its operations included a May 7 advertisement in the *New York Times*; a special citation at the AJC's annual meeting to the German Green Bundestag member Winfried Nachtwei, with whom the AJC had been working to keep the issue on the German political agenda, for his efforts on compensation; expanded meetings with German officials such as President Roman Herzog and Chancellery Minister Friedrich Bohl; increased lobbying with congressional leaders, including a press conference on Capitol Hill (with German Bundestag members, U.S. congressmen, and Jan Karski) and a letter from eighty-two senators to Chancellor Kohl; and overtures to President Clinton, resulting in agreement to place the topic of compensation on his agenda with Chancellor Kohl.[11] In fall 1997, Germany began to negotiate with the Conference on Jewish Material Claims Against Germany, and in January 1998 Germany agreed to provide compensation to approximately 18,000 forgotten victims.[12]

The AJC's ability to deal directly with the German government has been enhanced since January 1998 by the opening of an office in Berlin; the importance the German government attaches to the organization was demonstrated in the ceremonial opening. In the summer of 1998, Chancellor Kohl acknowledged the role of the American Academy and the American Jewish Committee in fostering new ties between Germany and the United States in his welcoming remarks to President Clinton on the fiftieth anniversary of the Berlin Airlift. American officials also displayed their support for the AJC's initiative at the 1998 opening, as they had in March 1997 when the Amerika Haus in Berlin hosted an AJC conference to inaugurate that organization's programs in Germany's new capital. The AJC's purpose in Germany involves monitoring anti-Semitism, supporting Israel, maintaining contact with Jewish communities in Eastern Europe, and providing a meeting point for American Jews.[13]

The Role of American Officials

Stuart Eizenstat, an honorary vice president of the AJC, emerged as the Clinton administration's key official on the issue of Holocaust-era assets, first during his ambassadorship to the European Union, when he was appointed President Clinton's special representative on Jewish property claims in Eastern Europe; then as Under Secretary of Commerce, when he oversaw the U.S. government report on "Nazi gold," and more recently as Under Secretary of State for Economic, Business and Agricultural Affairs, when he hosted the Washington Conference on Holocaust-Era Assets (November 30–December 3, 1998), which emphasized art, insurance, communal property, and Holocaust education, remembrance, and research.[14] In an article written after the publication of the U.S. government's report on gold, Eizenstat emphasized that priority should be given to the forgotten, or "double" victims (of Nazism and communism) who had received little or no compensation from Germany.[15]

Ambassador Eizenstat also has served as the chief American official interlocutor in lengthy and difficult negotiations with Chancellor Schröder's representatives (first Bodo Hombach, then Otto Lambsdorff) on the topic of slave and forced labor. Eizenstat changed his office again, finally serving as the Deputy Secretary of the Treasury, but his role in compensation questions continued.

The negotiations on slave and forced labor are part of the Social Democratic Party (SPD)/Green government's commitment to addressing issues of history. As a sign of moral remorse, but also as a highly pragmatic attempt to end "the campaign being led against German industry and our country," Schröder announced in February 1999 the creation of the "Remembrance, Responsibility and the Future" fund, to be financed by German companies and the German government. The German government and German industry were concerned about the incalculable effect of class action suits, and the efforts of Alan Havesi, the highest financial officer of the state of New York, to delay the merger of Deutsche Bank with Bankers Trust until clarification of compensation.[16] Just before talks in Washington in October 1999, the AJC placed a half-page advertisement in the Op-Ed section of the *New York Times*, entitled "Justice Delayed … Justice Denied." While lauding the progress in creating the fund, the AJC found German industry's response "insufficient" and called on it to be "forthcoming."[17] At the end of September, the AJC had appealed directly to 117 German companies on the slave and forced labor question. Other Jewish organizations placed similar advertisements in American newspapers. The negotiations reached a successful conclusion in July 2000, involving a pledge to pay DM10 billion to be shared equally by the government and industry.[18]

Given the perceived centrality of economic relations as the new post-unification "glue" in transatlantic ties, compensation for victims of Nazism, a key priority of the American Jewish Committee, has transformed from a sectional concern to a shaping element of German-American ties.[19] In light of the institutionalization of ties with the American and German governments, its physical presence in Germany, and a large agenda (from outstanding issues of restitution and compensation to the Middle East peace process, from human rights in Central and Eastern Europe to minority rights in Germany), the Jewish role in German-American relations, as exemplified by the activities of the American Jewish Committee, is likely to grow as the Berlin Republic takes physical shape.

Remembrance

Germans involved in a central aspect of the emerging Berlin profile—the decision and design concerning the memorial to Europe's murdered Jews—including Minister of State for Culture Michael Naumann, Mayor Eberhard Diepgen, and members of the Bundestag Cultural Affairs Committee, have already canvassed American Jewish views, particularly those of the American Jewish Committee; and the AJC co-sponsored a conference at Princeton University in April 1999 with the principal players. Michael Blumenthal, former Secretary of the Treasury in the United States, in his capacity as Director of the Jewish Museum in Berlin (designed by the American architect Daniel Libeskind), has mediated in the arduous process of altering the proposal of Peter Eisenman, the American architect. In the summer of 1999, a decision was made in favor of the proposal for a memorial and an educational site. The new Germany's interpretation of its history and its representation in contemporary politics and culture are thus also being filtered through the lens of American Jewish opinion and perceived American Jewish influence.

Conclusion

As to the future Jewish role in German-American relations, five probabilities emerge:

1. The AJC will continue as a major actor, with increased prominence and capacity given to its office in Berlin. There could well be more examples of the fall 1999 efforts of the AJC and German

organizations to act together in other areas, such as the joint activity in providing aid to Kosovo refugees in Macedonia and earthquake victims in Turkey.

2. The AJC will continue to act as a complement to the United States government, but there is also the increasing possibility that it can act as a conduit for the United States government—and be a source of conflict.

3. Increased tension has developed among American Jewish groups and between American Jewish and European Jewish representatives over the appropriate approach to restitution, and could grow as the compensation issue moves forward.[20]

4. With the presence of American Jewish organizations in Germany, American Jewish religious practices, particularly Conservative Judaism, may impact German Jewish religious preferences, which already are undergoing transformation for reasons of generational change and the influx of Jewish immigrants from the former Soviet Union and Soviet bloc. As the AJC furthers its ties *in situ* with the German government, it could also affect the way the German Jewish community deals with the German political elite.

5. In the future, our analytical scope must be widened from German-American relations to transatlantic ties, for American Jewish organizations have begun to recognize the importance of the European Union, whether on questions of minority rights or the Middle East peace process.

The Jewish role in German-American relations has been multifaceted and effective, and will continue to be a vital element reminding us of history while attending to the international issues of the twenty-first century. The attempt and reality of influence is a normal occurrence.[21] Other minorities play a similar role—Irish Americans regarding the peace process in Northern Ireland, for example. The multitude of voices in foreign policy is a sign of democracy at the end of the twentieth century.

Notes

1. For attitudes toward Germany, see The American Jewish Committee, *1997 Annual Survey of American Jewish Opinion* (New York, 1997). On the related issue of Jewish "power," see J. J. Goldberg, *Jewish Power: Inside the American Jewish Establishment* (Reading, MA, 1996).

2. Shlomo Shafir, *Ambiguous Relations: The American Jewish Community and Germany Since 1945* (Detroit, 1999).

3. The American Jewish Committee, "The American Jewish Committee and Germany: A Summary of Programs, 1945–1994" (New York, February 1994).

4. For Blaustein's role, see the contribution by Yeshayahu Jelinek to Axel Frohn, ed., "Holocaust and Shilumim: The Policy of *Wiedergutmachung* in the Early 1950s," German

Historical Institute, Occasional Paper no. 2 (Washington, D.C., 1991). On Goldmann's efforts, see Rolf Vogel, ed., *The German Path to Israel* (London, 1969), 36–37.

5. See, e.g., the November 1985 observations of Daniel Thursz, the executive vice president of B'nai B'rith, on return from his first visit to Germany since the 1950s, in Michael Neiditch, "Some Jewish Perspectives on Germany's Attempt to Come to Terms with Hitler and the Nazi Era," a paper presented to the conference on "Vergangenheitsbewältigung in Post–World War II German Literature," American Institute for Contemporary German Studies/Johns Hopkins University (Washington, D.C., April 1986).

6. The AJC's connection to the East German Jewish community, and therefore to the East German government, had already begun in 1983. See Angelika Timm, *Jewish Claims Against East Germany: Moral Obligation and Pragmatic Policy* (Budapest, 1997), 33–34.

7. The American Jewish Committee, "The American Jewish Committee and Germany," 1.

8. Statement by German Ambassador Günther van Well before the B'nai B'rith International, Washington, D.C., 21 May 1985. Since the early 1950s, Germany had been concerned about changing American Jewish opinion toward Germany, and employed American Jewish individuals in its public relations efforts (see Shafir, op. cit., chap. 10).

9. For details, see the *AJC Journal*, the organization's monthly publication.

10. For illustrations of AJC activities with Germany, see the organization's reports of meetings, including "Current Concerns in Germany and in German-American Jewish Relations," Summary of a Conference Held by the American Jewish Committee and the Atlantik-Brücke, New York, 17–19 January 1993; "Current Concerns in American Jewish-German-Israeli Relations," Summary of a Conference Held by the American Jewish Committee and the Atlantik-Brücke, Jerusalem, 9–12 March 1994; "The Jewish Dimension in German-American Relations: Perceptions and Realities," Amerika Haus, Berlin, 3–4 March 1997. See also The American Jewish Committee, "The American Jewish Committee and Germany" (New York, August 1998).

11. For details, see Andrew Baker's AJC pamphlet, *Unfinished Business: Compensation and Restitution for Holocaust Survivors* (New York, 1997); *AJC Journal*, June 1997, April 1998.

12. See *Süddeutsche Zeitung*, 13 January 1998.

13. On the opening of the AJC's Berlin office, see *New York Times*, 10 February 1998; *Frankfurter Allgemeine Zeitung*, 14 January 1998. On the inaugural conference of March 1997, see *Der Tagesspiegel*, 4, 5, 6 March 1997; *Süddeutsche Zeitung*, 3 March 1997; The American Jewish Committee, "The Jewish Dimension in German-American Relations"; The American Jewish Committee, "The American Jewish Committee and the AJC Berlin Office" (Berlin, 1998).

14. See Department of State, "U.S. and Allied Efforts to Recover and Restore Gold and Other Assets Stolen or Hidden by Germany During World War II," preliminary study, Publication 10468, Bureau of Public Affairs, Office of the Historian, May 1997; and the supplement of June 1998, Department of State Publication 10557. The Holocaust-era assets report is available on the State Department's web site: http://www.state.gov/www/regions/eur/holocausthp.html, where related remarks, testimonies, and briefings also can be found. For an overview of the issue of material restitution and compensation, see *CQ Researcher*, Congressional Quarterly, vol. 9, no. 12, 26 March 1999.

15. See "Reparations for Nazis' Victims," *International Herald Tribune*, 12 May 1997.

16. *New York Times*, 17 February 1999; *Süddeutsche Zeitung*, 15, 16 February 1999; *Financial Times*, 15, 16 April 1999.

17. *New York Times*, 4 October 1999, p. A31.

18. *The Washington Post*, 18 December 1999.

19. See "Der Faktor Glaubwürdigkeit," *Süddeutsche Zeitung*, 21 December 1998; Josef Joffe, "Ein guter Ruf ist Gold wert," *Süddeutsche Zeitung*, 18 February 1999; Heribert Prantl, "Die Zeit der Ausflüchte ist vorbei," *Süddeutsche Zeitung*, 17 February 1999.

20. See, e.g., Theo Klein, "Putting a Price on Holocaust Guilt," *New York Times*, 15 December 1998.

21. David A. Harris, "American Jews and U.S. Foreign Policy," in *Amerikanisches Judentum heute/American Jewry Today*, ed. Ursula Mantell-Oomen (Trier, 1999), 41–60.

Chapter 13

THE ISRAELI AND GERMAN HOLOCAUST DISCOURSES AND THEIR TRANSATLANTIC DIMENSION

Moshe Zuckermann

The recognition that Israel's and Germany's discourses on the Holocaust differ substantially can be considered merely obvious. Since Germany is grasped, canonized, and treated as the "country of the perpetrators" and Israel as the "country of the victims," the different perspectives in dealing with the memory of the Holocaust are as if inscribed into the abstract concept of the "country." No one would think of seeing Germany as *not* the country of the perpetrators, just as no one, or very few, would question whether Israel is the "country of the victims."

Of course, the latter claim raises substantial questions. As is well known, the *state* of Israel did not exist at the time when the mass annihilation of European Jewry took place in this century. And when Israel was founded in 1948, it was established on a territory far away from the historical region of the catastrophe. Thus, no Holocaust victims were Israeli citizens (or even members of the pre-state phase of the Jewish community living in Palestine). After 1945, many of the Holocaust survivors immigrated initially to Palestine and then to the just-founded state of Israel, but a large number of survivors did *not* do so, moving instead to other countries. From the beginning, Israel claimed a monopoly on official, state commemoration of the Holocaust, as well as the right to represent the interests of the survivors; this was not a logically necessary matter of course, though it is understandable against the background of the accelerated establishment of a "Jewish state" precisely as a consequence of the catastrophe.

Zionism, increasing in strength since 1945, not only viewed the Holocaust as the irrefutable argument justifying its own political solution to the "Jewish question" that had recently turned into a catastrophe; it also objectified this understanding of history through a massive co-optation and instrumentalization of the memory of the victims, as well as through a political-ideological way of dealing with the survivors. This resulted in an *objective* (i.e., *not* intentional) discrepancy between the Holocaust survivors who had arrived in Israel and the state-sustaining Zionist ideology: to the degree that state Zionism, based on the doctrine negating the diaspora, understood the Holocaust as the ultimate manifestation of what must be negated, it could, in the end see the surviving victims of the catastrophe only as examples of living warnings against what must be negated. The survivors personified everything that the so-called "national renewal" sought to overcome, and they paradigmatically embodied the "Diaspora Jews," who were to be replaced by the "New Jews." This historical confrontation had several dimensions, ranging from the ignorant, arrogant question of many Israelis, "How could you let yourselves be led like lambs to the slaughter?" and the thus implied coupling of "heroic courage" with the "Shoah" in the title of the official, state-established Holocaust memorial day, through Israeli silence about the Holocaust in the 1950s at the same time that German expiation was materialized in the restitution payment treaty of 1952, to the ideology, proclaimed with immense Zionist pathos, of the "new beginning" now possible in the new country. This must be understood correctly: that many of the Holocaust survivors needed precisely *such* an ideology to help them survive, and that many became Zionists as the "conclusion" drawn from the horror of their own biographies, does not change the fact that the objectively existing discrepancy indeed had an *objective* effect, namely of a chasm, almost impossible to bridge, between the individual realities of personal life worlds (or *psychological* grappling) and the official, state sphere, which not only had to ignore these worlds of life for material and political reasons, but which also had to work directly *against* the aspects of victimization, helplessness, shock and horror, disease, and despair that dominated the psychological-mental world of the survivors. The opposition between the image of the healthy, self-defending, productive "New Jew" and the (stereotyped) idea of the sick, weak, and helpless Holocaust survivor could be overcome only ideologically—specifically, through a unified ideology of "homecoming," a "melting pot," and a "new beginning." The Holocaust survivors' personal internalization of this state-mandated "overcoming" characterizes both the (aforementioned) socially legitimated *private survival strategy* and the collective ideological aspect of the "new consciousness" or the reformulated "new identity" demanded by the new state.

It is thus the "Jew after Auschwitz" that Zionism very soon could use to its own purposes. The "Jew after Auschwitz" became the irrefutable argument of the Jews' historical teleology as construed by the secular national movement: if anyone still needed proof of the urgent need to establish a Jewish national homeland, world history had furnished such proof incontrovertibly. But since this representation was formulated from an *objective* standpoint, the protagonists of what had been functionalized as a national argument had to be removed from their self-determined, subjective identities (whose contours would be very difficult to reconstruct). The anonymization of the victims, as manifested in the industrial mass destruction, paradoxically continued *mutatis mutandis* in the Zionist ideologization of their fate—a concomitant of adducing their memory as a national historical argument.

Thus seen, the historical event of the Holocaust and its Zionist ideologization were from the beginning complementarily coupled with the double-term of the Holocaust as turning point—in the sense of a breakdown of civilization (*Zivilisationsbruch*) on the one hand, and as the hub of modern Jewish national history on the other. To the degree that the Holocaust was not grasped as a catastrophe of humanity, but as the Shoah of the Jews, the structural foundations for co-optation by particularistic—i.e., nationalistic—interpretation were in a sense already laid. Since the individual group identities of the murdered victims evaporated in the "six million" code, making the "Jews" an overarching, discrepancy-eliminating category, and since, beyond that, those survivors who did *not* immigrate to Israel did not form any clearly identifiable, autonomous social group in their new countries, while those who *did* immigrate to Israel were, for years, not mentioned, Zionism could occupy the vacated historical space and fill it with meaning. Thus, senselessness as the culmination of civilizational development (namely, the orgy of murder for its own sake, and thus the certainty of the constant potential to regress into barbarity) was given a somehow "positive" secular sense, which made the (historically quite understandable) co-optation of the monstrosity a heteronomous ideology, not only in regard to the *particularistic* political interest, but also in regard to the nature of what happened in Auschwitz, in its *universalistic* civilizational context. This is hardly surprising, for the silence about the Holocaust (and the initial inability even to begin to understand what had happened) accompanied, from the beginning, a clear practical interest: the political solution of the "Jewish question," i.e., making the unprevented past catastrophe an argument for preventing a future one. But because this meant a fundamental rejection of all Jewish efforts at assimilation or acculturation, the universal perspective was automatically blocked. One could be in favor of the instrumentalization of the Holocaust by the newly founded Israel and the materialization of expiation by the so-called "other Germany" as the unspoken complementary relationship of *particularistic* interests, but Hannah Arendt's *Eichmann in Jerusalem*—the idea of a *universal* banality of evil arising from modern civilization—had to remain untranslated in Israel to the present day.

The reception of the Holocaust presented Israel supposedly unambiguously as the (new) country of the *victims*, and just as indubitably, Germany as the country of the *perpetrators* seemed obligated to wrestle with the past. But while Israel first had to be founded and the collective subject of enshrined memory constituted, the issue was quite different for Germany: there wasn't one Germany, but two. The German Democratic Republic understood itself as the heir of antifascist Germany, thus eluding the debate in passing. But the Federal Republic, bastion of the "other Germany" newly conceived by the West in the course of the cold war that had meanwhile broken out, saw itself forced to carry out the ideological-political purification ritual of "*Vergangenheitsbewältigung*," of "dealing with the past."

Early on, the division (and the reunification) of Germany proved to be the latent matrix of West German dealings with the past. The postwar era's government policy orientation toward a "smooth" transition was anchored to a striving for Germany's reunification and to a relationship with Israel aimed at "restitution." Meanwhile, running increasingly counter to the restorative climate of the 1950s, a new tone emerged in the politically articulated public arena of the old Federal Republic of Germany. The New Left's critique of existing conditions was explosively antiauthoritarian, whereby the rebellion against traditional authorities understood itself *mutatis mutandis* as a concrete grappling with the German historical catastrophe in the twentieth century and drew its moral legitimation partly from its uncompromising "score-settling" with the Nazi past of the parental generation. This topos later developed into an integral part of the political-ideological orientation of large segments of Germany's intellectuals. As late as 1988, a survey carried out among German writers asked them what it meant to them "to be a German writer at the present"; all the participants spoke of "shame, sorrow, a consciousness of guilt or of responsibility," or as the author Günter Kunert put it: "Inescapably, Heinrich Heine is mixed with Heinrich Himmler, Weimar with Buchenwald, grand masterpieces of art and simultaneously Death as a master from Germany."[1] The philosopher Peter Sloterdijk summed up the mental matrix underlying these feelings in December 1989, when he wrote: "If not for a whole generation, then at least for those now around forty, to be born so close to the horror means to have come into a world in which people have not yet relearned how to guarantee for themselves and for one another."[2] The mental pattern thus formed manifested itself above all in a widespread recoiling from the national, which made itself felt in the justification of German division as the price to be paid for the war begun by the National Socialists, as well as in a fundamental rejection of reunification. This rejection definitely also understood itself as a political expression of the more-than-latent fear of the nationalistic aggressive potential of a reunited Germany.

As politically loaded as this position may have been, it proved irrelevant in the concrete debate that arose when the unification of the two German states was imminent. Characteristic here was the connection many leftists made between Auschwitz and reunification. In his book *Volk ohne Zeit*, Lothar Baier makes the following assertion: "The Berlin Wall, although a product of the cold war, was consciously or unconsciously perceived by many as a construction standing in an unspecific relation to Auschwitz, as a symbol of a continuing and, considering the dimension of the crime, not disproportional punishment, which could be accepted."[3] Ever since the night the Wall was opened, he continues, considering the "impending solution" of the historic "German question," the Germans no longer seem to need to grapple with their past: "No more laments about missed historical chances and fateful exceptionalism." And that, it appears, is the crux of the matter: as a matter of fact, the GDR served Germany's left primarily as a welcome screen for projecting historical "lessons" to be learned from the German past. But after the Wall came down and these "lessons" had been *objectively* "revised," so to speak, when it had become unambiguously clear who had emerged as the victor in the cold war—in short, when the East German state dissolved (of "its own free will")—what little the left had was taken away—namely, the projection screen it had used in its futureless grappling with the past. This was not surprising at all. In its heyday, the New Left knew very well why those who did not want to speak about capitalism should remain silent about fascism; now, after it had established itself and turned into a pinkish-green quasi-left conglomerate, it not only quickly joined the camp of German Social Democracy, but also—and since 1998, quite concretely—set up quarters rather comfortably in the vehemently vigorous capitalistic establishment of the new German republic. Not for nothing did the journalist Ulrich Greiner laconically remark, about two years after unification, that the German left no longer existed.[4]

This political, though "extra-parliamentarily" determined, development of dealings with the past in the old Federal Republic of Germany should not lead us to forget that, while the political establishment early on "came to an arrangement" with the past (whereby Israel's instrumentalization of the Holocaust found its complementary counterweight in Germany's materialization of expiation), there were also public counter discourses opposed to the above leftist ideas. In this connection, the *Historikerstreit* (historians' debate) of the mid-1980s must be seen as the most explosive culmination *before* reunification. This debate, academically begun but very soon oriented toward media- and mass-effectiveness, differed from every earlier approach to the German past in that, for the first time, the relativization of the Holocaust (or the doubt cast on the doctrine of the Holocaust's singularity) was not only harshly formulated by voices bearing the charisma of competent position, but also in that its public discussion was legitimated. It matters little that the academic and journalistic camp resisting this approach appeared to remain the "victor": considering the eagerness with which, shortly after reunification a few years later, one began the discursive "replacement" of the brown's past with the red's past, i.e., of the Nazi with the Stasi past (thus creating a new, "more urgent," supposedly symmetrical and at any rate more comfortable object of "grappling"), the suspicion may arise that despite the (until recently) dominant critique of ideology, that the all-German discourse on the German past is rather more ideological—i.e., determined by heteronomous interests—than it may appear. The great public debates in the reunified Germany of the 1990s—the Goldhagen debate, the Wehrmacht exhibition debate, the Holocaust monument debate, and finally the Walser-Bubis debate—are eloquent testimony to this.

Much could be added to this. But one thing appears to emerge clearly from what I have already shown: despite all complementarity and a parallel ideological function of recalling the Holocaust in Israel and in Germany, we are apparently dealing with *two different Holocausts*. Not only the different perspectives of the "victim" or "perpetrator" countries play a substantial role here, and not only the difference between the Holocaust as a historical event and the "Holocaust" as a projection screen for heteronomously molded interests, but also, and connected with both, the primarily political-ideological dimension of "remembering" in Israel and of "disposing" (or, if you will, of "forgetting through remembering") in Germany. In a time when the generation of the perpetrators and the surviving victims is gradually dying off and the historical event of the Holocaust is thus irrevocably becoming the object of historical research or other forms of historical recollection, the ideological components of the two Holocaust perspectives elucidated here should be considered. They are the preconditions for any adequate memory.

Does all this have anything to do with the United States? The question can be examined only in the context of the world-historical situation of the early postwar period. I have already indicated that the *official state* Holocaust discourses in Israel and in Germany (to be clearly distinguished from the grapplings in the particular life worlds) stood in a relationship of complementary interests: the (initially primarily) material interest underlying Israel's ideological instrumentalization of the Holocaust correlated with the German interest in a materialization of expiation. Israel needed these material resources to erect infrastructure in the newly founded state and gradually emerging society (all the more so when, in the first decade after the state was founded, massive waves of immigration tripled the Jewish population of the country). Germany— meaning the old Federal Republic—could not hope for anything politically better than to be allowed to "pay off" the monstrous, world-historical guilt it had taken upon itself; *material* reparations enabled it not only to enter into "dialogue" with the representatives of the victims, but also—at least in its own eyes—to unburden itself. It is no coincidence that Germany and Israel signed their restitution agreement as early as 1952—all of seven (!) years after the gates of Auschwitz were opened— and that thirteen years later the two countries established full diplomatic ties. In the early 1950s, the just-emerging Federal Republic was not the only place using the phrase "other Germany"; it was no other than Ben-Gurion, Israel's first prime minister, who propagated the term in his own country (in light of the controversial public reaction to the aforementioned restitution agreement). Indeed, to this day there is no *official state* institution in Israel that gives expression to a relationship of hate or even mere resentment toward Germany; whatever may still reverberate powerfully in particular life worlds, and (sometimes) in individual exchanges, finds no equivalent expression on the official level of diplomatic and political relations between states (ignoring for the moment the instrumentalizing "obligation" of Germany toward Israel). Seen in this way, it is also no coincidence that, in the 1950s, Germany and Israel both more or less maintained public silence about the Holocaust. On both sides, the psychological inability (collective as well as individual) to deal with the trauma and the catastrophe played a substantial role; but it was also in the *interest* of both parties to avoid such dealings at first. The state-sustaining ideology of Zionism propagated and fueled the creation of the "New Jew" and dealt with the Shoah only in terms of its own ideological goals, while not knowing how to deal with the ailments of the Holocaust survivors; at the same time and for its part, the Federal Republic established as the "other Germany" had no use at all for any grappling with Germany's immediate past. The notorious climate of restoration in the Adenauer era played a role in this, but so did other motivations driven by more comprehensive geopolitical interests. This is the backdrop against which the "transatlantic" dimension of the German and Israeli Holocaust discourses appears.

Quite soon after the liberation of Auschwitz (but long before the beginnings of the exploration of its civilizational meaning), the "other Germany" was conceived (in the course of the cold war, which had already broken out) by the West as a "bastion of democracy" to be erected in Central Europe against the "advance of communism." Of course, to assume this function, Germany (i.e., the Germany of the English-, French-, and above all American-occupied zones) had to (re-)join the "community of nations." Certain measures were necessary to this end. Not only was the infrastructural foundation of the *material* establishment of this "other Germany" created by the Marshall Plan, but the *symbolic* basis of "having become different" was also launched. On the one hand, the prominent remnants of the top National Socialist leadership were liquidated in the framework of the Nuremberg Trials. On the other hand, the process of wholesale denazification began, enabling the almost seamless transfer of old Nazi economic, judicial, scientific, and in part political elites into the new Federal Republic, as well as the ideological consciousness of now being purified and chastened, or "different," or simply "denazified." Here, the legitimation of a restitution taking the form of the *materialization of expiation*, juridically completed with the restitution treaty of 1952, can be seen as a particular achievement: as we have seen, it implied an interaction with the representatives of the victims, thus legitimizing the "other Germany"; and it shifted dealings with the recent past to the sphere of reification and the exchange value, or trade. Germany's later culture of debate would unfold these dealings with the past to the point of excess, but first the *material* foundation was laid for the future "reconciliation" with the survivors and above all for Germany's renewed acceptance in the bosom of the "community of nations." This integration of Germany into the West not only made use of the Germans' smooth transition from the horrors of the global catastrophe to the repressing confidence of the "economic miracle"; it also lay in the geopolitical interest of the United States (and of the West led by the United States) in the newly emerged bloc system. This is the instrumentalizing character of the "transatlantic dimension" of the German and Israeli Holocaust discourses. The fact that *all* the parties discussed here were initially subject to the logic of this dimension may indicate why it would take years before the Holocaust discourses could be rid of at least part of their ideologically heteronomous character.

This does not mean that there was no genuine Holocaust discourse in the United States. Though it was some time before it became a public American *non*-Jewish "topic," America (containing by then the second largest Jewish community in the world) became, next to Israel and Germany, a third important center of Holocaust memory. As a matter of fact, when the Holocaust Museum in Washington was founded, certain grim voices in Israel asserted that the new institution would "compete" with the Israeli Yad Vashem Museum and undermine its monopoly of remembrance. Indeed, it has even been suggested that the Holocaust has replaced Israel itself as a major source of secular American Jewish identity. Needless to say, all this culminated in a vast corpus of American literature on the Holocaust and Holocaust-related themes, ranging from a socio-historical account of the so-called "eliminatory anti-Semitism" determining German history (as in Goldhagen's *Hitler's Willing Executioners*), through research on Holocaust survivors' lives in postwar America (as in William B. Helmreich's *Against All Odds: Holocaust Survivors and the Successful Lives They Made in America*), up to criticism of the prevailing American Holocaust ideology (as in Peter Novick's *The Holocaust in American Life*).[5]

However, it seems to me that the major "transatlantic" (i.e., genuine American) dimension of the Holocaust discourse pertains to something else: the absorption of the Holocaust into popular culture, or, to be more precise, into the culture industry. In order to reflect on that, some remarks on "culture industry" are necessary.

The diagnosis, which posits that works of art have always been, among other things *but not exclusively*, commodities, and that the products of the culture industry are by now nothing *but* commodities, was made over thirty years ago. Since then, it seems that its validity has only increased gradually: the culture industry has expanded and gained dimensions which even Adorno could not have foreseen. Nowadays, the "success" of any huge Hollywood production, for instance, is measured only in terms of the tremendous financial investments put into it and its income in the first week of its distribution. Even before the product itself is released to the market, the dramatic/entertaining/heroic documentation of its production ("behind the scenes") is circulated in the mass media (sometimes as a film in its own right), putting to work an immense apparatus of promotion and marketing, perfectly in control of each and every mode and nuance of the authoritarian fetishizing of the heroes, the immediate reification of its contents and messages into purposeful stimuli, and the aggressive commercialization of its thoroughly designed aura. This apotheosis of commodification knows no limits now, not even the limits of minimal respect toward the transition from reality to fiction, and from fiction to reality: just as one of these promotion movies reported that Steven Spielberg insisted on cutting rehearsals for the crowd scenes of *Schindler's List* because the real victims in the historical camps "had no rehearsals," so an invitation to a meeting with one of the Schindler survivors, held in the States some years ago, tried to attract the audience by stating, "You've seen the movie—now meet a survivor." And just as this survivor saw no harm in the promotional reification of the horrors of his private past, so the movie itself was well received and approved by many survivors because of its effectiveness—it is "doing the job well."

It may be argued, of course, that *Schindler's List* is not a very good example for a typical product of the culture industry; one could go even further to explicitly classify it into the realm of "high" culture. This is not the place to elaborate on this issue of the general expansion of the culture industry, its increasing domination of significant parts of "high" culture, the evident impact it has on it, and the connection between all these factors and the potential of the "low" inherent in "high" art itself. Not by coincidence did Adorno keep stressing that kitsch is not just a "waste product of art, originating from unfaithful accommodation; rather it lurks in it, waiting for the ever returning chances to leap out from art."[6] Yet, in the context of our discussion, the relevant question is whether the fate of Spielberg's work, however serious in its motivation, is not actually predestined since it is subjected to the structure of production, and, even more important, to the mode of perception and patterns of reception inherent in the very same industry, the raison d'être of which is to ideologically fabricate those "waste products" of art. Do not the cathartic purpose ("doing the job well") and the mimetic fixation (a quasi-realistic presentation of "what happened there"), the objective blending of affirmated habits of thought and memory with their fetishized representations, actually contain the entertaining dispersion of what cannot be expressed, the all-too-accessible diversion of what must not be forgotten, yet is so hard to remember? And, precisely for that reason, should the movie's (artistic) approach retain a certain degree of a never dissolving discontent, a persisting tension between the carefully conducted touch and that which should never be touched? The culture industry, by its own definition, does not engage itself with these kinds of problems. It is doubtful whether the assertion that after Auschwitz, writing a poem might be considered barbaric, was valid even then, when it was uttered in view of the extensive horrors, a short time after the Second World War. This is one of the very few assertions that Adorno is known to have withdrawn. Yet it is also clear that, since the dominant culture in the era "after

Auschwitz" has turned "Auschwitz" into a consumer item whose exchange value is embodied in the Hollywoodian Oscar statuette (and other forms of materialization of the Holocaust memory), barbarity is no longer a simple question of practice reflected in ideology, but rather a question of an ideology turned to practice.

The mediation of the Holocaust by Hollywood movies like *Schindler's List* is only one aspect of culture industry. A no less important one is that "the history of Auschwitz has become a material, a raw material, with which one can make as good politics as with any election campaign donation," as the German sociologist Detlev Claussen has put it.[7] No longer is this solely an American problem. It has been globalized by now, because the principle of the culture industry has been globalized. And it is this that may eventually turn out to be the true transatlantic dimension of today's Holocaust discourse.

Notes

1. Quoted in Moshe Zuckermann, *Zweierlei Holocaust: Der Holocaust in den politischen Kulturen Israels und Deutschlands* (Göttingen, 1998), 45.
2. Peter Sloterdijk, *Versprechen auf Deutsch* (Frankfurt, 1990), 17.
3. Lothar Baier, *Volk ohne Zeit: Essay über das eilige Vaterland* (Berlin, 1990), 69.
4. Ulrich Greiner, "Flucht in die Trauer," in *Die Zeit* 39 (1992): 69.
5. Daniel Jonah Goldhagen, *Hitler's Willing Executioners: Ordinary Germans and the Holocaust* (New York, 1996); William B. Heimrich, *Against All Odds: Holocaust Survivors and the Successful Lives They Made in America* (New York, 1992); Peter Novick, *The Holocaust in American Life* (Boston/New York, 1999).
6. Theodor W. Adorno, *Ästhetische Theorie*, 10th ed. (Frankfurt, 1990), 355.
7. Detlev Claussen, "Rache an der neuen Welt," in *Der Spiegel* 38 (1992): 12.

Chapter 14

THE PLACE OF THE HOLOCAUST IN THE AMERICAN ECONOMY OF EVIL

Manfred Henningsen

"Forgetting ... is a crucial factor in the creation of a nation," Ernest Renan said in 1882 in a now-famous lecture at the Sorbonne in Paris on the question: "What is the nation?" He continued: "... which is why progress in historical studies often constitutes a danger for [the principle of] nationality. Indeed, historical enquiry brings to light deeds of violence which took place at the origin of all political formations."[1] The never-ending reconstruction of German history since the end of the Nazi empire in 1945, the founding of the two postwar republics in 1949, and the reunification of Germany in 1990 provide an exceptional and negative illustration of Renan's thesis. Germans have tried, sometimes desperately, to forget, distort, or suppress their past. Yet the victims of and the victors over the Nazi empire have kept the memory of the "deeds of violence" alive. Germans were not allowed to master their past according to rules outlined by Renan and followed by almost all societies in the twentieth century, including the United States and the other victors of World War II. As a result of the growing pressure from outside and, later, inside Germany to recognize and process the memory of evil, Germany concluded the twentieth century by establishing a compensation fund for the surviving forced laborers from Nazi occupied countries and deciding to build a memorial near Berlin's Brandenburg Gate commemorating the six million victims of the Jewish Holocaust. Although these political decisions by the German government and parliament in 1999 were accompanied by public pressure, including pressure coming from American politicians, journalists, and intellectuals, they are supported by majorities in German society. But why did this strong pressure come from the United States, a society not known for its deviation from Renan's rule? Why did Americans consider it necessary that Germans recognize the memory of evil in their past while they themselves have difficulties coming to terms with their own economy of evil?[2] How did the Jewish Holocaust and other scenarios of terror that did not involve American victims gain this importance in the American public debate decades after the defeat of Nazi Germany?

The United States, after all, did not enter World War II in order to stop the "Final Solution" or other scenarios of terror from being carried out by Nazi Germany. The destruction of six million European Jews was not even at the center of the Nuremberg trials of the surviving leadership of the Nazi empire. The American chief prosecutor at the tribunal, Justice Robert Jackson, insisted in the International Conference on Military Trials in London, in the summer of 1945 before the Nuremberg trials, on sticking to a "general principle" which had been in place "from time immemorial," namely:

> that the internal affairs of another government are not ordinarily our business; that is to say, the way Germany treats its inhabitants, or any other country treats its inhabitants, is not our affair any more than it is the affair of some other government to interpose itself in our problems.... We have some regrettable circumstances at times in our own country in which minorities are unfairly treated. We think that it is justifiable that we interfere or attempt to bring retribution to individuals or states only because the concentration camps and the deportations were in pursuance of a common plan or enterprise of making an unjust war in which we became involved. We see no other basis on which we are justified in reaching the atrocities which were committed inside Germany, under German law, or even in violation of German law by authorities of the German state.

Raul Hilberg, who quotes these comments by Jackson in his study on the Holocaust, concludes:

> The London delegates were unwilling to recognize the destruction of European Jewry as a crime *sui generis*. In the end they were not even able to cover the pre-war anti-Jewish decrees under the count of aggression. During the trial the prosecution failed completely to establish any connection between these decrees and the "conspiracy" to make war. The "crimes against humanity" were dead wood.[3]

A casual reading of the history of American-German relations after 1945 seems to indicate that they have always been overshadowed by the memory of the Holocaust. This casual assumption, however, is contradicted by Peter Novick's book, *The Holocaust in American Life*. According to Novick, the Holocaust discourse played no important role until the 1960s. He writes: "Between the end of the war and the 1960s, as anyone who has lived through those years can testify, the Holocaust made scarcely any appearance in American public discourse, and hardly more in Jewish public discourse—especially discourse directed to gentiles."[4] This change came in the following decades:

Since the 1970s, the Holocaust has come to be presented—come to be thought of—as not just a Jewish memory.... Over the past twenty years every president has urged Americans to preserve the memory of the Holocaust. The operating expenses of the Washington Holocaust Museum ... have been largely taken over by the federal government. In Boston, the New England Holocaust Memorial is located on the Freedom Trail, along with Paul Revere's house and the Bunker Hill Monument.

Novick asks: "How did this European event come to loom so large in American consciousness?"[5] His book presents a detailed historical analysis of this American discourse formation. He mentions also the consequences it has for the processing of the American record of evil when he recognizes that "[the] identical talk of uniqueness and incomparability surrounding the Holocaust in the United States ... promotes evasion of moral and historical responsibility."[6] He specifically mentions the remarkable cultural affront against blacks: "The greatest symbolic affront was that while Jews had a federally funded museum memorializing their victimhood, proposals for a museum of the black experience never made it through Congress."[7] Novick was quoted in a *New York Times* article about contemporary German intellectual attitudes toward historical memory: "What would we think if the Germans said the Holocaust is a terrible thing, but chose to build a museum in Berlin commemorating American oppression of blacks? It would be grotesque."[8] The arguments of this essay address some of the "grotesque" features of the contemporary debate on German history.

In 1959, a new departure in the understanding of American slavery began. It was the time when the Holocaust slowly emerged as a central theme in the cultural debate of the nation. Right from the beginning of the new exploration of slavery in 1959, in Stanley Elkins's book *Slavery*, the parallel with German evil was suggested. Yet Elkins, who undertook the experiential comparison of the *Middle Passage* and West Indian slave plantations with the death world of German concentration camps, was mercilessly criticized for raising the issue. Elkins subsequently left the field of slavery scholarship. The comparison vanished from the mainstream black and white research agenda of slavery and receded into the circles of Afrocentric groups. Why was this possible, and what role did the Holocaust begin to play in the American discussion of evil?

Toni Morrison dedicated her award winning novel *Beloved* (1987) to "Sixty Million and more." The Nobel laureate obviously referred to the Africans who died on their long journey from capture in Africa to their utilization as slaves in the New World. She articulated the sense of outrage that dictated the dedication to the novel in the essay *Playing in the Dark* (1992) when she wrote:

traditional canonical American literature is free of, and unshaped by the four-hundred-year-old presence of, first, Africans and then African Americans in the United States. It assumes that this presence—which shaped the body politic, the Constitution, and the entire history of the culture—has had no significant place or consequence in the origin and development of that culture's literature.[9]

Morrison's outrage, however, which represents black sensibilities in the United States, echoes the sense of a culpability that Abraham Lincoln expressed at his Second Inauguration on March 4, 1865, one month before his assassination.

Lincoln recognized the American economy of evil on which the Republic was built. He emphasized in his inaugural address what generations of American historians from the Civil War to the 1950s downplayed when he said: "… slaves constituted a peculiar and powerful interest. All knew that this interest was somehow the cause of war."[10] But Lincoln did not stop here. He hoped and prayed "that this mighty scourge of war may speedily pass away." He was not certain, though, whether his hope and prayer would be answered, and therefore he issued a warning to his country:

> Yet, if God wills that it [the war] continue until all the wealth piled by the bond-man's two hundred and fifty years of unrequited toil shall be sunk, and until every drop of blood drawn with the lash, shall be paid by another drawn with the sword, as was said three thousand years ago, so still it must be said "the judgments of the Lord are true and righteous altogether."[11]

Lincoln's Second Inaugural is as important as his Gettysburg Address.[12] For the opening of the cemetery on November 19, 1863, Lincoln connected, in 272 words, the events of the Civil War with the beginning of the revolutionary formation, the Declaration of Independence ("Four score and seven years ago …"). At the height of the crisis of the Republic, Lincoln reinvented its meaning with a stroke of political genius. He did not simply wipe out the legitimacy of slavery in the Constitution. He undercut the symbolic sanctity of the document itself by committing the Republic to the language of the Declaration. Equality became one of the foremost founding principles of the United States. The text Lincoln crafted for the occasion in Gettysburg was obviously, in Plato's words, a noble lie. Lincoln's assassination, the following failure of the radical reconstruction policies for the South, and the emergence of Jim Crow laws in the South underline the unwillingness of the postbellum United States to accept Lincoln's revisioning of America. It took one hundred years for the majority of Americans to understand, grudgingly, Lincoln's noble lie as the saving tale for the Republic. The *Chicago Times* editorial of 23 November 1863 captured contemporary attitudes when it insisted on characterizing the speech as a sacrilegious lie. Lincoln had violated his oath of office:

> It was to uphold this constitution, and the Union created by it, that our officers and soldiers gave their lives at Gettysburg. How dare he, then, standing on their graves, misstate the cause for which they died, and libel the statesmen who

founded the government? They were men possessing too much self-respect to declare that negroes were their equals, or were entitled to equal privileges.[13]

The editorial provides an intriguing connection with the main author of the Declaration of Independence, Thomas Jefferson, who had the good luck of being the American representative in Paris during the time of the constitutional convention in Philadelphia. He therefore did not sign the draft of the Constitution that included encoded references to slavery. Instead, he did have the bad luck of publishing a book, *Notes on the State of Virginia* (1785), and shortly thereafter starting an affair with a slave he owned, who gave birth to their children.

To talk about Jefferson is to confront the honest dishonesty that surrounds the American founding, namely to proclaim equality and to accept slavery as the price of the unity of the Republic as white antifederalists pointed that out in the Philadelphia convention and in the public debate surrounding the ratification of the Constitution.[14] Black radicals echoed these comments throughout American history with specific reference to Thomas Jefferson as the main author of the Declaration.[15] Jefferson represents this dishonesty in an obvious and in a tragic way. He obviously indulges the prejudices and privileges of his slave-owning class when acknowledging in the *Notes* the dependency of the Southern economy on slave labor. He writes: "For in a warm climate, no man will labour for himself who can make another labour for him. This is so true, that of the proprietors of slaves a very small proportion indeed are ever seen to labour."[16] Recognizing this dependency, he justifies the exploitation of African slave labor in a straightforward racist discourse that was just beginning to become socially dominant all over the Western world.[17] Despite some signs of intellectual discomfort, he advances the "suspicion ... that the black whether originally a distinct race, or made distinct by time and circumstance are inferior to the whites in their endowments both of body and mind. It is not against experience to suppose, that different species of the same genus ... may possess different qualifications."[18] However, if the slave should ever be set free, the dangers of "staining the blood of his master" are present. Therefore, the slave owner Jefferson recommends as policy: "When freed, he is to be removed beyond the reach of mixture."[19] Jefferson had not yet started his affair with Sally Hemings, who was the offspring of his father-in-law and another woman of mixed parentage.[20] Still, despite this unwillingness to recognize widespread miscegenation in the American South and in his own family, Jefferson's bad conscience played tricks on him.[21] As if he was anticipating the fateful price that American society would have to pay in the future with the lives of 600,000 primarily white soldiers during the Civil War, he warns his contemporaries of violent things to come. Based on demographic reality, Jefferson indicated in 1785 that "a revolution of the wheel of fortune, an exchange of situation, is among possible events: that it may become probable by supernatural interference. The

Almighty has no attribute which can take side with us in such a contest."
He concludes his reflections with the ominous expectation of nearly
inescapable genocidal violence: "The spirit of the master is abating, that
of the slave rising from the dust, his condition mollifying, the way I hope
preparing, under the auspices of heaven, for a total emancipation, and
that this is disposed, in the order of events, to be with the consent of the
masters, rather than by their extirpation."[22]

Whatever the reasons may have been that led Jefferson to this rather
startling conclusion, there is no question that he realized how distorted
American life had become due to the evil of slavery. Yet equally surprising, if not tragic, is the fact that he did absolutely nothing to change it
during the next forty-one years of his life, including the two terms of his
presidency. The first president, George Washington, who was also a slave
owner (and was recently charged with having fathered a son with one of
his slaves)[23] seems to have had a similar attitude toward slavery. However, though recognizing the dependency of the Southern economy on
the evil of slavery, he came clean, at least personally, by not treating his
slaves as capital and selling them, as Jefferson mandated in his last will,
as a down payment on his debts. Emancipating all his slaves by decree of
his last will was obviously based on Washington's "aversion" to the institution of slavery altogether.[24]

Jefferson resembles the presidents who followed Lincoln and did nothing to improve the life of former slaves. As Ulysses S. Grant, a military hero
of the Civil War, proclaimed in his Second Inaugural on March 4, 1873:

> Social equality is not a subject to be legislated upon, nor shall I ask that any-
> thing be done to advance the social status of the colored man, except to give
> him a fair chance to develop what there is good in him, give him access to the
> schools, and when he travels let him feel assured that his conduct will regulate
> the treatment and fare he will receive.[25]

Grant's unkind, but symptomatic words about the former slaves contrast badly with the generous social welfare package that was developed
for the veterans, widows, and orphans of the Union troops in the Civil
War.[26] How it was possible to release the slaves into freedom without providing them with any means of economic and social support is, in light
of Lincoln's and Jefferson's recognition of the American dependency on
slave labor, astounding. Most abolitionist plans in the 1840s and 1850s for
the return of freed slaves to Africa or some settlement in Central America
called for capital funding by the federal government. In any case, there
was certainly no prosecution of any Southern slave owners, politicians or
judges after the Civil War. The president of the Southern Confederacy, Jefferson Davis, was not put on trial, though he was detained for two years.
He died a natural death twenty-four years after the war in 1889. Amnesty
by amnesia was the response of society to the regime of terror that had
defined the life of blacks in America. The watershed of the Civil War did
not mean the end of terror for blacks; yet no American president after the

Civil War had the political will even to introduce or support federal anti-lynching legislation. The violence that Leon Littwack has recently described in his book *Trouble in Mind* went on unabated from 1890 to 1940, counting more than 3,200 black lynching victims, the tip of the iceberg of violence against African Americans.[27] Apartheid had set in by 1880 and continued to characterize life in the South until the 1960s, when the civil rights movement forced Congress to finally deliver the legislation that was promised in the Fourteenth and Fifteenth amendments.

The unwillingness of historical America to compensate former slaves for the labor they had performed for the national economy, or at least to issue a national apology, continues to the present. This American unwillingness to pay up its historical debts may sometimes have international consequences. One of the major reasons that the United States refused for decades (from 1948 to 1988) to sign the UN "Genocide Convention" had to do with the fear of Southerners in the U.S. Senate that civil rights activists would use it against their own country. Samantha Power recently summarized this syndrome when she wrote:

> Southern Senators especially were afraid that lawyers might use the Convention, which on its face appeared to count the infliction of mental harm ... as genocide, to target the architects of southern segregation.... [A] vocal band of southern Senators ... joined the American Bar Association in leading the anti-ratification charge. These men were afraid for themselves, and for their southern way of life. Opponents of the Convention played on the Senators' insecurity, and argued that Senate passage would hand African-Americans a weapon in their struggle, enabling the victims of segregation to drag the United States before an international court on genocide charges.[28]

A similar resistance is led by North Carolina Senator Jesse Helms against the acceptance of the International Criminal Court, a proposal signed by a German-led coalition of UN member states in the Rome Treaty of 1998.

When President Clinton suggested, both in 1997 and during his 1998 visit to Africa, that he contemplated apologizing in the name of the nation to African Americans for the violence of slavery that was perpetrated on their ancestors, he ran into widespread opposition. Clinton said in August 1997:

> An apology under right circumstances, those things can be quite important. Surely every American knows that slavery was wrong, and that we paid a terrible price for it and that we had to keep repairing that.... Just to say it's wrong and that we're sorry about it is not a bad thing, it doesn't weaken us.[29]

The then Speaker of the House, Newt Gingrich, labeled an apology "emotional symbolism," "an avoidance of problem-solving," and a "dead end."[30] The *New York Times* columnist Russell Baker summed up the arguments against an apology when he wrote:

Like every country, the United States has a lot of history to apologize for. After apologizing for slavery, we could move ahead to apologizing for what our forebears did to the Indians. Was it genocide? No, the word hadn't been invented until it was all over. The words that had Americans spellbound back then were "manifest destiny." Destiny had given us a continent to populate. The Indians were in the way. Destiny demanded their removal. Such was the argument, anyhow.[31]

Baker did not mention Germany in his column. Germany was strangely absent from the apology debate. It was almost as if Americans wanted to prove to themselves that there is a qualitative difference between the processing of the German and the American economy of evil. But before I return to the German memory, I want to take a last look at an American apology that was issued and accompanied by the payment of compensation to individual members of an entire victim group.

Why did Congress agree to apologize to Japanese Americans who were interned in camps during World War II, and to pay "$20,000 in redress payments to 82,219 eligible claimants, totaling more than $1.6 billion"?[32] A professor of philosophy at the University of Hawaii, Rodney C. Roberts, compared the African-American and Japanese-American cases and came to the conclusion that more was involved than racism or even the political clout of Asian Americans. For Roberts, it is the civilizational meta-understanding of Africa, Africans, and African Americans that lies at the roots of the American unwillingness to compensate those people on whose labor and freedom the United States was founded.

Roberts's argument is intriguing for many reasons. He argues that attempts to rectify the injustice perpetrated on blacks will get nowhere because white Americans are "ascribing a *prima facie* inferior status" to blacks.[33] Not only are blacks the offspring of an "inferior" social group in the United States, namely slaves, but they were captured on a continent that was, in the eyes of white Americans, devoid of all civilizational achievements, and which became totally dominated by Western powers. Compared to the Japanese and Japanese Americans who regained their equal status vis-à-vis Europeans and Americans, Africans and African Americans remained "losers." And Americans as winners are ideologically incapable of apologizing to "losers." According to Roberts, this social-Darwinian reasoning explains why Japanese Americans received compensation and an apology, while African Americans are still waiting. A ranking Democrat, Congressman John Conyers, introduced in 1989 a legislative initiative, "Commission to Study Reparation Proposals for African-Americans Act," which still has not received a hearing in the House Judiciary Committee. Roberts's thesis on the alleged inferiority of Africa and Africans echoes, in an almost ironic way, the inferiority charges that were raised against Americans and the American continent in the second half of the eighteenth century,[34] provoking Jefferson to write his *Notes on the State of Virginia*.[35] Yet Roberts's thesis has a contemporary German dimension also.

A front-page article in *The New York Times* (17 February 1999) covered an announcement that German Chancellor Gerhard Schröder made in Berlin in the presence of a group of corporate executives. The headline read: "German Companies Adopt Fund for Slave Laborers Under Nazis. Chancellor Sees 'Campaign' against his Nation." The author of the article wrote:

> The Chancellor ... said a main function of the fund was to "counter lawsuits, particularly class action suits, and to remove the basis of the campaign being led against German industry and our country." The Chancellor did not say who was behind the "campaign" against Germany, but his suggestion appeared comparable to the response of some Swiss officials who said they saw a darkly orchestrated anti-Swiss movement in the legal actions by Holocaust survivors against Swiss banks...."[36]

The reporter did not charge Schröder with anti-Semitism but saw in his statement a reflection of the "ambivalent mood of a Germany anxious to put the past behind it, irritated over what some intellectuals have called the 'popularization' of the Holocaust, yet still conscious of its inescapable historical responsibilities." One day later, the same newspaper printed an article about the attempts of major corporate firms to hire bona fide historians to sort through their corporate files for any evidence of direct ties to the Nazi concentration camps. This time the article appeared in the business section, probably because American companies like Ford and General Motors were mentioned also.[37] Without question, most, if not all, of these claims are based on legitimate requests for compensation and will now be paid. The German response to American threats, however, indicates that former slaves, with the help of American lawyers and historians, can successfully use American courts to get compensation only if they were Nazi slaves. Freed American slaves had and have no such recourse, and Congress still refuses to even discuss the issue. Unlike Eastern Europeans and European Jews, Africans were, if one follows Roberts's argument, considered "inferior." The generally dismissive response to the apology and compensation requests may also explain the public indifference to movies that cover slavery and the Jim Crow experience, such as Singleton's *Rosewood* (1997) and Demme's *Beloved* (1998). Not even a movie like Spielberg's *Amistad* (1997), which celebrated a former American president as a heroic critic of the European role in slavery, made it at the box office or the Oscar nominations. Spielberg had to return to a theme from World War II in *Saving Private Ryan* (1998) to regain his place as Hollywood's prime mythopoet. Fighting the "Good War" against the evil empire of the Holocaust has replaced the conquest of the West as a core narrative of American mythology. Overcoming slavery and its aftermath of Jim Crow-Apartheid never made it to the theme reservoir of American self-interpretation.

Can Germans reclaim their history from the Americans or, better, do they want to? As suggested before, if Germans had a choice they probably would not mind being relieved of the need to process the memory of their Nazi past. They would thereby follow a pattern that manifests itself as the collective will to "forgetting" in cases like the gulag regime in Russia, imperial Japanese violence in Asia, terminal terror in revolutionary China, left fascism in Pol Pot's Cambodia, and slavery and Indian removal in America. Most societies are getting away with amnesia. Germany does not have this option because of the identity of the Holocaust victims.

The memory of the Jewish Holocaust has become part of the spiritual self-understanding of Jews everywhere. The Holocaust has entered Western memory through the spiritual importance it has gained since the 1960s for Jewish communities in Israel, Europe, the United States, and elsewhere. However Germans may deal with this memory, it will not affect the permanent presence of the German *Reich* of evil as the culminating experience of Jewish persecution in their history.

European Jewish memory of the Holocaust is directly connected with German political self-understanding, but American-Jewish memory is not. However, the United States is, next to Israel, the society with the second largest constituency of European Holocaust survivors. According to 1998 estimates, 58,000 reside in America. Survivors' organizations have been the driving force behind the creation of the Holocaust memorials and museums all over the country and, according to Novick, contributed heavily to the initial funding. The authentic motives of this constituency of survivors have been merged with the symbolic interests of the political culture at large. The Holocaust Memorial Museum in Washington, D.C., is located in the Mall area, the most prominent gathering space of the Republic and in clear proximity to the Washington, Jefferson, and Lincoln memorials. The prescribed exhibition itinerary in the museum begins in the elevators to the fourth floor with a video that shows General Eisenhower's visit to Ohrdruf, an affiliated labor camp of Buchenwald, on 15 April 1945. This visit took place four days after the abandonment of Buchenwald by the SS troops, the takeover of the camp by the inmates, and the anticipated arrival of contingents of George Patton's tank battalion; it happened three months after the arrival of the Red Army in Auschwitz on 27 January 1945—now Germany's national remembrance day. The newsreel footage of Eisenhower shows him looking in anger at piles of corpses. The symbolic meaning of this short news clip at the beginning of the museum tour seems to suggest that the American Supreme Commander of the Allied Forces in Europe, later president of the United States, fulfilled the mission of his assignment when the American troops reached Buchenwald.

This American appropriation of the Holocaust memory, which works itself through the media of the culture industry, recasts U.S. reasons for entry into World War II and revises the record of the actual disengagement from any military rescue operations during the war for the people in Buchenwald and other camps, especially the death camps in the east. The thrust of David Wyman's book, *The Abandonment of the Jews* (1984), is deflected by the suggestion that the United States had been fighting to save the lives of the inmates of concentration camps of Nazi Germany. This triumphant symbolic revisionism, which one encounters frequently in products of popular culture, is not helped by the absence of a comparative perspective in most Holocaust studies. The refusal of scholars to question the uniqueness thesis has contributed to an obsession with the macro- and micro-history of the Holocaust that has been translated into Holocaust classes at universities, colleges, and high schools all over the United States. This obsession does not make it easier to understand why Germans did not stop the events when they began, and why others did not intervene, nor why, since 1945, millions have died and are dying under similarly "unique" circumstances in Europe, Asia, and Africa. At a recent conference on the Holocaust, the twenty-ninth annual conference of the hosting organization, not one paper among the 179 scheduled for presentation had a comparative perspective.[38] The danger of redundancy and, worse, Holocaust fundamentalism has become obvious.

Let me finish my discussion of the place of the Holocaust in the American economy of evil with some observations about the difficulties Germans have with this evil segment of their history. Whatever the intentions of German politicians, historians, and writers might be when they speak about "normalization" of German history, Ron Rosenbaum, in his remarkable book about the authors who are "explaining Hitler," expresses a global suspicion when he writes: "... however much ordinary Germans might feel they've normalized, absolved themselves, explained themselves to others, to many they still need to prove they're not a people of the Devil."[39] Germans cannot do anything about this suspicion. They can only do what nations, according to Ernest Renan, rarely do, which is to include in their narratives of historical meaning the "deeds of violence" that are the root cause of the suspicion. The German decisions in 1999 to establish a compensation fund for forced laborers and, especially, to start with the construction of a German Holocaust Memorial in Berlin in the year 2000 provide such occasions.

Berlin already has an abundance of buildings, places, and streets that directly connect the present with the past of Nazi terror. At many of these sites today one finds museums, permanent exhibitions, or other reminders of history. Not far away from the planned memorial, for example, the new Jewish Museum was built in an architectural style that aesthetically evokes and transcends experiences of terror. In walking distance from the memorial site, the permanent exhibition, *Topography of Terror*, is located at the place of the former SS Headquarters and other institutions of the Nazi empire of evil, including a Gestapo prison. The memorial itself will be in the proximity of the space where Hitler's chancellery stood and where he finally committed suicide in the underground bunker. This ominous topography, however, will not be part of the memorial site. According to plans discussed in late 1999, it will be treated with concealment, probably covered with asphalt.

Will the Holocaust Memorial Museum in Berlin prove that Germans are not "a people of the Devil"? If Germans build it with global approval in mind, probably not. Building this structure, however, with its multiple symbolic and intellectual functions at the most visible place of the new and old German capital, may establish a unique precedent. For the first time in history, a society will not only rhetorically recognize the evil deeds of its own history. It will actually identify these victims and invite the citizens of the Berlin Republic to remember the millions who were killed, to study the circumstances under which it was possible, and to remind us that the world has not learned much, if anything, from the German economy of evil.

Will the German Holocaust Memorial have an impact on American attitudes toward the processing of their own past? Will Congress, for example, reconsider its refusal to discuss proposals for a slavery memorial in the Washington Mall area? The presence of the Holocaust Memorial in Berlin next to the prominent sites of historical and contemporary Germany will provoke continuous discussion inside and outside of the country. Tourists and official visitors will suddenly be confronted with a new uniqueness phenomenon. The uniqueness claim that has been attached to the Holocaust as the crime of the century will be raised in view of its German memorial. Why are Germans able and willing to commemorate their past in such a demonstratively unique way? Members from victim populations in other societies may look at the Berlin memorial and the other sites of German historical memory as a challenge. They may request similar symbolic representations in their own societies, including the United States of America. One could borrow a memorable phrase from Berlin's most famous philosopher, Hegel, and call this impact the "cunning of history."

Notes

1. Ernest Renan, "What is a Nation," in *Nation and Narration*, ed. Homi K. Bhabha (London/New York, 1990), 11.

2. My use of the phrase "economy of evil" has caused some uneasiness. I intended to provoke this reaction. Lincoln's explicit connection of moral and economic arguments justifies this language. He makes it possible to see the evil core of American slavery. Since the modern use of the term economy means the management of society's resources, American chattel slavery certainly belonged to these resources. Yet in the American "economy of truth" (Edmund Burke, 1796), the core of slavery is not seen from the perspective of the victims as a "regime of terror." I want to challenge this economic treatment of truth, comparing the American self-interpretation of slavery with the American treatment of the German empire of evil. Americans have no difficulties of symbolic representation when it comes to the Nazi past and political demands that Germany should meet. This juxtaposition does not blur the qualitative differences between slavery and Nazi evil and is therefore not another attempt to relativize the Holocaust.

3. Raul Hilberg, *The Destruction of the European Jews*, revised and definitive edition, 3 vols. (New York/London, 1985), 1065f.
4. Peter Novick, *The Holocaust in American Life* (Boston/New York, 1999), 103.
5. Ibid., 207.
6. Ibid., 15.
7. Ibid., 194.
8. Roger Cohen, "The Germans Want Their History Back," *The New York Times*, 12 September 1999.
9. Toni Morrison, *Playing in the Dark: Whiteness and the Literary Imagination* (New York, 1993), 4f.
10. Abraham Lincoln, "Second Inaugural Address," in *Inaugural Addresses of the Presidents of the United States from George Washington to Lyndon Baines Johnson* (Washington, D.C., 1965), 127.
11. Ibid., 120.
12. See Gary Wills, *Lincoln at Gettysburg: The Words That Remade America* (New York, 1992), 32ff.
13. Ibid., 38f.
14. See the references to the slavery issue in Herbert J. Storing, ed., *The Complete Anti-Federalist*, 5 vols. (Chicago/London, 1981).
15. See especially David Walker, *David Walker's Appeal, in Four Articles*, from 1829, which has been reprinted in numerous editions.
16. Thomas Jefferson, *Notes on the State of Virginia*, ed. William Peden (Chapel Hill/London, 1982), 163.
17. See Ivan Hannaford, *Race: The History of an Idea in the West* (Baltimore, 1996).
18. Jefferson, *Notes on the State of Virginia*, 143.
19. Ibid.
20. See Annette Gordon-Reed, *Thomas Jefferson and Sally Hemings: An American Controversy* (Charlottesville/London, 1997), 158–209.
21. The black writer Connie Briscoe claims that the same honest dishonesty that characterizes Jefferson's behavior manifests itself also in the life of James Madison, her personal ancestor and co-author of the *Federalist Papers* and fourth president of the United States; see: Felicia D. Lee, "A Novelist Fills in Slavery Blanks with Imagination," *The New York Times*, 1 September 1999.
22. Jefferson, *Notes on the State of Virginia*, 163.
23. See Nicholas Wade, "Descendants of Slave's Son Contend That His Father Was George Washington," *New York Times*, 7 July 1999.
24. Robert F. Dalzell, Jr. and Lee Baldwin Dalzell, *George Washington's Mount Vernon: At Home in Revolutionary America* (New York/Oxford, 1998), 211.
25. Ulysses S. Grant, "Second Inaugural Address," *Inaugural Addresses of Presidents*, 133.
26. See Theda Skocpol, *Protecting Soldiers and Mothers: The Political Origins of Social Policy in the United States* (Cambridge/London, 1992).
27. Leon Littwack, *Trouble in Mind. Black Southerners in the Age of Jim Crow* (New York, 1998), Chapter 6.
28. Samantha Power, "The United States and Genocide Prevention: No Justice without Risk," *The Brown Journal of World Affairs*, vol. 6 (1999): 23.
29. Steven A. Holmes, "Idea of Apologizing for Slavery Loses Steam," *The New York Times*, 6 August 1997.
30. Sam Fulwood III, "Gingrich scoffs at idea of apologizing to blacks," *Los Angeles Times*, 14 June 1997.
31. Russell Baker, "Sorry About That," *New York Times*, 1 July 1997.
32. "U.S. pays 82,219 WWII internees," *The Honolulu Advertiser*, 20 February 1999.
33. Rodney C. Roberts, "Why Have the Injustices Perpetrated against Blacks in America Not Been Rectified?" paper to be published in the *Journal of Social Philosophy*.
34. See James W. Ceaser, *Reconstructing America: The Symbol of America in Modern Thought* (New Haven/London, 1997), 19–42.

35. Ibid., 43.
36. Roger Cohen, "German Companies Adopt Fund for Slave Laborers Under Nazis," *New York Times*, 17 February 1999.
37. "Chroniclers of Collaboration: Historians Are in Demand to Study Corporate Ties to Nazis," *New York Times*, 18 February 1999.
38. The 29th Annual Scholars' Conference on the Holocaust and the Churches, 6–9 March 1999, Uniondale, New York.
39. Ron Rosenbaum, *Explaining Hitler: The Search for the Origins of His Evil* (New York, 1998), 358.

Part Three

The New Transatlantic Predicament

INTRODUCTION
Politics, Communication, and Scholarship

Frank Trommler

In the first two sections of this book, the contributors focus on the perspective of one nation vis-à-vis the other, of the presence of one nation *in* the other. In this section the angle of vision changes again, with the focus on the interaction in the present. The eight authors are in one way or another wrestling with more integrated views and politics of the German-American encounter, reflecting the increasing diffusion of economic, intellectual, and moral power that characterizes our age of post–cold war globalization and the Internet. This diffusion, though usually defined by the comparison with the priority-setting politics of the period before the fall of the Berlin Wall, refuels the thinking in historical discontinuities in dramatic and unexpected, yet intellectually stimulating ways.

Most of the drama lies in the disintegration of the notion of Atlantic bipolarity that carried the political and intellectual relationship during the East-West tensions and allowed the concept of Americanization to become a heuristic tool for understanding modernization as an outgrowth of the transatlantic power structure. As political elites on both continents engage in reformulating the bipolarity in terms of a new relationship between a unifying and revitalized Europe and the United States as the senior partner, they run into the conceptual challenge of losing a traditional foreign-relations vocabulary to a new sense of Atlantic politics as domestic politics. Karsten Voigt, the German Coordinator for German-American Cooperation, articulates the most optimistic take on this uneven power constellation when he declares friction to be the unavoidable concomitant of the increasing closeness and emphasizes the multinational input as a guarantee of a new kind of alliance beneficial to all partners. Hinting at the notion of a generational change with which the Schröder government undergirded the projection of the new Berlin Republic as a more self-confident international partner, Voigt omits the ritualistic evocation of gratitude toward the United States during the cold war, insisting instead on a vocabulary of mutuality, where foreign relations start to look more and more like domestic issues.

With his call for a "cultural dialogue," Theo Sommer, editor of the weekly *Die Zeit*, directs the attention to many open areas of misunderstandings that cannot easily be subsumed under the "two-pillar alliance" whose time has come. Sommer, a committed Atlanticist, answers the question of whether the acceptance of the continuous existence of an Atlantic Community will be strengthened more by discussing its disintegration than its resilience. He balances current concerns about economic, military, and political frictions with a bold agenda for a "new Atlantic covenant" between Europe and the United States. Meanwhile, Konrad Jarausch engages in an unusually critical and revealing exploration of the alienating factors that undermine the weight of political cooperation. Jarausch's assessment that "some of the cultural underpinnings of the German-American relationship have begun to erode during the last decade," resonates with Sommer's call for a "cultural dialogue." Indeed, the recognition of discontinuities and inconsistencies is a prerequisite for a new comprehensive view of the post-cold war situation, in which the languages of globalization and mutuality signal as much rivalry as cooperation.

The increasing importance of "cultural and attitudinal aspects of the European-American relationship" (Sommer) finds its full reflection in the contributions to this section. As political arguments lose pungency in the global web of legal and regulatory negotiations, the growing weight of technological, attitudinal, and generational criteria demands different analytical responses. One of the crucial, if not *the* crucial concept of the traditional bipolar discourse that is being challenged by the authors is that of Americanization. It has run its course as a tool for grasping modernization as a force from the outside. It has various histories in various countries and a twofold history in postwar Germany, West and East. It can mean almost anything. Yet it has a strong following in the United States, dispersed between intellectual musings about the outside world and economic triumphalism. Berndt Ostendorf systematizes its German uses in a generational framework, pointing to the various narrative habits of societies whose positive or negative conceptualizing of American influence always also functions as a reflection of themselves. Ostendorf delineates its understanding as commodification of culture, but also questions its scholarly usefulness beyond the confirmation of established polarities.

Tracing America's leading role in both the advancement of popular and mass cultures and the communication revolution is one thing. Defining Americanization as the core dynamic of social and cultural modernization is quite another, less assured enterprise. Even at the height of the American expansion in these areas, the transformation of culture and communication as the basis of the new post-industrial age did not progress in one direction but was rather shaped by many economic and intellectual forces in cross-Atlantic, cross-Pacific exchanges. The technological advances of the Japanese in the 1980s were as much a part of this exchange as the European insistence on the public responsibility of culture—in contrast to American notions of culture. Frank Trommler summarizes these developments since the 1960s with an eye on the transformation that the mediators themselves have undergone during and since the cold war and by in the course of the digital revolution. Elliott Shore concentrates on the Hollywood movie and demonstrates, through the prism of its presentation in the German language in Germany, that its character as a cultural composite with a clearly mediated American bias manifests itself not only in its production but also in its reception.

The last part of the section sheds light on the ways in which the other country is studied, focusing on German studies in the United States and American studies in Germany. In the context of reviewing the state of German studies, Russell Berman sounds a warning about the questionable effects of concepts of Americanization: "a self-assured triumphalism increasingly gets in the way of any strong engagement with other cultures." Under the aegis of the American embrace of multiculturalism, the temptation is indeed strong to apply American criteria to other societies. The results might not be too different from the misperceptions about American culture—or, rather, non-culture—that nineteenth-century Europeans derived from the application of their cultural paradigms to the New World. Reflecting on two decades of Americanizing the engagement with German literature and culture, Berman indicates the limits of this practice. His warning resonates with the worldwide concerns about preserving individual cultures against the unifying tendencies of globalization.

There could not be a better conclusion of the discourse on bipolarity, Americanization, multiculturalism, and the encounter of two societies in the age of globalization than the dialogic presentation of Günter Lenz and John Carlos Rowe on American studies. Both authors, set against a "unidirectional" application of American notions of multiculturalism to global contexts, attempt to assimilate current cultural and intellectual trends with a strategy for a "dialogic cultural critique." What Rudy Koshar, in his analysis of American encounters with war-torn Germany in the decade after 1945, calls intercultures, lays out the territory for the experience of cultures not as "static, enclosed networks of meanings, or 'texts,' but force fields of open, contested, transnational 'cultural flows' that are articulated and negotiated in specific local (or local-global) situations and that ask for 'hybrid,' 'creolized,' and 'creolizing' discourses and a dialogical reorganization of knowledge."

Entering the twenty-first century engaged in a multitude of intercultural encounters, we need to adjust the perception of ourselves and the other within a more flexible set of defining categories, which enables the dialogic process to lead to better understanding, more innovative scholarship, maybe even better politics. As Americanization and bipolarity lose their stringency as defining concepts for social and cultural interaction, Lenz and Rowe give a model for the kind of cross-cultural conversation that this volume as a whole intends to encourage.

— *Chapter 15* —

INTELLECTUAL DISSONANCE
German-American (Mis-)Understandings in the 1990s

Konrad H. Jarausch

O n the surface, transatlantic relations in the late 1990s seemed to be moving on "an even keel." With the election of Gerhard Schröder, a spirit kindred to President Clinton had taken power in Germany, a new brand of centrist politician from the left who understands the importance of courting the media. If diplomatic insiders can be believed, even the formerly anti-American Greens, such as Foreign Minister Joschka Fischer, were behaving as paragons of Atlanticism when visiting Washington.[1] Both governments appeared to be groping for an economic modernization strategy with a social conscience, giving in to neoliberal market demands to make their countries competitive without cutting the social net for the weaker citizens. The well-publicized tensions over German reluctance to participate in the Gulf War, the rapid recognition of Croatian independence, and clashing economic interests over bananas and beef seemed all but forgotten. The enormous goodwill resulting from American support for German reunification[2] and the success of the joint Kosovo intervention appeared to augur well for cooperation in the future.

Behind the impressive façade of German-American amity, closer scrutiny might nonetheless detect an almost imperceptible drifting apart of intellectual perspectives. In spite of global village rhetoric, instant electronic communication, and ease of transatlantic flight, the cultural discourses in Germany and America remain remarkably different. For instance, U.S. media concerns, such as the millennial hysteria about the Y2K problem, evoked only a bemused smile on the old continent. Yet major intellectual events in Europe, such as the controversies about François Furet's *Le passé d'une illusion* or the *Schwarzbuch des Kommunismus*, went unnoticed in the United States because the texts were not yet available in English translation.[3] Due to such cultural distance the elites, and to some degree also a great majority of people in both countries, see each other through a prism of misleading clichés. Their international perspectives are diverging, and learning processes remain one-sided, with Europe becoming more American rather than vice versa.[4] These trends create the risk of future misunderstandings that could render pragmatic agreement difficult.

Because the optimism of policymakers and the skepticism of cultural critics operate on different planes, there is a profound disconnect between the two views. In a debate on "the future of German-American relations," Karsten Voigt, German Coordinator for German-American Cooperation, gave an upbeat account of common problem solving in democratizing the Balkans and spreading NATO structures to Eastern Europe that suggested a complementarity between American global interests and German regional priorities. While other panelists criticized U.S. financial unilateralism or European military weakness, John D. Bindenagel of the State Department sought to reassure them that there were no fundamental contradictions. The academic commentators stressed the "soft power" of the Berlin Republic, debated the German uncertainty about their role, and wondered what might go wrong.[5] But the entire session ignored the erosion of the cultural underpinnings of the German-American relationship, the changes in mutual images and emotional attitudes that undergird such policies. Werner Weidenfeld has therefore perceptively warned that "a transatlantic cultural split in Euro-American relations appears inevitable" unless the causes of divergence are confronted openly.[6]

The following remarks, more personal than academic, will explore some important facets of the drifting apart of attitudes and feelings in the transatlantic relationship. Without spreading a simplistic alarmism, they propose to break through the self-congratulatory after-dinner rhetoric of German-American amity, propounded by such organizations as the American Council on Germany, the German-American Council, or the American Academy in Berlin. Such an effort to capture changing moods must draw on an impressionistic reading of public discourses among intellectuals and literati in the electronic media, printed newspapers or magazines, and institutional experiences in Potsdam and Chapel Hill, as well as private conversations on both sides of the big ditch.[7] By addressing shifts in undercurrents of opinion, these observations intend to pose some elusive questions that are rarely raised in polite transatlantic company.[8]

Mutual Clichés

One source of intellectual dissonance in both countries is their general publics' profound mutual ignorance about each other, which leaves the field open to misleading clichés. In the United States, reporting on Central Europe is at best intermittent and crisis-driven, German language study is rapidly declining, and as a tourist destination Germany ranks behind Britain, France, and Italy.[9] Only the remaining United States soldiers stationed in Germany and a part of the business community are personally acquainted with the Germans. In Germany, the media provide more American coverage, but tend to exploit the bizarre; English language training is almost universal, but somewhat dominated by Britain; and United States tourism is largely limited to Florida, New York, San Francisco, and the national parks. Former exchange students play an important role, but are not numerous enough to overcome Hollywood images that are both sugarcoated and repulsively violent at the same time.[10] The resistance of this cognitive gap to educational efforts raises the question: Which clichés govern mutual perceptions that could be leading to serious misjudgments?

Over the five decades since the Nazi genocide, American views of Germany have become increasingly dominated by the perspective of the Holocaust. The media are full of stories about indictments of National Socialist collaborators from Eastern Europe, efforts to reclaim victims' gold in Swiss banks, and demands for compensation for German slave labor, which are finally compelling leading firms to create a humanitarian fund to avoid class-action suits. In spite of academic criticism of its many flaws, Daniel J. Goldhagen's blanket indictment of "eliminationist anti-Semitism," which turned Germans into willing executioners, scored a phenomenal publishing success.[11] Countless educational programs in high schools and colleges focus on the annihilation of the European Jews, and major museums in Washington, D.C., and Los Angeles dramatize this most extreme instance of man's inhumanity to man. The intensity of this concern makes one forget that the notion of the "Holocaust," as well as its Americanization, are recent constructs that assign the role of victims primarily to Jews, of executioners to the Nazi-Germans, and of rescuers to United States GIs.[12]

This counter-intuitive strengthening of the memory of Hitler's crimes begs for an explanation, since World War II recollections seemed to be fading after the fiftieth anniversary celebrations of Allied victory. Many explanations have been advanced for the recent intensification of Holocaust consciousness. Some commentators, like Peter Novick, point to the identity politics of a Jewish diaspora that can appeal to the suffering of the past in order to create support for Israel in the present. Other critics, like Bernhard Giesen, argue that the German left has also created a Holocaust identity as a kind of negative identification with the history of its own people.[13] Observers also suggest that the last survivors finally feel free to talk about this painful subject and that the generation of the grandchildren has to experience the horrors anew in order to be emotionally moved by them. Of course, less noble elements of commercialization and political gain also play a role by exploiting the issue, as Norman Finkelstein has asserted in his provocative book.[14] Yet perhaps the most significant aspect is the shift from uniqueness to universalization of the Holocaust as negative exemplar of absolute evil in the modern world, which speaks to American liberals who were neither victims nor perpetrators.

Laudable as it may be in ethical terms, this Holocaust perspective creates considerable problems for American understanding of contemporary Germany. As the books by Jane Kramer and Marc Fischer show, it fixes public views in a terrible past, thereby making it more difficult to appreciate recent efforts to learn from it.[15] The subtext of Elizabeth Pond and David Schoenbaum's protestations of normalcy is the fundamental concern that the Germans might fall back into their prior errors at any time.[16] This kind of perspective looks for indications of the persistence of racism, such as skinhead violence against foreigners, and exaggerates it into an acute danger, even if such incidents are less frequent and severe than in neighboring France. Behind official protestations of friendship, there lurks an undercurrent of private unease among intellectuals and some policymakers that can not be assuaged by German contrition, because such apologies themselves prove the suspicion to be justified. The metahistorical perspective of the Holocaust suggests a timeless association between Germans and ultimate evil. As a result, from Serbia to Britain, anyone who resents Berlin's policies can invoke Hitler to warn against the recrudescence of German power.[17]

On the other side of the Atlantic, some traditional undercurrents of anti-Americanism seem to be assuming a new shape and intensity as well. Since the emigration of the Krefelders in 1683, Germans have alternated between praising the United States as a land of freedom and opportunity and condemning it as a modernist threat to culture, exemplar of economic greed, and/or imperialist oppressor. Currently, left-wing intellectuals who are tired of having American job creation held up as a shining example in the context of an intractable 11 percent unemployment, are ridiculing the American world of "McJobs" according to the motto: "Sure, thousands of jobs have been created, but I hold three of them." Social Democratic critics like the former finance minister Oskar Lafontaine castigate the "casino capitalism" of speculators that is running rampant in business, producing fluctuations in international currency markets, and forcing company mergers. Reinforced by media reports of spectacular violence, death penalties to German citizens and recurrent natural disasters, this "McJob" perspective suggests that America represents a Darwinian world of struggles for survival from which any educated European ought to recoil in horror.[18]

The reasons for the resurgence of anti-American rhetoric have much to do with the difficult process of economic adjustment to the pressures of worldwide competition, which is reinforcing traditional leftist skepticism. During the cold war, the Right had admired Washington's leadership and security guarantee but loathed American popular culture, while the Left had welcomed the informality of U.S. lifestyles and protest culture but railed against capitalist imperialism.[19] Now the business community has embraced neoliberalism and is using the argument of Germany's lack of competitiveness in the global economy in order to call for reductions in taxes and regulations that would dismantle the extensive welfare state, characteristic of the social market economy.[20] In this domestic power struggle, the labor unions and intellectuals find themselves on the defensive, having to reject the American example to maintain their hard-won privileges. In order to uphold their model of social policy, they claim the continental pattern of caring for the weaker members of the community to be morally superior and accuse the United States of heartless pursuit of profit.

Though it has been overshadowed by close military cooperation in the Kosovo war, the painful German emancipation from American tutelage also fosters intermittent resentment against "superpower arrogance." For instance, the unyielding insistence on a wider security perimeter for the embassy of the United States to be built at the Brandenburg Gate in Berlin created much negative publicity, since it would mean shifting a couple of roads into the Tiergarten and into the plot of the German Holocaust memorial.[21] When commenting on incidents like the impeachment proceedings and the Lewinsky affair, media reporting in *Der Spiegel* or *Die Zeit* was often dismissive of American politics, since such conflicts seem ridiculous and incomprehensible to European elites. The cumulative effect of consistent carping about U.S. "unilateralism" or "inconstancy" is a growing disbelief in the moral superiority of American protestations of human rights, an increasing resentment against being bullied by a larger ally, and a still subterranean reluctance to follow U.S. leads.[22]

Beyond the rhetoric of German-American friendship, one can therefore discern a rising sense of ambivalence about the respective partner. Mutual perceptions are becoming more critical in the media and intellectual circles, not because of particular actions on one side or the other, but due to different domestic preoccupations within the respective country.[23] Elements of real difficulties, such as the German burden of the past or the proliferation of American minimum-wage jobs, are exaggerated out of proportion because they fit into agendas that can be justified by spreading such clichés. On the German side, the continual harping on Holocaust guilt is likely to strengthen the covert resentment over being endlessly reminded of the unsavory past, resonating with Martin Walser's statement of 1998 that enough contrition ought to be enough.[24] On the American end, foreign criticism of racial divisions, urban ghettos, and the lack of health insurance among the poor might very well reinforce older patterns of nativist disdain for European cultural affectations, especially on the Right.

Divergent Priorities

The clichés above are compounded by a gradual divergence of interests and priorities between the United States and Germany. Washington still has to come to terms with its post–cold war position as the sole remaining military and economic superpower, simultaneously courted and criticized by its friends and adversaries. Berlin faces the adjustment to the return of normalcy as a continental nation-state that is expected to exercise leadership due to its size and prosperity, but is damned if it actually uses its increased power. The benign construct of mutual complementarity of worldwide American leadership and a limited regional German role seems to function well enough—as long as the fundamental interests of these two partners do not clash. However, the concurrent reconstructions of national identity combined with trying challenges to economic interests pose the question: What kinds of visions are beginning to inform the international outlooks on both sides of the Atlantic?[25]

In recent years, the American public has started to view the world in "global" terms, making "globalization" one of the buzzwords of the 1990s. On the positive side, this McLuhanesque concept suggests a widening of horizons beyond national frontiers to the worldwide implications of economic developments and communication flows, i.e., a broadening of intellectual perspectives. In response to the growing racial diversity of immigrant groups in the United States, many Americans are suddenly becoming curious about remote corners of the globe to which they had never before paid attention, since now they might have repercussions for their own lives. In a secularized version of the old missionary drive, the social sciences have developed a problem-perspective that no longer treats hunger, ecological damage, and diseases like AIDS as local phenomena, but as linked and transcending threats that can only be met by global cooperation.[26] Needless to say, in this globalization of perspectives, Europe has started to lose its privileged conceptual place.

At times American academics have been a bit oblivious to the dark underside of the globalization rhetoric that essentially functions as justification for a neoliberal agenda. Based on Adam Smith's precepts, advocates of global perspectives seek to liberate the market forces from their constraints in order to enter an era of worldwide exchange of goods and services and to exploit the advantages of location (raw materials, labor costs), thereby benefiting consumers worldwide. Among those who stand to profit from this vision are limited number of transnational corporations that want to operate without regard to national laws or social costs, and a small group of financial speculators who intend to cash in on the rise and fall of national currencies or stock markets. In some ways this is but a continuation of the American Open Door policy before World War I, which was a form of indirect, economic imperialism that avoided incurring the cost of a formal empire. While some individuals and companies make enormous fortunes from the current trend, the hype ignores that globalization is also leading to a loss of manufacturing jobs in high-wage countries, a breakdown of social services, and an increase in competition between regions.[27]

The intellectual benefits of the globalization perspective have also been somewhat exaggerated. Of course, it is better to be informed about developments in the wider world and to have a sense of human interdependence around the globe.[28] But much of the practice of global studies has been culture blind—conducting the discussions in English and assuming that the rest of the world shares the moral and cultural values embedded in this lingua franca. In the field, the disasters of ethnocentric theorizing have been dramatic, most prominently the failure of the Harvard Business School to reconstruct the Russian economy due to its glaring ignorance of Slavic customs. On campus, the global perspective has, for all of its good intentions, often meant a projection of internal American agendas of race and gender onto the rest of the world, irrespective of whether these problems were similarly pressing elsewhere. Curiously enough, the category of social class and the question of exploitation seem to have gotten lost in the global shuffle. While some problems like environmental damage must, indeed, be tackled on a worldwide level, the globalization perspective appears to have led, as an unintended byproduct, to a kind of *globalized parochialism* that defines everything as essentially the same and fails to come to terms with the profound otherness of the other.[29]

The German reaction to this globalization challenge has been an intensified commitment to Europeanization. Originally, the turn to Europe was also a constructive impulse to prevent the recurrence of war on the devastated continent in the early 1950s through some kind of supranational organization that would ban the ghosts of nationalism once and for all. Who could forget the touching picture of the diminutive French president François Mitterand hand in hand with the massive German chancellor Helmut Kohl, paying their last respects to the dead of the First World War at its quintessential battlefield in Verdun? This kind of idealism was also reinforced by a keen sense of self-interest that led France's farmers and Germany's industrialists, plus Benelux's traders, to found the Common Market that has metamorphosed into the European Union with fifteen members and a new currency of its own. Compared with the boundless aspirations of globalization, European integration seems more like a modest project, somehow suited to the shrunken power of the Old Continent.[30]

In practice, however, the European enterprise has also narrowed into a form of economism with serious unemployment problems and democratic deficits. When the ambitious initial effort to create a European defense and political community foundered on the French veto in the 1950s, the functionalist strategy of combining economic interests proved more successful in constructing first a free trade zone and eventually an integrated market. The beneficiaries of these integration steps were by and large the big European-wide companies and some American subsidiaries rather than the workers, because capital flows and production relocation proved much easier than the movement of labor. The high agricultural tariffs and subsidies for agriculture (butter mountains and milk lakes) not only angered American competitors, but also dearly cost European consumers, while postcolonial preference schemes further distorted trading patterns. At the same time, a massive European-wide bureaucracy arose in Brussels and tried to regulate everything from French Camembert to the purity of German beer. Until recently, the European parliament has been unable to oversee the commission, which is more responsive to the wishes of individual member states than to the elected representatives.[31] Toward the outside, Europeanization therefore has often meant a raising of barriers in order to keep the forces of globalization at bay.

As an ideology, Europeanism may actually function as the present-day equivalent of nineteenth-century nationalism. Beyond calculation of gains or losses, the German dedication to integration is based on a faith that every problem is better served if addressed on a European level. Of course, much of this attitude is a result of the excess of nationalism that was discredited by Nazi genocide, and has left intellectuals without a sense of transpersonal mission—a void filled by the attractive vision of a European community at peace. Moreover, as survey research shows, this conviction is carried more passionately by the economic and academic elites than by the publics for whom Europe means at best a wider selection of vegetables in the supermarket or an easier crossing of former frontiers.[32] One flaw in this scenario is the fact that French and British intellectuals, who are not traumatized by World War II to the same degree, do not share this supranational fixation. Though generally ready to concede the utility of removing economic barriers, they are loath to part with sovereignty or to abandon their cultures to an international melange, let alone give up their sense of national identity.[33] The sizable gap between the holiday rhetoric in favor of integration and the practical problems with its implementation makes the European project still rather embattled on the inside.

Though their economies and defense systems are more strongly intertwined than ever, these divergent views are moving the old and new worlds further apart psychologically. Perhaps the conception of a common set of Western values that was shared on both sides of the Atlantic and promoted to American students in Western civilization courses was an artifact of the cold war and underlying differences are beginning to reassert themselves with its passing. No doubt the United States is a global power and economy with many more multilateral responsibilities, while Germany, after the bloody failure to achieve this rank, would be well advised to content itself with a more circumscribed European role.[34] But there is a danger that, in the globalization perspective, the old continent will gradually disappear from sight and that the Europeanization drive will, under French influence, assume an anti-American edge. The reasoned and nuanced voices of the academic specialists on both sides of the Atlantic are hardly strong enough to counter this continental drifting apart, since they are themselves caught up in promoting globalization and European integration projects.

One-Sided Convergence

Cultural stereotyping and differences in outlook might not matter, if there were strong economic or political forces pushing both societies toward some kind of convergence. At first blush the prospect for such a development might look favorable, since American music dominates

European radio, Hollywood movies crowd continental television screens, and American software is present on every German computer. At the same time, a goodly number of German luxury cars race along American superhighways, upscale supermarkets sell European delicacies, and the pages of women's magazines continue to display continental fashions. But the heyday of the Europeanization of American lifestyles among the yuppie generation, which produced a slew of so-called Euro-products such as Euro-Sport for soccer equipment or Euro-Coffee for continental lattes, seems more than a decade past. In contrast, the spread of McDonald's franchises to ancient city centers indicates that the Americanization of consumer tastes and popular culture appears to continue unabated on the continent. If they are correct, these impressions point to a potentially troubling problem: Can convergence continue to prove beneficial if it proceeds largely in one direction, making Europe more American rather than vice versa?

On the cultural level, the postmodern wave, if one can use this shorthand for linguistic and post-structuralist theories, appears to have long since crested.[35] In the United States, as the names of Derrida, Foucault, Lyotard, and others show, these philosophical perspectives and analytical methods have been associated with French theory rather than with their Germanic antecedents in Heidegger or Nietzsche. In contrast, only a small group of American thinkers has tried to discuss the counterpositions of a Habermas or a Gadamer. Moreover, in their feminist and especially postcolonialist variant, the American postmodernists have constructed the "dead white European male" as ideal-type enemy in order to hold him responsible for the disasters of Western civilization and the repression of women and other races around the world. The somewhat ironic consequence of the reception of French theory has therefore been a deconstruction of European canons as male-centered and exclusively white.[36] While much of the effort to broaden cultural horizons was long overdue, it has nonetheless led to students no longer conversant with the Western classics.

On the political level, the Republican revolution of the 1990s, for all of its cultural conservatism, has been utterly resistant to European influences. The whole neoliberal project has been directed toward the dismantling of the state—not the cutting of business subsidies, but rather the elimination of even the relatively weak welfare system that does exist in the United States.[37] To be sure, the success of the Common Market helped inspire the creation of the North American Free Trade Association (NAFTA), notoriously weak in labor regulations and environmental protections. But other attempted transfers of European models have foundered: the effort at health care reform that sought to provide insurance for the bottom quarter of the populace that is not covered—an unparalleled scandal in the civilized world! Also, the brief flirtation with the German system that combines apprenticeship and trade schooling has gone nowhere, and the import of fast commuter trains has been limited to the route between Boston and Washington, D.C. In certain political circles, it seems to be enough to attach the word "European" to an initiative in order to kill it, because it smacks of liberalism, or even worse, socialism!

In contrast, Germans continue to respond to American influences on many levels—even if examples from the United States are invoked for conflicting purposes. In the political area, Washington's reversal from opposing military involvement to actually demanding participation has contributed to resolving the question of deployment within the NATO umbrella. Since the *Grundgesetz*, the federal constitution, prohibited German soldiers from being used for any but defensive purposes, it took a long struggle to overcome the resistance of the pacifist Greens, the left wing of the Social Democratic Party, and the remnants of the religious and trade union-based peace movement. Dramatized by the Bosnian horrors, U.S. calls for German involvement in peacekeeping in the Balkans led to an incremental change that started with hospital and supply units and gradually moved up to fuller participation. When politicians could come to no agreement, the German Supreme Court had to rule on the question in order to authorize participation in peace missions, provided they were legitimized by the United Nations. With this decision, Germany has left behind its postwar exceptionalism of economic powerhouse and political dwarf, and has begun to become a more "normal" nation state.[38]

Another area in which the American multicultural example has played a crucial role has been the contested issue of immigration and citizenship. The U.S. model of a legislatively controlled in-migration coupled with a rapid naturalization of foreign-born migrants has been a powerful argument against conservative Germans who oppose immigration as well as the granting of citizenship to foreigners. While there is still no immigration law, the asylum compromise of returning migrants to safe countries through which they have passed and the more stringent language requirements for ethnic re-migrants seem to have decreased the influx considerably. More importantly, recent legislation, supported by a solid Social Democratic Party (SPD), Green, and Free Democratic Party (FDP) majority in the Bundestag and Bundesrat, has transformed the *jus sanguinis* into a *jus soli*, offering citizenship to those foreigners' children who are born in Germany (if they choose before the age of 23), while making the naturalization of their parents easier. This is a fundamental change in German political culture that would not have been possible without frequent references to the positive American experience of integrating immigrants.[39]

A final example of positive U.S. influence is the still seemingly intractable issue of university reform. By allowing the extension of the West German system to the new Eastern states, German unification only postponed the day of reckoning for a system that was still rhetorically dedicated to Humboldtian ideals of personal cultivation while practically engaging in mass professional training.[40] But the arrival of the truly integrated market in Europe is forcing the convertibility of academic degrees across countries in order to permit the free movement of people as well as capital or goods. In addition, the vast overcrowding of the German system, its underfunding in the humanities and social sciences, and the prolonged time taken for students to finish degrees are also calling for some drastic action. As a result, an informal consensus has been building on freeing institutional leadership from bureaucratic tutelage, introducing the B.A. as a preliminary degree, giving the institutions lump sum budgets, and allowing the universities some voice in the selection of future students. While the concept of charging tuition is still in ideological limbo, blocked by a rear guard of sixty-eighters, there is some hope that state-level reforms will at last make the system more flexible and responsive.

Yet if it remains one-sided, such convergence will lose its constructive effect and ultimately risk creating fresh resentment rather than partnership. In part, the asymmetry in size and power between the United States and the Federal Republic of Germany makes it logical that the former should have more formative influence on the latter than the other way around. Also, technological leadership, the glamorization of popular culture, and the spread of consumerism, not to mention the resilience of democracy, give the American example reasons to be imitated by others. But there are German virtues to be admired as well in the quality of labor training, the comprehensiveness of welfare provisions, the success of environmental protection, and the efficiency of public transportation—areas in which Americans might well learn from Europe.[41] Of course, the cold war arrangement in which the United States provided military protection and economic help while the old continent offered historical sites and high culture has disappeared, never to return. But a new set of mutualities that go beyond a one-sided copying will need to take its place in order for viable ties to survive the next half-century.

Living with Difference

Though there is no reason for undue alarm, the indicators discussed above suggest that some of the cultural underpinnings of the German-American relationship began to erode during the last decade. Instead of ushering in a harmonious "partnership in leadership," to paraphrase George Bush,[42] unexpected tensions have arisen that have widened the gap in mutual perceptions, created divergent policy priorities, and complicated processes of learning from each other. In the high-pressure environment of international politics, the discernable indifference between the transatlantic partners may quickly turn into a substantive policy difference. The much heralded "successor generation," which lacks the memories of cold war comradeship, is being socialized into a world in which transatlantic solidarity is no longer an automatic result of shared values, but a consequence of deliberate choices between competing alternatives. Since calls for "founding the transatlantic community anew" have foundered on domestic preoccupations, it might be wiser to acknowledge the emerging differences, and to discuss their implications in order to learn to live with them.[43]

For Americans, such self-reflection might mean an acceptance of the passing of their tutelage over Germany that still seems hard for some former administrators, soldiers, or even intellectuals.[44] The laudable Holocaust-education efforts should be complemented by equal attempts to make the public aware of the rehabilitation of the Germans after 1945, lest frozen images from a terrible past prevent an understanding of the current dynamics of a major partner. Also, the globalization perspective would become more constructive if it did not lose sight of Europe, engaged the issue of who will lose from the process, and stopped "naturalizing" its own agenda as an inevitable phenomenon. Instead of constructing the old continent as the cultural enemy, the critical perspectives, based on a gender, race, and a revived class analysis, ought to develop a more complex picture of the New Europe as riven by tensions similar to those of contemporary America. Finally, a dose of modesty would make it easier for the United States to learn from those positive European examples that do provide interesting solutions to vexing problems.

For the Germans, such self-examination would imply a growing recognition of their own responsibility in Europe without hiding any longer behind the terrible legacy of the past.[45] This maturing process also presupposes a deeper understanding of the United States as the leading power of the free world, an appreciation that would finally break out of the traditional love-hate relationship fueled by sensationalist media clichés. Neither fawning idealization nor disappointed denigration of U.S. motives and actions will be helpful. What is needed is a sympathetic yet critical sense of the tension between noble dreams and practical shortcomings in the American experiment.[46] A less ideological approach to the European integration project would also be more constructive, since the transnational super-state may not be the answer that the German neighbors really want. Instead, a looser and more open-ended structure may turn out to be more viable, if it allows different tiers of power and identity to persist within a larger whole.[47] Finally, learning from American examples need not be a slavish imitation of every latest fashion, but a more self-assured and selective borrowing of what really works.

What is therefore required is a *new curiosity* on both sides that is ready to explore the differences arising out of the return to normalcy. Markers such as location, size, ethnic composition, and religious orientation make the Federal Republic of Germany and the United States of America too distinctive from one another to ever be completely in agreement on everything. But current intellectual dissonances need not be a threat, if the mediators between cultures openly confront them as a challenge to the imagination.[48] Instead of taking traditional assumptions of common values, intertwined histories, and shared problems for granted, German-American cooperation will flourish only if both sides come to terms with the shifting perceptions, priorities, and learning processes of the present. Compensating for the drying up of immigration, military stationing, and other older ties requires much investment from the American side as well, in the infrastructure of student exchanges, academic research centers, and people-to-people encounters, to create a "transatlantic learning community." But most of all, the relationship needs a more candid acknowledgement of some of the present divergences in order to manage them for the sake of a common future.[49]

Notes

1. Robert D. Blackwill, *The Future of Transatlantic Relations: Report by an Independent Task Force Sponsored by the Council on Foreign Relations* (New York, 1999), 9ff. See Michelle Raffino, "The United States and Germany: Foreign Policy and Domestic Determinants," American Council on Germany *Occasional Paper*, no. 4 (1999).
2. Konrad H. Jarausch, "American Policy Towards German Unification: Images and Interests," in *Transatlantic Images and Perceptions: Germany and America since 1776*, ed. David Barclay and Elisabeth Glaser-Schmidt (Cambridge, MA, 1997), 333–52.
3. They are now available: François Furet, *The Passing of an Illusion: The Idea of Communism in the Twentieth Century* (Chicago, 1999), and Stéphane Courtois et al., eds., *The Black Book of Communism: Crimes, Terror, Repression* (Cambridge, MA/London, 1999).
4. Werner Weidenfeld, *America and Europe: Is the Break Inevitable?* (Gütersloh, 1996), 9ff.
5. Special session of the 1999 meeting of the German Studies Association in Atlanta on "Recasting the Alliance: The Future of German-American Relations," organized by Wolfgang-Uwe Friedrich with panelists Karsten Voigt, Jürgen Stark, Peter Göbel, J. D. Bindenagel, James A. Cooney, Jackson Janes, and Carroll Brown.
6. Weidenfeld, *America and Europe*, 99ff.
7. For the classical "image" literature see Willi Paul Adams and Knud Krakau, eds., *Deutschland und Amerika: Perzeption und historische Realität* (Berlin, 1985).
8. For instance, American Council on Germany, *1998 Annual Report* (New York, 1999), as well as Kristin L. Archick, "The XX American-German Young Leaders Conference," American Council on Germany *Occasional Paper*, no. 9 (1998).
9. According to Richard Brod and Bettina J. Huber, "Foreign Language Enrollment in US Institutions of Higher Education, Fall 1995," *ADFL Bulletin* 28 (1997): 55–61, German enrollments declined by 27.8 percent between 1990 and 1995, continuing a retreat from the all-time high of 1968.
10. As background see Klaus Weigelt, ed., *Das Deutschland- und Amerikabild: Beiträge zum gegenseitigen Verständnis beider Völker* (Melle, 1986), especially 10ff., 95ff.
11. Daniel J. Goldhagen, *Hitler's Willing Executioners: Ordinary Germans and the Holocaust* (New York, 1996).
12. Mariam Niraumand, *The Americanization of the Holocaust* (Berlin, 1995).
13. Peter Novick, *The Holocaust in American Life* (Boston, 1999); Bernhard Giesen, *Die Intellektuellen und die Nation: Eine deutsche Achsenzeit* (Frankfurt, 1993).
14. Norman G. Finkelstein, *The Holocaust Industry: Reflections on the Exploitation of the Jewish Suffering* (New York, 2000); Charles S. Maier, "Das Spiel finsterer Mächte?" *Süddeutsche Zeitung*, 16 August 2000.
15. Jane Kramer, *The Politics of Memory: Looking for Germany in the New Germany* (New York, 1996); Marc Fischer, *After the Wall: Germany, the Germans and the Burdens of History* (New York, 1995).

16. David Schoenbaum and Elizabeth Pond, *Annäherung an Deutschland: Die Strapazen der Normalität* (Stuttgart, 1997).
17. Andrei S. Markovits and Simon Reich, *The German Predicament: Memory and Power in the New Europe* (Ithaca, 1997).
18. See the coverage in *Der Spiegel, Die Zeit* and on German TV.
19. Dan Diner, *Verkehrte Welten: Antiamerikanismus in Deutschland. Ein historischer Essay* (Frankfurt, 1993).
20. "Competitiveness—Defining the Terms, Shaping the Policies: A German-American Dialogue," American Institute for Contemporary German Studies *Seminar Paper*, no. 11 (Washington, D.C., 1995).
21. Roger Cohen, "Germans Are Balking at US Embassy Blueprint," *New York Times*, 28 October 1999. The conflict has been resolved by greater flexibility on the part of the Bush administration.
22. Andrei S. Markovits, "Anti-Americanism and the Struggle for a West German Identity," in *The Federal Republic of Germany at Forty*, ed. Peter H. Merkl (New York, 1989), 35–54.
23. Even the otherwise optimistic report of the Council on Foreign Relations sees this development as a potential danger. Blackwill, *Future of Transatlantic Relations*, 12ff.
24. See the text of Martin Walser's 1998 peace prize speech at the Frankfurt book fair and the controversial reaction to it. In Frank Schirrmacher, ed., *Die Walser-Bubis-Debatte: Eine Dokumentation* (Frankfurt, 1999).
25. For the German side, see Konrad H. Jarausch, ed., *After Unity: Reconstructing German Identities* (Providence, 1997).
26. Essays in Stefan Immerfall, ed., *Territoriality in the Globalizing Society: One Place or None?* (Berlin, 1998).
27. Paul Krugman, *The Accidental Theorist: And Other Dispatches from the Dismal Science* (New York, 1998).
28. For a positive example, see Charles Bright and Michael Geyer, "World History in a Global Age," *American Historical Review* 100 (1995): 1034–60.
29. Konrad H. Jarausch, "Globalization: Premise or Problem?" *Global Perspectives* (April 1997). See also J. K. Gibson-Graham, "Querying Globalization," in *The End of Capitalism (As We Know It): A Feminist Critique of Political Economy* (Cambridge, MA, 1997), 120–47.
30. See, for instance, Derek W. Urwin, *The Community of Europe: A History of European Integration since 1945* (London, 1995).
31. Tony Judt, *A Grand Illusion: An Essay on Europe* (New York, 1996).
32. Konrad H. Jarausch, "From Empire to Europe: The Taming of German Power," in idem and Michael Geyer, *Shattered Pasts: Reconstructing German Histories* (Princeton, forthcoming).
33. Gary Marks, "Territorial Identities in the European Union," in Jeffrey Anderson, ed., *Regional Integration and Democracy: Expanding the European Experience* (Boulder, 1999), 69–91.
34. Max Otte, *A Rising Middle Power? German Foreign Policy in Transformation, 1989–1999* (New York, 2000), 199ff.
35. Joyce Appleby, Lynn Hunt, and Margaret Jacobsen, *Telling the Truth About History* (New York, 1994), 198–237.
36. Paul Berman, ed., *Debating PC: The Controversy over Political Correctness on College Campuses* (New York, 1992), and the special issue of the *Partisan Review* on "The Changing Culture of the University," no. 2 (1991).
37. Newt Gingrich, *Lessons Learned the Hard Way* (New York, 1998).
38. Markovits and Reich, *The German Predicament*, 137ff.
39. Jeffrey Peck, Mitchell G. Ash, and Christiane Lemke, "Natives, Strangers, and Foreigners: Constituting Germans by Constructing Others," in Konrad H. Jarausch, ed., *After Unity: Reconfiguring German Identities* (Providence, 1997), 61–102.
40. Konrad H. Jarausch, "The Humboldt Syndrome: West German Universities, 1945–1990 – An Academic *Sonderweg*?" in *German Universities Past and Future – Crisis or Renewal?*

ed. Mitchell G. Ash (Providence, 1997). See also Hans-Peter Söder, "Wie modern ist die deutsche Universität?" *Universitas* 54 (1999): 269–81.

41. Weidenfeld, *America and Europe*, 54ff.
42. Gerald R. Kleinfeld, "Partners in Leadership? The Future of German-American Relations," in *The Federal Republic of Germany at Forty-Five: Union Without Unity*, ed. Peter H. Merkl (New York, 1995), 60–79.
43. Weidenfeld, *America and Europe*, 115ff.
44. A case in point is the CIA's foot-dragging on returning the foreign espionage files of the Stasi to the German government. Robert Gerald Livingston, "The Quest for Stasi's Old Files," *Los Angeles Times*, 27 December 1998, and "Akt der Freundschaft," *Der Spiegel*, no. 32 (1999): 116.
45. Markovits and Reich, *The German Predicament*, 203ff; Schoenbaum and Pond, *Annäherung*, 184ff.
46. Diner, *Verkehrte Welten*, 168ff.
47. It is the continuing disunity of the Europeans on issues of defense, sovereignty, and the like that renders hopes for a "global strategic partnership" illusory. Blackwill, *The Future of Transatlantic Relations*, 3ff.
48. Lothar Bredella, ed., *Mediating a Foreign Culture: The United States and Germany* (Tübingen, 1991).
49. Frank Trommler, "Unification Policies and the German Image: Comments on the American Reaction," in Barclay and Glaser-Schmidt, *Transatlantic Images and Perceptions*, 353–61; and Weidenfeld, *America and Europe*, 125ff.

Chapter 16

EUROPE AND THE UNITED STATES
Looking beyond 2000

Theo Sommer

Introduction

At the beginning of the twenty-first century, the Atlantic Alliance stands at an important crossroads. What is at stake far transcends the narrow field of German-American relations, which continue to be important but have been dissolving progressively into the wider scope of European-American relations. The fact that I was invited to speak on "German-American Relations in the Future European Context" reflects this momentous innovation. It also reflects the recognition that since 1989, the world has undergone profound change: new factors have upset the premises of the old transatlantic partnership, and for this relationship to endure we shall have to recast its very foundations.

The Post–Cold War World

At the end of the 1980s, the world that we had come to know since 1945 was still intact: the world of the cold war with its familiar risks, its comfortable certitudes, and the acknowledged need to huddle together. But in the very year of 1989, the rumblings of impending change began to resonate through Eastern Europe. Within six months the Berlin Wall came down; within eighteen months Germany was reunified and Eastern Europe freed from the shackles of communism; within thirty-two months the Soviet Union fell apart.

It was a famous victory for the West. Yet with communism dead and Russia but a pale shadow of its previous powerful self, the West suddenly found itself in the same predicament the Athenians found themselves in upon the discovery that there were no longer any Persians on their doorstep. Like the Greeks 2,500 years ago, we have come to lament, to quote Constantine Cavafy's famous line: "And now what shall become of us without any barbarians? Those people were a kind of solution."[1] Reflecting the deep concern of many, Mark Nelson argued in *Foreign Policy*: "With no common enemy, Europe and America are coming unglued."[2]

At roughly the same time, a second phenomenon started to change the existing terrain. The onset of globalization signaled a fundamental change of paradigms. Geopolitics and geostrategy receded into the background; geo-economy became the name of the game. "It's the economy, stupid"—that admonition was stuck on the bulletin boards of chancelleries all over the world, not only in the White House.

We all know that warding off a common threat unites nations. By contrast, fighting for market share is inherently divisive. Commenting on the "strategic traders" in Clinton's Washington and the protectionist afflictions of the Brussels Commission, Daniel Bell coined the apt phrase: "Economics has become the continuation of war by other means." Indeed, if formerly the essential task was military containment of enemy states, now it is all too frequently conceived as economic containment of partner nations. There is a real danger that the cooperative triangle United States/Europe/Japan-Asia will break up and give way to a constellation in which three rival blocs engage in all-out competition. At the very least, we must expect a great deal of severe interdependence friction.

In addition to the end of the cold war and the rise of globalization, a third phenomenon completes the picture of change during the past ten years: the gradual but unstoppable rise of Europe. The European Community was already on the way to the "Single Market" when the Berlin wall came down and the Soviet Empire disintegrated. Its leaders immediately decided to push ahead toward full monetary and political union—partly to tie in, or tie down, united Germany even more firmly in the West European association, partly to provide a staunch and stable basis for the piecemeal integration of newly liberated Central and Eastern Europe. This was the whole purport of the Maastricht Treaty. It entered into force on November 1, 1993; on that date, the European Community became the European Union. And 365 days before the end of the century, the Monetary Union sprang into existence, comprising from the very outset the astonishing number of eleven members, all of whom met the tough Maastricht criteria.

I have always been convinced that the European Monetary Union (EMU) would come about. I am as firmly convinced now—never mind the initial weakness of the euro—that the Monetary Union will be a success and will evolve into "a more perfect union," a political union. In the year 2020, give or take five years, it will be a reality. By then, the European Union (EU) will count two dozen or even two-and-a-half dozen members. It will have a palpable security and defense identity. And it will be a global actor in its own right; not in opposition to the United States, but autonomous—an equal partner at long last.

Points of Friction

The past decade has highlighted a number of issues on which the allies do not see eye to eye. As human beings tend to be alarmist about the future and nostalgic about the past, it is perhaps useful to remember that transatlantic relations have never been trouble-free. Europeans and Americans quarreled about nuclear strategy. They differed about the handling of out-of-area problems. They never ended wrangling about how to deal with the Soviet Union. The recent squabbles over bananas and hormone-fed beef were long ago preceded by "chicken wars" and tariff tiffs over soybeans. Thus we have always had our difficulties with each other—but we have always overcome them. The question is whether our differences are categorically more serious at present, and whether we shall once again be able to overcome them.

Let me make two general remarks before I deal with the three main differences—and "differends"—in Euro-American relations:

1. The United States is now the sole remaining superpower. Its unilateralist attitudes are no longer checked by the Soviet Union. There is a powerful temptation "to perceive the national role in hegemonic terms" (William Pfaff); to "throw its weight around" (Volker Stanzl); to deduce from the primacy of American military power a natural right to call the shots—by fiat, rather than by catalytic leadership, persuasion, or patient coalition building. There is no denying the fact that the United States is "the indispensable nation" and will remain the pivotal power on the world scene. But the Balkan crises of the 1990s should have made it clear to everyone that the United States cannot act alone with any hope of success. It needs allies to prevail. The argument put forth by Madeleine Albright that Americans deserve to lead because they "stand taller and see farther" is by no means universally shared. Others cannot help notice the highly erratic nature of U.S. foreign policy in recent years, the waning inclination of the American public to see their country engage in the world beyond their own shores, and the disturbing tendency to treat foreign affairs chiefly as a sop to specific ethnic constituencies around election time. While Joe Joffe's remark that the United States "irks and domineers, but it does not conquer" is of course true, Europeans do feel overwhelmed at times—if not conquered, then badgered, buttonholed, and railroaded.[3]

2. Europeans gratefully acknowledged President Clinton's declaration of support for the European Union in 1994: "I believe our best partner, as we look toward the twenty-first century for prosperity and peace, is a Europe united in democracy, in free markets, in common security." Yet in this field, as in many others, the administration does not always speak with one voice. Statements from the seventh floor of the State Department like "Europe is not the world" or "The twenty-first

century belongs to the Pacific nations" were hardly apt to inspire European confidence. The Americans have habitually been of two minds about the venture of European integration. On the one hand they welcomed it, on the other they begrudged the Europeans their progress toward "an ever closer union" (Maastricht) whenever they took another step forward. One remembers Henry Kissinger's complaint about not having a single telephone number to ring when he wanted to talk to Europe. But whenever the Europeans did agree on a particular issue, he came storming out of meetings, griping "They are ganging up on me."

The pre-history of the EMU could also be cited as a case in point. For a long time, Americans totally ignored the project. When it could not be overlooked any more, they tried to belittle or ridicule it. Finally, when the EMU became a reality, we read Martin Feldstein's absurd theory that it would lead to war between the United States and the European Union. There were, of course, more positive utterances. William Pfaff foresaw increased rivalry and competition on account of the euro, which is a reasonable case to be made. Euroland has 290 million inhabitants compared to the United States' 270 million. Its aggregate GNP tops that of the United States ($8.1 trillion as against $7.8 trillion). Its share in world GNP, at present 20 percent, is larger than that of either the United States or Japan. As Fred Bergsten, an outright fan of the euro, pointed out, it is likely to become, over time, a powerful rival to the dollar.[4] Certainly it is going to spur on the process of political integration. Harmonization of economic, fiscal, and tax policies is bound to follow the creation of a common currency. And since the EU's Cologne and Helsinki summits in 1999, there can no longer be any doubt that the European Union is on the way to acquiring a distinct identity in the field of defense and security as well.

Americans tend to scoff at Europe's inability to get its act together. But, from our vantage point, Washington, too, is frequently quite unable to get its own act together. The coexistence of mighty institutional power centers like the White House, the Congress, the Pentagon, and the State Department creates complications no less bothersome than the existence of fifteen national governments within the European Union. True, more centralized power has already been acquired by or accumulated with the Brussels Commission than the citizens of the United States have ever seen fit to grant to their federal government in Washington. This does not yet hold true for foreign and security policy, but give us another ten or twenty years and we shall get there, too.

I would like to draw your attention to three specific arenas in which Europeans and Americans are likely to clash unless they make a conscious effort to resolve their differences. The first arena of discord is

NATO. What is its mission supposed to be in the early twenty-first century? The second potential field of battle is trade and economics. Can we address the problems arising in this field in a spirit of collaboration rather than in a beastly zero-sum game mood? The third battleground lies in the realm of cultural and attitudinal discrepancies, where self-images, historical identities, and divergent value scales tend to assume more prominence.

The Future of NATO

In the 1990s, the alliance was revamped. In the absence of an existential threat, force levels were steeply lowered; the American garrison in Europe was reduced from 350,000 personnel to less than 100,000; the Europeans halved the number of men and women in uniform. In this regard, NATO has adjusted to the new dispensation which has emerged in the post–cold war era. What it has not been able to achieve is unanimity about NATO's future role.

At the fiftieth anniversary jubilee of the North Atlantic Treaty Organization in 1999, the allies tried to map out a new strategy and define a new purpose for NATO. They failed, however, in their attempt to re-forge NATO into an instrument for projecting allied power in the service of human rights, democracy, and stability. The documents signed at the Washington Summit in April 1999 were replete with high-sounding rhetoric, but they were barely able to conceal a fundamental dissonance. While the U.S. administration tried to upgrade NATO to a kind of global policeman, to act wherever and whenever there is ethnic or religious conflict, the Europeans are wary of boundless out-of-area interventionism to stop genocide, ethnic cleansing, or humanitarian horror. Small wonder that the Washington Declaration did not get too specific on what the defense diplomats call the "expanded core function" of the alliance. Where exactly does the "Euro-Atlantic space" begin and where does it end? Extraordinary threats emanate "from many directions," the document says—but it does not say whether they all rate the same vigorous reaction. "Non-article V contingencies" are to become the norm henceforth, yet there is no agreement on what this means in actual practice.[5]

The United States as the "sole remaining superpower" may feel compelled to react in a wide arc of crisis around the world, although the mood in 1999 on Capitol Hill and popular sentiment would seem to militate against this. Europe, at any rate, is going to limit its forays beyond the borders of the alliance to its immediate vicinity. There are few common European-American interests around the world. Barring a major conflict threatening the free flow of oil from the Middle East or the existence of the state of Israel, Europeans will prefer to stay on the sidelines in most out-of-area contingencies. This forebodes acrid debates each time such a contingency arises.

Against this background, no one should be surprised at the Europeans' reluctance to undertake the kind of arms modernization the Pentagon has been urging on them. Nor should the rather cool welcome Europe has extended to the "revolution in military affairs" that the Americans pushed in the 1990s come as a surprise to anybody. Europeans also remain wary of new American plans for a downsized Star Wars project to provide an antimissile shield against crazy rogue state dictators. And they were horrified by U.S. Senate's vote against ratifying the Comprehensive Test Ban Treaty (CTBT). It is indeed a reasonable question how the world's leading power expects to maintain pressure on nuclear proliferators like India, Pakistan, or Iran if it insists for itself on the right to test forever.

NATO's original mission was the defense of its members' territory against attack, and prior to such defensive action the deterrence of any armed aggression. The defense of its own real estate, as envisaged in Article V, was the only binding obligation members took upon themselves. Other missions were perhaps permitted under Article IV, but were neither mandated nor mandatory. This was especially true for out-of-area missions, which other than strictly defensive ones in the narrow territorial sense, were outright unthinkable. Now the Americans would like to broaden the brief of the alliance. This idea finds little favor in Europe. Europeans balk at reforming NATO into an instrument for projecting allied power in the service of human rights, democracy, and stability. They insist that defense is and should remain NATO's basic task. If the alliance were to serve other purposes, military action could only be taken on the basis of an explicit UN mandate. In the Kosovo war, the Europeans waived this requirement, as the powder keg was too close for comfort. But we should not delude ourselves that it would be brushed aside as easily in many other out-of-area contingencies. Prior commitment to such interventions will be impossible to attain. In the same vein, a formal rephrasing of the North Atlantic Treaty would be unlikely to pass most national parliaments. Europe will remain an Atlantic partner, but it will not become a global partner.

The European Union installed Javier Solana, the former Secretary General of NATO, as "Mr. Common Foreign and Security Policy." The job is a bit nondescript so far. But the new buzzword ESDI—European Security and Defense Identity—points in the direction in which Mr. Solana will take the EU partners. They want the capability to address and solve problems without always requiring U.S. combat involvement.

Many Europeans also harbor grave doubts about NATO's future strategy, in particular with regard to the role of nuclear weapons. They have some residual role, given the possibility that a resurgent Russia might once again turn against the West. However, their usefulness as a deterrent to the employment of chemical or biological weapons by "rogue states" seems limited. NATO's first-use doctrine has already come under attack. Like the stationing of U.S. nuclear weapons in Europe, this is likely to become a bone of transatlantic contention in the post–cold war environment.

For the alliance to survive, it will have to evolve toward the "two pillar" system envisaged by John F. Kennedy almost forty years ago, when the Europeans were not yet ready. But they have been preparing the ground for a two-pillar alliance ever since the Maastricht Treaty of 1991. One of the goals of this treaty is the development of a Common Security and Foreign Policy (ESFP) "including the eventual framing of a common defense policy, which might in time lead to a common defense."[6] For a long time, this phrase remained a mere rhetorical flourish. But as Europe intensified the search for its future identity, it has suddenly sprung to life. This was the result of Tony Blair's reversal of the previous British position. In December 1998, he agreed at Saint Malo with French president Chirac that "the Union must have the capacity for autonomous action backed up by credible national forces, the means to decide to use them, and a readiness to do so, in order to respond to international crisis."[7] The two leaders underlined their intention to thus "contribute to the vitality of a modernized Atlantic Alliance which is the foundation of the collective defense of its members." Similar sentiments pervaded a number of Franco-German statements. Chancellor Schröder put his view this way: "We want a new Europe for a new NATO, and we want the new NATO for the new Europe."[8]

It would seem the two-pillar alliance is an idea whose time has finally come. The Americans are entitled to say that they want to see both the new Europe and its novel defense architecture first. But they will themselves have to overcome their ambivalence about the two-pillar scheme—an ambivalence that has at times envenomed the protracted transatlantic talks about Combined Joint Task Forces (CJTF), a concept allowing the Europeans to use NATO assets for operations in which the Americans show no interest in participating.

The lessons of both Russia and Kosovo would seem to be that Europe and America must work together if they want to affect a particular situation. Proceeding separately invites stagnation or failure; working at cross-purposes means courting disaster; only cooperation leads to success. It will take a determined effort to prevent the deep structural forces which are currently at work on the world scene from pulling us apart.

Trade Friction and Economic Rivalry

As the world moves from geopolitics to geo-economics—which is what globalization is basically all about—bread-and-butter questions assume primary importance: employment, the trade balance, tariffs, a level playing field on the world market. Nations are tempted to interfere with Adam Smith's "invisible hand": whenever they feel that the jobs of their own workers and farmers are threatened, protectionism rears its ugly head. And trade strategists just love commercial conflicts, justifying, in the process, Daniel Bell's dictum about economics as the continuation of war by other means.

Economic issues have been a bone of contention between the United States and Europe for more than thirty years. Just remember the "chicken wars" of the early postwar years, the tariff battles over soybeans, or various squabbles over edible oils and steel exports. Our trade relations have never been entirely free of tension. Inflation, monetary policies, and the dollar exchange rate have frequently been the object of vociferous exchanges. Thus we should not be overly surprised that Europe and America are once again at loggerheads over economic matters.

In recent years, a number of specific transatlantic irritations have given rise to considerable bluster and brinkmanship by trade negotiators on both sides. There was, for instance, the interminable "banana issue." Since 1993, the European Union has been discriminating against Latin American bananas distributed by American companies, ostensibly to protect the interests of small Caribbean and African banana producers. In March 1999, the United States, frustrated after seventeen months of EU procrastination (and egged on by Chiquita, Dole, and Del Monte), imposed sanctions on exports from Europe. Only a modest 191 million dollars' worth of trade was at stake (out of a total transatlantic trade volume of $400 billion). But these punitive measures hit the manufacturers of French and Italian leather goods, German coffee machines, and British batteries very hard.

At the same time, Europe and America were embroiled in a battle over hormone-treated U.S. beef. When the EU failed to produce scientific evidence that hormone-treated beef presents a hazard to health, the United States imposed 100 percent duties on a range of European food products. Beef, pork, canned tomatoes, and mustard—annual value $110 million— mainly from Germany, Italy, and Denmark were affected. As in the banana case, American retaliation had the full backing of the World Trade Organization (WTO).

In another controversy, this time over American offshore tax arrangements for exporting companies, a WTO panel backed the Europeans. They claim that the American law permitting the creation of foreign sales corporations permits U.S. companies to channel 10 billion dollars' worth of profits through these corporations, annually saving themselves about $2 billion in taxes. Another dispute still simmering concerns the E.U.'s decision to ban older American aircraft fitted with expensive noise reduction devices known as "hush kits."

There are plenty of other contentious issues. Americans and Europeans have fallen out over mobile telephones. They quarrel about data privacy, aerospace subsidies, and champagne. A full-fledged war is in the offing over gene-modified foods. The tiff over Monsanto's "terminator" seeds was merely the first battle. The reports about Echelon, a surveillance network the United States uses to spy on the telecommunications of its allies to obtain industrial and economic secrets, has drawn heated protests in continental Europe.

The Americans object to European intransigence and inflexibility. The Europeans, in turn, fear that the traditional consensus for liberal trade has vanished in the United States. There is a lot of mutual spitballing. Many Americans worry about the possible effect a strengthening euro will have on the predominance of the U.S. dollar. European banks fret about the application of American rating systems to the European market. The competition between Boeing and Airbus is likely to heat up after the recent merger of Germany's Dasa and France's Aérospatiale. Transatlantic mergers and acquisitions are changing the givens. There is talk of a "war chest" raised for American buyouts in Europe, but more and more European companies are extending their activities to America (just think of Daimler-Benz or Bertelsmann). Lobbies set the tone on both sides of the Atlantic, while political leadership is all too often conspicuously absent. It is high time to put an end to all this bickering.

There is no denying it: the Atlantic nations are allies, yet they are also rivals. This fact was powerfully underscored in spring 1999, when the clash over banana exports came to a head precisely at the moment when America and Europe were engaged in fighting their war against Serbia. Shoulder to shoulder in war, at loggerheads in peace—this is a perverse situation. It jeopardizes an association that has proved its inestimable worth during the past half century.

A Cultural Divide?

The danger of cultural disunion is the greater because today, when we no longer need to fear Russia's military ambitions, we seem to think that we can yield to the temptation of indifference or arrogance. During the cold war, the Atlantic Alliance was frequently defined as a "community of values." There could be little doubt about this community, as members compared their value order to that of the communist adversary. But after the demise of bipolarity, considerable differences arose in the Western camp, and cracks and crevices became visible where previously we had closed our eyes to them. While the communist threat hung over us, Americans and Europeans used to suppress their occasional bouts of snootiness; now they give them free rein. Celebrations of American exceptionalism and French insistence on *l'exception culturelle* are but different sides of the same coin.

The fact of the matter is that cultural and attitudinal aspects of the European-American relationship have gained more and more prominence. Different mindsets, inherited predilections, divergent traditions, value systems, and intellectual perspectives impinge on the nuts-and-bolts issues.

My least worry, in this context, is the elitist disdain many European intellectuals—on the right as on the left—manifest with regard to "McWorld," "McJobs," and McDonald's. Most of them just love to take their children to the nearest burger place. Nor do I get overly agitated when reading texts by American gurus like Daniel Rothkopf singing the praises of U.S. "cultural imperialism."[9]

FIGURE 19. The Main Hall of the German Society of Pennsylvania

The main hall of the 1888 building of the German Society of Pennsylvania in Philadelphia at the occasion of the conference, "The Future of German-American History," on April 15–17, 1999. At the podium is Theo Sommer, editor of the Hamburg weekly, *Die Zeit*. The German Society hosted the conference at the conclusion of a five-year restoration and cataloguing project of its library, which, with 70,000 volumes, is arguably the largest private German-American library in the United States. (Cliff Mauthner)

I am more seriously concerned by that hardy perennial, the never-ending debate about how much Hollywood Europeans should suffer in their cinemas and on their television screens. In the last analysis, it is a debate about globalization. To the extent that it means simply Americanization, globalization induces all other nations to think hard about how much of their national patrimony, their cultural identity, their linguistic purity they want to maintain. It is a serious problem, and there are no easy answers. On the other hand: Who and what is Hollywood? Sony? German directors, German actors making films there? Parochialism cannot be the solution.

Then there is a whole range of issues that Europeans and Americans approach from radically different points of departure. In some respects, a cultural divide seems to determine political views and attitudes. This goes, for example, for the whole gamut of questions connected with raising animals, processing food, and gene-modified plants. "Food remains to this day not merely the staff of life but the very stuff of cultural identity and difference"—Martin Kettle, writing in the *Washington Post*, got it absolutely right.[10] Or take the issue of capital punishment. Europeans abhor it. Russia, before it could join the European Council, had to abolish it. The European Union has started a campaign in the United Nations for worldwide abolition. The ghastly imposition and execution of the death penalty in the United States would prevent the country from joining the European Council.

European and American attitudes also diverge when it comes to international organizations, institutions, and control regimes, especially the United Nations. Washington has a tendency to hijack the UN's course of action whenever convenient and to ignore it whenever inconvenient. Europeans deplore the failure of the Test Ban Treaty in the U.S. Senate; they are aghast at the protracted congressional refusal to pay more than $1 billion in back dues to the UN; they cannot muster much sympathy for Washington's decision not to support the establishment of an international court of justice to deal with war crimes and human rights violations. They were aghast at the acquittal of the air force pilot responsible for sending twenty people to their deaths in the ski lift catastrophe in Cavalese in the Italian Alps. Nor does Europe share Washington's sanctions mania, in particular when sanctions—e.g., in the Iran-Libya Sanctions Act and the Helms-Burton Act on Cuba—have a penalizing extraterritorial effect on America's allies. Then there is the whole field of environmental policy. Here again, Europe feels that the United States is less than cooperative and that it is undermining the Kyoto agreements.

Finally, Europeans respect and admire America's stunning economic success in the nineties. Yet with the exception of Britain, they take a wary view of the social costs that go hand in hand with the American way of running the economy. They are about to reform their own system, at different speeds and with varying degrees of success so far, but it will basically remain what it has been for the last half century: "Rhenish capitalism," that is to say, capitalism with a human face. They recognize the magic of the marketplace, but they remain clear-eyed about its risks. Nobody wants the neoliberal harshness of the American economy.

And there are other incompatibilities. The details they learned about the investigations and interrogations of Monica Lewinsky reminded many Europeans of the wicked practices employed by evil empires of past epochs. The Germans fumed when the State Department branded Germany as a violator of human rights because it had the cheek to make the Church of Scientology—a non-nonprofit organization if there ever was one—pay taxes. There is widespread anger at the U.S. stance on child soldiers.

If we want to avoid further acrimony of this sort, there is only one lesson we can, and should, draw from these squabbles: We urgently need a cultural dialogue between the two halves of the Atlantic Community. Such a dialogue should reinforce the community of values without which our affiliation would lose much of its vitality and viability.

Conclusion

Europeans and Americans should not allow themselves to be overwhelmed by their differences. Rather, we should try to compose them and strike a new transatlantic deal to shore up and give new momentum to a consociation that has served both extremely well for more than fifty years. All the old reasons for American-European partnership are still valid and compelling today save one, the communist threat.

Of course, America's preponderance is formidable. But the lone superpower cannot do much alone—Samuel Huntingdon is quite right about that. The world is not really unipolar, he argues.[11] To deal with any important global issue, the United States needs the support of at least a few other major powers. Indeed, if it refuses multilateral commitments in favor of unilateral action, it is likely to wind up as a "leader with no one to lead," as *The Economist* put it recently.[12]

Conversely, for all its efforts at integration, at acquiring a defense and foreign policy profile of its own, at getting its act on the world scene together, Europe continues to need America as a partner. The Europeans cannot act alone either: they need the reassurance provided by their link with the United States. Only in close association of Europe and the Americans is there any hope of bringing some minimal order to our turbulent world.

The three historical events mentioned—the end of the cold war, the onset of globalization, and the rise of Europe—are bound to have a continuing significant impact on the relationship between Europe and the United States. We have to ensure that this impact will be positive; that it will strengthen the transatlantic connection rather than destroy it; and that it will provide the impetus toward a new Atlantic synthesis able to carry us into the new century.

What we need at this juncture is a serious debate about the future of the Atlantic Community. This debate ought to lead to a new Atlantic Covenant. In my view, the renewed partnership should be constructed around three central propositions. The first proposition is to build a modernized NATO—an alliance acknowledging the emerging European reality by elevating Europe to the rank of equal partner under the common umbrella of the North Atlantic Pact. The second proposition is to tame economic rivalry and conflict by creating an Atlantic Free Trade Area. It would be a profitable scheme. Perhaps even an agreement on narrower corridors for the exchange rate between the dollar and the euro might make some sense. The third proposition is to create a political organization analogous to NATO's military organization: a kind of North Atlantic Authority for Civilian Affairs, which would first unsnarl and then tie together the numerous tangled wires and lines in order to deal with issues beyond the ken of military men or diplomatists.

After fifty years of NATO, there is battle fatigue in the United States and in Europe. There is a tendency, after our joint triumph in the cold war, to indulge in spitballing and mutual recrimination. And there is a disquieting trend to consider our proven partnership expendable. We must resist those temptations. If we raise our eyes beyond our own borders, imagining what is likely to happen out there in the next twenty years or so, Europe will understand that it still needs America because the challenges on its eastern and southeastern periphery are too much for the Brussels Union to master by itself. America, however, will understand why it will continue to need Europe: the "unipolar moment" will not last, new challengers will arise, and to contain them, allies will be indispensable. We may be rivals, but we must remain partners. Our interests are likely to diverge on occasion, but in essential areas they will always coincide. The European-American relationship will remain the key relationship for the twenty-first century.

Notes

1. Constantine Cavafy, "Expecting the Barbarians," in *The Complete Poems of Cavafi*, trans. Rae Dalven (San Diego/New York/London, 1989), 19.
2. Mark Nelson, "Transatlantic Travails," *Foreign Policy*, no. 92 (Fall 1993): 75.
3. Josef Joffe, " How America Does It," *Foreign Affairs* 76:5 (Sept./Oct. 1997):16.
4. *International Herald Tribune*, 8 May 1998.
5. Washington Summit Communiqué, 24 April 1999 (NATO Press Release NAC-S [99] 64).
6. "Vertrag über die Europäische Union," in *Bulletin der Bundesregierung*, 12 February 1992 (Presse- und Informationsamt der Bundesregierung, Bonn), 114–84.
7. Joint Declaration on European Defense, issued at the British-French Summit, Saint Malo, 3–4 December 1998.
8. Chancellor Schröder at the Munich Conference on Security Policy on 6 February 1999, in *Bulletin der Bundesregierung*, 22 February 1999 (Presse- und Informationsamt der Bundesregierung, Bonn), 91.
9. Daniel Rothkopf, "In Praise of Cultural Imperialism," *Foreign Policy*, no. 107 (Summer 1997): 38–54.
10. Martin Kettle, "A World of Difference," in *Washington Post*, 8 May 1999.
11. Samuel Huntingdon, "The Lonely Superpower," *Foreign Affairs* 78:2 (March/April 1999): 35–49.
12. "America's World," *The Economist*, 23 October 1999.

— Chapter 17 —

GERMANY AND THE UNITED STATES IN THE EURO-ATLANTIC COMMUNITY

Karsten D. Voigt

Ten years after the fall of the Wall, the relationship between the United States and Germany has reached a new stage. The inevitable conflicts that accompany such a development do not indicate that the two sides of the Atlantic are drifting apart. Neither are they hints of a cultural rift between Europe and the United States. Instead, they are the "labor pains" of a new Atlanticism, one whose foundations remain the same as always: common values, as laid down in our constitutions; and common interests, whether they are political, economic, or cultural. The old Atlanticism had been characterized by power politics, the opposition of Eastern and Western political systems. The new Atlanticism will be largely about economics, culture, and society, issues that will fundamentally change both sides of the Atlantic in the coming decades.

Questions of security will continue to play an important role in the Euro-Atlantic partnership. But the danger of another world power attacking Alliance territory will no longer be in the foreground, as it was during the cold war. Instead, the key question will be how the United States and Europe can—within the framework of the North Atlantic Treaty Organization (NATO), the European Union (EU), the five-nation contact group (Germany, Russia, France, Britain, and the United States), and also the Organization for Security and Co-operation in Europe (OSCE)—coordinate their actions in the case of regional conflicts like Bosnia or Kosovo. At the same time, it will be necessary to cooperate in the containment of global security risks, as is obvious in the case of environmental dangers, the proliferation of weapons of mass destruction, international terrorism, international crime in general and the drug trade in particular. Global security risks are real, but talk of a global NATO is misleading. The governments of Germany and the United States agree on this issue.

What this new Atlanticism will actually be is a matter of contention. But the development of the discussion in Germany on foreign policy and security issues, including all the aspects of the Euro-Atlantic relationship, indicates an overall possibility that the new Atlanticism will rest on a broad consensus. Some of these developments relate to NATO and its future tasks: the role of the European Union in Euro-Atlantic relations; the eastern expansion of the EU and of NATO; as close a cooperation with Russia (and Ukraine) as possible; and finally, the military interventions in Bosnia and Kosovo.

What has changed, compared to the old Atlanticism? And what are the missions and tasks of the new Atlanticism? Germany is united. It is not threatened by any of its neighbors; on the contrary, for the first time in its long history it is surrounded only by friends and allies. In terms of foreign policy and security issues, this is the best situation for Germany since the start of the Thirty Years' War in 1618, the beginning of the first great catastrophe in German history. This improved situation has resulted in the fact that today there are one million fewer soldiers on German territory than there were before 1989. And by now almost all of the nuclear weapons against which there have been demonstrations since the 1950s have been destroyed or removed from Germany.

The presence of U.S. troops is no longer necessary to defend Germany in the case of an attack at the Fulda Gap. But it remains important to give a visible military expression to the Euro-Atlantic link in security issues. Furthermore, their presence is in the interest of Europe because it will stay dependent on American support, even in the long term, in the case of larger military conflicts like Bosnia or Kosovo. In addition, the U.S. military presence in Europe acts as a further deterrent to the re-emergence of inter-European rivalries: when the unification of Germany became imminent, some of its European partners reacted not in a way that looked forward to a greater integration of Europe, but rather in the tradition of balance-of-power politics. Luckily, these older, conventional ways of thinking have lost more and more ground during the last ten years. The Europe of the past was the Europe of alliances and wars. The Europe of the future will be the Europe of integration and cooperation.

The United States and Germany share an equal interest in stabilizing democracy and economic systems in the countries east of the pre-1989 borders of the EU and NATO. Because of their geographic proximity, Germans will be more concerned with problems of everyday life in these countries than about questions of nuclear strategy. But this does not change the fundamental convergence of American and German interests toward Central and Eastern Europe. Nor is it a coincidence that the United States and Germany were the driving forces behind the eastern expansion of NATO and the establishment of the Russia-NATO Council, just as they are advocating a speedy expansion of the European Union. Maybe the United States exerts even more pressure in this case than the Germans, since Americans are not concerned with the practical problems associated with this attempt to integrate East and West. The United States may not welcome the practical consequences of increased German self-confidence in every instance, but it is easier for the United States to accept the larger role of post-1989 Germany than it is for some of Germany's European partners, as not even a united Germany wants to or could contest the status of the United States as the only remaining superpower.

The importance of the European Union has been growing steadily. Europe now has a common currency. In the future, this currency will not only stand on equal footing with the dollar, but it will be just as strong. This is good for the Euro-Atlantic partnership. "Euroland" will be not just a regional but a global player. Germans will increasingly need to learn to think and act globally as an integrated part of Europe. Traditionally, this has been less difficult for Germany in matters of economic and financial policy than it has been in the areas of foreign and security policy. Here too, Germans will have to broaden their frame of reference and reconceptualize their sphere of action, which has been narrowed to the size of the Fulda Gap!

Without a working common identity in matters of foreign, security, and defense policy, the European Union will not be able to do justice either to its own goals or the interests of the United States. The biggest problem in the development of a European Security and Defense Identity (ESDI) is not American strength but the weakness of Europe. This weakness cannot be overcome by criticizing the United States, but only through common goals and actions within Europe. As always, progress will be painfully slow, but I am optimistic that there will be several important steps forward in the years ahead. This seems to be possible mostly because everybody involved is starting to become more realistic. Europeans have realized that due to their limited military capabilities, they will be able to conduct only limited military operations in the foreseeable future without direct American participation. And the United States recognizes the fact that there is a growing movement, especially in the U.S. Congress, that demands that the Europeans take a greater or even exclusive responsibility in the event of a crisis in Europe like the ones in Bosnia and Kosovo.

European economies are by far the biggest foreign investors and employers in the United States, as is true for the United States in Europe. Today, German companies have invested more in the United States than American companies in Germany. The Daimler-Chrysler merger is only the most conspicuous example of the growing economic integration. This increase in the quantity of economic connections will lead to a change in the quality of the political and cultural relations between the United States and Europe.

Most of the current trade conflicts are the result of friction in the face of growing closeness. Both sides will find this kind of friction even more painful when it also involves cultural differences. The banana war had been an exclusively economic conflict, different from the case of the debates over hormone-treated beef, genetically altered foods, privacy protection, and the noise levels of airplanes. In these instances, different economic interests *and* different sets of cultural values collide with one another. In almost all of them, there is potential for the emotions of large parts of the populations to be easily mobilized, which makes it more difficult for the respective governments to compromise with one another. The driving forces behind the passage of the Iran-Libya Sanctions Act and the Helms-Burton Act were the political and moral convictions of members of Congress. With these laws, the U.S. Congress claims extraterritorial rights, in violation of international law. In fact, Congress interferes here with the legislative powers of European parliaments.

But if—as was the case with the decisions of American courts regarding the accident at Cavalese* and the executions of German citizens in Arizona—moral indignation in Europe arises from the impression that officials in the United States claim different rules for themselves than for their European allies (who are less powerful but in theory possess equal rights), then there is the danger that an emotional reaction could turn into political alienation. Such developments should be avoided at all costs.

German and European perceptions of American decisions are only part of the problem. When the substance of American decisions is the issue, Germans and Europeans will not be satisfied by a change in the public tone of American politics, but will press for a change in the decision itself. For example, based on its own understanding of religious freedom, the United States has in the past criticized the treatment of the Scientology organization in Germany, even though Germany was acting consistently with its own legal tradition, protecting its democracy in an active way against anti-democratic forces. There is a similar conflict between the American priority of freedom of speech and German striving for an international accord to stop the dissemination of child pornography and acts of racist hatred on the Internet. These conflicts between equally legitimate sets of values remain unresolved.

The death penalty is yet another area of unresolved conflict. There are many proponents of the death penalty in Europe, and many opponents of it in the United States. But all European judicial systems have bound themselves to reject the death penalty, contrary to the development in the United States, where the number of states that allow the death penalty has increased again. Europeans are offended more by executions in the United States than by executions in other countries, because Europeans and Americans are rightfully convinced of a community of values between the democracies. Europeans and Americans experience their differences all the more painfully not because their value systems are so dissimilar, but because there is so much common ground.

---

*An American military jet cut the cable of a ski lift in Italy, killing twenty people. The crew members were later acquitted by an American military court.

The connections between the European and American societies are now so close that they have taken on the character of more quasi-domestic than foreign relations. Economic, social, and cultural discussions and decisions in the United States are the subject of internal debates in Europe and especially in Germany. This aspect of American domestic policy as the often-controversial point of reference for discussions and decisions regarding German domestic policy will not diminish, even if there is more progress toward European integration. Therefore, even more so than in the past, we should introduce social, legal, and cultural issues into the German-American dialogue.

In both societies, conflicting priorities are normally resolved through elections, parliamentary majorities, or legal rulings. But this institutional approach is not suitable, or is limited in its effectiveness, in dealing with the aforementioned conflicts in the Euro-Atlantic relationship. Thus it is extremely important to talk about these conflicts more intensively than before. This dialogue should include politicians, but it will be crucial to do this primarily on the level of nongovernmental organizations.

One area in which Germans are currently getting much closer to Americans is the reform of citizenship law. This law redefines not only the notion of citizenship, but the whole identity of Germans, which is why it is controversial. A point of interest: the percentage of resident aliens in Germany is now almost identical with that percentage in the United States.

Germans can also learn from the greater flexibility and mobility in many areas of the American economy and society. This does not at all mean that Germany could or should copy the economic or social structures of the United States. The American ability to ameliorate local, social, or political problems through the private initiative of individuals or groups is very impressive. Germany can learn a lot from this approach, too, without having to give up its social welfare state.

In the early 1970s, Germans protested against the war in Vietnam. In the early 1980s, the overwhelming majority of my friends demonstrated against the NATO *Doppelbeschluss* (the stationing of Pershing II rockets and cruise missiles on German soil). In the early 1990s, many of those who today, as members of the SPD and the Greens, are part of the government and of the majority in parliament, criticized the U.S.-led military action against Iraq. Can a generation that has been defined to such an extent by criticism of American foreign and security policy become the foundation of a new Atlanticism? I think it can.

The end of the East-West conflict has rendered irrelevant many of the differences that polarized the debate over German foreign policy for forty years. Fifty years after the founding of the Federal Republic, the majority of Germans feel so confident about the German army being an integral part of German democracy that the decision of whether to deploy German soldiers alongside American ones is no longer made primarily against the background of the unspeakable crimes of the Second World

FIGURE 20. The Reagans at Hambach Castle in 1985

President Ronald Reagan and his wife Nancy Reagan at Hambach Castle in 1985. On his state visit to West Germany, Reagan paid homage to a symbol of the German search for liberty and democracy with a speech to 10,000 young Germans. He referred to the political demonstration of liberals at the Hambach Fest of 1832 as part of an important common tradition. (Bilderdienst Süddeutscher Verlag)

War, but with the goal of preventing new crimes. This is the decisive reason that a broad majority of parliament is willing to allow the deployment of German soldiers in the Balkans.

As important as this moral justification is for the deployment of German troops, it cannot be the sole reason for the decision to risk the lives of those soldiers. Just as important are a careful weighing of the political and military risks, a thorough examination of the basis for such a proceeding in international and constitutional law, and a clear definition of the goals and interests involved. The priority of the political decision-making process, even in a military conflict, must never be lost from sight. The United States has a long tradition of allowing these different aspects of military actions to be judged from within the government and by the elected representatives of the public as well as the public itself. A similar process has taken place in the German government and parliament regarding the decision to send German troops into their first combat action.

All German political parties are experiencing a growing desire to present their own democratic traditions and legitimate interests with self-confidence, even when dealing with the United States. This increased self-confidence of German politics does not endanger German-American relations, since the United States has no problem cultivating stable partnerships with politicians from other democracies who represent their interests and goals.

However, having equal rights does not mean having equal power. It is obvious that German politics is in need of a multilateral framework. That is why Germany cannot afford to take a unilateral position, something the United States is often tempted to pursue. In my opinion unilateralism is not only a temptation, but also a reality of American politics. I do not claim that there is a dominant concept of unilateralism in American foreign policy. The United States prefers to be supported by as broad a coalition of partners as possible. The United States also tries to accomplish its policies within multilateral institutions. But it has a hard time accepting limits to its own freedom of action through multilateral institutions or rules, which is where it is tempted to resort to unilateralism. The interests of the United States would be better served if it always acted from within multilateral institutions like the UN, NATO, or OSCE, or at least after consultation and coordination with its partners. When Germany presses the United States for more multilateralism, it does not act only in its own interest, but also serves the cause of their mutual interest.

In the future, the United States will remain Germany's most important non-European partner and ally. From an American point of view, Germany's role has changed since 1989, but not only has it not diminished, in many areas the values, goals, and interests of the United States and Germany are identical. Where there are differences of opinion, Germany will make its views known with increasing self-confidence, even vis-à-vis the United States, since both Germany and the United States have equally legitimate interests. After the introduction of the euro, European partners and allies of the United States are in need of more freedom of action, especially in their foreign, defense, and security policies, so that their specific European interests and viewpoints will be acknowledged in the United States.

The two sides of the Atlantic are not drifting apart. There are no serious signs of a cultural rift between Europe and the United States. The problems, where they exist, are the result of differences of perception and of interest in the face of a growing closeness, not of a growing alienation. As a stable democracy, connected in friendship to partners in NATO and in the EU, Germans have every reason to look beyond the problems and conflicts that are unavoidable in every close relationship, and toward common perspectives and opportunities in the German-American and Euro-Atlantic relations.

Translated from the German by Maria Sturm

Chapter 18

BRIDGING INTELLECTUAL AND MASS CULTURES ACROSS THE ATLANTIC

Frank Trommler

The Global Village as Idea and Reality

There was a time, after World War II, when a preoccupation with America's well-being was regarded as consistent with a genuine concern for, and general interest in, the rest of the world. America as the Western superpower was confident not only in its strength but also in its ability to build, together with others, a world of shared duties and rights, and to be ready to carry the major burden in this enterprise. It was an era when Marshall McLuhan's vision of the global village was just dawning, when it was still reasonable to dream of a world community in which geographical and social distances were rendered meaningless by methods of communication that promoted understanding.

Looking at today's eclipse of distances thanks to the high-tech and television expansion of the 1970s and 1980s and the Internet explosion of the 1990s, the notion of a global village for which the United States takes responsibility seems quaint. As long as the cold war lasted, American dominance in international communication was, though grudgingly, accepted. In fact, this dominance was built and protected, especially in the Reagan years, with a strong link to cold war rhetoric. When the Berlin Wall fell and the Iron Curtain disappeared, moral claims for communication politics promoting an international order for information lost their appeal. Even in the 1980s, American communication politics did not hide its pursuit of national interests at the expense of the much-promoted mission of the free flow of information. The high point—or low point—of this national communication politics occurred in 1984, when the United States decided to leave the most important international organization for cultural exchange and politics, UNESCO, because it could not stand UNESCO's new, democratic, third-world-inspired information charter.

Instrumentalization of communication did not just serve the cold war defense of the West; rather, it served the interests of the American information and communications industry, as Zbigniew Brzezinski asserted in 1970 in his influential book *Between Two Ages: America's Role in the Technetronic Era*. As a consequence, talking about communication and its transforming power for transatlantic cultural relations in recent decades cannot be done without reflection on American business interests. However, one should also understand that the United States, in the age of the Internet, does not single-handedly set the parameters of information policies anymore. The new forms of transatlantic communication are characterized by both decentralization and a lack of moral mission.

Future generations might be better equipped to appreciate fully the crucial importance of the communications revolution for both the redefinition of culture and transatlantic relations in the last decades of the twentieth century. They will be able to sort out the relationship between cultural innovations and mutual influences, and the perception of distance between the two sides of the Atlantic. While the revolution in communications technologies, especially the Internet, has instituted immediacy as a global phenomenon, the experience of distance is increasingly becoming a subject of new cultural expressions. Negotiating cultural distance while the much longed-for economic closeness of societies has been achieved only seems a paradoxical agenda. Eventually, it will become part of a future system of international mediation, since its diffusion in time and space will have to cope with many forms of ethnic, social, and cultural self-assertion.

Bridging intellectual and mass cultures across the Atlantic has become a different enterprise from what it was in the 1960s. It is my thesis that its most contentious phase between the 1960s and the 1980s was also its most productive one. Since then, the two continents have been wired together more closely than ever before but appear mentally farther apart than in the days of transatlantic contentions over the Vietnam War and the European resistance to America's cultural imperialism. The cold war gave the mutual dependency a charge. Much of it was a confirmation of a political stalemate, but it also provided direction and a reflection of common benefits. The following observations will pay particular attention to the changing relationship between culture and communication and the changing predicament for the cultural mediators and their institutions.

Redefining Culture as a Transatlantic Project

When Daniel Bell followed up his pathbreaking volume, *The Coming of Post-Industrial Society* (1973), with a study about late capitalism, his readers and critics were surprised by the intensity with which he emphasized the role of culture in contemporary society. Under the title *The Cultural Contradictions of Capitalism* (1976), Bell highlighted culture as the area which, on the basis of the modernist revolution, had contributed most impressively to creating a modern consciousness, but which also was, with its focus on individual self-fulfillment, responsible for diluting the effectiveness of Western economic and political structures. Bell's broad definition of culture was bound neither by the criteria of high culture nor by the commercial mechanism of mass culture—though he frequently referred to both. Unlike critics such as Dwight Macdonald or Clement Greenberg, who had attacked mass culture as a threat to high culture in the debates of the 1950s, Bell asserted that cultural activities were part of a democratizing agenda and that democratization of culture reflected the American spirit. In his take on the democratizing quality of culture, Bell opened his neoconservative analysis toward the upheavals in lifestyles and popular entertainment of the 1960s. His complaints focused primarily on the loss of economic efficiency, less on the loss of high culture. It was, by all measures, a sanguine acknowledgement of Alexis de Tocqueville's warning that a true democratization of culture could entail the slide into mediocrity.

Bell's work can serve as a guidepost pointing toward the paradox that, for a short period in the second half of the twentieth century, culture enjoyed enormous prestige as a social force in the democratization of traditional Western society, despite the demise of the hierarchy of cultural distinctions. With different orientations, public discourse in both the United States and Western Europe focused on culture as crucial element of change; without this understanding, the student rebellion of 1968 would not have become the reference for many social and political transformations that resulted from unrelated conflicts. Against grudging recognition on the part of political establishments, movements that initially were part of counterculture gained political influence and eventually legitimacy, from feminism and civil rights politics in the United States to the Greens in Germany. Rock and pop music became powerful instruments in the protest movement against the Vietnam War and the fight for recognition of the rights of minorities. The terms "culture" and "cultural" attained new associations with America's spirit of democracy.

In Europe, the public discourse on culture still carried more of the universalist principles that had been associated with high culture. It found its political application not only within the democratization of education, public services, and support of the arts, but also in the growing resistance to the military and ideological petrifications of the cold war. Whereas politics gravitated around the stale maneuvers of the superpowers, culture effected broad contacts across the East-West divide, used by UNESCO and the Helsinki Conference in an official capacity.

Clearly, the condemnation of the commercialization of culture in the "culture industry," once a centerpiece of Horkheimer/Adorno's *Dialectic of Enlightenment*, absorbed many energies of the intellectual opposition. Used to ascribe public significance to cultural products, oppositional criticism added substantial importance to American mass culture as an expression of imperial power.[1] When France took the lead in opposing

American dominance of the international market of popular and mass culture, especially television and film, it expressed its fears of economic subjugation and invoked the mandate of cultural democracy, which resonated widely in Europe and the developing countries. In 1983, the French government brought together in a conference at the Sorbonne "women and men of culture": writers, artists, historians, economists, and sociologists from all over the world. In the presence of President Mitterand, the two-day conference *Creation et developpement* was designed to lay down the principles of an international cultural policy whose objectives, according to Culture Minister Jack Lang, should be "to prevent market mechanisms and the economic power struggle from imposing stereotyped, culturally meaningless products on individuals of other nations."[2] The participants agreed to complement the notion of cultural identity with that of cultural democracy, aware of the fact that cultural self-expression has great potential for economic gains or can, at times, compensate for insufficient economic gains.

The 1980s became the crucial decade for a twofold readjustment of the redefined and broadened concept of culture that had been extricated from the dichotomies of high and mass cultures in the 1960s. Both readjustments originated in the United States and were routinely attributed to this origin, often with open resentment. The first was, under the strong international dominance of American music, film, and media culture, the wide acceptance of the commercial conditions of cultural production, including those of high culture and art. The obligation to provide support for arts and culture, which state institutions and cities had traditionally assumed and broadly extended in the 1970s and early 1980s, was increasingly questioned and put under financial scrutiny. By the 1990s, the established system of arts sponsoring—in Germany, about 90 percent from public, 10 percent from private sources—was beginning to unravel. In the United States, where about 10 percent of outlays for arts and culture come from public and 90 percent from private sources, the few national agencies of public arts sponsoring, like the National Endowment for the Arts, were almost shut down by the Republican Congress. Only heavy emphasis on the social usefulness of culture, which also informed the public commitment in European legislative bodies, saved public sponsorship on the national level. Demonstrating the economic benefits of arts and culture—both high and popular—for a city or region emerged as the most effective counterargument.

The other readjustment of the broadened concept of culture occurred, under even stronger U.S. influence in the area of communication, where technological advances, especially the "digital revolution," transformed notions of time and space on a global scale. Communications technology reconstituted the relationship between economic, political, and cultural actors, absorbing functions and practices that traditionally had been considered to belong to the cultural realm. In his analysis of this process, Armand Mattelart illuminates how both technological and non-technological factors contributed to the readjustments of the 1980s, which resulted in the realization that communication, long associated only with its technologies, would have to be considered part of culture:

> Communication is also *culture*. Placing thought about communications under the sign of culture, however, was not a major concern of the theories and strategies of international communications in the course of their history, because of their technicist and economistic drifts. It was only recently, in the 1980s, that the recentering on culture acquired its legitimacy, as centralized models of the management of culture in the welfare states entered into a crisis and as the world market became a space of transnational regulation of the relations between nations and peoples.[3]

Although Europeans were more resistant to recognizing communication as culture, they did not hesitate to muster the old arguments from the cultural realm against American commercialism and cultural imperialism in this sphere as well. The conservatives and Marxists, though separated by different social goals, found themselves to be companions in the offensive against American dominance in mass culture and communication. American responses ranged from the plea for "exporting the American model" through the "Global Information Infrastructure"[4] to the insistence of the truly global, i.e., decentralized growth of communication technology that culminated in the explosive expansion of the Internet in the second half of the 1990s.

One of the most influential responses had already been formulated in 1970 in the volume *Between Two Ages*, in which Zbigniew Brzezinski projected the crucial role of the United States in disseminating the technetronic revolution. It would lead, Brzezinski conceded, to a "new imperialism," which, however, would soon be challenged and replaced as the new communication practices enabled other nations to compete and catch up. He described America's impact as disseminator of the technetronic revolution in this contradiction:

> [I]t both promotes and undermines American interests as defined by American policymakers; it helps to advance the cause of cooperation on a larger scale even as it disrupts existing social or economic fabrics; it both lays the groundwork for well-being and stability and enhances the forces working for instability and revolution.[5]

Brzezinski's projection of enormous advancements of global economic and social policies on the basis of the communications revolution, and his insistence that the role of the United States as disseminator would not go unchallenged, have held their ground for more than thirty years. His listing of stabilizing and destabilizing factors can be applied to the age of the Internet, as can the response on the Left that also "the new communication technologies are, in fact, the product and a defining feature of global capitalism that greatly enhances social inequality."[6] What has become more concrete with the Internet is the potential of overriding "the anti-democratic implication of the media marketplace." Whether more democratic media and a more democratic political culture will ensue, however, remains to be seen.[7]

Both adjustments of the extended concept of culture were anchored and monitored in the realm of political economy, not in traditional humanities or liberal arts discussion. As a consequence, academic and educational communities that engaged in cultural studies as a new heuristic and theoretical device were left in a precarious position of entrenchment. It is hardly surprising that the adversarial promotion of culture as diversity took shape in the 1980s, most prominently and polemically in the academic world, which found it a convenient vehicle for renewing the tradition of cultural pluralism as part of the democratic ideal. The contest between cultural conformity, intensified by the growth of mass culture and communication, and cultural diversity, enhanced by the academic yearning for distinction and *différence*, absorbed a great deal of critical energy. Eventually it became the terrain on which multi-culturalism shifted the frame of reference away from the Eurocentric basis of American education toward the concept of culture as a vehicle of personal, ethnic, or racial identity.[8] The so-called cultural wars of the 1980s, which were fought over the definition of American identity either from the traditional consensus position or from the multicultural fabric of the country, made this terrain part of the confrontations, as it reflected America's close ties to the cultures of Europe. These ties, weakened by the end of the cold war, were seriously threatened by both technocultur-alism and multiculturalism.[9]

It has been called a great irony that "America's belated attention to its multicultural makeup ... occurred just when the electronic media and technology are perfecting our ability to obliterate diversity."[10] Upon a closer look, the connection is less ironic than causal. The fact that multi-culturalism became the focal point of the American democratic agenda should not obliterate this dialectic. Europeans did not overlook the connection, although they found the American model of multiculturalism especially appealing at a time when ethnic clashes in the Balkans triggered the worst atrocities in Europe since World War II. With the debate about globalization, the arguments about obliterating cultural diversity have again turned against the United States, although globalization has been increasingly conceptualized under the decentering omnipresence of the Internet, not only under the principles of corporate expansionism. Among the many irritations that surface in the transatlantic quarrels about directing globalization, one question clearly reflects the recent shifts in the conceptualization of culture: whether Europe still participates in defining the universalism of which it was the guardian for centuries, or whether it has shifted to enforcing culture in its resistance potential against economic globalization. Slavoj Žižek has formulated it for the case of France, always the most alert critic of American hegemony:

The paradox is that the proper roles seem to be reversed: France, in its republican universalism, is more and more perceived as a *particular* phenomenon
threatened by the process of globalization, while the United States, with its
multitude of groups demanding recognition of their particular, specific identities, more and more emerges as the universal model.[11]

And yet, France is not the emerging Europe. What is threatened by globalization, Žižek avers, is not the particularity of a region or culture but
"universality itself, in its eminently political dimension."[12] As Europe
increasingly tries to unite nationalities and not just ethnic cultures, it
needs to reformulate and institute a universalism beyond the economic
and technological agendas. The ability to integrate socially determined
goals into international politics will determine the measure of success as
will the ability to reshape the concept of culture and activate its prospec-
tive and anticipatory qualities.

Academics, Mediators, and the Loss of a Public Mission

The ascent of a political notion of culture as a catalyst for social and
mental transformations in the second half of the twentieth century has
run its course. Due to changing concepts of work, leisure, and the public sphere, deeply rooted practices in politics, arts, and lifestyle have
given way. The catchall terms "culture" and "cultural," traditionally
endowed with universalist values associated with high culture—
though more in Europe than in the United States—helped new forms of
emancipatory politics find broad appeal, particularly among members
of the younger generation who felt stifled by the East-West gridlock.
Their anthropological focus in the American usage was as much part of
the emancipatory appeal as the universalist connotations in Europe.
Clearly, the dialectic between high and popular culture, unifying and
diversifying tendencies, was linked across the Atlantic. Its historical
extension, roughly between the 1960s and the 1980s, is marked by the
cold war. Without the common confrontation with a third power, the
use and overcoming of distances would not have fashioned such a
forceful momentum.

Before the virtual eclipse of spatial and temporal distances in the era
of the Internet, the transatlantic divide was creatively used in the negotiation with traditional cultural forms. Much of it was reconfigured in the
much debated juxtaposition of modernism, as a mainly European heritage enmeshed in Enlightenment rationalism and universalism, and
postmodernism, as the expression of unrestricted access to art and culture and their reworking without traditional aesthetic hierarchies. The
withering away of the battles about modernism and postmodernism at
the end of the century seems connected, in a not yet fully explored manner, to the fading of the transatlantic dialectic in the cold war era.

Although the transatlantic dynamic deeply affected transformations on both sides, one needs to reflect on the institutionalized forms of information about the other side of the Atlantic in order to draw conclusions about mutual interest in the age of communication saturation. If it had not been for America's century-old cultural dependence on Europe, the postwar alliance with Western Europe would not have given the British, French, German, and other European cultures such weight in American society and higher education. But if it had not been for the cold war, and especially the "Sputnik shock" in reaction to the first Soviet space rocket in 1957, the information establishment devoted to the Old World would not have been built up to this extent. The cold war became the golden period of U.S. education in which the middle classes were fully engaged; this also meant their participation in furthering the transatlantic perspective. As U.S. education about Europe had once originated in the college and high school curriculum—when modern languages like German and French replaced Latin as the educational backbone in the late nineteenth century—familiarity with European culture grew out of the liberal arts agenda, which did not substantially change until the 1980s.

With the end of the cold war, however, this kind of information transfer has lost its funding structure and political lobbies. The universities have had to refashion themselves from institutions with a public/political mission within the Western political formation into education enterprises under the strictures of economic accountability.[13] Doubtless an important factor for the well-being of academic institutions, economic accountability favors standards that tend to discard the acquisition and dissemination of "mere" cultural knowledge without specific application. Reprivatization has made American universities economically healthier but culturally poorer due to the loss of political and intellectual accountability.

At the same time, it is worth noting that Europeans traditionally did not include America in their educational philosophy. It has been customary for them to learn about America through media, books, and the press, through tourist and personal information, in the mode of immediacy and accessibility. As a matter of fact, since Kennedy's assassination, America has been understood through its audiovisual articulation—or master-coding—of the present. American information policy in Germany has gone from extreme government control after 1945, when all information was conveyed through American sources (instead of the teaching of America being handed over to Germans, it remained the domain of *Amerika Häuser* and other American institutions), to a kind of abdication of public responsibilities in this realm. This loss of political accountability of the information conveyed to Europeans raises the question of whether the commercial information sector does indeed provide the full picture, which is more than an addendum to the marketing strategies of big commercial sponsors. After all, commercialization of information tends to select its product according to its capacity to serve as a public relations carrier. Given the weak presence of American studies at European universities, it is unsurprising that knowledge about America is strongly tied to the vagaries of media fashions. And yet, the fact that Europeans have seldom been formally educated to a more historical and systematic understanding of America has not diminished their obsession with making America part of their presence—on the contrary, it might have increased it.

As the American doctrine of the free flow of information through commercial channels has helped dislodge the European tradition of public service broadcasting, it remains to be seen whether the "impression that in Europe broadcast news and current affairs have not been overwhelmed by depoliticization, personalization and sensationalism in the wake of commercially driven multi-channel competition,"[14] can be maintained. Also in the case of radio and television, privatization disbands essential ingredients for comprehensive information about the other society. Differences in political culture—"the valuation of politics as such"[15]—might keep European publics more receptive than the American electoral audience to news agendas led by serious politics. While building media channels to other countries was an American prerogative in the postwar decades, critical information about the United States has been left to only a few enterprising groups on both sides of the Atlantic—which gives the information establishment of American universities all the more responsibility, despite dwindling resources. Aware of the receding American interest in Germany, the Kohl government characteristically invested in select academic institutions in the United States to further the study of Germany, giving state-sponsored organizations like the German Academic Exchange Service and the Goethe Institute leeway in their intercultural work.

Despite the recent proliferation of theoretical activity in globalization discourse, the new information explosion of the Internet has not yet led to a broad understanding of its impact on the encounter with other societies. The effect on the role of universities as mediators of knowledge and reflection, though assumed to be profound, is still hard to ascertain. Bypassed by easy-to-access information on the Web, universities are trying to re-situate themselves as indispensable access centers. It seems that their investment in cultural studies, which has resulted in a plethora of theories and studies of cultural resistance, can only be recovered by intensifying work on approaches that build on creative complication and differentiation of knowledge in lieu of the Web's pretense of eliminating hurdles and distances vis-à-vis the other culture. Expanding on the definition of culture as "the concept of difference, a contrastive rather than substantive property of certain things,"[16] the real classroom can offer a live experience of practicing this difference as no virtual classroom can. No doubt, however, the offer to eliminate distances to other cultures is more popular than the one to complicate them in a world of easy access. Only the social rewards of organizing the real classroom as part of education can guarantee continuity in funding the necessary scholarship. The threat in the mid-1990s of eliminating sponsorship of area studies, in which the Social Science Research Council was heavily invested, revealed not only the financial vulnerability of academic programs in foreign studies but also their weak political justification as foreign policy sank to the lower end of Washington's totem pole.[17]

So far, internet technology seems to change modes of access but not to intensify interest in the outside world. Neither interactivity nor virtuality prevents the decrease in attention, asserts Claude Moisy, the former director of Agence France-Press, in his exploration of the myths of the global information village. If the selection of information is completely left to the consumer instead of being prepared by professional mediators, the foreign news budget will deteriorate further. Moisy expects the interface of public opinion and the management of international relations to continue to take place on two levels:

> On the one hand, the day-to-day conduct of most of the country's international relations will remain the preserve of a small, informed establishment with the tacit consent of a relatively indifferent public. On the other hand, circumstances will arise in which the public at large stirs and makes itself heard on foreign policy matters out of perception, right or wrong, that the very *raison d'être* of the nation is at stake. In these causes the public will not necessarily react on the basis of knowledge and pertinent information but more likely on the basis of collective emotions aroused by the mass media. Whether the decisions made at either the élite or the popular level will be wise is another story.[18]

The dream of the global information village and its benefits for conducting reasonable politics on a global scale has lived on. It was rarely accepted by the caste of professional mediators in newspapers and universities, whose terrain is increasingly washed away while corporations and governments engage in building their own access to the "Global Information Infrastructure," as the American government has called it. McLuhan spoke of the global village, not of the global town, indicating a re-created domesticity that media critics were not willing to accept in view of the wide-ranging battles over world communication markets. And yet, considering the inward turn that the Internet has intensified in the last decade, it might just be that the communications revolution has indeed created only global villages, not a global town.

Notes

1. Richard Pells, *Not Like Us: How Europeans Have Loved, Hated, and Transformed American Culture Since World War II* (New York, 1997); Rob Kroes, Robert W. Rydell, and Doeko F. J. Bosscher, eds., *Cultural Transmissions and Receptions: American Mass Culture in Europe* (Amsterdam, 1993).
2. Chantal Cinquin, "President Mitterand Also Watches *Dallas*: American Mass Media and French National Policy," in *The Americanization of the Global Village: Essays in Contemporary Popular Culture*, ed. Roger Rollin (Bowling Green, 1989), 19.
3. Armand Mattelart, *Mapping World Communication: War, Progress, Culture* (Minneapolis/London, 1994), xv.
4. "The United States should not hesitate to promote its values. In an effort to be polite or politic, Americans should not deny the fact that of all the nations in the history of the world, theirs is the most just, the most tolerant, the most willing to constantly reassess and improve itself, and the best model for the future." David Rothkopf, "In Praise of Cultural Imperialism," *Foreign Policy*, no. 107 (Summer 1997): 38–53, here 48.
5. Zbigniew Brzezinski, *Between Two Ages: America's Role in the Technetronic Era* (New York, 1976), 34 (Penguin ed.).
6. Robert W. McChesney, "The Internet and United States Communication Policy-Making in Historical and Critical Perspective," *Journal of Communication* 46 (1996): 98–124, here 99.
7. Ibid.
8. David A. Hollinger, *Postethnic America: Beyond Multiculturalism* (New York, 1995), 100.
9. Stephen Langley, "Multiculturalism versus Technoculturalism: Its Challenge to American Theatre and the Functions of Arts Management," in *The American Stage: Social and Economic Issues from the Colonial Period to the Present*, ed. Ron Engle and Tice L. Miller (Cambridge, 1993), 278–89; Frank Trommler, "Multiculturalism and the European Connection: Theme Park or Dual Citizenship?" *Multiculturalism in Transit: A German-American Exchange*, ed. Klaus J. Milich and Jeffrey M. Peck (New York/Oxford, 1998), 167–89.
10. Langley, "Multiculturalism versus Technoculturalism," 279.
11. Slavoj Žižek, "A Leftist's Plea for 'Eurocentrism,'" *Critical Inquiry* 24 (1998): 988–1009, here 1007. For the contrary view of France's exception as resistance, see James Petterson, "No More Song and Dance: French Radio Broadcast Quotas, *Chansons*, and Cultural Exceptions," in *Transactions, Transgressions, Transformations: American Culture in Western Europe and Japan*, ed. Heide Fehrenbach and Uta G. Poiger (New York/Oxford, 2000), 109–23.
12. Žižek, "A Leftist's Plea," 1008.
13. Michael Geyer, "Multiculturalism and the Politics of General Education," *Critical Inquiry* 19 (1993): 499–533.
14. Jay G. Blumler, "Political Communication Systems All Change: A Response to Kees Brants," *European Journal of Communication* 14 (1999): 245.
15. Ibid., 246.
16. Arjun Appadurai, *Modernity at Large: Cultural Dimensions of Globalization* (Minneapolis/London, 1996), 12.
17. Jacob Heilbrunn, "The News from Everywhere: Does Global Thinking Threaten Local Knowledge?" *Lingua Franca* 6:1 (1996): 49–56.
18. Claude Moisy, "Myths of the Global Information Village," *Foreign Policy*, no. 107 (Summer 1997): 78–87, here 87.

Chapter 19

THE AMERICANIZATION-OF-GERMANY DEBATE

An Archaeology of Tacit Background Assumptions

Berndt Ostendorf

The following reflections were prompted by two books, one German, one American, dealing with transatlantic perceptions and relations.[1] Why was the act of reading these books at the same time so engrossing and irritating? There was no quick answer. And thereby hangs my tale, which, however, deals less with the contents of the books than with my spontaneous, even uncontrollable, reactions. To rein these in I designed a graduate course, hoping to test my responses within a more analytical framework and against that of younger Germans. Of the thirty-five students that registered (many more were turned away), about one-third were of Turkish, Kurdish, Croatian, Greek, Italian, and Spanish German background. A handful of visiting U.S. students balanced the multiethnic ticket. They turned out to be an interesting control group both in age and makeup. The German students, all born after 1970, seemed to me Americanized in ways that I was not, which they fervently denied. Despite my assessment, which they considered condescending and somewhat unkind, they seemed to feel more comfortable in their German skins than my "skeptical" generation did, a curious contradiction that needed to be explored. How could these Americanized youths be so obviously German, I asked myself, and how could they generate new types of boundary maintenance vis-à-vis America from within their Americanized selves? As Americanized as they were, some voiced neonationalist, anti-American sentiments. How could one be Americanized and anti-American at the same time? We realized quickly that our detectors of what constituted Americanization were calibrated quite differently. When I argued that even their detectors seemed to me Americanized, they insisted on their rigorous perception of transatlantic cultural difference and on their ability to identify an "Americanized German when they saw one." This incongruity of perspectives led me to my first conclusion, that there must be a generational gradient in the perception, diagnosis, and definition of Americanization. Could it be that those who happen to run the country use Americanization as a differential marker against the younger generation, a habit of social distancing they pass on to the next generation? Indeed, I had to admit that our parents had bitterly complained about our Americanization: "Son, turn off that American noise." And had we not fervently denied any such influence? Americanization, nonsense! We simply did not want to be mistaken for older Germans and made sure to distance ourselves from the residual Nazi style and rhetoric of, say, the *Fox Tönende Wochenschau*. I had to realize that each postwar generation has defined Americanization differently and that the historical time, place, and social station from which the perception of Americanization is diagnosed are of strategic importance.

The hyphenated Germans in my class had undergone an even more complicated, if not antagonistic, acculturation. By bringing them into the picture the plot of Americanization thickens. Their socialization adds an element of ethnic self-reflexivity: their Americanization may have occurred as an integral part of their Germanization as they rolled along with their Americanizing German cohorts, but things American could be used also as a contestation and denial of Germanization, as a means of breaking away from Germany. Furthermore, individual elements of German or American culture, or of a Germanized or Americanized ethnic "creole," could be instrumentalized in myriad ways to challenge the purism and traditionalism of their ethnic parents. Doing Turkish rap in their own idiom, Turkish-German, would drive both their German teachers and their Turkish parents to distraction. Their story was multilayered, shot through with a double consciousness and a fractured, triply ironic perspective on America, Germany, and their country of origin. A girl of Serbo-Croatian background, born and raised in Germany, did her report in English on an all-male, Turkish-German break dance group whose motto, "fight the power," was drawn from Spike Lee's film *Do the Right Thing*. Her infectious enthusiasm made me wonder about the complications of identity formation in multiethnic Germany.

A second motive for teaching this course had to do with Europe looming large. American studies programs at ten European universities have embarked on a project of cooperation to develop a European master's degree in American studies. The group is currently designing a set of course modules on topics and issues that entail a common European perspective above the national horizon. This initiative is remarkable, for it rests on the assumption that next to its currency, the euro, there is also a common European perspective on America and on Americanization ready to replace a previous set of parallel binational relations.[2] A welcome side effect of such curricular cooperation will be a harmonization of European grading and credit systems via the creation of a European credit transfer system (ECTS). All these are serious steps in the Europeanization of American studies.

One of these projected modules deals with the American presence in Europe. It will have a common European core, which constitutes about 50 percent of the course work and deals with the common European experience and perception of Americanization. The second section deals with the national variants and local particulars of Americanization (Italian, French, Spanish, Dutch, German or Basque, Bavarian, Scottish, etc.). Why this sudden interest on the part of multinational and regional Americanists in the Americanization of Europe? The reasons are fairly obvious, though they bear repeating. First, the end of the cold war called for a redefinition of the role of the United States in Europe and of the role of Europe toward its eastern flank. Second, the unification of Germany triggered a realignment in the relationship, in both culture and politics, between the United States and Europe, the United States and Germany, and Germany and other nations.[3] Third, European unity looms large, calling for a set of political, economic, and bureaucratic harmonizations. Finally, globalization, whether perceived as a threat or a chance, has for many observers in Europe an American face. Hence a tacit agenda of the course serves to explore a European alternative to American globalization.[4]

A library search came up with some thirty new publications on the Americanization of post–World War II Germany. These included scholarly books by German and American authors or teams of scholars about all aspects of transatlantic relations. Then there were popular books situated somewhere between coffee table books and patriotic tracts. Finally, I noticed a near-constant journalistic preoccupation with the topic, a steady stream of articles and special numbers of journals. All of these added up to a rather motley spectrum and an ambivalent score. There was a noticeable difference between the *discourses* on Americanization, which seemed to me more enmeshed in narrative habits than in historical facts, and the conscious and, more frequently, unconscious *behaviors* of the Americanizing subjects or Americanized objects. Often the public discourses of Americanization and the private Americanizing practices did not match. Therefore it seemed reasonable to look first at the *talk about Americanization*, then ask *what* was being Americanized and *who* did it to *whom*. An interesting trajectory from hard to soft evidence emerged. On the side of hard evidence, Americanization referred to the manifest and measurable American influences on the political, civil, and economic *institutions* in European countries. But how did this influence affect political and economic *cultures*? Was Americanization perhaps softer, less tangible, more insidious, because its invisible and covert influence was of the sort that can only be observed over an extended period (*longue durée*)? Following Sigfried Giedion, we could call it the submerged part of the iceberg of history, a sea change shaping individual behaviors and performance styles, habits of the heart, imaginaries, realms of desire, fantasies, body languages, fashions, new pursuits of happiness? While pondering this methodological can of worms, it occurred to me that two topics were folded into each other and needed to be unpacked. One was the *Americanization-of-Europe* debate. The second concerned the production of transatlantic *attitudes, images, and stereotypes of the other* each driven by older traditions of national iconography, imagology, and influencology. The latter seemed to me the hidden motor of the first debate and the agent responsible for its rather consistent choreography. All these methodological caveats strengthened my conviction that in order to understand the *current* Americanization debate, one needed to take a long view. Americanization discourses and Americanizing practices have been going on for a long time. In fact, the transatlantic exchange has played itself out in a compulsive *folie à deux* for over three centuries with a remarkably stable set of choreographies, but with a rather uneven, historically specific set of performances. The stability of these "forests" of habit is often forgotten when looking at one particular "tree" of stereotype, yet there are clearly differences which must be historicized.[5] Over time there emerged a curious dialectic echo between the past significance of America and its present meanings for each successive German generation.

Three Patterns of the Transatlantic Debate

What are these compulsive cognitive patterns? What is the deep structure of the transatlantic relationship, and what are the epistemological "habits of the heart," which have inscribed themselves in the choreography of this debate? I notice three larger clusters of background assumptions. The first such habit I would identify as a preference for *killer oppositions*. Both of the aforementioned books fall into a binary pattern: *Traum vs. Alptraum*, dream vs. nightmare, love vs. hatred, us vs. them. Behind this dichotomy lurks the most primitive and compulsive form of boundary maintenance, well known in anthropological fieldwork. It reflects the binary structure of all ethnic othering according to the ethnocentric logic of personal achievement (we Germans) and outside ascription (those Americans). Its binary logic is essentially lopsided, call it partisan or patriotic. It compares the sterling virtues of one's own culture (which we know deep in our hearts) with the worst excesses of the others (which are so obvious and apparent to the eye). Claude Levi-Strauss sighed that after forty years of ethnographic research he had found but one human universal: ethnocentrism. This existential habit is responsible for creating the filiopietism of the Germans-can-do-no-wrong school, a parochial sentiment most cosmopolitans would rather do without. Such patriots are endowed with a strong libidinal fixation on their ethnic identity, whatever collective or personal construct that may be. Their character type has had nine lives and is currently experiencing a remarkable rebirth in American identity politics. I would name their advocates, the no-fault-identity school or pass-the-buck-to-the-others school. They are most often dressed in national garb, and though in the past the "others" were most often ethnically or racially defined, the enemy today may be an identifiable set of DWEMs (dead white European men) or the system *tout court*. Whatever faults there may be, always chalk them up to those others on the other side of difference. As Fritz Stern writes: "Such enemy images are based on a convenient resentment."[6] Such no-fault-identity advocates are at home in a comfortable moral fundamentalism designed by the Daniel Goldhagens or Kenneth Starrs, whose world accepts only opposites such as "we vs. them," "victims vs. perpetrators," and nothing in between. The binary trap (or refuge) is quite pervasive in time and place since it warms the patriotic heart, radicalizes the moral choices, and keeps nations going.

This binary logic has dogged the transatlantic debate since colonial times. In fact, the first comment on the project of the peopling of the Americas was morally divided. At the quincentennial of the so-called "discovery" of America, the public debate soon became a shouting match between hostile camps, laying bare a colonial double consciousness between the *leyenda rosa* and *leyenda nera*. The America-as-utopia-or-dystopia opposition, its essentialized trope, is a mere variant of this initial moral charter. And this pattern continues to energize political rhetoric throughout American history, as Detlef Junker reminded us when he called attention to a Manichaean trap in American policymaking.[7]

Upon modest reflection it is clear that such killer oppositions constitute self-serving, ahistorical, and tired thinking, which may account for their longevity and popularity. They are a form of mood simplification for those at a loss in a complex age, and they are a welcome journalistic shorthand in the age of the sound bite. Picture Larry King Live: "Professors Barber and Huntington, we have thirty seconds left in our program. In fifteen seconds, where is the world going?" Professor Barber: "Jihad vs. McWorld." Professor Huntington: "Clash of Civilizations." How can we escape this binary trap of easy answers for complex problems? We need a metadiscursive, bilateral, balanced approach in order to deconstruct the predictable cognitive results of such self-serving, Manichaean thinking. As I will try to demonstrate later, this has over the ages remained and continues to be a tall order, easier said than done. Habits involved in stabilizing our identity die hard.

A popular strategy for avoiding the original sin of ethnocentric nativism has been the *binary switch*, which drives out the devil with Beelzebub. Patriots become critics of the *patria*, filiopietists turn to jeremiads and step right into the next contradiction, which I would call the *Persian Letters* trap. The binary moral options remain in place, but the charges are reversed. Now a German might project an idealized America to call attention to the deficits of his own culture. This utopian construction of an idealized Other serves—as did the *Persian Letters* of Montesquieu—to instrumentalize an abstract and utopian version of other cultures as a foil against which to identify, make visible, and measure the dark faults and deep wounds of one's own culture.[8] Indeed, this narrative posture "from the other's point of view" marks the origin of most utopian fantasies from Thomas More onwards, and is at work in a certain type of anthropological pastoralism. Such a projection of a moral space into an imagined other from which to make self-criticism figurable has had important political uses. But on a deep structural level such books reflect the same ethnocentric patriotism as the previous set, only now in a self-critical, jeremiadic habit. Epistemologically this posture is a twin of pastoral desire. Virgil reports that Roman city-dwellers dressed as rural shepherds. Their creation of an idealized rural space allowed them to implicitly criticize the city while remaining urbanites untouched by the blood, sweat, and tears of rural labor. Similarly, the Persian letter posture allows you to have your cake and eat it, too.

A curious subgenre has emerged. Here a visitor to the United States such as Carl Gustav Jung might throw a "curve ball" and openly praise Americans for habits of which they are secretly ashamed. After a short visit to the United States in the late twenties, Jung considered himself expert enough to wax eloquent on "Your Negroid and Indian Behavior," praise that was shipwrecked on the stony silence of the Americans. And Jean Baudrillard paid a left-handed compliment to outraged Americans in his *L'Amerique*, where he summarizes all the terrible things the French have said about Americans over the ages, and presents these put-downs as fulsome praise. How to avoid these traps? We need a mutual interaction or appropriation model, or better yet, a cosmopolitan model that investigates the borrowing and exchanging between free agents over time while identifying structural or normative constraints, be they cultural, political, or economic, in the public arena where these agents have to operate. And in doing so we should not put too much trust in the evidence of Gallup polls. Influences work secretly and subversively, more on the level of competence than performance. There is a process at work that linguists have called "structural amnesia."[9] People simply forget ideas and habits that are dysfunctional and constantly invent new traditions. George Devereux called attention to the fact that acculturation often proceeds in an "antagonistic" fashion. This term is particularly appropriate for culture contact in asymmetrical power relations. Turkish rap in Berlin "fights the power" of three agencies: the German school, the public arena (street, police), and domestic parental authority, all at the same time. Yet in that very act the young Turks acculturate to their constitutional freedoms and, when successful as recording artists, join a popular German youth culture industry. To understand these subtle dialectical workings of cultural influence is easier said than done.

The third habit of thought has sedimented as a world-historical determinism. These tropes fall into an evolutionary trap, one of the oldest cognitive sinkholes in the business. Bishop Berkeley (1685–1753) put the trope on its victorious track: The poem "On the Prospect of Planting Arts and Learning in America" begins as follows:

Westward the course of empire takes its way;
The four first acts already past,
A fifth shall close the drama with the day:
Time's noblest offspring is the last.

Berkeley, a proper patriot, was referring to the British in America as time's noblest offspring. Friedrich Wilhelm Schlegel picked up the notion in 1820 when he voiced the "world-historical conjecture which presumes that the life of the mind and higher level of civilized humanity, which started in Asia and flourished in Europe, will continue to wander westwards to America. There it will develop with renewed vigor. Europe will, on the contrary, continue to age and will, like Asia today, wither and die." Shortly before his death in 1918, Georg Simmel expressed his belief to Hermann Graf Keyserling, "that this suicide of Europe in favor of America is the beginning of that next stage of world history, which continues its movement from East to West." Keyserling seconded the notion in 1930 with his book *Amerika, der Aufgang einer Neuen Welt*, a belated counterpoint, it seems, to Oswald Spengler's equally deterministic *Untergang des Abendlands*. This belief that evolution moves toward the west, toward a manifest destiny, was shared in America, albeit in unexpected ways. Owen Wister, author of the classic western novel *The Virginian*, saw in the Anglo-Saxon cowboy the classic end result of such world-historical evolutionary logic.[10] John Wayne would give this trope of natural aristocracy a somewhat wooden incarnation. It would also feed the longest running advertising campaign in American history. This evolutionary trope has by no means run its course, Fukuyama and the end-of-history school chime in. According to them, we have reached "the end point of mankind's ideological evolution and universalization of Western liberal democracy as the final form of human government."[11] Jean Baudrillard, taking his cue from Alexandre Kojève, recognizes in postmodern, hyperreal America "utopia achieved." Folks in Peoria will be glad to find out from Paris that they are already there.

The Degeneracy Thesis

After identifying three major types of such writing and their near-compulsive logic, the question arises: What drives it? What do Europeans hope or fear when they use "Americanization" as a beacon of orientation or a defensive club? There are certain recurrent hidden agendas, either deep anxieties or deep yearnings. Four clusters may be identified, but there may well be more. The first, an apocalyptic, worst-case scenario, pictured the New World in terms of degeneration and decline, a threat best to avoid. By way of contrast, the integrated, progressive faction hoped for modernization and progress, and looked to the United States as its engine and model. The third, the evolutionary model, has currently found a welcome new home in the end-of-history-plus-globalization debate. All three topoi are accompanied by or embedded in American-style commodification, which causes revulsion or desire, or both. Of these four, let me run the degeneracy thesis through historical changes, leave the next two for homework, and return to the commodification scare last. The degeneracy thesis was first prompted toward the end of the eighteenth century by Count Buffon's research in natural history. Abbé Raynal picked it up, and it was written into dogma by a Francophone Dutch clergyman who lived in Germany, Cornelius DePauw. The latter's elaboration of the thesis became a popular bestseller all over Europe. The basic idea rests on physiocratic logic: that the wretched climate of the New World had led to a general degeneracy of all species, including man. He adduces as evidence the small size and the mortality rate of Indians, or the size and bizarre shape of animals such as armadillos and llamas. These, he claimed, were proof that the climate was not conducive to either physical strength or aesthetic beauty. Creole dogs, he concluded, were not only ugly, but they had also unlearned how to bark. And human Creoles had lost the moral hardiness of their parents.[12] Thomas Jefferson bridled at such French chutzpah and composed his *Notes on the State of Virginia* as an explicit rebuttal of the degeneracy thesis. By way of proof he sent Buffon the bones of a bull moose pickled in rum. Hamilton, a native Caribbean Creole, reacted rather testily to this transatlantic putdown in the *Federalist Papers*. Hence, as James Ceaser writes, two central documents of American politics arguing for a new, exceptional American Adam grew out of a rebuttal of the degeneracy thesis.[13]

One should think that a thesis of such poor merit had seen its day, but it is alive and well to this day. Only when we consider the ongoing metaphorization of this belief over time do we realize the stability of the degeneracy trope in a displaced and translated form. While it begins in the late eighteenth century as a physiocratic argument ostensibly judging the American climate, there is a smooth transfer in the nineteenth century from nature to nurture, then to race and gender, subsequently to culture and social organization, and ultimately to politics. Incidentally, the specter of degeneracy not only energized the anti-American mood in Europe, but also fueled American self-doubt. The latter runs from the Anti-Federalists, through Thoreau's *Civil Disobedience* and Timothy Leary's dropout generation, to critical legal studies. Consider furthermore the fear of mongrelization of the national ideal and of the white race that culminated in Madison Grant's *The Passing of the White Race* and continues to lead a secret life in William Faulkner's novels. Residues of the mongrelization fear are currently alive in predictions that the demographic profile of the United States will soon tip from white to brown due to Hispanic border crossing. The projected date depends less on empirical evidence than on the level of nativist paranoia, and may extend anywhere from 2010 to 2050. Such nativist anxiety, I should hasten to add, is a function of nationalist boundary maintenance and enjoys transnational currency. It is alive and well in Bavaria, France, and Austria, where the new Right invokes the dangers of *Durchrassung*, miscegenation, albeit in guarded, historically adjusted terms.

Throughout the nineteenth century there was a gendered semantic cluster that equated the fear of being weak with the feminine. The countervailing effort gave us the "strenuous" decade, progressive social control, and Teddy Roosevelt's dude ranch. This anxiety may have been spurred by an older fear that the colonial situation, that is, the warm climate plus miscegenation, would "feminize" or "creolize" the colonizers. Elias Chr. van Haven, a Dane, extended this idea to foods from the colonies in 1792, when he claimed that the consumption of certain imported goods turned people "womanish."[14] Most recently the trope has re-emerged in the rhetoric of the radical right: William Pierce writes in the *Turner Diaries* (the book that inspired Timothy McVeigh to bomb the federal building in Oklahoma) that the basic American creed, liberalism, is "feminine and soft." In Germany Rolf Winter makes the claim that American liberalism is *ordnungsunfähig*, incapable of establishing order in society, tacitly assuming, I submit, that *Ordnung*, order, is masculine. The degeneracy idea is also alive and well in the rhetoric of cultural influencology. Throughout Europe, American "McCulture" is said to drive out European high culture, and even cultivated Americans regret this waning of European cultural authenticity under the onslaught of American commodification. Disneyland was greeted by French intellectuals as a cultural Chernobyl, Heidegger diagnosed American culture (and society) as *katastrophenhaft*, and even Adorno, who owed his survival to the United States, understood the political gains of a *Dialektik der Aufklärung* as a cultural loss. As usual, such European challenge begets American responses. Curiously enough, the alumni professor of English at Florida State, James Twitchell, chimes in with two books, *The Trashing of American Culture* and another, published by Columbia University Press, *Adcult: The Triumph of Advertising in American Culture*. The alumni professor comes across as a deviant pilgrim exulting in the Vanity Fair, or as Pigpen with a Ph.D., who in a rash of cultural masochism confirms all the dire things the Germans and French have said about the commodified degeneracy of American culture with one interesting twist—he approves of it. I hope the alumni know what they are doing.[15] During the early twentieth century in the United States, but also in the Weimar Republic, the fear of a mongrelization of white, good music by black and Jewish soft, womanish music fueled the American and German national debates. Carl Gustav Jung's essay "Your Negroid and Indian Behavior" clearly did not help to allay those fears. Even in the realm of politics we find permutations of this idea. American proprietary individualism, thus went German fears, degenerates to the point of egotism. "We don't want a pushy society," said Gerhard Schröder, echoing American communitarians such as Amitai Etzioni and Robert Bellah, who would restore a civil religion that never existed. The laissez-faire liberal economic order is a mere guise for social

Darwinism and thus barefaced *Heuchelei* (hypocrisy), say European Social Democrats from the late nineteenth century up to Oskar Lafontaine. Liberal democracy is *ordnungsunfähig* and hence breeds a subculture of crime, counters the new Right in 1995 in the person of Rolf Winter, who adopts the arguments advanced by German socialists in the nineteenth century. From liberty to libertinism, from freedom to the Darwinist jungle, the fear of civic decline is pervasive. And on and on the stories of decline continue in a weaving motion across the ideological spectrum.

The degeneracy argument has left its traces in the story of labor. Here the degradation or dehumanization of labor through Taylorism or Fordism was a big topic from the teens to the fifties in the American Left. It gave us the very European film *Modern Times*. The development from unique craftsmanship to mass production was seen by many Cassandras as a loss of creativity or, *pace* Benjamin, of aura and authenticity. And the same trajectory of decline inspires the current stakeholder to shareholder debates. Generally there is the complaint that globalization is sending us on the way from meaningful safe occupations to meaningless hire-and-fire jobs of the McWork sort. The specter of global commodification engulfs all human practice and ends in a one-dimensional world: so runs a fear in the wake of Herbert Marcuse that day by day gains credibility. The degeneracy thesis is in full swing today, albeit as *gesunkenes Kulturgut* in Rolf Winter's 1995 book *Little Amerika: Die Amerikanisierung der deutschen Republik*, or in Gustav Sichelschmidt's rightist *Deutschland eine amerikanische Provinz: Der große Seelenmord*, also of 1995.

The Weakening of Language Identity

Finally, the fear of decline concerns language, and here the anxiety may have a real base. Harald Weinrich, a German professor of French, complained in his presidential address to the 1997 Romanistentag about "the anglophonic mono-culture, in which the viruses of ignorance multiply." He asks: "Is not the neglect, in theory building and agenda setting, of language and of linguistic form as the one conditioning factor of human knowledge one such virus of parochialism that thrives in the milieu of agendas exclusively promoted in English, agendas that have become resistant to all criticism from the outside?"[16] Carl Schmitt, a man I do not normally trust, observed in 1932: "It is an indication of genuine political power when a great nation determines the rhetoric and the thinking of other peoples, their lexicon, their terminologies and their concepts."[17] He may not have been aware that he echoed Alice in Wonderland, who in her reading of *Jabberwocky* explains to Humpty-Dumpty that it is not what words mean, but who has the power to make them mean that is important. Indeed, the global introduction of English as a *lingua franca* seems unstoppable now as many European universities switch to English as the language of instruction in order to remain competitive on a global educational market. One side effect is the tacit assumption that agendas that are not figurable in English do not exist or are of no importance, not only to Americans, but also to the rest of the world. The citation index ignores scholarship in languages other than English. This fact has serious repercussions in the teaching of foreign languages and other cultures in the United States. If the emerging world culture draws its plots from Hollywood, its interior decor from a transnational commodity culture, and its information from CNN, why should Americans want to take notice of regional or particular cultures—let alone teach them? Why should an American student learn German or bother to go to Germany if the entire world, including most Germans, speaks English? One consequence has been the subtle Americanization of American *Germanistik* under the new label "German cultural studies." Some of its adherents believe that the new and improved approach beats doing it the older, more strenuous way. The problem is that such cultural studies operate with that American epistemological template Harald Weinrich warns against. When the questions, paradigms, theories, and language all are American, the German language and the methods of *Germanistik* appear as mere obstacles to better, marketable knowledge. This Americanization of the tracking devices and of the human interest clearly would tend to consider the original German literary masterpieces as obsolete, particularly when the insult of a difficult language is added to the injury of their being written by dead white males. The bundling of these synergetic tendencies, so Frank Trommler argues, has accelerated the decline of *artes liberales*, which in the age of economic legitimation have already lost much of their political clout in the academy.

This demise of particular cultures by an Americanization via cultural studies is of course stabilized by the growing anglophonic parochialism. But why worry—because this is bad news even for patriots. The *Aufhebung* of other cultures in cultural studies denies Americans an important position from which to locate self-criticism of the Persian letter type. Like a vast cognitive Bermuda triangle, the new uni-dimensionality swallows all particular differences—a practice of repression of the truly other at the very moment when cultural studies is waxing eloquent about multiculturalism and diversity. Werner Sollors has recently embarked on a project to rescue American literatures in languages other than English, and as the German Society library in Philadelphia bears witness, there are many literary treasures of American provenance in German among them. He called attention to the irony that the purely anglophonic discourse and the neo-orthodox ideology of multiculturalism have driven out the real existing language cultures.[18] And his plea to the American Studies Association to devote a conference or workshop to America's old and new multilingualism was refused outright on the grounds that few people spoke foreign languages and that linguistic particularism was divisive. In this climate of hostility toward the *real* other (as opposed to the representational other *auf Englisch*), German cultural policy in the United States has been either defensive or accommodating. German yearning for nor-malcy and a tendency to indulge in a psychology of self-denial conspire to repress the "Germanness" of German culture, or mark it as "nothing special," "really quite European." The closing of the Goethe Institutes at various locations merely acknowledges such failure of nerve and con-firms the self-annihilation of German cultural difference in America.

Unpacking the Concept of "Americanization"

After all is said and done, the time has come to ask: How useful is the term "Americanization"? Not very, as the previous unpacking of a com-plex problem makes clear. Throughout the course of history, the follow-ing larger issues have been found hiding behind the blanket term Americanization. These have to do with European reactions to the his-torical unfolding of the project of American liberalism. Here we have, to quote Mephisto, *des Pudels Kern*, the heart of the matter. Again let me identify three clusters:

1. The applied enlightenment project of individual rights of (male) whites. The post-enlightenment spread of civil rights for women and minorities; egalitarianism and populism (democratization and mass culture); "girl power" and feminism. In short, civil rights lib-eralism and its consequences.
2. A "market-oriented capitalism" as the dominant order (e.g., also extending to education and social services); the American system of production: seriality and replaceable parts; Fordism, mass pro-duction, and the assembly line; Taylorism and the commodification of labor; consumer society and commodification *à l'americaine*; technological and economic progress; multinationalism and transnationalism; globalization with America as its motor. In short, the American version of economic liberalism.
3. Mongrelization and race mixture; creolization, hybridity, multieth-nicity; individualization of life styles; popularization and egalitar-ian mass culture. In short, pluralism and creolization as a consequence of the above.

This seems a bit much to pack into one term and blame on one people. Sometimes it may be useful to avoid the term Americanization as an operational tool altogether and treat the more specific agendas that hide behind the term—and do so without the presumption or ascription of guilt. The proof of the pudding is in the eating. My pudding will be Richard Pells's book, *Not Like Us*. Before I measure him against my typologies, let me express my admiration for his work, particularly his study of American cultural politics in the cold war era and his work on Hollywood. And yet, with this book he has crossed a Rubicon. Half of it is brilliant and half of it is irritating. There is an interesting critical seesaw effect: the brilliant half has received rave reviews, notably in the American scholarly press, while European critics have come down heavily on the irritating part of the book.[19] Here we encounter the chief problem of the new anglophonic age. In his account of *transatlantic* relations, Pells relies exclusively on *English*-language sources. Hence from the very beginning there is in the book a grave imbalance of the we-they type. While he uses all available American sources and historical data expertly and at times brilliantly, he only gets hold of a small part of the European elephant, and often identifies its parts wrong. Briefly put, his main sources of information on postwar Germany are Peter von Zahn and Herbert von Borch. Though I do not bear a historical grudge against the lower East Elbian aristocracy (as well I might), they do not represent or speak for my Germany. Of historians, Pells's main source is Willi Paul Adams—not at all a bad one—but even Willi Paul may well shudder at the thought of having to shoulder what all of postwar Germany thinks. Weinrich's worry touches on a serious and sore point: there is a new linguistic imperialism that travels incognito under the promise of a worldwide lingua franca, a fact many Americans tend to ignore, yet that all neighbors of the United States, south and north, are well aware of.

A focus on postwar Europe from the perspective of American historical agendas easily falls into another trap. Terence Martin writes in *Parables of Possibilities* of the "American Need for Beginnings." Just a small, even trivial item may suffice. Pells suggests that Coca-Cola struck Europeans in 1945 as "genuinely novel." Indeed, the image of GIs liberally handing bottles of Coke to Nazi Germans is a popular icon of the zero hour myth. However, Coca-Cola was bottled and marketed in Nazi Germany from the early thirties until 1942 under the slogan "Blitzschnell und Eiskalt." Traces of Coke advertising had not been fully eliminated from the *Sportpalast* in Berlin where Goebbels did his "Do you want total war?" number. The Devil, even the transatlantic one, is in the details. His chapters on American policy are brilliant, as are his answers to the question of why American popular culture was so successful in postwar Europe. The imbalance is also strategic, since he meant to and has written a patriotic book suggesting between the lines that the Americanization of Europe, particularly of its film industry, is probably a good thing. Not everyone in Europe will be convinced.

The book leaves many important questions unanswered. Let me outline some of them. We need a new historical archaeology of deep-seated political assumptions, a comparative history of the two political cultures and their national wounds. In America a successful revolution and liberalism for white males (not for blacks, Indians, or women) stands opposite a failed revolution and a fall of liberalism in Germany. Many Germans react viscerally to the totality of American liberalism by criticizing any one of its (popular) cultural spin-offs; many Americans do not understand the normative and stratified nature of the German ideological and cultural spectrum and shudder at the thought of an entrenched bureaucracy. Hence political signposts such as "left, right, liberal" seem to point in different directions. The terms do not have the same semasiological range. To Germans the American (liberal) Left seems too conservative, and to Americans the German (Christian-Democratic) Right seems too liberal.[20] We need more studies that explain why this misapprehension between the American and German political systems seems inevitable.[21]

A second area that needs attention is the role of returnees in the re-education of Germans. There are studies of individual returnees, but not on their effect as a national cohort. I am thinking of Arnold Bergstraesser, who founded the Bergstraesser Institute in Freiburg, of Theodor Adorno and Max Horkheimer and their Institut für Sozialforschung in Frankfurt (probably studied best), of Ernst Fraenkel and the Otto Suhr Institut in Berlin, of Eric Voegelin and the Geschwister Scholl Institut in Munich, of Kurt Shell and the Zentrum für Nordamerikaforschung in Frankfurt, of Friedrich Georg Friedmann and the Amerika Institut in Munich. Concurrently we should study the role and contribution of returnees to the Eastern Zone and German Democratic Republic (Stefan Heym, Ernst Bloch), including those radical Americans who fled McCarthy America. The (West) German Association of American Studies, which was founded by these returnees, has been in operation for forty-five years and needs a full history. We need an account of the charter generation of Americanists, among them Hans Galinsky, Hans-Joachim Lang, and Ursula Brumm in the West, and Eberhard Brüning, Horst Ihde, and Heinz Wüstenhagen in the East.[22]

In Pells' s book, the fifty years of the postwar period are blurred like a bad watercolor. Here my initial observation of a differential Americanization of age cohorts comes to bear. We need to pay closer attention to the sequence of age groups, their changing image of America, and their staggered Americanization. Based on my own observation, I would argue that each age cohort after the war had a distinctive image of America and an attitude toward it that could be at cross purposes during times of domestic crisis. While our parents loved American foreign policy and hated its popular culture, we loved rock 'n' roll and hated the Vietnam war. I would differentiate the following cohorts in postwar socialization *and* Americanization:

1. The parent generation and older, born before 1925, who experienced the Nazi regime and its collapse firsthand.
2. The generation of *Flakhelfer*, anti-aircraft auxiliary, born between 1927 and 1929, who sat between stools, neither completely in the war nor quite yet members of the postwar generation.
3. Those who were adolescents at the end of the war, born between 1930 and 1935. This cohort had the hardest lot and most difficult experience, growing up at a time of extreme scarcity.
4. The *Schulspeisungskinder*, children who got their meals at school, born between 1935 and 1940, who were the first to benefit from the

impact of postwar recovery and the first to participate in exchange programs. Groups three and four both remained, ideologically speaking, skeptics.
5. Not so the children of Elvis and Marx, born between 1940 and 1950, who turned radical and helped usher in the ideological wars of the sixties.
6. The post-60s generation, born to affluence and comfort between 1950 and 1960. They raised neither eyebrows nor emotions.
7. The postmodern groups born after 1960, already Americanized in my view, yet at the same time more comfortable in their new German identities.[23]

All of the above trajectories of change are caught up in the inexorable process of commodification. Much of the debate may in fact be a displaced reaction to its global effects and its secret attractions.[24] But here lies the crucial problem. Whereas at home, American style commodification is part and parcel of the American liberal dream in a land packed with natural resources, its export worldwide raises new issues. Clearly American culture is so popular because its message to consumers the world over resonates with the promise of consumption at American levels. In popular culture and its most important outlet, advertising, utopian dreams are channeled into a myth of salvation through commodities, a promise that gives American commodities worldwide a quasi-redemptive aura. American culture carries as a subplot the promise of not only personal fulfillment (from Cinderella to *Pretty Baby* and *Forrest Gump*), but also material wealth. This message of material promise is, within America, taken with a grain of salt, as is all self-congratulatory puffery of American exceptionalism. But it is particularly seductive for non-Americans who miss the ironic tease, and particularly to those who suffer acutely from material want. As a pragmatic charter of behavior, American culture projects the material utopias that are part and parcel of its civic eschatology. The problem is that American levels of wealth and comfort cannot be universalized without straining the ecological limits of growth. Therefore, this promise within an American exceptionalism can never become a world dream: its utopian promise of abundance simply cannot be kept and must be deferred. But this prime tease in Americanization is what makes it so effective. "In its heyday in 1960 the USA with approximately one-fifteenth of the world's population was using about one third of the world's resources," writes Peter Taylor. "Obviously this provides no basis for general imitation. In fact, one estimate of the carrying capacity of the world assuming American standards of living is 600 million people, a figure passed in 1675, before the USA, let alone the American dream, was ever thought of."[25] The larger issue of Americanization as commodification still awaits a thorough European analysis.

It is a unique and somewhat irritating experience to read books from both sides of the Atlantic that treat one's own life cycle as sedimented history. Every reading of such books battles with a knee-jerk reaction, a dual response, one from the body private, as a subject that experienced the impact of Americanization, one from the body politic, as a member of the academic cohort that shaped policy. Add to this the self-critical recognition that in the very reading of these books, each reader falls into the very cognitive traps that I outlined initially. While reading, I catch myself slipping into the three traps, all of them annoying from the perspective of the broken and fractured patriotism so typical of the skeptical generation to which I belong. But these very reactions, which need to be debated openly and publicly, are in themselves the center of an ongoing negotiation between national cultures that have eyed each other curiously, but always suspiciously. It is not quite "the more things change, the more they stay the same," but we need to identify the compulsive and persistent patterns, identify the fears, and mark the traps in the Americanization-of-Europe debate before we can identify and outline the real social and political changes, including the changes in perspective.

Notes

1. Alf Lüdtke, Inge Marßolek, and Adelheid von Saldern, eds., *Amerikanisierung: Traum und Alptraum im Deutschland des 20. Jahrhunderts* (Stuttgart, 1996), and Richard Pells, *Not Like Us: How Europeans Have Loved, Hated, and Transformed American Culture Since World War II* (New York, 1997). A longer critique may be found in "'The final banal idiocy of the reversed baseball cap': Transatlantische Widersprüche in der Amerikanisierungsdebatte," *Amerikastudien/American Studies* 44 (1999): 25–48. There is a veritable cottage industry on the topic of transatlantic relations and imagology: e.g., Frank Krampikowski, ed., *Amerikanisches Deutschlandbild und deutsches Amerikabild in Medien und Erziehung* (Baltmannsweiler, 1990); Willi Paul Adams and Knud Krakau, eds., *Deutschland und Amerika: Perzeption und historische Realität* (Berlin, 1985). See also my "What Makes American Popular Culture so Popular? A View from Europe," in *American Popular Culture*, ed. U. Haselstein, B. Ostendorf, and P. Schneck, forthcoming.
2. Some fifteen years ago, Mike Weaver of Oxford University, Paul Levine of Copenhagen University, and I from Munich were ready to form a "European American Studies Consortium" for the purpose of advising Eastern European universities in setting up graduate programs in American studies. This European initiative toward the East made United States Information Agency (USIA) in Washington exceedingly nervous. It was USIA policy to keep all transatlantic relations in binational, separate compartments at arm's length. Today, after the end of the cold war, the American fear of such European bonding has declined.
3. The closing of the USIA *Amerika Häuser* is one such typical post–cold war change. It is interesting that the erstwhile reluctant client of re-education, Germany, was more interested in maintaining USIA-run houses than was the American Congress.
4. Hermann Schwengel, *Globalisierung mit Europäischem Gesicht* (Berlin, 1999).
5. Niklas Luhmann attributes our epistemological woes to the invention of a self-reflexive concept of culture: "We speak of culture as if we did not know that the concept was invented in order to duplicate everything and expose it to historic or national comparisons—ergo to render everything insecure." Dirk Baecker, "Gesellschaft als Kultur," *Lettre* 45, no. 2 (Summer 1999): 56–59.

6. Fritz Stern made this comment in his acceptance speech of the Peace Prize at the 1999 Frankfurt Book Fair: "It may be attractive in the short run to lapse into old anti-American clichés, placing the blame for the shrinking of one's own identity on U.S.-driven globalization. Such enemy images are based on a convenient resentment" [volume editors' translation], *Süddeutsche Zeitung*, 18 October 1999, 19.

7. Detlef Junker, *Von der Supermacht zur Weltmacht: Amerikanische Außenpolitik im 20 Jahrhundert* (Mannheim, 1995).

8. Nietzsche used France as a foil to show the faults of Germany.

9. The folklorist Victor Green, while studying the Polish polka, interviewed a couple of Polish-American polka players, who were then about seventy-five years old, and had emigrated in their youth. He asked them whether they were still, after all these years in America, playing genuine Polish polkas. "Genuinely Polish is what we play," they insisted. Green wanted to test the claim, so he raised some money and took them along to a Polish polka festival in Warsaw, their first time back in the old country. When they arrived they were appalled at their compatriots who, in their views, had betrayed the genuine Polish polka by modernizing it, while the Poles thought the music of their American compatriots was hopeless Americanized kitsch. That is structural amnesia.

10. Owen Wister, "The Evolution of the Cowpuncher," in Ben Merchant Vorpahl, *My Dear Wister: The Frederic Remington-Owen Wister Letters* (Palo Alto, 1972), 77–96. Berndt Ostendorf, "Ein Mythos der Versöhnung: Owen Wisters Cowboyroman 'The Virginian'" in *Wirklichkeit und Dichtung: Studien zur englischen und amerikanischen Literatur*, ed. U. Halfmann, K. Müller, and K. Weiss (Berlin, 1984), 273–87.

11. Even the levelheaded *The Economist* joins the evolutionary end-of-history debate and asks politely, "Has economic liberalism won the argument?" 10 April 1999, 77.

12. Berndt Ostendorf, *Creolization and Creoles: The Concepts and Their History with Special Attention to Louisiana* (Odense, 1997).

13. James W.Ceaser, *Reconstructing America: The Symbol of America in Modern Thought* (New Haven, 1997), 19–42.

14. This culinary boundary maintenance has, on the European side, given rise to the song "C A F F E E, trink nicht so viel Caffee...."

15. The alumni professor would fail, proudly perhaps, the cultural literacy test of E. D. Hirsch, for he attributes the "Ode to Joy" to Johann Sebastian Bach. My review is in *Amerikastudien* 44 (1999): 182–84.

16. Harald Weinrich, "Von der schönen fremden Freiheit der Sprachen," *Süddeutsche Zeitung*, 4–5 October 1997.

17. Schmitt quoted in Ernst Fraenkel, *Amerika im Spiegel des deutschen politischen Denken* (Cologne/Opladen, 1959), 307. See David Crystal, *English as a Global Language* (Cambridge, 1997). At a conference on the global consequences of digitalization, an American historian opined that the brave new global village of information networking would be of benefit to mankind. When I asked him what language this new world would use, he did not understand my question. When I prodded: "Finnish or Portuguese?" he said: "Why, of course English."

18. Berndt Ostendorf, "Der Preis des Multikulturalismus" (Sonderheft: GegenModerne? Über Fundamentalismus, Multikulturalismus und Moralische Korrektheit) *Merkur* 46 (1992): 846–62.

19. Pierre Guerlain, "Review of *Not Like Us*," *American Studies International* vol. 36 (1 February 1998): 86–87.

20. Let me give a telling example. In 1987 George McGovern accepted the Eric Voegelin professorship at the Amerika Institut. This fact received a short notice in the *New York Times* mentioning my name as host. Soon I received a barrage of letters from American readers of the *Times*. One letter from a German American professor of philosophy at a college in the Midwest asked how I could as a German educator, invite this "leftist pervert, this destroyer of the Democratic Party, this seducer of American youth and give him a platform." As a parting shot he reminded me of my moral responsibility as a German, raising the specter of National Socialism that drove his parents to America.

Then McGovern called from the Emirates to say that he would not be able to meet his first lecture class, which I then met myself. Four hundred people showed up. By way of introduction I told them about George McGovern's career, then read them the hate mail I had received. On the way out, a member of the Marxist-Leninist group (small in Munich) said with anticipation, "I am really looking forward to this leftist." McGovern began teaching his course on U.S. foreign policy after 1945. After two weeks a delegation of students showed up, headed by the Marxist-Leninist student, who was visibly puzzled. "You told us McGovern was a radical. We have listened to him. He is not. On domestic issues we would place him at best on the liberal side of the CDU, and in foreign policy he is about as radical as Franz Josef Strauss." A few weeks later we paid a courtesy call to the same Franz Josef Strauss. On the way to the *Staatskanzlei*, I told McGovern where the Bavarian minister president stood on sundry issues. The two hit it off immediately, rollicking through foreign policy and finding much agreement. At the end they talked about the need of principles in politics. Strauss said: "You know, Herr Senator, principles are important and I hang them high. So high that I can easily slip under them when necessary." McGovern thought this was sound pragmatic advice. On the way home he mused: "You have told me about Franz Josef Strauss being on the German right wing and I believe what you said, but you know deep down he is a closet liberal."

21. After listening to Elliott Shore's paper, which is reprinted in this volume, I see some virtue in a cultural history of transatlantic mistranslations. In my view, though, many great authors, Freud and Mann among them, were gravely mistranslated. So was Ralph Ellison, whose German translator rendered Jim Crow as "Jim Krähe" and the blues as "traurige Lieder." But not all is lost in translation, as Shore argues.

22. A useful beginning is made in Rainer Schnoor, ed., *Amerikanistik in der DDR: Geschichte-Analysen-Zeitzeugenberichte* (Berlin, 1999). It is striking that there are no women in the group of returnees: Hannah Arendt could have made a career in Germany, but she chose not to, perhaps in view of the rehabilitation of Heidegger, a man who—as she confided to Jaspers—was devoid of any character. Moreover, postwar Germany was not exactly a land of opportunity for professional women.

23. Age is of course just one variable, but crucial in an argument about the sequential change in perspective. Class, gender, and rural-urban settings need to be considered. My focus is on the educated, urban, book-reading upper middle class.

24. Hans Dieter König, "Der amerikanische Traum. Eine tiefenhermeneutische Analyse gesellschaftlich produzierter Unbewußtheit," in *Bilderflut und Sprachmagie*, ed. Hans A. Hartmann and Rolf Haubl (Opladen, 1992).

25. Peter J. Taylor, "What's Modern about the Modern World System? Introducing Ordinary Modernity through World Hegemony," *Review of International Political Economy* 3:2 (Summer 1996): 283.

— Chapter 20 —

GAINED IN TRANSLATION
Hollywood Films, German Publics

Elliott Shore

On the last evening of the 1998 Cannes Film Festival, the Golden Palm was awarded to the Greek filmmaker Theo Angelopoulos. This was a film festival that included such films as *Life is Beautiful*, which won the Grand Prize for Roberto Benigni, and *The School of Flesh*, a vehicle for Isabelle Huppert.[1] The vote was unanimous for the Greek auteur film *An Eternity and a Day*. Right after Jean Reno, the action hero of the film *Godzilla*, awarded the prize to Angelopoulos, the room went dark and an atom bomb exploded red onto the same screen that the auteur films had just graced, engulfing the audience in Reno's Hollywood flick.[2]

At Cannes, the independent film or director's film—the American language does not translate this idea very well—the *Autorenfilm*, as it is known in German, beat the Hollywood film unanimously. But, as the German film critic whose description of this scene at Cannes I am paraphrasing asserts, along with David Putnam,[3] the Englishman who was chairman of Columbia Pictures for two years in the late 1980s and who produced such films as *Chariots of Fire* and *The Killing Fields*, the war over the images must produce a winner and a loser, which means that the peaceful competition in Cannes will not last. This is a war, a war in which the *Autorenfilm* can only take on the Hollywood action film with a contrary silence, while one swish of Godzilla's tail can sweep a hundred *Autorenfilme* off the table—though not (yet) at Cannes, where a whole generation of film critics know which film is better.

That was in 1998. In order to complicate and celebrate a long and intertwined history of two countries, two peoples, it might be useful to think back a century or more to the period before the *Autorenfilm* and the Hollywood film, when what constituted a national film industry was under construction in Philadelphia, for example. The United States' first movie company, Lubin Cineograph Company, was founded by an immigrant to and from Berlin, son of an optician, graduate of the University of Heidelberg, a man with only one eye but an enormous desire to make money. He developed Lubinville, the largest production site in the first twenty years of filmmaking in the United States, the remnants of which succumbed to the wrecking ball in 1995.

But Lubin stopped producing films, for all intents and purposes, during World War I, in spite of Lubinville's state-of-the-art production facilities; in spite of a huge "back lot" called Betzwood that Siegmund Lubin had bought up along the Schuylkill River across from Washington's encampment at Valley Forge, the palatial estate of the Philadelphia German American brewer John Betz and his wife, the former Countess of Beroldingen; in spite of subsidiary operations in Florida and California. Lubin, who had turned out hundreds of films since mid-1897, was chased out of film production by the very elements of what would become known as a Hollywood film: high production values, continuity, spectacle, and length. Four Italian films that came to America—starting in 1911 and culminating in 1915 with *Quo Vadis?*—rang the death knell for Lubin and others like him in the United States who had concentrated on a form of entertainment that catered to other tastes. Other American producers of films were quicker and more agile than Lubin, who for many reasons, some having to do with his place in the Philadelphia German American community and his desire to demonstrate loyalty to Thomas Edison, did not react in time to become a producer of what would become known as "Hollywood" films.[4]

What happened at Cannes in 1998 and in Philadelphia in 1895 begins to explain the world beyond the standard mantras of our academic age, which see the Hollywood film specifically and American popular culture in general as a totalizing, deadening, and ultimately destructive form of cultural imperialism that is homogenizing and flattening out the forms of human expression that have flourished around the globe. We can complicate each of at least three of the categories upon which this culturally despairing argument is premised: that the Hollywood film is a purely American form of entertainment, that the audiences in countries other than the anglophone parts of the United States receive the films as foreign entertainments, and that there are unidirectional meanings embedded in these films that are somehow expressive of a way of life that is foreign to those who see them and that somehow corrode what is local, what is distinctive.

The Hollywood film is not a simple American creation. Lubin succumbed to the influence of the Italians on the American film industry. But the Hollywood film would be as much a work of such "German" directors and producers as Ernst Lubitsch, F. W. Murnau, and Carl Laemmle, who came to these shores in the 1920s, when the film industry in the United States was one of at least three competing for international supremacy. One of the many factors missing from the popular debate about the globalization of culture today is the fact that from the first moment that film seemed to be a lucrative product, it was the object of international, cutthroat competition. Lumière against Edison, Edison against Lubin, the Germans against both, the Americans and the French ganging up on the Germans.

The Hollywood film that lost at Cannes is an example of this phenomenon. The director of *Godzilla* was Roland Emmerich. Emmerich is not an American director. He is a Swabian. His other recent film, *Independence Day*, was a huge moneymaker. He started his career with a group of German filmmakers in the 1980s, copying Hollywood with his film *Joey*.[5] *Godzilla*, panned in the United States by highbrow critics, is praised by a German critic, who finds the film much better than his U.S. counterparts did. The categories that seem fixed in some minds are not fixed in his.

It is not just the production of films, but the context in which they are seen that matter to the filmgoer. Seeing a Hollywood film in a contemporary German theater is not the same experience as viewing it in the United States. Watching a despised American film like *Täglich Grüßt das Murmeltier* (Groundhog Day) or *Titanic* begins well before the credits roll. The film does not start anywhere near the time its listing says it will; instead, commercials are shown for up to a half-hour beforehand, including those that have long been banned in the United States: the Marlboro man almost always appears, sometimes in the original American television versions of the 1960s and 1970s, with the original music but with German narration, and there is the *de rigueur* showing of the Langnese ice cream advertising spot that appears very amateurish to an American viewer but uproariously funny to German filmgoers, especially if they have seen it several dozen times before. This practice of showing seemingly endless spots before the feature film starts has made its debut in the United States, and is starting to imitate its German forerunners in length and amateurishness.

When the feature film begins, there is a nine in ten chance today in a German theatre that it will be a Hollywood production dubbed, or, to use the German root word, "synchronized" into German. This practice is the preferred method of the overwhelming number of German filmgoers, who have been polled to find out their thoughts on this matter. The Dutch prefer it the other way, the way preferred by most German and American intellectuals and film critics: the subtitled version keeps the "authentic" film intact, allowing the viewer, it is said, to enjoy the "real" film with the help of the words burned into the print. German academics who have taken the matter seriously raise objections to print being added to the audio and visual basis of the sound film culture and argue for dubbing as a more enjoyable experience for the filmgoer. Germany's dubbing industry is said to be the largest and best in Europe; it may be that in countries like Holland, where the market is much smaller, the relatively inexpensive method of subtitling is the only cost-effective way to operate.[6]

Now, what are we about to see? What is a Hollywood film dubbed into German? Is it something that is distinctly American, or does the practice of dubbing change this cultural artifact into something else? What does the German audience of today experience in the darkened theater after seeing a long string of badly produced commercials? The scholarship on the dubbed film has concentrated on technical aspects of the question, and the "censoring" and "changing" of the "original" film into something that is somehow "inferior." I want to resist that language and think of the dubbed film as something that acts on the people who see it and is actively interpreted by them. It does that in two different ways: over time in a larger cultural context, and in an individual viewer watching a particular film in a personal and visceral way. The language of the translation of the film can, over time, become integrated into the language of the "other" culture, as we will see shortly in an example from *Casablanca*. Cultural "misunderstandings," "mistranslations," can become new ways of thinking and communicating, and can enrich a language and a culture in ways that are not immediately condemnable as forced globalization.

The wonder of the movies is that the pictures stay the same—most of the time, though not always—while the language in which one hears them can change. But the voice of that actor or actress stays the same throughout the career of his or her films in Germany: one hears and can identify with the actor who is Humphrey Bogart or the actress who is Lauren Bacall—it is a familiar voice, not a strange one, that is coming from the screen. And to the Germans who see only that version of the film that is dubbed, it is *the* voice of those actors—it becomes their personal experience of it. It can be strange and unsettling, to someone who had only seen the dubbed version to be confronted with the "real" actor later in the original language version.

The argument that preceded the dubbing of American movies into German at the end of the 1920s did not concentrate on the question of globalization as we now think of it, but rather on this question of who gets to say what in which language. Then there was open talk about the desire to carve up the market, a market that seemed, and may actually turn out to be, virtually limitless. One very early incident of the dubbing of the film *Im Westen Nichts Neues* is instructive of the confluence in the late 1920s of the development of sound pictures and the bankruptcy of the German film industry, the one European film industry that looked to be of promise in giving Hollywood a run for its money.

Silent pictures spoke a universal language, one that relied on gestures and conventions that most any filmgoer anywhere could learn after a reel or two. The practice of intertitles allowed the pictures to flow seamlessly from land to land, with a few words of dialog inserted in the local language, or spoken by the master of ceremonies at the screening. Sound rocked the international market for films, threatening to make the national film industries just that: national again, not able to compete in other markets because of the inability to cross the sound barrier. Hollywood, Neubabelsberg, and others tried to film simultaneously in several languages (Lubin had experimented with sound in films a full twenty years earlier), using actors and actresses who were native speakers, refilming the same sequences that more famous stars had just completed.

This soon proved to be too expensive, and when it did work, it only meant being able to add one or two more markets to the national market for the film, since only German or French or English versions were produced in this manner. Moreover, the motion picture industry had already developed into one that was marketing "stars," faces familiar to the entire world, who were "bankable," their presence in a film assuring financial success, as far as anything could. By replacing these actors, in whom millions had been invested in publicity, with lesser-known faces, this basic underpinning of the youthful industry was kicked loose.

Dubbing started in Germany as early as 1930, in the landmark film *Im Westen Nichts Neues*, a "Hollywood" film by German émigré Carl Laemmle, based on a novel written in German that became an important element in the history of Weimar Germany. The film won the Academy Award for the best picture of 1930 and is generally considered the greatest antiwar film ever made.[7] Siegfried Kracauer did not think much of the dubbing effort, though: "Unfortunately, the German words, inserted after the fact, often fit very badly into the mouth movements of the Americans." He went on to say:

> If sound films are to retain the international nature of the silent film, one either has to emphasize the images and the background sounds at the cost of the dialog, or each film has to be filmed in all major languages. Trying to pass off Americans as speakers of German is preposterous (*ein Unding*).[8]

This absurdity, this *Unding*, has become *the* way of watching film in Germany. Was the fact that these actors were speaking German a factor in the sensational unrest to which this film led? One can only speculate. Technical improvements certainly overcame some of Kracauer's objections, if not the central one. But I would like to make a different argument, one that starts to reassert what we already know in another form: that the Swabian Laemmle, the Westphalian Murnau early on, that Fritz Lang later, and Billy Wilder after that, and Fred Zinneman, and the scores of other, lesser-known figures who became part of this massive new, internationally minded industry, helped to transform American cinema, to create much of what would later become known as Hollywood production values, helped to produce the Hollywood film that was re-exported to Europe and all over the world.[9] So, is the Hollywood film really German? Of course not. The relations between and among those who made films were fluid—the Germans went to America, the Americans to Germany; the French, Russians, and Italians all learned from one another and shared new techniques. The movement back and forth across the Atlantic and throughout Europe was continuous.

The debate at the end of the century seems to go one way only. But we need to keep in mind that films have always been made for export, in several versions; that film in each country has a more or less commercial face—Italy less, the United States and Germany more—and that commercial wars have been waged over it since at least the 1920s; that because

Hollywood films no longer make a profit in America, they are made with a certain sense that they must be shown in other countries; that "foreign imports" can have beneficial effects on changes in language.[10] One classic example of this is the story of the German saying *Seh mir in die Augen, Kleines*, which has entered German as a sweet nothing spoken to one's lover. It is the way that "Here's looking at you, kid," was dubbed into German for the film *Casablanca*. The original English expression conveys much more the sense of *Prost!* or *Zum Wohl!* than anything remotely loving. Furthermore, Bogart utters it with heavy irony. Did the German audience lose something in the translation? Yes. But they gained something in the way of talk between lovers. Did the translation miss the fact that one major subtext of the film is heavy drinking? Maybe so, and maybe not.

When a Hollywood film comes to a German public, it has been Germanized in language and it appears to be a "natural phenomenon" to its audience. Film may in fact be, like automobiles, laundry detergent, and jeans, another form of universal product (as Kracauer seems to have implied) that is driven, used, and worn to different cultural meanings in different parts of the world, and differently even within different regions of the same country. It may be only those intellectuals who are multilingual who see the Hollywood film shown in Germany as dangerous, because only they "know" what the "real" film is like, and that what the audience is getting in the other part of the world is either "watered down" or somehow "changed" to make the whole thing more "insidious."

How is the Hollywood film domesticated in Germany? What does a German public see and hear when it goes to the movies? They hear their own language spoken by actors who speak the same parts for years and years, who are Robert Redford, or Humphrey Bogart, or Kim Basinger to the audience. How much does this matter? How much does this change what they are seeing into something other than was originally intended?

The Hollywood film seems to be moving in the last few years into the direction of more action and less plot, to fewer movies and bigger movies, to movies in which dialog is at a minimum, plot development secondary, and special effects most potent. Can we see this as a way of redeploying film, taking it back to the period just before sound became important? Is the action film the new silent film, the film carried by its pictures and background sounds, as Kracauer would have it, and not by its language? If that is the case, does someone like Emmerich, who comes to America to make blockbusters, reinvigorate the Hollywood film by bringing spareness, close attention to detail, and a vocabulary of economy from Germany back to the United States, thereby making it more possible to sell the film to the entire world,[11] and helping along a process that was once celebrated in a different way, when film appeared to speak a universal language? Maybe the movement of a director back and forth from one country to the other and the enriching of language from cross-cultural influences are two ways of thinking of Hollywood films and German publics as gaining something from each other in translation.

Notes

1. For a list of winners, see: http://www.cannesfest.com/1998/actu/palmares.htm.
2. This description and the ideas that follow are paraphrased from Tobias Kniebe, "Für die Echse gibt es keinen Ersatz," *Süddeutsche Zeitung*, Feuilleton, 26 May 1998.
3. See David Putnam, *Movies and Money* (New York, 1998).
4. Joseph P. Eckhardt, *The King of the Movies: Film Pioneer Siegmund Lubin* (Madison/Teaneck, NJ/London, 1997). See also Eileen Bowser, *The Transformation of Cinema* (New York, 1990).
5. Eric Rentschler, "Film der achtziger Jahre," in *Geschichte des deutschen Films*, ed. Wolfgang Jacobsen, Anton Kaes, and Hans Helmut Prinzler (Stuttgart/Weimar, 1993), 294.
6. The major work on German dubbing is Guido Marc Pruys, *Die Rhetorik der Filmsynchronisation: Wie ausländische Spielfilme in Deutschland zensiert, verändert und gesehen werden* (Medienbibliothek: Serie B, Studien; Bd. 14) (Tübingen, 1997). This monograph focuses on the technical and historical aspects of dubbing, but does not venture into questions of the possible meanings of these films to German audiences.
7. James Pallot et al., *The Movie Guide* (New York, 1995), entry for *All Quiet on the Western Front*.
8. Siegfried Kracauer, "'Im Westen Nichts Neues': Um Remarque-Tonfilm," *Frankfurter Zeitung* 6 (December 1930), as quoted in Pruys, *Die Rhetorik der Filmsynchronisation*, 149. The German text: "Soll der tönende Film die Internationalität des stummen bewahren, so muss man entweder das Schwergewicht von den Dialogen zurück auf die Bilder und auch auf die Geräusche verlegen oder jeden Film von vornherein in allen Hauptsprachen drehen. Der Versuch, amerikanische Sprecher für deutsche auszugeben, ist ein Unding."
9. Even if all of the other Hollywood films were to vanish from their periods of active filmmaking, the filmography of just two German American filmmakers, Billy Wilder (*Double Indemnity*, 1944; *Sunset Boulevard*, 1950; *Sabrina*, 1954; *The Seven Year Itch*, 1955; *Some Like It Hot*, 1959; *One, Two, Three!* 1961; *The Fortune Cookie*, 1966) and Fred Zinneman (*High Noon*, 1952; *From Here to Eternity*, 1953; *Oklahoma!* 1955; *A Man for All Seasons*, 1966; *The Day of the Jackal*, 1973) could stand as a reliable guide to the genre. The list could be greatly expanded to include some of the leading titles in such genres as horror, film noir, and schlock.
10. In the late nineteenth century, this was an argument that supported the benefits of the invention of new words in American English.
11. See Desmond Ryan "Multinationals Are Changing the Movies and Film Fans Are Not Going to be Pleased," *Philadelphia Inquirer*, 28 March 1999.

Chapter 21

TRADITION AND CRITICISM

German Studies in the Age of Globalization

Russell A. Berman

Evaluating the prospects for German studies in the United States, one can identify many positive aspects of the current state of the profession. American-born or trained scholars are making vigorous contributions to the study of German literary and cultural history with significant publications on major authors, often with quite innovative or even provocative approaches.[1] Recent publications in various university press monograph series demonstrate a vibrant interest in literary history. More prominent in the overall intellectual landscape, however, are articles in the important professional journals as well as recent books that point to a complex research agenda. These projects combine cultural studies, discourse theory, gender studies, and multicultural approaches to minority phenomena in German-speaking Europe. The study of film, once a controversial addition to the literature curriculum, is now fully integrated, if not commonplace, in German departments, and research is expanding to consider other forms of popular culture and everyday life. Other formerly marginalized or excluded topics have similarly moved to the center of attention: anti-Semitism and the Holocaust, German colonialism, and Nazi "culture."[2]

It is difficult to generalize about this rich and dynamic field, characterized by an emphatic plurality of methodologies: feminism and postcolonialism, deconstruction and the new historicism exist side by side. Given the scope of methodological innovation, it is fair to say that while scholarship on canonic literature continues, it is rarely approached as part of a somehow self-evident canon, i.e., a set of literary works linked in a diachronic intertextuality and corresponding to a shared and definitive taste. Instead, scholars increasingly approach literary evidence as cultural objects, understood to be imbricated in larger cultural or discursive structures. The material is approached less as an object of a specifically aesthetic reflection, and more as a symptom of a larger, non-literary condition. Contrary to expectations, however, the condition or frame within which literature is analyzed is not defined in primarily social-historical terms. Instead, contemporary scholarship posits discursive or quasi-philosophical paradigms within which literature is placed. The irony here is that the erstwhile opposing methodological positions from the 1960s—the canon on the one side, social history on the other—have both been overshadowed by a postmodern perspective and its theoretical approaches, which countenance neither aesthetic autonomy nor social contextualization. The attention of scholarship has therefore undergone a "decentering" away from individual works of literature that formerly made up the canon. Literature has lost its privileged or "auratic" status, and larger cultural and historical issues are raised without any necessarily strong link to social history.[3] Meanwhile, the center of gravity of scholarly interest continues to shift toward twentieth-century studies while attention devoted to older historical tradition shrinks. This loss of historical scope parallels similar tendencies toward "presentism" in other humanities fields.

This shift from German literary history to German studies—understood as a variant of cultural studies—is often presented as the emergence of a distinctly American perspective in the study of German culture. This claim in turn implies a perceived break from *Germanistik* in the Federal Republic, which, not long ago, still exercised considerable influence on American scholarship. This rupture with the profession in Germany can even be traced in appointment patterns. The prominence in the profession of German-born and trained scholars, i.e., emigrants of both the prewar and postwar periods, has given way to a generation of American-trained scholars who are primarily American born but include some Europeans who pursued graduate education in the United States. This demographic shift alone carries with it certain consequences: a less insular status for German departments, with scholars more prepared to build bridges to other units within the university, but at the same time a diminished connection to professional colleagues in Europe. Moreover, as the number of native speakers of German in American departments declines, the use of German as a language of scholarship, i.e., conducting graduate seminars in German, becomes less frequent. This decline exacerbates structural tensions between the competing elements of the departmental mission: second language acquisition and literary or cultural scholarship. The "Americanization" of German studies is at best, therefore, a double-edged sword.[4] Yet, a full understanding of what may be distinctly American in the situation of American German studies requires reflection on some other structural shifts in higher education in the United States. For just at the point when an American German studies has come into its own with its unique methodological agenda, larger underlying tendencies have come to the fore, raising worrisome questions for the future, not only for German but for the study of all other cultures and the humanities at large.

Changes in Higher Education

Foremost among the challenges that the study of German culture faces in the university is the profound transformation of the spirit of undergraduate education. American college education was based during most of the century on a liberal arts program, combining general education with the pursuit of a specialized topic, a major, which was not at all understood to be necessarily linked to career goals. Professional, career-oriented training took place after attaining the B.A., in professional schools, such as law school, medical school, business school, or—for the aspiring researcher—in a graduate department within the faculties of the arts and sciences. Undergraduate students were free to choose a major independent of any subsequent plans. Majors in German (or in other humanities departments) had no commitment to Germanist careers, but would instead regularly proceed toward other professional vocations.

For complex reasons, including both cultural and economic changes, public appreciation of a liberal arts education is no longer as evident as it was in the past. Undergraduates frequently have much more specific professional plans for their college career. The link between college education and career goals has become much stronger, exerting a more direct influence on course selection. If students once calculated that a degree from a prestigious college would be enough to get a job or admission into professional school, now they speculate that individual course choices (and grades) determine their subsequent options. The college degree in the past certainly responded to the pressure of the market place, but only to the extent that it represented a valuable sign of status. The substance of the educational process, course selection and content, was relatively shielded from economic calculation. By the end of the century, however, students were making substantive educational choices in economic terms, with an eye to career plans. Between 1969/70 and 1994/95, the number of B.A.s awarded in the modern foreign languages dropped by 36.7 percent; B.A.s in history fell by 38.6 percent and in English by a relatively small 9.7 percent—during a period in which the overall number of B.A.s awarded had in fact increased.[5] Given this move away from the traditional humanities, the temptation arises to justify the value of the study of foreign languages in vocational terms. Yet the credibility of such arguments has never been great, and would be, perhaps, lower than ever in an era of an ascendant American economy in which it is assumed that English is the language of global business.

The erosion of liberal arts education and the increased emphasis on pre-professionalism are compounded by an additional shift due in part to the growing prominence of the Hispanic minority in the United States: enrollments in Spanish have increased dramatically, with a corresponding decline in both French and German. German language enrollments amount to about 10 percent of current undergraduate language enrollments in the United States, down from the 22.5 percent of 1965, and the profession is quite concerned about future enrollment patterns.[6] Scholars in the field continue to grapple with the question of how to proceed, or, given decreasing student numbers, how to attempt to retrieve some of the enrollment that has been lost. Yet the language question is not only about gross numbers. The historic reluctance of Americans to learn foreign languages is arguably taking a turn for the worse. If, as Spanish advocates argue, Spanish should not be designated a "foreign" language because it is the first language of so many Americans, then the attractiveness of Spanish does not indicate a growing interest in "foreign" cultures but a fascination with internal, American cultural diversity. Similarly, since growth in some of the less commonly taught languages, such as Chinese, Japanese, and Arabic, depends disproportionately on heritage learners, the engagement with the second language involves a search for roots and identity, rather than an encounter with a fully different way of life. In various ways, a dialectic is therefore played out, permitting students to engage themselves more in domestic diversity and feed a personal sense of multiculturalism, even as they grow increasingly indifferent to the languages and cultures of the rest of the world.

Thus, the current situation of German studies in the United States is complex, split between vibrant and innovative scholarship, and the changing undergraduate perspective, in particular, a weakening of interest in learning the language at all. The situation is emblematic of the challenge that the advocates of learning about any foreign culture face within the American university. Phrased positively, the ethical mission of the study of a foreign language and literature involves imparting to students the ability to recognize and respect the other inhabitants of the world. Yet, for all of the American talk of diversity and multiculturalism, a self-assured triumphalism increasingly gets in the way of any strong engagement with other cultures. Why learn other languages if English is adequate around the world? Why assume the burden of learning another culture, if professional life will take place in a uniform international culture, linked to the self-evident superiority of American cultural choices? Questions like these are fundamental to any serious reflection on the future of the study in the United States of languages, literatures, and cultures.

There is a way to answer these questions: the opportunity to be engaged with alternative traditions by studying another literature and language provides a chance to learn about tradition and experience in general. The student who grows through foreign language study gains an inward knowledge as well as a familiarity with another culture, permitting in turn a more critical perspective on one's own culture.[7] This is, however, a liberal arts argument for the humanities, i.e., for the American version of personal *Bildung*, as a pedagogic goal. It is still a plausible answer today, if not as unquestioned as it may have been in the past. It is a humanistic argument that might be made more forcefully if scholars themselves were not encumbered by the sort of antihumanism associated with current interpretive methodologies. American Germanists cannot take an undergraduate public for granted, especially given the changing character of higher education. The major challenge facing the field involves finding the courage to make the argument for the value of liberal arts education while developing strategies to restructure curricula in ways that can reinvent German studies as an attractive option for students.

Traditions, Criticism, and Scholarship

The split between undergraduate education and a research agenda, particularly in German studies, is quite significant. The future of the field will depend on an adequate reflection on the relationship between the two. The research project of cultural studies, as it is generally practiced, directs a hermeneutics of suspicion toward German cultural traditions, which are subjected to criticism from an increasingly American point of view. Instead of examining German literary and intellectual traditions on their own terms in order to translate them to an American public, German studies has intentionally become a project to aim American theoretical perspectives and norms at German culture. The study of German minorities, for example, becomes an opportunity to try out the categories of contemporary American multiculturalism on the quite different German experience and, not surprisingly, to find a discrepancy with American models that is interpreted as inadequacy.[8] Yet if the lessons of the research enterprise amount to a perpetual suspicion toward German culture, measured against an ultimately unproblematized American standard, then a persuasive rationale for students to study German culture, enter the field, and continue the project quickly disappears. The research wing of the profession is not only distinct and distant from undergraduate education (which alone is unfortunate), but the tendency of "cultural studies" to objectify cultural material and diminish it as an expression of a problem rather than as an indication of achievement (aesthetic or otherwise) also undermines the undergraduate project by discouraging positive identifications with the culture.

While the adversarial relationship to the literary or cultural tradition derives from the critical self-understanding of a German studies devoted to a critique of Germany (operating with a variant of *Sonderweg* argumentation), the consequences turn out to be quite affirmative and decidedly uncritical vis-à-vis the United States, which is cast as the political and cultural norm for which Germany is expected to strive. Nor is this de facto Americanism of American German studies surprising, since its advocates have consistently argued that, as a field, it should free itself from German influences and participate in the larger American discussion. As a strategic agenda, however, this Americanization of German studies is quite problematic, for it stifles the undergraduate program and sacrifices distinct intellectual traditions on the graduate level.

Instead of the Americanization of German studies, an alternative strategy for the future can focus on the value inherent in the study of other cultures and traditions, both as a vehicle for individual growth (the liberal arts argument) and as a salutary corrective to an aspect of contemporary American culture with its frequent ignorance about the rest of the world. Here German studies, as an example of the study of any foreign culture, can maintain a critical agenda. The pivotal question remains: Should German studies be a field primarily concerned with German culture as a problem? The receptiveness of the American public to Daniel Goldhagen's account of German culture certainly indicates a predisposition to a summary condemnation of German cultural traditions as hopelessly tainted with anti-Semitism and anti-democratic authoritarianism. The alternative future of German studies entails defining the field as concerning valuable aesthetic and intellectual traditions, which themselves represent critical responses to specific historical experience. A critical redemption of tradition requires an engagement with the cultural material through a complex integration of positive reappropriation, awareness of internal contradictions and surrounding contexts, and the urgency of translating the substance of German material to American students.

A critical reappropriation of tradition would fundamentally revise a defining trope of modernity. It is much more familiar to treat tradition and criticism as binary and incompatible opposites. Yet, there exists a dialectical relationship between criticism and tradition, which is itself a focal point of cultural transfer between Germany and the United States. For example, in his 1937 essay "Traditional and Critical Theory," Max Horkheimer posited a basic opposition between two distinct modes of philosophical thinking. The predominant view, holding sway in public opinion and in established scholarship, defined theory as a set of abstract statements, standing in a descriptive relationship to the objective world, where precise and empirical observation could always confirm or disprove such theoretical claims. This so-called "traditional theory" represented a generalization concerning the already given. In contrast, Horkheimer invoked a "critical theory," deemed anticipatory, that points toward the future and the immanent goal toward which society innately develops. It is hardly surprising that he presented this stark contrast as heir to an opposition between Descartes and Marx. The novelty in the essay is that Horkheimer did not rest with mere assertions of class interest and a conflict between bourgeois and proletarian perspectives, which would have been compatible with standard Marxism since the late nineteenth century. He associated the "Marxist" or proletarian position with a proleptic criticism, an aspirational orientation toward a future, while "traditional theory" was understood as Cartesian formulations. These provide descriptive repetitions of the status quo, and thus became a reassertion of the merely given. This reassertion took the form of increasingly mathematical descriptions, emptied of details, of homogenized and abstract space.[9]

Horkheimer associated traditional theory with social domination because it reaffirmed the status quo as it engaged in a process of abstraction that removed the specificity of detail. This characteristically German neo-Marxist amalgamation combines a romantic suspicion of science with the dialectical politics of class opposition. Parallel forerunners might have been found twenty years earlier in Lukács's *Theory of the Novel*, or in Spengler's cultural pessimism, or in a whole range of German irrationalist thinking since Nietzsche at least. From the perspectives of critical theorists, the civilizing process that transformed German culture throughout its entry into modernity appears quite problematic or, at worst, tantamount to the termination of traditional culture. There is a remarkable antinomy inherent in Horkheimer's title: the position of conventional theory, the "other," so to speak, to "critical theory," is named "tradition." However, the socio-cultural process against which Horkheimer protests is none other than modernization, i.e., the process of cultural and social transformation marked above all by the destruction of tradition. Can it be that "traditional theory" is complicit in the annihilation of traditions? Horkheimer wields "critical theory" as an alternative to a mathematicizing modernity, much as did Husserl in his *Crisis of the European Sciences*, of the same era. It is therefore not a genuinely "traditional theory" that Horkheimer dismisses, i.e., the theorization of tradition or a theory that places tradition somehow in the center of cultural analysis. Rather, when Horkheimer attacks "traditional theory," he means merely conventional theory, in particular, the theory of modernization, to which tradition stands as an excluded antagonist. To rephrase the problem: the process of abstraction to which Horkheimer objects—from the standpoint of critical theory—is none other than the progressive destruction of tradition.

It is odd to see Horkheimer labeling this modernization process as "traditional," a gesture comprehensible only if we assume that he is using the term "traditional theory" in a simplistic sense. His imprecise terminology would appear to mask the dialectic. Instead of regarding criticism as the alternative to tradition (as in the binary of "traditional and critical theory"), we should recognize how tradition and criticism turn out to be allied against a logic of conceptual leveling and a homogenizing modernity.

The consequences of this inversion are of profound importance for the study of German culture in the American university and the strategic choices it faces for the future, and not only because of the influence of Frankfurt School critical theory in the United States. The labile status of the study of any national cultural tradition within the contemporary academy has to be seen within the larger frame of the dialectic relationship between particular cultures and universal theory. The impetus to theorization and rationalization, which are inherent in the process of modernization, and which are especially cultivated within the university, take the form of a perpetual skepticism toward the particularity of foreign traditions. The predominance of general literary or cultural theory—as opposed to national philologies—coupled with U.S. undergraduate students' turning away from the traditional humanities, represents an aversion to particularity, an aversion that is concurrent with the Enlightenment process criticized by Horkheimer. When cultural studies denounces traditions, treating them as merely "invented" or as expressions of illegitimate power structures, the process of judgment frequently falls short of substantive criticism, since the denunciation of other traditions never challenges the American context itself. American values systems, their intellectual frameworks, and their "Americanized" participants are set as the norm against which alterity is judged. To cultivate a self-sustaining critical scholarship, a more complex relationship to culture and tradition will be necessary, one that recognizes the particular importance of maintaining a dynamic and productive relationship with the alterity of foreign languages and literatures. Such a dialectic of cultural transfer is the necessary basis for any viable future German studies.

The Future of National Philology

Not tradition as the opposite of criticism, but tradition in itself as the source of criticism and the logic of abstraction and identity is the key concern of critical theory, with its insistence on the priority of particularity. Concerning American German studies, recovering the status of tradition as criticism allows for rethinking the project of national philologies. Undoubtedly, nineteenth-century historiographies of national literatures relied on grand narratives of progress in a way that, from our contemporary perspective, undermined their credibility. We now see how their exaggerated claims regarding historical continuity served nationalistic purposes. The suggestion that American German studies develop a positive engagement with the literary and cultural tradition does not mean a return to a Borussocentric historiography. Nevertheless, the romantic insistence on a special relationship between identity, popularity, language, and literary expression found value and meaning in participating in the national community, and thus simultaneously took on a democratic nature. If universal suffrage polled the national will, national literary history measured the national soul. Whitman's *Democratic Vistas* gives the clearest expression to this credo, but it also pervades the writings of the young Thomas Mann, with his concerns for German specificity precisely at the moment of democratization. Mann could link Whitman to Novalis and democracy. The project of the *Kulturnation* is no less democratic for its being cultural. Tradition is the historicity based on which the national will emerges. There is no democracy without tradition.

This assertion runs counter to the tendency of modernity to render traditions obsolete, and this is precisely the battle being fought in the universities with regard to the legitimacy of individual departments devoted to the study of particular linguistic and literary traditions. Should universities offer instruction in single literatures, implicated deeply in their national and linguistic traditions, or should curricula be restructured to study only "literature" or "culture" in general (the latter being ultimately impervious to the language of expression or the historical experience it embodies)? The viability of the project of national literature, tied as it was to both cultural identity and political self-determination, has lost much of its credibility, and it faces strong challenges from theoretical models that cast linguistic and historical specificity as merely external contingencies rather than constitutive determinants of the literature. No matter how strong the arguments may be for the critical or emancipatory nature of national cultural perspectives, and no matter how one may insist on an ethical mission to the project of teaching foreign literatures in the increasingly insular American university, the study of national literatures is under extraordinary pressure and may very well disappear. We should not be blind to these pressures or the proximity of such a regrettable outcome.

The challenges that scholarship on Germany must surmount in the United States derive from the logic of modernity and its ambivalence regarding tradition as it is played out within the methodological debates and administrative pressures of the university. This process is compounded by the historically problematic relationship of America to other cultures. These tendencies are embedded in the larger process of globalization. Is there room for national philology if all solid and local traditions are melting into the air of a new internationalism? Of course, there are plenty of reasons to retain skepticism toward the exaggerated claims of global networks. In fact, in many parts of the world, a resurgence of local or ethnic identity might be taken to represent quite the opposite of a globalized culture. Yet the appearance is deceptive. Zygmunt Bauman argued that the weakening of the standard nation-state due to the proliferation of globalization (particularly in the economic sphere) is concomitant with regionalist or separatist movements, which can mobilize local identities, ethnic or otherwise, to justify their irredentist projects. Far from representing ancient animosities, these resurgent ethnicities, for example, in the Balkans, are byproducts of the modernizing breakdown of nations, which may undermine the inherited cultural landscape.[10] Are these new and smaller nationalisms likely to develop strong cultural profiles that will rise to the level of the older nation-states, or will the smaller and perhaps therefore weaker units just become easy pickings for global culture and Hollywood cinema? Their smaller size, lack of economic resources, and weak or nonexistent institutions of cultural mediation all indicate that the proliferation of new local identities is likely to subvert the paradigm of national literatures and their insistence on long historical traditions. If an independent French film industry can only survive with the help of a controversial protectionism, the prospects for autonomous cultural production in poorer regions are slim indeed.

The revised cultural topography in the era of globalization is pertinent to the structure of scholarship in the American university because in the postcolonial (including post-Soviet) world, the legitimacy of maintaining independent departments for the languages and literatures of some nations (France, Germany, Russia) and not others (e.g., Poland, Nigeria, Indonesia) is no longer as clear as it may have been in the past. The honest response that certain fields of scholarship have long disciplinary histories and constitute particularly rich domains of knowledge is valid but not necessarily compelling in the face of administrative and political pressures. Yet it is hardly imaginable that universities will proceed to form individual departments devoted to all nations and languages. The alternative, the consequence of globalization for scholarship, may end up taking the form of calls for literature in general, or global or world literature, probably separated from any specific language knowledge, and largely disconnected from any possible local traditions.

To the extent that globalization undercuts nation-states, bypassing them in order to engage regions or cross borders, it also undermines the legitimacy of national traditions. In the place of national traditions emerge vague notions of a global culture, the parameters of which are difficult to describe. At times the cultural corollary to globalization appears to entail little more than the migrations of celebrity intellectuals, although there is certainly no evidence of a unified cultural public sphere. Alternatively, global culture can be taken to indicate the export of certain sorts of marketable American cultural icons; "Americanization," as a topic of scholarship, is reminiscent of the "culture industry." But surely the study of foreign cultures includes more than their susceptibility to American forms. Even more cynically, global culture can be understood to be simply the reflection of the hermetic capsules of generic identity in business-class hotels around the world, with the same international news networks, regardless of locations. Within such a frame (recall Horkheimer's vision of mathematized uniformity), any local or national cultural specificity takes on an atavistic air, a backwardness or even reactionary residue that stands in the way of globalizing history. From the standpoint of the advocates of global culture, the study of a national philology probably has the same credibility that the Taliban has for the editorial board of the *New York Times*. Learning another language becomes a rather odd project, at best a matter of acquiring a particular skill, and therefore only a transaction cost for international business. It is certainly not a qualitative engagement with a different way of life. The paradox of globalization is that while it transcends provincial national frames, it cultivates a dismissive disregard for local differences. Globalization optimists avoid encountering the sectors of the population that are locked into local languages and lack advanced technological skills. Yet the tension between the international economy and those excluded from it remains a source of political and economic instability that cannot be understood by a consciousness that intentionally ignores local traditions.

We can think of globalization as a process that tends to suppress or conceal local specificities across the world. In the process, teaching and research on specific local traditions and cultures, the historical core of the mission of foreign language and literature departments, are undermined within the American university. The future of German studies in the United States is therefore a function both of shifts specific to American higher education and to the reconfiguration of the status of local traditions, and of knowledge within the political, economic, and cultural regime of globalization. However, betwixt the specific American situation and the larger global transformation there remains a German aspect to all of this that exacerbates the situation for the teacher of German in the United States. It is hardly surprising, of course, that the nature of the object of study influences the process of study itself. It has been the case in the past as well: the abrupt decline of the scope of German study in the United States can be traced to Germany's enemy status in the First World War. Both the Nazi era and the cold war, with the division of Germany, similarly, if less dramatically, influenced the nature of the Germanist's field. The character of a post–cold war German studies can be linked to a range of factors: access to archives in the former GDR, the changing status of literature in unified Germany, a diminished American military presence in Germany, and the process of European unification, which may tend to eclipse national identities.

Factors such as these pertain to transformations in German society and culture and to American interests in Germany, both of which may influence the nature of American scholarly approaches to Germany. The example of Russia is sobering: with the collapse of the Soviet Union as the military rival, student interest in learning Russian declined dramatically, despite the fact that Americans could travel to Russia and engage in business relatively freely for the first time since 1917. Are there lessons for Germany and for German studies? Predictions are difficult: either the loss of Germany's front-line status may render it less interesting for Americans, or its potential vitality in a European economy may make it more attractive. Whether business prominence can translate into increased scholarly interest remains to be seen. Moreover, the nature of future German support for American scholarship is an open question. The Federal Republic and its cultural institutions have been extraordinarily generous in support of the study of Germany in the United States: Deutscher Akademischer Austausch Dienst (DAAD) funding, for example, rebuilt intellectual bridges after the war. This is one of the grand cultural-political successes of the century. American scholars of Germany are indebted, both personally and institutionally, for that support. Given the American tendency to disregard other cultures and particularly the diminished focus on Europe, American scholarship on Germany will be able to flourish only if German support remains forthcoming. Meanwhile, Germany faces new neighbors to the east, where cultural political activities are also expanding and therefore competing for the same funding.

The vibrancy of contemporary American scholarship on German literature and culture is a promising sign for the future. Nevertheless, that future can only be thought of in relationship to several other crucial dimensions with less sanguine implications. Second language acquisition is a crucial component of the field; it has too often been relegated to the margins or treated dismissively from the standpoint of putatively more important scholarship. Yet the viability of the field depends on the vitality of this section of the enterprise, not only for reasons of administrative justification but also in terms of the cultivation of future scholars. An assessment of future prospects cannot ignore larger trends in American universities as well, particularly the transition from liberal arts to pre-professional models. How language learning and the study of foreign cultures will adapt are open questions. In the final analysis, however, the future of German in academia depends on the status of the study of cultures in general, not merely as "cultural studies," but as the positive engagement with traditions as an urgent component of our lives in communities and our temporal experience as humans.

Notes

1. From a list of examples that could be extended, consider: Stanley Corngold, *Franz Kafka: The Necessity of Form* (Ithaca, NY, 1988); Stephen D. Dowden, *Kafka's Castle and the Critical Imagination* (Columbia, SC, 1995); John Fuegi, *Brecht and Co.: A Revolutionary Portrait of One of the World's Greatest Theater Artists* (New York, 1994); Anna K. Kuhn, *Christa Wolf's Utopian Vision: From Marxism to Feminism* (Cambridge, MA, 1988); David E. Wellbery, *The Specular Moment: Goethe's Early Lyric and the Beginnings of Romanticism* (Stanford, CA, 1996); W. Daniel Wilson, *Das Goethe-Tabu: Protest und Menschenrechte im klassischen Weimar* (Munich, 1999).
2. Leslie A. Adelson, *Making Bodies, Making History: Feminism and German Identity* (Lincoln, 1993); Julia Hell, *Post-fascist Fantasies: Psychoanalysis, History, and the Literature of East Germany* (Durham, 1997); Patricia Herminghouse and Magda Mueller, eds., *Gender and Germanness: Cultural Productions of Nation* (Providence, 1997); Wolfgang G. Natter, *Literature at War, 1914–1940: Representing the "Time of Greatness" in Germany* (New Haven/London, 1999); Eric Rentschler, *The Ministry of Illusion: Nazi Cinema and Its Afterlife* (Cambridge, MA, 1996); Linda Schulte-Sasse, *Entertaining the Third Reich: Illusions of Wholeness in Nazi Cinema* (Durham, 1997); Maria M. Tatar, *Lustmord: Sexual Murder in Weimar Germany* (Princeton, 1995); Arlene Akiko Teraoka, *East, West, and Others: The Third World in Postwar German Literature* (Lincoln, 1996); Sabine von Dirke, *All Power to the Imagination! The West German Counterculture from the Student Movement to the Greens* (Lincoln, 1997); Marc A. Weiner, *Richard Wagner and the Anti-Semitic Imagination* (Lincoln, 1995); Susanne Zantop, *Colonial Fantasies: Conquest, Family, and Nation in Precolonial Germany, 1770–1870* (Durham, 1997).
3. Marc A. Weiner, "From the Editor," *German Quarterly* 69 (1996): vi.
4. See Peter U. Hohendahl, "The American-German Divide," in *The Future of Germanistik in the USA: Changing Our Prospects*, ed. John A. McCarthy and Katrin Schneider (Nashville, TN, 1996), 19–28; John A. McCarthy, "Double Optics: The Americanization of Germanistik—The Germanization of Americans," in *Future of Germanisitik*, 1–13; Lynne A. Tatlock, "Response to Hohendahl," in *Future of Germanisitk*, 29–34; John Van Cleve and A. Leslie Willson, *Remarks on the Needed Reform of German Studies in the United States* (Columbia, SC, 1993), 15–23.

5. National Center for Educational Statistics, *Digest for Education Statistics* (U.S. Dept. of Education, 1997), 311–312, 316.

6. Hugo Schmidt, "A Historical Survey of the Teaching of German in America," in *The Teaching of German: Problems and Methods*, ed. Eberhard Reichmann (Philadelphia, 1970), 7.

7. See Hohendahl, "The American-German Divide," 26.

8. Hinrich C. Seeba, "Cultural versus Linguistic Competence? Bilingualism, Language in Exile, and the Future of German Studies," *German Quarterly* 69 (1996): 403.

9. See Max Horkheimer, "Traditionelle und kritische Theorie," in Horkheimer, *Kritische Theorie: Eine Dokumentation*, ed. Alfred Schmidt, vol. 2 (Frankfurt, 1968), 137–91.

10. See Zygmunt Bauman, *Globalization: The Human Consequences* (New York, 1998), esp. 55–76.

— *Chapter 22* —

TEACHING CULTURAL DIFFERENCE
Multiculturalism and the Internationalization of American Studies

Günter H. Lenz and John Carlos Rowe

In the following essay, we consider some of the problems of conducting research and instruction in two different societies, Germany and the United States. We examine the discipline of American studies and the significant perspective the field contributes to our understanding of what it means to be present in another culture. American studies plays crucial, albeit different, roles in German and U.S. educational institutions and their curricula, and these different functions are not discrete but rather subtly related. As professional organizations such as the American Studies Association and the European Association for American Studies develop protocols for transnational cooperation, understanding of the similarities and differences of these two different national approaches to American studies can construct a microcosm for the larger project of internationalizing the field.[1] How to interpret the often unnoticed, even unconscious ways in which the discipline in the United States depends on assumptions not always appropriate for American studies in Germany should be a critical methodological question for both Americanists and Germanists.

No single scholar, however cosmopolitan, can address these questions; the topics demand scholarly cooperation. Thus, the following two sections are intended to be read in dialogue with each other, representing German and U.S. views of how American studies figures differently in the modern educational institutions of the two nations, and in the dialectical relationship between John Carlos Rowe's pedagogical and Günter Lenz's theoretical approach. In the dialogue that follows, Rowe provides an *Erfahrungsbericht*, report, about the problems facing a group of scholars conducting a transatlantic research and teaching project between the United States and Germany. Lenz provides a theoretical framework in which he suggests some solutions to the problems this research group encountered.

I. John Carlos Rowe

Günter Lenz and I discussed the possibility of a transatlantic research project following a June 1992 conference in Ebernburg, Germany, organized by Günter, then of the Johann Wolfgang Goethe Universität in Frankfurt. (Günter Lenz and Klaus J. Milich edited the papers given at the conference and compiled them in the volume entitled *American Studies in Germany: European Contexts and Intercultural Relations*, which outlines the conference's main concerns.)[2] That same month, the German American Studies Association's annual convention at the Free University of Berlin discussed the topic *Multikulturelle Gesellschaft: Modell Amerika?* the title under which the proceedings were published.[3] In these two volumes I published my presentation (in English along with a German translation), "A Future for American Studies: The Comparative United States Cultures Model"—*Die Zukunft der 'Amerikastudien': Die Kulturen der USA im Vergleich.* I proposed a general topic for our transatlantic research project, based on the work I started in the preceding essay, that would revolve around theoretical and practical considerations of multiculturalism in the United States and Germany.

American studies in the United States, where the United States is the primary focus, is not as broadly conceived of as in Germany, where Latin American, Caribbean, and Western Hemispheric studies are considered part of the "American studies" enterprise. We examined the question of multiculturalism from several angles. The question of "multiculturalism," therefore, was a complex one involving the juxtaposition of multifarious theoretical, historical, institutional, and national notions of the word. For our project, we considered several definitions of the term "multiculturalism" that included the specific history of diverse cultures and their encounters in the United States; an examination of the theories that surround and underline these various encounters; and a comparison of multiculturalism in the U.S. and other nations of the Western Hemisphere. Moreover, we analyzed the differences between the institutional and methodological approaches of German and U.S. institutions in exploring these issues, *including* prevailing United States myths about German multiculturalism and German myths about multiculturalism in the United States, which complicated matters further.

As we corresponded about these problems subsequently, we were tempted by expediency and the restrictions of most grant applications to focus on only one of these areas, each of them being large enough to involve a wide variety of interesting colleagues in valuable intellectual exchanges. Because one of our long-range goals in setting up such a research project was to establish a network of scholars that would eventually include graduate students and advanced undergraduates, we thought it might make sense to refine our definition of the topic.

We also asked such questions as who our colleagues in this project would most likely be? From what fields would we most likely attract graduate and undergraduate students interested in possible international exchanges, year-long residencies at foreign universities, and possible appointments as teaching or research assistants? Assuming that most of the German students interested in exchange programs in the United States would be American studies majors, we concluded that the U.S. students would have to be recruited to Germany to learn more about how American studies works in scholarly, curricular, and pedagogical terms in Germany. Our study of "multiculturalism" had quickly been reduced to understanding the term as it is employed in the American studies departments of U.S. and German institutions. The "intercultural relations" of Günter Lenz and Klaus Milich's subtitle for the aforementioned volume had been condensed to those of professional scholars and their students (in the course of being professionalized) working in a common academic discipline (or set of disciplines).

But could the term "multiculturalism," with its potential relevance to any social experience, including that of an apparently monocultural society, be abridged in this fashion as an "academic" topic, where the differences in theory and definition might be studied exclusively in terms of German and U.S. approaches? Frank Trommler has pointed out how "multiculturalism has been institutionalized as an American venture with a problematic relationship to the multiculturalism of other countries and continents."[4] German *Anglistik* and *Amerikanistik* and English and American studies in the United States have contributed to this Americanization of "multiculturalism," often by reinforcing its English-language bias. Too often this version of multiculturalism is a thinly disguised version of what Günter Lenz terms the liberal ideal of "cultural diversity" and "pluralism." Practical considerations were effectively causing us, against our best intentions, to equate the popular identification of "multiculturalism" with "American" society in our project.[5] This conflict between intellectual ambitions and institutional conventions was not adequately resolved by our research group, and we are convinced it is a problem that must be addressed in future work, not only in intellectual but in institutional terms.

The early nineties, when we embarked on our endeavor, was also the period of the so-called "culture wars" and inflammatory public campaigns against "political correctness" in the United States. Across the Atlantic, this was the post-1989 period of immigration to Germany from many of the former Soviet satellites, a time that marked the genesis of the restructuring of the German Federal Republic as a consequence of the reunification of Germany. The term "multiculturalism" was impossible to specify in terms of a particular academic specialization or even a particular nation, because it raised so many heated issues that spilled over national boundaries and disciplinary specializations. Our confusions and problems were not, then, simply consequences of our inability to focus our topic; they derived from the "contact" of the public sphere with intellectual discourse, the transgression of strictly "professional" domains by political urgencies. Although not usually considered a "border discourse" in the sense in which Günter Lenz uses the term, the border between academic and public domains involves complex negotiations. The intersection of the public and academic spheres differs in Germany and the United States. Americans are isolated from other peoples, in part because the mass media keep U.S. issues at the center of our attention, and thus we tend to assume that U.S. multiculturalism is archetypal of the phenomenon. German news media are far more attentive to U.S. events, often because U.S. hegemony so threatens German autonomy and cultural identity. The absence of Europe in the U.S. public sphere must be taken into account in any study of multiculturalism from an international perspective, just as the often oppressive presence of the United States in the German public sphere has to be considered a crucial factor in an understanding of multiculturalism. In our experience in this research project, it is remarkable how often Germans, whether scholars or interested citizens, declared "multiculturalism" to be an "invention" of the United States and denied the relevance of the concept to contemporary German society.

Our grant proposal, which was accepted by the American Council of Learned Societies-Deutscher Akademischer Austausch Dienst (ACLS-DAAD) transatlantic cooperation initiative, was entitled "Multiculturalism, Transdisciplinarity, and Teaching in an Intercultural Perspective." As this title suggests, we understood the theorization of multiculturalism to be related to methodological claims for *inter*disciplinarity, *trans*disciplinarity, and *multi*disciplinarity in various areas of the humanities and social sciences. We also understood multiculturalism to involve reconsideration of how we teach, as well as what we teach. Multiculturalism had in fact become a central topic in the culture wars, in part because it challenged canonical texts, and established knowledge and the concept of the nation as the primary paradigm for understanding culture. Multiculturalism cannot be properly understood without comparative contexts, as the phrase "Intercultural Perspective" suggests.

Although we attempted to avoid any initial specification of nation-based "multiculturalism" in hopes of encouraging a wide variety of approaches and contexts for comparing the United States, Canada, Germany, Australia, the Caribbean, and Africa, among others, we ended up working with a group of scholars primarily from English departments and American studies programs in the United States and Germany. Jeffrey Peck of Georgetown University, a strong advocate of German studies, tried to keep us focused on the differences between multiculturalism in Germany and the United States. The papers delivered at a conference organized by Peck at Georgetown in October 1996 on behalf of our research group included fine contributions from scholars working on the subject of Turkish culture in Germany, the political, legal, and cultural status and identity of guest workers in Germany (*Gastarbeiter*) and attitudes among the German public toward recent foreign immigration to Germany. Such topics are good examples of Günter Lenz's "border discourses" and "discourses of global localism," which go beyond the familiar examples in U.S. cultural studies.

But emphasis on multiculturalism in the United States prevailed as we fell into discussion of United States-oriented notions of multiculturalism, to which we were accustomed as German and U.S. Americanists. From our first meeting in early August 1995 at the University of California, Irvine, it was clear that our professional training in a common field constituted us as a cohesive group familiar with the current theoretical and methodological debates in American studies. However comforting, that was still disastrous. It was likely that we would end up reproducing the sorts of friendly, esoteric debates typical of many academic conferences. Despite educational, institutional, and national differences, including the professionalization of several members of our group in the universities of the German Democratic Republic, we had too much in common, at least as far as multiculturalism as the focus of the new American studies was concerned.

What saved us from this sort of intellectual provincialism, with its potential for ignoring or trivializing public debates regarding multiculturalism in the United States, Germany, and other nations, was the strong emphasis we placed on developing the new pedagogies and curricula demanded by the methods of the new American studies, cultural studies, and the reconfiguration of American culture as situated in the different multicultural societies of the Western Hemisphere. During that first organizational meeting at Irvine in August 1995, I was simultaneously conducting a summer institute, funded by the National Endowment for the Humanities (NEH) and local sources, designed to bring high school, community college, four-year college, and university teachers together to discuss changing pedagogies and curricula at their different levels. The aim of the "Bridging the Gaps" summer institutes in intersegmental higher education was to assess and then overcome the disparities in the curricular definition of various fields in the humanities and social sciences at the different levels of higher education.[6]

Although German colleagues in our transatlantic initiative were only able to participate in the last week of our five-week summer institute, they recognized that the understanding of multiculturalism in California's high schools and community colleges differed significantly from that of many faculties in the University of California. University faculty debated the curricular and scholarly importance of independent ethnic studies programs—African American, Asian American, Latin American, Women's, Native American, Gay and Lesbian studies—relative to synthetic, integrative American studies programs, and questions relevant to the theorization of "multiculturalism," such as intersectionality and transdisciplinarity, and to specific theories such as poststructuralism, postmodern theory, queer theory, and cultural studies. High school and community college teachers relied on very few theoretical models and had relatively little freedom (or time) to design new curricula, but they were teaching a wide range of non-canonical literary texts and combining literature and history programs in new team-taught ventures that suggested a kind of populist New Historicism. These changes were occurring at these levels of higher education not because of a sudden influx of new teachers trained in the new American studies, but primarily because the demographics of these schools demanded it. California's multiculture was changing the texts. California high school teachers were not as successful at reaching students with William Shakespeare, Jane Austen, and Henry James as they were with Sandra Cisneros, Maxine Hong Kingston, Harriet Jacobs, Frederick Douglass, Helena Viramontes, and Louise Erdrich, even when these works were as difficult lexically and historically as Shakespeare's, Austen's, and James's. Multicultural education was building in California, even as attacks on affirmative action in education and employment and efforts to undo indispensable programs in bilingual education were mounting.

These and other experiences led many of us in this research group to realize that transformations in intellectual fields do not occur exclusively— and in some cases, not even primarily—by way of top-down developments from the most sophisticated scholarship and theory to the college and university classroom, to eventually finding their ways into high school and community college pedagogies and curricula. This "trickle-down" theory of knowledge was particularly inappropriate to changes in the so-called "human sciences," which are fields dramatically affected by transformations in public attitudes, which in turn are influenced strongly by changes in demography, immigration, economy, and politics.

Post-1989 Germany is an excellent example of just how such changes in the public sphere influence the everyday practices of higher education and scholarship, even in a field like American studies, which is not directly related to the social, economic, and political changes of reunified Germany. Thus, we applied practical teaching experience and discussions with teachers at different levels of higher education in both Germany and the United States to our collaborative research project. This included a June 1996 conference in Berlin with gymnasium, or German secondary school teachers, as well as several experiments in international "team-teaching," utilizing whenever we could new electronic technology for communication. For example, Günter and I planned two courses together that focused on modern U.S. literature, each pursuing different concerns within that sphere. Günter's focused on the critical revision of traditional Anglo-American modernism, concentrating on the plurality of American modernisms. My course focused on modernist responses and/or contributions to U.S. territorial and cultural expansionism in the first half of the twentieth century.

Because the seminars served different institutional purposes, they could not be organized with identical readings and arguments; therefore, we overlapped several assignments, such as oral reports given by students in the different seminars, and included four common texts: John Dos Passos's *Manhattan Transfer*, Alfred Döblin's *Berlin Alexanderplatz*, William Faulkner's *Absalom, Absalom!*, and James Agee and Walker Evans's *Let Us Now Praise Famous Men*. Our purpose in selecting four texts by canonical white male modernist writers was to test new theories of art and culture—especially those attentive to issues of race, class, and gender—as ways of revising the established understanding of literary modernism. We were also interested in finding out how our German and American students would interpret these familiar works in light of more recent theories of multiculturalism. The results were quite interesting. Students in my seminar interpreted all four modernist classics critically. Often identifying modernist literary techniques with ideological limitations of the authors, my students interpreted each text as divided between its progressive aesthetic aims and the political consequences of its reception. Günter's students were more tolerant of these works' historically specific achievements as aesthetically and sometimes politically avant-garde. The German students wanted to understand American and German modernism as an anticipation of multicultural social values and postmodern aesthetic practices; the American students were anxious to deconstruct modernism to make room for more progressive forms of multiculturalism and postmodernity.

Despite some problems with the mechanics of communication by electronic mail, our students actively exchanged ideas with each other and the two professors. I visited Berlin in June 1996 for the several events associated with our research project, such as the conference with gymnasium teachers, a public conference entitled "Cultural Studies in Comparative Perspective" sponsored by Humboldt University, and closed working sessions by the members of the research group. I was able to conduct one of the regular meetings of Günter's seminar, for it was still in session as a *Sommersemester* course.

This collaborative and international teaching venture was moderately successful, as well as easy enough to plan and complete. Andreas Müller-Hartmann of the University of Giessen and I planned an electronic "teacher sharing" program in the fall of 1997.[7] Andreas and I were both teaching seminars on postmodernism and multiculturalism in the United States, and we agreed to use a common film, John Sayles's *Lone Star*, in both seminars. Despite very different reading lists and different formal assignments, our courses shared similar concerns relating to the definition of U.S. multiculturalism in the postmodern period.

There are numerous conclusions to draw from the combination of scholarly research and teaching practices in a research project of the sort

Günter and I designed for German and U.S. scholars, but I will concentrate on three. Students in Germany and the United States brought to the seminars we taught on U.S. multiculturalism a wide variety of "background information"—personal prejudices and attitudes, "local" knowledge specific to their regions and ethnicities, habits of thought reflecting the kind of education they had received, and cultural assumptions about foreign cultures that anticipated and thus prejudiced their readings of the texts. Our students taught us what Günter Lenz means by the necessary "dialogic cultural critique" appropriate to a "multicentered world." When such "background information" was entertained as part of the educational process, it suggested the need for other disciplines, such as history and sociology, to help students overcome their own cultural misunderstandings and misconceptions. Allowing such background information to enter classroom debates also had the consequence of revealing similar assumptions in some scholarly approaches.

The conceptualization and theorization of research in the humanities and social sciences in terms of the ultimate use of such research in teaching practices—including the wide range of non-classroom "educational" settings with which we are familiar and yet often neglect in this regard (museums, conferences, internet exchanges, professional journals, readers' reports for scholarly presses, grant writing and evaluation, etc.)—not only reintegrate teaching and research for their properly educational ends, but they remind university scholars how much we have to learn from our students. This is a commonplace among high school and community college teachers in the United States and the gymnasium teachers with whom we met in Berlin. The classroom, wherever it may be, is always a site of multicultural, comparative, and theoretical work, and it should be an integral part of most research projects in the humanities and social sciences, especially those with specifically transnational participants and topics.

The most committed and self-conscious efforts to treat multiculturalism from comparative perspectives that respect its different meanings in specific societies and historical periods cannot be successful in exclusively English-language contexts (whether these be research protocols or teaching practices). As Günter Lenz points out, we must avoid a "unidirectional" application of U.S. multiculturalism to global contexts. Cultural studies must stress the importance of foreign language instruction in conjunction with the work of multicultural understanding across national boundaries, stressing the tendencies of monolingual approaches to commodify and misrepresent other cultures, often transforming them into versions of U.S. multiculture (and just as often "judging" these other cultures to be deficient when measured by this "standard"). American studies and cultural studies need foreign languages and cultures to be studied regularly and carefully in the postmodern university, especially (but not exclusively) in the United States, in order to provide students with the "broad understanding of peoples" that multiculturalism promises but often fails to deliver when the concept refers exclusively to a pluralistic, English-language, and U.S.-specific notion.[8]

II. Günter Lenz

In recent years, American historians have widely debated the "internationalization of American history," with strong support from David Thelen's *Journal of American History.* In literary and cultural studies, the increasing prominence of "minority discourses," of the New Historicism, of postcolonial discourse, and the impact of British cultural studies have opened up critical perspectives for recognizing the intercultural dimensions of U.S. literatures and cultures, in the plural, for placing them into a transnational frame of analysis, and for conceiving new ways of doing "comparative literature in the age of multiculturalism."[9] For years, the American Studies Association and the journal *American Studies International* have emphasized the need for an "internationalization of American Studies" (Robert H. Walker) and provided the framework for developing American studies programs all over the world and for discussing the complex issues of American studies at home and abroad. Since 1989, the European Association for American studies has expanded its geographical scope to include Eastern European countries and initiated a debate on the specific potential of something like European American studies. Yet, from my perspective as a German, or European, American studies veteran, the various efforts to "internationalize" American studies deserve closer scrutiny of their theoretical legitimization and the institutional implementation of their vision and program. In the following, I will offer a brief critical account of what I see as the most important achievements and open questions in recent "trans- and postnational" American studies in redefining the meaning of (U.S.) "American culture(s)" and its role in a global force field of intercultural relations. Then I will indicate the dimensions and objectives of what I define as the "dialogics" of inter- or transdisciplinary international(izing) American cultural studies, and, finally, discuss some of their directions and "comparative" projects, seen from a European, or a German, perspective.

American Multicultural Critique, Border Discourses, Cultures of United States Imperialism

Multiculturalism should not be understood as a "liberal" version of "cultural diversity" or a "pluralism" of (more or less) independent group cultures, but be taken in its radical, transformative version as being characterized by contested and provisional negotiations of the various, conflicting dimensions of cultural difference and of the organization and institutionalization of social heterogeneity. When defined in this way, its critical cultural practices have most powerfully been articulated in the border discourses that have been worked out in their intercultural as well as trans- and postnational dynamics, mostly by critics positioned at the boundaries of cultures, in cultural "contact zones," at defining moments of the clash, the mixing, and the reconstitution of cultures.[10] These border discourses explore the analytical and political potential of concepts such as cultural translation, transculturation, border cultures, mestizaje/mestiza consciousness, cultural hybridity, creolization, and diaspora. They address the processes of the construction of cultural difference and otherness in the encounters of cultures, and elaborate the various dimensions of intracultural as well as intercultural difference in the constitution and reconstitution of multivocal cultural identities and communities. All of them point to the effects of power, of imperialism and (post)colonialism, but they also can dramatize the dialectical processes of the de- and reconstruction of cultures of resistance.

All of these border discourses have been conceived in specific material, historical, and political contexts. However, it is crucial to realize that they do not only address problems and perspectives of various minorities and marginalized positionalities. They are not identical with "minority discourses" in the sense of giving direct expression and voice to the experience and the perspectives of ethnic or cultural minorities themselves. All of them engage important dimensions and problems of contemporary societies and rearticulate the complex intercultural and intracultural dynamics of difference and otherness of their cultures at large. These border discourses and their central analytical concepts are not, in isolation, constitutive of the various politically engendered interdisciplinary programs in academia such as African-American studies, Asian American studies, Chicano/a studies, Native American studies, women's studies, or queer studies. On the contrary, they deconstruct in their complex interactive dynamics the tendency toward a "monocausal" essentialism or identity politics in terms of race, ethnicity, gender, sex, or territory that has often been characteristic of these programs, and re-engage them by recognizing and exploring their multiple interactions.

The border discourses in their inherent hybridity also pose the questions of the meaning of "America" in American studies, of the intercultural interrelationships that have characterized U.S. American culture, and of the transnational entanglements of U.S. culture(s) on a global scale. Richard P. Horwitz and several contributors to the volume *Exporting America: Essays on American Studies Abroad* (1993) have exposed the ideological premises and different strategies of the federal government and other agencies in "exporting the American Dream" during the cold war era.[11] Yet, important as this critique of the imperial "politics of international American Studies" is, it has to be extended to a more radical investigation of the mutual implications of the construction of American culture(s) at home and the dynamics of transnational cultural critique. It is not sufficient in a time of globalization processes to trace the cultural impact of the United States on other nations all over the world in order to reintroduce the history of American imperialism into the debates about postcolonialism. It is also a matter of showing how the global processes of American (cultural) imperialism have had a formative impact on the political organization and the academic institutionalization of U.S. cultures of difference and the study of American multiculture at large.

The essays in the volume *Cultures of United States Imperialism* (1993), edited by Amy Kaplan and Donald E. Pease, relate the "internal differences and conflicts, structured around the relations of race, gender, ethnicity, and class" that have been emphasized and analyzed in recent years in the work of the new Americanists and the border discourses' critique of "the global dynamics of empire-building."[12] Thus, a crucial consequence of the focus on the interrelation of intracultural differences and the global dynamics of empire building is the rigorously transnational, intercultural, and comparative reconstitution of American studies that Kaplan and Pease outline.[13] If the heterogeneity of cultures at home "asks" for an assertion of a common national culture by way of the construction of cultural difference and alterity abroad, the imperialist appropriation of other cultures also predetermines the terms and perspectives used in defining the contours and fault lines of difference that, in the common understanding of multiculturalism, have displaced histories with myths and social conflicts with the rituals of cultural dissent and diversity.

Kaplan and Pease's approach to the cultures of U.S. imperialism has complemented and reconfigured in a more radically political way what in recent years has established itself as the "discourse of global localism."[14] However, the focus on the workings of U.S. imperialism in American studies should not lead to a unidirectional approach in which the more recent insight into the inherent "self-difference" of a multicultural U.S. society is transferred to a global perspective and the interrelations between cultures (and the repercussions of American imperialism on the reconstitution of cultures at home) are explored only from the perspective of the "influence" or "impact" of a politically and economically more powerful culture on other cultures. If "modernization" has turned out not to have been identical with "Americanization," as many foreign observers had claimed earlier during this "American century," the more recent globalization processes are also not to be seen simply as processes of "Americanization" of a new post-Fordist capitalism of the one remaining world power, but as changes happening in different ways in a multicentered world.

Toward a Dialogics of International American Culture studies

What is needed is a genuinely dialogic notion of cultural critique and of inter- and postnational American culture studies in order to bring into view the two-directional processes of transculturation and rearticulation of the political role of American media and of the products of popular/mass culture in various parts of the world, as well as the cultural repercussions and preconditions of the different processes of what is summarily called globalization. Dialogic in this context is to be understood in the vein of Bakhtinian notions of dialogism, heteroglossia, and hybridization, of the intertextual relations between discourses, and of the internal differentiation of discourses in their specific historical and social contexts. But it equally refers to the encounter, confrontation, or clash of different cultures enacted in the critical debates between representatives of these different perspectives and discursive positions. It asks us to revise our traditional notions of a comparative approach to literary and cultural studies. Clearly, comparative analyses can no longer consist in putting "independent," "stable," "unified" cultures side by side and judging them according to common, seemingly objective and universal criteria and standards. Cultural identities and communities are never stable, unified, isolated, or continuous. Cultures are always hybridized, multicultural, intercultural, and changing, and they work and function less through a consensus on shared values and a "common core culture" than through debate, controversies, and negotiations. In a time of globalization (and the concomitant processes of relocalization) in the economy and in communication, when the very notion and the public roles of "culture" have undergone fundamental transformations, there is no "objective" "outsider" position from which critics could conduct a comparative survey. It is exactly the force field of multiple, contested, and unequal interactions among cultures that has to be uncovered and articulated from different positionings. In this sense, any critical non-American discourse is always already implicated in U.S. culture, but in spite of its impressive power, what is called, or constructed as, "American culture" is never "omnipresent" and is always in contested relationships with other cultures. There is no "global culture"; there are only cultural products and practices that can be found throughout the world, yet are variously recodified and refunctionalized in different contexts.

These critical reflections ask for a dialogic redefinition of "comparative" in terms of interculturality, cultural encounters, and "contact zones" (Mary Louise Pratt, John Carlos Rowe).[15] "Comparative" American culture studies has to be reconceived in a dialogic manner in the context of what Jane C. Desmond and Virginia R. Domínguez call, following Benjamin Lee, a "shared critical internationalism" that in its work and its directions in research and teaching "resituates the United States in a global context."[16] American comparative and international culture studies in this sense investigate the agency of other, non-American cultures in responding to and recodifying the increasing presence of U.S. mass media and products of popular culture. Next, they recognize and explore in critical cross-cultural dialogues between U.S. cultural studies scholars and representatives of other cultures (drawing on the work of cultural critics, travelers, immigrants, migrants, and exiles), how these "other" cultures articulate alternative modes of cultural representation and alternative cultural practices, interactive processes that have been transforming their own cultures as well as U.S. American cultures.

The potential of border discourses and of these intercultural, comparative approaches for defining the project of future American studies has important consequences for a reconceptualization of inter- or transdisciplinarity and, as John Carlos Rowe has elaborated in the first part of the essay, for the pedagogy and curriculum development of American studies. They also help redefine the role of American studies scholars and scholarship in reconstituting public cultures and citizenship in ways no longer based on the notion of the normative power of a common national culture, and of citizenship in a nation-state, as that exclusionary "identity which subordinates and coordinates all other identities—of religion, estate, family, gender, ethnicity, region, and the like—to its framework of a uniform body of law," as James Holston and Arjun Appadurai have put it.[17] Thus border discourses, conceived from an intracultural as well as intercultural perspective by American radical, feminist, and minority critics or by foreign American studies scholars, address in a self-critical, self-reflective manner the question of "authoring," of "authorizing" cultural critique, the problem of "speaking for others" or for your own "group," the logic of multiple subjects, and the dialogics of competing critical discourses.[18]

These discourses achieve their critical power by being and remaining "hybridized discourses" that cross disciplinary lines in order to define and explore the analytical and political questions and projects posed in and for American culture(s). Moving beyond the old notion of interdisciplinarity as the (re-)combination of methods from several academic disciplines in the pursuit of an overarching research project is to confront what Clifford Geertz has called the "blurring of genres." This means that we recognize that cultures are not so much static, closed networks of meanings, or "texts," but force fields of open, contested, transnational "cultural flows" (Ulf Hannerz) that are articulated and negotiated in specific local (or local-global) situations and that ask for "hybrid," "creolized," and "creolizing" discourses and a dialogical reorganization of knowledge.[19] American studies should not look for a new totalizing metatheory or synthesizing metadisciplinary cultural studies program, or acquiesce in a non-committed dispersion and fragmentation of the field in the vein of "postmodern" or "postnational" social and cultural processes of "globalization." They must transcend the parochialism of the many multiculturalist debates on cultural difference that lack an explicitly comparative, intercultural perspective. The task of American studies is instead to provide a forum and force field for explicitly addressing the workings of American public culture as a dialogue of competing discourses under conditions of unequal power, and for studying the interrelations among the various, politically authorized minority discourses and interdisciplinary studies programs that are engaged in, and transcend, U.S. national culture(s). American studies should, at the same time, organize its institutional and professional activities as sites for the interchange of cultural critique articulated from different and conflicting comparative positionings, realized from American and non-American, national and postnational perspectives of cultures as cultures of difference. The pedagogical potential of border discourses and comparative intercultural approaches and their consequences for reasserting the public role of American studies intellectuals have been addressed in suggestive ways by Henry Giroux, Paul Lauter, and John Carlos Rowe, especially in his "comparative U.S. cultures model."

This is a project that has to be pursued not only in the United States, but also among the international community of American studies scholars. Foreign scholars who work outside the United States and confront the problem of understanding how "national" U.S. American multiculture is constituted and reconstitutes "itself" in the interplay of heterogeneous "local" cultures or "subcultures" and in different intercultural and transnational discourses, can play a challenging role in exploring the impact of the United States on cultures and societies all over the world and the question of how processes of resistance, transculturation, and articulation of alternative visions have worked. But they also confront the question of how a heterogeneous multicultural and "transnational" society like the United States has made and remade itself as a national (not necessarily a "common") culture and state, which, even in an era of globalization, still has to confront the problems, and perhaps the opportunities, of cultural difference and social heterogeneity within its borders.[20] However, foreign scholars can make an important contribution to dialogical inter- and postnational American studies only when they move beyond the often justified complaint that their work has more or less consistently been ignored by their colleagues in the United States or confined to studies of immigration and direct intellectual influences, or that they are immediately marked in U.S. American academic contexts, by way of their national, ethnic, or racial "origin," as specialists in "their" fields of ethnic or minority studies and discourses. Foreign American studies scholars have to investigate and articulate more rigorously than they have done in the past their own positionings in the interchanges between U.S. American cultures and their own (and other) cultures, and to define more clearly the political and cultural function of conceptualizing and institutionalizing interdisciplinary American studies programs in their own national or transnational contexts.

Internationalizing American Studies—A View from Europe

Too often, charges of "Americanization" have functioned for scholars abroad as strategies of displacing, of "othering" unwanted processes and effects of social change, of the economic and social "modernization" or "globalization" happening in countries all over the world, as the result of the impact of outside forces—namely, the powerful United States—instead of exploring the specific complex and contradictory historical dynamics of their own countries. In the case of Western Europe, the continuing charges of an almost total "Americanization," of U.S. "cultural imperialism," or of politically diverse versions of so-called "anti-Americanism" have for a long time prevented us from seeing how strikingly different cultural and social developments have been in various European countries, especially after World War II. If we compare the debates on multiculturalism in the United States (or Canada) and in European countries, we realize that they emphasize different dimensions of multiculturalism, and that their notions of "cultural difference" are differently encoded and politically charged, as Berndt Ostendorf has pointed out.[21] They are grounded in different historical experiences of, and dealings with, ethnic and cultural heterogeneity (e.g., the increasing heterogeneity of "multicultural" European nation-states due to mass migrations from former colonies, immigration, people seeking asylum, or, for Germany, of so-called "repatriated nationals") and based on different legal constructions of citizenship and different culture concepts. In the case of Germany, citizenship continues to be based on a closed culture concept (*Volksnation*) that has repressed alternative traditions of cultural pluralism. Confronting multicultural differences, social heterogeneity, and transnational interrelations in the United States forces foreign American studies scholars, particularly in Europe, to radically revise their traditional ideological constructions of a homogeneous culture as the basis for their own nation-states, which, as it is argued, have only recently come under attack from "outside" by forces of heterogeneity and cultural difference. It is here that *Germanistik* as practiced in Germany can learn a great deal from American German studies.

In the public debate in Germany, multiculturalism has often been reduced to diversity of lifestyles and a plurality of "exotic" customs, or to the "*Ausländerproblematik*," the "integration" into German society of foreigners, but without full citizen rights. However, Germany seems to me to present a challenging case study in the politics of multiculturalism, as it forces us to come to terms with the legacies of the cold war in the country most exposed to its confrontational ideological politics, and to reconceive the consequences and problems of reunification after 1989 as a special and unprecedented project of multiculturalism.[22] What this can tell us is that the very differences that motivate the discourses of multiculturalism in the United States, Canada, and European countries demand a mutually critical dialogic engagement that can contribute to correcting and reassessing the objectives and organization of cultures and societies today.

The charges of "Americanization" have also obscured the complex dialectics of the modes of intercultural understanding, of the constructions, deconstructions, and reconstructions of competing metaphors, visions, and ideologies of "America" and "Europe" (or the "West"), and of their cultural functions and political repercussions. While the media of communication and the products of U.S. American (mass) culture may be "everywhere," and some Western European countries may (deceptively) look totally "Americanized," this notion of "Americanization" is often based on the worst kind of European prejudices and stereotyping of what constitutes "American culture." Yet, the products and performative modes of American popular/mass culture have always been, as Rob Kroes puts it in his book *If You've Seen One, You've Seen the Mall: Europeans and American Mass Culture* (1996), "creatively manipulate[d], reinterpret[ed], and recontextualize[d]."[23] Also, American culture is not the homogenized, powerful, imperializing, or globalizing "other," but "it" is in "itself" multiple, inherently differentiated and conflicted, and always changing in active responses to alternative, multicultural, and intercultural experiences and discourses.

Two of the key terms describing these processes are transculturation and traveling theory. The "impact" of American modernist culture, including popular and mass culture, was not only part of the American postwar "re-education program" or of American "cultural imperialism," but it also had a liberating effect on the reconstitution of modernism in West Germany after World War II and helped to redefine the elitist, closed concept of "high culture" ("Kultur" with a capital K) of the German tradition. Yet not only was American modernism "transformed" and "appropriated" in the different European contexts; it was also, in some places, reinterpreted—against the grain of so-called (white) "classic" Anglo-American modernism dominant in the United States at the time— as multicultural (as we would put it today), as a fascinating (non-European) way of encompassing and interrelating the radical avant-garde in the arts, Hollywood film genres, and black music (especially modern jazz), or, to use Hans Magnus Enzensberger's example, Faulkner and the Katzenjammer Kids.[24] If transculturation is always a bi- or multidirectional process, the same is true for what Edward W. Said has called "traveling theory." If Said emphasizes the "deradicalization" of European critical theories such as neo-Marxism, poststructuralism, or, we could add, British cultural studies, in the American context, the same could be argued for, e.g., the fate of American multiculturalist and minority discourses and of feminist theory in Germany. Yet the question is less one of misunderstanding or perversion, but of processes of recodification and refunctionalization in different contexts. However, these intercultural encounters do not happen between two more or less unified national bodies of theory, but in the frame of a multicentered, transnational world of competing discourses. It is the role of wide-ranging, often vaguely defined theoretical concepts such as postmodernism, postcolonialism, and multiculturalism to remind us of the need to approach questions of "traveling theory" and of intercultural relationships in the wider contemporary horizon of the dynamics of the global and the local that are addressed in the various border discourses of hybridity, creolization, and diaspora referred to above.

In a time of the redefinition of the political relations of the U.S. government to Europe after the end of the cold war and of the effects of unifying the countries of the European Community and extending its borders to include Eastern European states (where the repercussions of "Americanization" processes have worked in fundamentally different ways), the scope, objectives, and organization of American culture studies must be reconceived. The task of scholars in American studies outside the United States is to reassess the objectives and the forms of institutionalization of American studies, especially as the teaching of a foreign culture, society, and language, and of cultural studies programs in their own countries. American studies outside the United States can vitally contribute to a dialogical critique of the intricate and highly charged workings of U.S. cultural imperialism and of the questionable repercussions of new versions of "American exceptionalism." But they also have to pursue the question of how far their own American studies programs, often founded as "area studies programs" in the period of the cold war, have been implicated in these imperial politics. If American studies scholars in the United States have opened up their critical perspective beyond traditional relations with Europe to the Black Atlantic (Paul Gilroy), to Latin America (José David Saldívar), or to the Asian countries of the Pacific Rim (Rey Chow, Lisa Lowe), the various national American studies communities in Europe must not only contribute to this internationalizing, decentering critical vision of their work, but also confront the question of the meaning of European American studies.[25]

The challenge of "European American studies" is manifold. It sets European scholars the task of depending less in their work on the agenda-setting of American studies in the United States in terms of theoretical approaches, cultural politics, and curricular decisions, and of articulating much more clearly than in the past the specific outside perspective and different cultural work American studies should perform in countries where English is a foreign language and a different set of the institutionalization of cultural differences. But the question of "European American studies" also seems to have paradoxical implications. The closer cooperation of the various national American studies associations in the EAAS has led to a stronger awareness of something like a "common" European perspective on the United States, of cultural "otherness," in spite of the far-reaching differences among the various national cultures, particularly if we include the countries of Eastern Europe. Yet, ironically, in important ways this feeling of something like a "common" European culture in our time is based on the notion of the omnipresence of U.S. mass/popular culture, consumer goods, cultural rituals, mass media, and modes of communication, or, more precisely, on common, or comparable, processes of the transculturation of products and practices of U.S. culture. However, the paradox of the "Europeanization of American Studies" is even more complicated. If it reinforces the notion of a common, or widely shared, European response to the powerful influences of American culture, it also reveals the "parochialism" of a vision of "European American studies" as something more or less unified vis-à-vis U.S. American culture, as something like the traditional limited national perspective writ somewhat larger, but conceived of in an equally bi-directional manner that is oblivious of its manifold implications in the rest of the world.

Certainly, American studies, even when it is "internationalizing" in the ways suggested, cannot claim priority in studying the dynamics of the global/local processes of cultural change and the changing role of culture, but they can critically reflect on the political implications of the current call for the internationalization of cultural studies in the post–cold war period of a globalizing American capitalism and provide crucially important models for future intercultural studies. Seen in this way, German and European American studies offer a chance and a vision of turning their work and their programs into "contact zones" of the encounter, the interactions, and the study of cultures, and of vitally contributing to the future of German-American history.

Notes

1. See "Discussion of EAAS-ASA Cooperation," in "National Council Meeting Minutes," 19 November 1998, Seattle, Washington, *American Studies Association Newsletter* 22:3 (September 1999): 19–20.
2. *American Studies in Germany: European Contexts and Intercultural Relations*, ed. Günter Lenz and Klaus J. Milich (New York/Frankfurt, 1995).
3. Berndt Ostendorf, ed., *Multikulturelle Gesellschaft: Modell Amerika?* (Munich, 1994).
4. Frank Trommler, "Multiculturalism and the European Connection: Theme Park or Dual Citizenship?" in *Multiculturalism in Transit: A German-American Exchange*, ed. Klaus Milich and Jeffrey Peck (New York, 1998), 178.
5. Trommler, "Multiculturalism and the European Connection," 179. Trommler points out how "multiculturalism has become a drawing card of a department that does not teach a foreign language. It assumes competence in teaching many works of foreign cultures in English. The engagement with the other occurs on safe ground." Even as we understood this as a problem to be overcome in our research group, conventions of university curricula (in both the United States and Germany) and of extramural research foundations, especially with their criteria for grants, worked against us and in favor of what Trommler observes as a problem endemic to English departments.
6. I explain the intellectual and educational purposes of these summer institutes, conducted on the Irvine campus in the summers of 1995 and 1996, in "Research and Pedagogy in the New Partnerships," *On Common Ground* 8 (Winter 1998): 21–23.
7. The notion is adapted from Gerald Graff's suggestion of "teacher-swapping" as an alternative to "team-teaching," which often requires more advance notice and poses bureaucratic problems of granting credit to faculty in such team-teaching arrangements for their labor. See Graff, *Beyond the Culture Wars* (New York, 1992).
8. Trommler, "Multiculturalism and the European Connection," 178. For an excellent critique of multiculturism in this context, see Avery F. Gordan and Christopher Newfield, "Multiculturalism's Unfinished Business," in *Mapping Multiculturalism*, ed. Avery F. Gordan and Christopher Newfield (Minneapolis, MN, 1996), 76–115.

9. See the Charles Bernheimer Report for the American Comparative Literature Association, published with critical reponses as *Comparative Literature in the Age of Multiculturalism*, ed. Charles Bernheimer (Baltimore, MD, 1995).

10. See Günter H. Lenz, "Transnational American Studies: Negotiating Cultures of Difference—Multicultural Identities, Communities, and Border Discourses," in Milich and Peck, *Multiculturalism in Transit*, 129–66. For a perceptive and challenging account of a "strong" version of a "transformative" multiculturalism, cf. Gordan and Newfield, "Multiculturalism's Unfinished Business," 76–115.

11. See Richard P. Horwitz, "The Politics of International American Studies," in *Exporting America: Essays on American Studies Abroad*, ed. Horwitz (New York, 1993), 377–418.

12. Amy Kaplan, "'Left Alone with America': The Absence of Empire in the Study of American Culture," in *Cultures of United States Imperialism*, ed. Amy Kaplan and Donald E. Pease (Durham, NC, 1993), 15–16.

13. Donald E. Pease, "New Perspectives on U.S. Cultures and Imperialism," in *Cultures of United States Imperialism*, 22–37. For recent essays emphasizing the need for American studies to become more international and more comparative, see Jane C. Desmond and Virginia R. Domínguez, "Resituating American Studies in a Critical Internationalism," *American Quarterly* 48 (1996): 475–90; from Great Britain, Paul Giles, "Reconstructing American Studies: Transnational Paradoxes, Comparative Perspectives," *Journal of American Studies* 28 (1994): 335–58, and "Virtual Americas: The Internationalization of American Studies and the Ideology of Exchange," *American Quarterly* 50 (1998): 523–47; from the Netherlands, Rob Kroes, "National American Studies in Europe, Transnational American Studies in America?" in *American Studies in Germany*, 147–58 (cf. other essays in this volume), and Mel van Elteren, "American Studies in Europe: Its Vital Role in Internationalizing the Field," *Journal of American Culture* 20:4 (Winter 1997): 87–96.

14. Pease, "New Perspectives," 26.

15. See John Carlos Rowe, "A Future for 'American Studies': The Comparative U.S. Cultures Model," in *American Studies in Germany*, 262–78.

16. Desmond and Domínguez, "Resituating American Studies," 475. For a "more international model of cultural studies," see also Chicago Critical Studies Group, "Critical Multiculturalism," *Cultural Inquiry* 18 (Spring 1992): 530–55. See Benjamin Lee's essays "Critical Internationalism," *Public Culture* 7 (1995): 559–92, and "Between Nations and Disciplines," in *Disciplinarity and Dissent in Cultural Studies*, ed. Cary Nelson and Dilip Parameshwar Gaonkar (New York/London, 1996), 217–33.

17. See James Holston and Arjun Appadurai's suggestive essay "Cities and Citizenship," *Public Culture* 8 (1996): 187–204; 187.

18. See the contributions to *Who Can Speak? Authority and Critical Identity*, ed. Judith Roof and Robyn Wiegman (Urbana/Chicago, 1995).

19. See Ulf Hannerz, *Cultural Complexity: Studies in the Social Organization of Meaning* (New York, 1992), and *Transnational Connnections: Culture, People, Places* (New York/London, 1996).

20. See Kwame Anthony Appiah's reflections on distinguishing between "nation" and "state," between "common culture" and "dominant culture," and between "common culture" ("I am inclined to say that there is not now and there has never been a common culture in the United States") and "citizens committed to common institutions" or a shared "political culture": "Against National Culture," in *Text and Nation: Cross-Disciplinary Essays on Cultural and National Identities*, ed. Laura García-Moreno and Peter C. Pfeiffer (Columbia, 1996), 175–90; 184, 186, and *Identity Against Culture: Understandings of Multiculturalism*, Avenali Lecture (Berkeley, CA, 1994).

21. See, e.g., Berndt Ostendorf, *The Costs of Multiculturalism*, Working Paper no. 50 (1992), John F. Kennedy-Institut für Nordamerikastudien der Freien Universität Berlin, 1–30, and "Inclusion, Exclusion and the Politics of Cultural Difference," in *Fusion of Cultures?* ed. Peter O. Stummer and Christopher Balme (Amsterdam/Atlanta, 1996), 205–23.

22. See, for a first effort of dealing with the problems of a "German-German multiculturalism," Dieter Thomä, "Multikulturalismus, Demokratie, Nation: Zur Philosophe der deutschen Einheit," *Deutsche Zeitschrift für Philosophie* 43 (1995): 349–63.
23. Rob Kroes, *If You've Seen One, You've Seen The Mall: Europeans and American Mass Culture* (Urbana/Chicago, 1996), 156.
24. See Günter H. Lenz, "Refractions of Modernity-Reconstituting Modernism in West Germany After World War II: Jackson Pollock, Ezra Pound, and Charlie Parker," in *Living with America, 1946–1996*, ed. Cristina Giorcelli and Rob Kroes (Amsterdam, 1997), 139–70.
25. Paul Gilroy, *The Black Atlantic: Modernity and Double-Consciousness* (Cambridge, MA, 1993); José David Saldívar, *The Dialectics of Our America: Genealogy, Cultural Critique, and Literary History* (Durham, NC, 1991) and *Border Matters: Remapping American Cultural Studies* (Berkeley, 1997); Rey Chow, *Writing Diaspora: Tactics of Intervention in Contemporary Cultural Studies* (Bloomington, 1993); Lisa Lowe, *Immigrant Acts: On Asian American Cultural Politics* (Durham, NC, 1996). On the role of "European American Studies" see the essays by Kroes, van Elteren, and Giles mentioned above.

CONTRIBUTORS

Volker R. Berghahn is Professor of History at Columbia University.

James M. Bergquist is Professor of History at Villanova University.

Russell A. Berman is Walter A. Haas Professor in the Humanities and Dean of Undergraduate Studies at Stanford University.

Kathleen Neils Conzen is Professor of History at the University of Chicago.

Daniel Fallon is Chair of the Education Division at the Carnegie Corporation of New York.

Lily Gardner Feldman is Professor of Political Science and Senior Fellow at the American Institute for Contemporary German Studies, Washington.

Michael Geyer is Professor of History at the University of Chicago.

Manfred Henningsen is Professor of Political Science at the University of Hawaii.

Patricia Herminghouse is Professor Emerita of German and Comparative Literature at the University of Rochester.

Konrad H. Jarausch is Lurcy Professor of European History at the University of North Carolina and Director of the Zentrum für Zeithistorische Studien in Potsdam.

Hartmut Keil is Professor of North American History at Universität Leipzig.

Rudy Koshar is Professor of History at the University of Wisconsin, Madison.

Günter H. Lenz is Professor of American Literary and Cultural Studies at Humboldt Universität Berlin.

Berndt Ostendorf is Professor of American Cultural Studies at Ludwig-Maximilians-Universität Munich.

Brent O. Peterson is Associate Professor of German at Ripon College, Wisconsin.

A. Gregg Roeber is Professor of History at Pennsylvania State University.

John Carlos Rowe is Professor of English and Comparative Literature at the University of California, Irvine.

Elliott Shore is Professor of History and Director of Libraries at Bryn Mawr College.

Werner Sollors is Henry B. and Anne M. Cabot Professor of English Literature and Afro-American Studies at Harvard University.

Theo Sommer is Editor of *Die Zeit*, Hamburg.

Frank Trommler is Professor of German and Comparative Literature at the University of Pennsylvania.

Karsten D. Voigt is the German Coordinator of German-American Cooperation, Auswärtiges Amt Berlin.

Moshe Zuckermann is the Director of the Institute for German History at Tel Aviv University.

SELECTED BIBLIOGRAPHY

Abelshauser, Werner. *Wirtschaft in Westdeutschland*. Stuttgart, 1975.

Abenheim, Donald. *Reforging the Iron Cross: The Search for Tradition in the West German Armed Forces*. Princeton, 1988.

Adams, Willi Paul, ed. *Die deutschsprachige Auswanderung in die Vereinigten Staaten: Berichte über Forschungsstand und Quellenbestände*. Berlin, 1980.

Adams, Willi Paul, and Knud Krakau, eds. *Deutschland und Amerika: Perzeption und historische Realität*. Berlin, 1985.

Adelson, Leslie A. *Making Bodies, Making History: Feminism and German Identity*. Lincoln, 1993.

Adorno, Theodor W. *Ästhetische Theorie*, 10th ed. Frankfurt, 1990.

Ahlstrom, Sidney. *A Religious History of the American People*. New Haven/London, 1972.

Allen, Ann Taylor. *Feminism and Motherhood in Germany, 1800–1914*. New Brunswick, NJ, 1991.

Ambrosius, Gerold. *Die Durchsetzung der sozialen Marktwirtschaft in Westdeutschland*. Stuttgart, 1977.

Anderson, Benedict. *Imagined Communities: Reflections on the Origin and Spread of Nationalism*. London, 1983.

Anderson, Jeffrey, ed. *Regional Integration and Democracy: Expanding the European Experience*. Boulder, 1999.

Anneke, Mathilde Franziska. *Die Gebrochenen Ketten: Erzählungen, Reportagen und Reden (1861–1873)*, ed. Maria Wagner. Stuttgart, 1983.

Anthony, Katharine. *Feminism in Germany and Scandinavia*. New York, 1915.

Appadurai, Arjun. *Modernity at Large: Cultural Dimensions of Globalization*. Minneapolis/London, 1996.

Appel, John J. *Immigrant Historical Societies in the United States, 1880–1950*. New York, 1980.

Appleby, Joyce, Lynn Hunt and Margaret Jacobsen. *Telling the Truth About History*. New York, 1994.

Arendt, Hannah. *Besuch in Deutschland*. Translated by Eike Geisel. Berlin, 1993.

Armed Forces Information and Education Division, ed. *A Pocket Guide to Germany*. Washington, D.C., 1951.

Arweck, Elisabeth, and Peter B. Clarke. *New Religious Movements in Western Europe: An Annotated Bibliography*. Westport, CT/London, 1997.

Ash, Mitchell G., ed. *German Universities Past and Future – Crisis or Renewal?* Providence, 1997.

Bach, Jr., Julian. *America's Germany: An Account of the Occupation*. New York, 1946.

Bade, Klaus J., ed. *Deutsche im Ausland–Fremde in Deutschland: Migration in Geschichte in Gegenwart*. Munich, 1992.

Baedeker, Karl, ed. *Munich and Its Environs: Handbook for Travellers*. Hamburg, 1950.

_____, ed. *Northern Bavaria: Handbook for Travellers*. Hamburg, 1951.

_____, ed. *Southern Bavaria: With Excursions to Innsbruck and Salzburg*. Hamburg, 1953.

Baier, Lothar. *Volk ohne Zeit: Essay über das eilige Vaterland*. Berlin, 1990.

Barclay, David, and Elisabeth Glaser-Schmidt, eds. *Transatlantic Images and Perceptions: Germany and America since 1776*. Cambridge, 1997.

Barnouw, Dagmar. *Germany 1945: Views of War and Violence*. Bloomington/Indianapolis, 1996.

Barry, Colman. *The Catholic Church and the German Americans*. Milwaukee, 1953.

Bauman, Zygmunt. *Globalization: The Human Consequences*. New York, 1998.

Beatty, Barbara. *Preschool Education in America: The Culture of Young Children from the Colonial Era to the Present*. New Haven, 1995.

Bednarowski, Mary Farrell. *New Religions and the Theological Imagination in America*. Bloomington/Indianapolis, 1989.

Belgum, Kirsten. *Popularizing the Nation: Audience, Representation, and the Production of Identity in Die Gartenlaube, 1853–1900*. Lincoln, 1998.

Berghahn, Volker R. *The Americanization of West German Industry, 1945–1973*. New York, 1986.

Berghahn, Volker R., and Paul J. Friedrich. *Otto A. Friedrich: Ein politischer Unternehmer, 1902–1975*. Frankfurt, 1992.

Bernheimer, Charles, ed. *Comparative Literature in the Age of Multiculturalism*. Baltimore, 1995.

Bethge, Eberhard. *Dietrich Bonhoeffer: Man of Vision, Man of Courage*. Translated by Eric Mosbacher et al. New York/Evanston, 1970.

Bhabha, Homi K., ed. *Nation and Narration*. London/New York, 1990.

Blackwill, Robert D. *The Future of Transatlantic Relations: Report by an Independent Task Force Sponsored by the Council on Foreign Relations*. New York, 1999.

Blaschke, Monika, and Christiane Harzig, eds. *Frauen wandern aus: Deutsche Migrantinnen im 19. und 20. Jahrhundert*. Bremen, 1990.

Boernstein, Henry [Heinrich]. *The Mysteries of St. Louis*. Translated by Friedrich Münch. Chicago, 1990.

Bohlman, Phillip, and Otto Holzapfel, eds. *Land without Nightingales: The Musical Culture of German Americans*. Madison, 2000.

Bonn, Moritz S. *Das Schicksal des deutschen Kapitalismus*. Berlin, 1930.

Boorstin, Daniel J. *America and the Image of Europe: Reflections on American Thought*. Gloucester, MA, 1960.

Brancaforte, Charlotte L., ed. *The German Forty-Eighters in the United States*. New York, 1989.

Brecht, Martin et al., eds. *Die Geschichte des Pietismus: Der Pietismus im achtzehnten Jahrhundert II*. Göttingen, 1995.

Bredella, Lothar, ed. *Mediating a Foreign Culture: The United States and Germany. Studies in Intercultural Understanding*. Tübingen, 1991.

Brooke, John L. *The Refiner's Fire: The Making of Mormon Cosmology, 1644–1844*. Cambridge/New York, 1994.

Brzezinski, Zbigniew. *Between Two Ages: America's Role in the Technetronic Era*. New York, 1970.

Buchheim, Christoph. *Die Wiedereingliederung Westdeutschlands in die Weltwirtschaft*. Munich, 1990.

Buhle, Mary Jo. *Women and American Socialism*. Urbana, 1982.

Burgess, John P. *The East German Churches and the End of Communism*. New York, 1997.

Burkholder, John R., and Barbara N. Gingerich, eds. *Mennonite Peace Theology: A Panorama of Types*. Akron, PA, 1991.

Carter, Erica. *How German Is She? Postwar West German Reconstruction and the Consuming Woman*. Ann Arbor, 1997.

Cayton, Mary Kupiec, Elliott J. Gorn, and Peter W. Williams, eds. *Encyclopedia of American Social History II*. New York, 1993.

Ceaser, James W. *Reconstructing America: The Symbol of America in Modern Thought*. New Haven, 1997.

Chow, Rey. *Writing Diaspora: Tactics of Intervention in Contemporary Cultural Studies*. Bloomington, 1993.

Clifford, James. *Routes: Travel and Translation in the Late Twentieth Century*. Cambridge/London, 1997.

Conzen, Kathleen Neils. *Immigrant Milwaukee, 1836–1860: Accommodation and Community in a Frontier City*. Cambridge, MA, 1976.

Cooper, Frederick, and Ann Laura Stoler, eds. *Tensions of Empire: Colonial Cultures in a Bourgeois World*. Berkeley, 1997.

Corngold, Stanley. *Franz Kafka: The Necessity of Form.* Ithaca, NY, 1988.

Courtois, Stéphane, et al., eds. *The Black Book of Communism: Crimes, Terror, Repression.* Cambridge, MA/London, 1999.

Crystal, David. *English as a Global Language.* Cambridge, 1997.

Dahrendorf, Ralf. *Die angewandte Aufklärung: Gesellschaft und Soziologie in Amerika.* Munich, 1963.

Danyel, Jürgen, ed. *Die geteilte Vergangenheit: Zum Umgang mit Nationalsozialismus und Widerstand in beiden deutschen Staaten.* Berlin, 1995.

Debouzy, Marianne, ed. *In the Shadow of the Statue of Liberty: Immigrants, Workers, and Citizens in the American Republic, 1880–1920.* Urbana, 1992.

Delbrück, Jost, Knut Ipsen, Wilhelm A. Kewenig, and Georg R. Bluhm, eds. *Abschreckung und Entspannung: Fünfundzwanzig Jahre Sicherheitspolitik zwischen bipolarer Konfrontation und begrenzter Kooperation.* Berlin, 1977.

Delius, F. C. *Der Held und sein Wetter: Ein Kunstmittel und sein ideologischer Gebrauch im Roman des bürgerlichen Realismus.* Munich, 1971.

Diedrich, Maria. *Love across Color Lines: Ottilie Assing and Frederick Douglass.* New York, 1999.

Diner, Dan. *Verkehrte Welten: Antiamerikanismus in Deutschland. Ein historischer Essay.* Frankfurt, 1993.

_____. *America in the Eyes of the Germans: An Essay on Anti-Americanism.* Princeton, 1996.

Dirke, Sabine von. *"All Power to the Imagination!" The West German Counterculture from the Student Movement to the Greens.* Lincoln, 1997.

Dobbert, Guido A. *The Disintegration of an Immigrant Community: The Cincinnati Germans, 1870–1920.* New York, 1980.

Doering-Manteuffel, Anselm. *Wie westlich sind die Deutschen? Amerikanisierung und Westernisierung im 20. Jahrhundert.* Göttingen, 1999.

Driedger, Lee, and Donald B. Kraybill. *Mennonite Peacemaking: From Quietism to Activism.* Scottdale, PA/Waterloo, Ontario, 1994.

Dulles, Foster Rhea. *Americans Abroad: Two Centuries of European Travel.* Ann Arbor, 1964.

Easum, Chester V. *The Americanization of Carl Schurz.* Chicago, 1929.

Eckhardt, Joseph P. *The King of the Movies: Film Pioneer Siegmund Lubin.* Madison/Teaneck, NJ/London, 1997.

Emmer, P. C., and M. Mörner. *European Expansion and Migration: Essays on the Intercontinental Migration from Africa, Asia, and Europe.* New York, 1992.

Engle, Ron, and Tice L. Miller. eds. *The American Stage: Social and Economic Issues from the Colonial Period to the Present.* Cambridge, 1993.

Engler, Wolfgang. *Die Ostdeutschen: Kunde von einem verlorenen Land.* Berlin, 1999.

Enzensberger, Hans Magnus. *Politik und Verbrechen.* Frankfurt, 1964.

Erhard, Ludwig. *Wohlstand für alle.* Düsseldorf, 1957.

Ermarth, Michael, ed. *America and the Shaping of German Society, 1945–1955.* Providence/Oxford, 1993.

Ettelt, Werner, and Hans-Dieter Krause. *Der Kampf um eine marxistische Gewerkschaftspolitik in der deutschen Arbeiterbewegung 1868 bis 1878.* Berlin, 1975.

Evans, Richard J. *The Feminists: Women's Emancipation Movements in Europe, America and Australasia, 1840–1920.* New York, 1977.

Fallon, Daniel. *The German University: A Heroic Ideal in Conflict with the Modern World.* Boulder, 1980.

Fehrenbach, Heide, and Uta G. Poiger, eds. *Transactions, Transgressions, Transformations: American Culture in Western Europe and Japan.* New York/Oxford, 2000.

Finkelstein, Norman G. *The Holocaust Industry: Reflections on the Exploitation of the Jewish Suffering.* New York, 2000.

Finzsch, Norbert, and Dietmar Schirmer, eds. *Identity and Intolerance: Nationalism, Racism, and Xenophobia in Germany and the United States.* Washington, D.C., 1998.

Fischer, David Hackett. *Albion's Seed: Four British Folkways in North America.* New York, 1989.

Fischer, Marc. *After the Wall: Germany, the Germans and the Burdens of History.* New York, 1995.

Flitner, Andreas, and Klaus Giel, eds. *Wilhelm von Humboldt: Werke in fünf Bänden*, vol. 4. Stuttgart, 1964.

Flynn, Gregory, and Hans Rattinger, eds. *The Public and Atlantic Defense*. Totowa, NJ, 1995.

Fodor, Eugene, ed. *Germany 1953*. New York, 1953.

Fogleman, Aaron Spencer. *Hopeful Journeys: German Immigration, Settlement, and Political Culture in Colonial America, 1717–1775*. Philadelphia, 1996.

Foner, Eric. *Free Soil, Free Labor, Free Men: The Ideology of the Republican Party before the Civil War*. New York, 1970.

Foner, Philip S., ed. *The Autobiographies of the Haymarket Martyrs*. New York, 1969.

Ford, Henry. *My Life and Work*. New York, 1922.

Fraenkel, Ernst. *Amerika im Spiegel des deutschen politischen Denken*. Cologne/Opladen, 1959.

Franz, Eckhart G. *Das Amerikabild der deutschen Revolution von 1848/49: Zum Problem der Uebertragung gewachsener Verfassungsformen*. Heidelberg, 1958.

Frederiksen, Elke, ed. *Die Frauenfrage in Deutschland 1865–1915: Texte und Dokumente*. Stuttgart, 1981.

Freese, Peter, ed. *Germany and German Thought in American Literature and Cultural Criticism*. Essen, 1990.

Freit, Norbert. *Vergangenheitspolitik: Die Anfänge der Bundesrepublik und die NS-Vergangenheit*. Munich, 1996.

Fridenson, Patrick. *Histoire des usines Renault*. Paris, 1971.

Friedman, Susan. *Mappings: Feminism and the Cultural Geographies of Encounter*. Princeton, 1998.

Fröbel, Friedrich. *Autobiography of Friedrich Froebel*. Edited and translated by Emilie Michaelis and Henry Keatley Moore. Syracuse, NY, 1889.

Fromme, Friedrich K. *Von der Weimarer Verfassung zum Bonner Grundgesetz*. Tübingen, 1962.

Fuegi, John. *Brecht and Co.: A Revolutionary Portrait of One of the World's Greatest Theater Artists*. New York, 1994.

Furet, François. *The Passing of an Illusion: The Idea of Communism in the Twentieth Century*. Chicago, 1999.

Gabaccia, Donna. *From the Other Side: Women, Gender, and Immigrant Life in the U.S., 1820–1990*. Bloomington, 1994.

Gaddis, John Lewis. *We Now Know: Rethinking Cold War History*. Oxford/New York, 1997.

García-Moreno, Laura, and Peter C. Pfeiffer, eds. *Text and Nation: Cross-Disciplinary Essays on Cultural and National Identities*. Columbia, SC, 1996.

Garreau, Joel. *The Nine Nations of North America*. Boston, 1981.

Gassert, Philipp. *Amerika im Dritten Reich*. Stuttgart, 1997.

Gatzke, Hans W. *Germany and the United States: A "Special Relationship"?* Cambridge, MA/London, 1980.

Geitz, Henry, Jürgen Heideking, and Jurgen Herbst, eds. *German Influences on Education in the United States to 1917*. Cambridge, 1995.

Gerber, David A. *The Making of an American Pluralism: Buffalo, New York, 1825–60*. Urbana, 1989.

Gerbi, Antonelli. *The Dispute of the New World: The History of a Polemic, 1750–1900*. Translated by Jeremy Moyle. New York, 1973.

Gibson-Graham, J. K. *The End of Capitalism (As We Know It): A Feminist Critique of Political Economy*. Cambridge, MA, 1997.

Gienapp, William E. *The Origins of the Republican Party, 1852–1856*. New York, 1987.

Giesen, Bernhard. *Die Intellektuellen und die Nation: Eine deutsche Achsenzeit*. Frankfurt, 1993.

Gilroy, Paul. *The Black Atlantic: Modernity and Double-Consciousness*. Cambridge, MA, 1993.

Gimbel, John. *A German Community under American Occupation: Marburg 1945–52*. Stanford, 1961.

Giorcelli, Cristina, and Rob, Kroes, eds. *Living With America, 1946–1996*. Amsterdam, 1997.

Gjerde, Jon. *The Minds of the West: Ethnocultural Evolution in the Rural Middle West, 1830–1917*. Chapel Hill, 1997.

Gleason, Philip. *Conservative Reformers: German-American Catholics and the Social Order.* Notre Dame, 1968.

Golay, John F. *The Founding of the Federal Republic of Germany.* Chicago, 1958.

Goldberg, Jonothan J. *Jewish Power: Inside the American Jewish Establishment.* Reading, MA, 1996.

Goldhagen, Daniel J. *Hitler's Willing Executioners: Ordinary Germans and the Holocaust.* New York, 1996.

Gordan, Avery F., and Christopher Newfield, eds. *Mapping Multiculturalism.* Minneapolis, 1996.

Graff, Gerald. *Beyond the Culture Wars.* New York, 1992.

Gries, Rainer, Volker Ilgen and Dirk Schindelbeck. *"Ins Gehirn der Masse Kriechen!" Werbung und Mentalitätsgeschichte.* Darmstadt, 1995.

Gutman, Herbert, ed. *Work, Culture and Society in Industrializing America: Essays in American Working-Class and Social History.* New York, 1977.

Häderle, Irene. *Deutsche kirchliche Frauenvereine in Ann Arbor, Michigan, 1870–1930: Eine Studie über die Bedingungen und Formen der Akkulturation deutscher Einwanderinnen und ihrer Töchter in den USA.* Stuttgart, 1997.

Hahn, Steven, and Jonathan Prude, eds. *The Countryside in the Age of Capitalist Transformation: Essays in the Social History of Rural America.* Chapel Hill, 1985.

Halfmann, Ulrich, Kurt Müller, and Klaus Weiss, eds. *Wirklichkeit und Dichtung: Studien zur englischen und amerikanischen Literatur.* Berlin, 1984.

Hannaford, Ivan. *Race: The History of an Idea in the West.* Baltimore, 1996.

Hannerz, Ulf. *Cultural Complexity: Studies in the Social Organization of Meaning.* New York, 1992.

_____. *Transnational Connnections: Culture, People, Places.* New York/London, 1996.

Harper, Ida Husted. *The Life and Work of Susan B. Anthony,* 3 vols. Indianapolis, 1908.

Hartmann, Hans. *Amerikanische Firmen in Deutschland.* Cologne, 1963.

Hartmann, Hans A., and Rolf Haubl, eds. *Bilderflut und Sprachmagie.* Opladen, 1992.

Harzig, Christiane. *Familie, Arbeit und weibliche Öffentlichkeit in einer Einwanderungsstadt: Deutschamerikanerinnen in Chicago um die Jahrhundertwende.* St. Katharinen, 1991.

_____, ed. *Peasant Maids—City Women: From the European Countryside to Urban America.* Ithaca, 1997.

Hauser, Heinrich. *The German Talks Back.* New York, 1945.

Heffer, Jean, and Jeanine Rovet, eds. *Why Is There No Socialism in the United States? Pourquoi n'y a-t-il pas de Socialisme aux États-Unis?* Paris, 1988.

Heimreich, William B. *Against All Odds: Holocaust Survivors and the Successful Lives They Made in America.* New York, 1992.

Heineman, Elizabeth D. *What Difference Does a Husband Make? Women and Marital Status in Nazi and Postwar Germany.* Berkeley/Los Angeles/London, 1999.

Hell, Julia. *Post-fascist Fantasies: Psychoanalysis, History, and the Literature of East Germany.* Durham, NC, 1997.

Henke, Klaus-Dieter. *Die amerikanische Besetzung Deutschlands.* Munich, 1995.

Henningsen, Manfred. *Der Fall Amerika: Zur Sozial- und Bewußtseinsgeschichte einer Verdrängung.* Munich, 1974.

Herminghouse, Patricia, and Magda Mueller, eds. *Gender and Germanness: Cultural Productions of Nation.* Providence, 1997.

Hertle, Daniel. *Die Deutschen in Nordamerika und der Freiheitskampf in Missouri.* Chicago, 1865.

Herzstein, Robert E. *When Nazi Dreams Come True.* London, 1982.

Hilberg, Raul. *The Destruction of the European Jews.* Revised and definitive edition. 3 vols. New York/London, 1985.

Hobsbawm, Eric, and Terence Ranger, eds. *The Invention of Tradition.* Cambridge, 1983.

Hochgeschwender, Michael. *Freiheit in der Offensive? Der Kongreß für kulturelle Freiheit und die Deutschen.* Munich, 1998.

Hoerder, Dirk, ed. *American Labor and Immigration History, 1877–1920s: Recent European Research.* Urbana, 1983.

_____, ed. *Labor Migration in the Atlantic Economies: The European and North American Working Classes during the Period of Industrialization.* Westport, CT, 1985.

_____, ed. *"Struggle a Hard Battle": Essays on Working-Class Immigrants*. DeKalb, 1986.

Hoerder, Dirk, and Christiane Harzig, eds. *The Immigrant Labor Press in North America*. 3 vols. Westport, CT, 1987.

Hoerder, Dirk, and Leslie Page Moch. *European Migrants: Global and Local Perspectives*. Boston, 1996.

Hoerder, Dirk, and Jörg Nagler, eds. *People in Transit: German Migrations in Comparative Perspective, 1820–1930*. New York, 1995.

Hofstadter, Richard, and Walter P. Metzger. *The Development of Academic Freedom in the United States*. New York, 1955.

Hollander, Paul. *Anti-Americanism: Critiques at Home and Abroad, 1965–1990*. New York, 1992.

Hollinger, David A. *Postethnic America: Beyond Multiculturalism*. New York, 1995.

Holt, Michael F. *Forging a Majority: The Formation of the Republican Party in Pittsburgh, 1848–1860*. New Haven, 1967.

Holt, Michael F. *The Rise and Fall of the American Whig Party: Jacksonian Politics and the Onset of the Civil War*. New York, 1999.

Hopkins, C. Howard. *The Rise of the Social Gospel in American Protestantism, 1865–1915*. New Haven, 1967.

Horkheimer, Max. *Kritische Theorie: Eine Dokumentation*. Frankfurt, 1968.

Horwitz, Richard P., ed. *Exporting America: Essays on American Studies Abroad*. New York, 1993.

Hostetler, Beulah Stauffer. *American Mennonites and Protestant Movements: A Community Paradigm*. Scottdale, PA/Kitchener, Ontario, 1987.

Humboldt, Wilhelm von. *Ideen zu einem Versuch, die Grenzen der Wirksamkeit des Staats zu bestimmen*. Stuttgart, 1967.

_____. *The Limits of State Action*. Edited and translated by J. W. Burrow. London, 1969.

Huyssen, Andreas, and Klaus R. Scherpe, eds. *Postmoderne: Zeichen eines kulturellen Wandels*. Reinbek, 1986.

Ignatiev, Noel. *How the Irish Became White*. New York, 1995.

Immerfall, Stefan, ed. *Territoriality in the Globalizing Society. One Place or None?* Berlin, 1998.

Inglehart, Ronald. *The Silent Revolution: Changing Values and Political Styles among Western Publics*. Princeton, 1977.

International Kindergarten Union; Committee of Nineteen. *Pioneer of the Kindergarten in America*. New York/London, 1924.

Jacobson, Matthew Frye. *Special Sorrows: The Diasporic Imagination of Irish, Polish, and Jewish Immigrants in the United States*. Cambridge, MA, 1995.

_____. *Whiteness of a Different Color: European Immigrants and the Alchemy of Race*. Cambridge, MA, 1998.

James, Harold. *A German Identity, 1770–1990*. New York, 1989.

Jarausch, Konrad H., ed. *After Unity: Reconstructing German Identities*. Providence, 1997.

Jarausch, Konrad, and Hannes Siegrist. *Amerikanisierung und Sowjetisierung in Deutschland 1945–1970*. Frankfurt/New York, 1997.

Jarausch, Konrad H., and Michael Geyer, *Shattered Pasts: Reconstructing German Histories*. Princeton, forthcoming.

Jensen, Richard. *The Winning of the Midwest: Social and Political Conflict, 1888–1896*. Chicago, 1971.

Johnson, Charles Thomas. *Culture at Twilight: The National German-American Alliance, 1901–1918*. New York, 1999.

Judt, Tony. *A Grand Illusion: An Essay on Europe*. New York, 1996.

Junker, Detlef. *Von der Supermacht zur Weltmacht: Amerikanische Aubenpolitik im 20. Jahrhundert*. Mannheim, 1995.

Kaes, Anton, Wolfgang Jacobsen, and Hans Helmut Prinzler, eds. *Geschichte des deutschen Films*. Stuttgart/Weimar, 1993.

Kamphoefner, Walter. *The Westfalians: From Germany to Missouri*. Princeton, 1987.

Kamphoefner, Walter D., Wolfgang Helbich, and Ulrike Sommer, eds. *News from the Land of Freedom: German Immigrants Write Home*. Translated by Susan Carter Vogel. Ithaca, 1991.

Kanigel, Robert. *The One Best Way: Frederick Winslow Taylor and the Enigma of Efficiency*. New York, 1997.

Kaplan, Amy, and Donald E. Pease, eds. *Cultures of United States Imperialism.* Durham, NC, 1993.

Kaplan, Marion A. *The Jewish Feminist Movement in Germany: The Campaigns of the Jüdischer Frauenbund, 1904–1938.* Westport, CT, 1979.

Kapp, Friedrich. *Geschichte der Deutschen im Staate New York bis zum Anfange des neunzehnten Jahrhunderts.* 3rd ed. New York, 1869.

Kaufmann, Franz Xaver. *Sicherheit as soziologisches und sozialpolitisches Problem: Untersuchungen zu einer Wertidee hochdifferenzierter Gesellschaften.* Stuttgart, 1970.

Kazal, Russell A. *Becoming "Old Stock": The Waning of German-American Identity in Philadelphia, 1900–1930.* Ann Arbor, 1998.

Keil, Hartmut, ed. *German Workers' Culture in the United States 1850 to 1920.* Washington, D.C./London, 1988.

Keil, Hartmut, and John B. Jentz, eds. *German Workers in Chicago: A Documentary History of Working-Class Culture from 1850 to World War I.* Urbana, 1988.

Keil, Hartmut, and John B. Jentz, eds. *German Workers in Industrial Chicago, 1850–1910: A Comparative Perspective.* DeKalb, 1983.

Kleppner, Paul. *The Cross of Culture: A Social Analysis of Midwestern Politics, 1850–1900.* New York, 1970.

Kocka, J. *Industrial Culture and Bourgeois Society.* Oxford/New York, 1999.

Krakau, Knud, ed. *The American Nation - National Identity - Nationalism.* Münster/New Brunswick, NJ, 1997.

Kramer, Jane. *The Politics of Memory: Looking for Germany in the New Germany.* New York, 1996.

Krampikowski, Frank, ed. *Amerikanisches Deutschlandbild und deutsches Amerikabild in Medien und Erziehung.* Baltmannsweiler, 1990.

Kroes, Rob. *If You've Seen One, You've Seen The Mall: Europeans and American Mass Culture.* Urbana/Chicago, 1996.

Kroes, Rob, Robert W. Rydell, and Doeko F. J. Bosscher, eds. *Cultural Transmissions and Receptions: American Mass Culture in Europe.* Amsterdam, 1993.

Krugman, Paul. *The Accidental Theorist: And Other Dispatches from the Dismal Science.* New York, 1998.

Kuhn, Anna K. *Christa Wolf's Utopian Vision: From Marxism to Feminism.* Cambridge, 1988.

Laslett, John H. M., and Seymour Martin Lipset, eds. *Failure of a Dream? Essays in the History of American Socialism.* Berkeley, 1974.

Leidecker, Kurt F. *Yankee Teacher: The Life of William Torrey Harris.* New York, 1946.

Lenz, Günter, and Klaus J. Milich, eds. *American Studies in Germany: European Contexts and Intercultural Relations.* New York/Frankfurt, 1995.

Lerda, Valeria Gennaro, ed. *From 'Melting Pot' to Multiculturalism: The Evolution of Ethnic Relations in the United States and Canada.* Rome, 1990.

Levenstein, Harvey. *Seductive Journey: American Tourists in France from Jefferson to the Jazz Age.* Chicago/London, 1998.

Levi, Carlo. *The Two-fold Night: A Narrative of Travel in Germany.* Translated by Joseph M. Bernstein. London, 1962.

Levine, Bruce. *The Spirit of 1848: German Immigrants, Labor Conflict, and the Coming of the Civil War.* Urbana, 1992.

Lidtke, Vernon L. *The Alternative Culture: Socialist Labor in Imperial Germany.* New York, 1985.

Liebknecht, Wilhelm. *Ein Blick in die Neue Welt.* Stuttgart, 1887.

_____. *Leitartikel und Beiträge in der Osnabrücker Zeitung 1864–1866.* Hildesheim, 1975.

_____. *Erinnerungen eines Soldaten der Revolution.* Berlin, 1976.

Light, Dale B. *Rome and the New Republic: Conflict and Community in Philadelphia Catholicism between the Revolution and the Civil War.* Notre Dame/London, 1996.

Littwack, Leon. *Trouble in Mind: Black Southerners in the Age of Jim Crow.* New York, 1998.

Lowe, Lisa. *Immigrant Acts: On Asian American Cultural Politics.* Durham, NC, 1996.

Lowenstein, Steven M. *Frankfurt on the Hudson: The German-Jewish Community of Washington Heights, 1933–1983.* New York, 1989.

Lüdtke, Alf, Inge Marßolek, and Adelheid von Saldern, eds. *Amerikanisierung: Traum und Alptraum im Deutschland des 20. Jahrhunderts.* Stuttgart, 1996.

Luebke, Frederick C. *Bonds of Loyalty: German Americans and World War I*. DeKalb, 1974.
_____. *Germans in the New World: Essays in the History of Immigration*. Urbana, 1990.
_____, ed. *Ethnic Voters and the Election of Lincoln*. Lincoln, 1971.
Maase, Kaspar. *BRAVO Amerika: Erkundungen zur Jugendkultur der Bundesrepublik in den fünfziger Jahren*. Hamburg, 1992.
Maizlish, Stephen E. *The Triumph of Sectionalism: The Transformation of Ohio Politics, 1844–1856*. Kent, OH, 1983.
Mallinckrodt, Anita M. *From Knights to Pioneers: One German Family in Westphalia and Missouri*. Carbondale, 1994.
Mantell-Oomen, Ursula, ed. *Amerikanisches Judentum heute/American Jewry Today*. Trier, 1999.
Markovits, Andrei S., and Simon Reich. *The German Predicament: Memory and Power in the New Europe*. Ithaca, 1997.
Marschalck, Peter. *Deutsche Überseewanderung im 19. Jahrhundert: Ein Beitrag zur soziologischen Theorie der Bevölkerung*. Stuttgart, 1973.
Marsiske, Hans-Arthur. *Eine Republik der Arbeiter ist möglich: Der Beitrag Wilhelm Weitlings zur Arbeiterbewegung in den Vereinigten Staaten von Amerika 1846–1856*. Hamburg, 1990.
Mason, Timothy. *Social Policy in the Third Reich*. Oxford, 1993.
Mattelart, Armand. *Mapping World Communication: War, Progress, Culture*. Minneapolis/London, 1994.
McCarthy, John A., and Katrin Schneider, eds. *The Future of Germanistik in the USA: Changing our Prospects*. Nashville, 1996.
McCormick, E. Allen, ed. *Germans in America: Aspects of German-American Relations in the Nineteenth Century*. New York, 1983.
McMaster, Richard K. *Land, Piety, Peoplehood: The Establishment of Mennonite Communities in America, 1683–1790*. Scottdale, PA, 1985.
McSeveney, Samuel T. *The Politics of Depression*. New York, 1971.
Mehring, Franz. *Geschichte der deutschen Sozialdemokratie II: Von Lassalles "Offenem Antwortschreiben" bis zum Erfurter Programm 1863 bis 1891*. Berlin, 1960.
Merkl, Peter H., ed. *The Federal Republic of Germany at Forty*. New York, 1989.
_____, ed. *The Federal Republic of Germany at Forty-Five: Union Without Unity*. New York, 1995.
Merritt, Anna J., and Richard L. Merritt, eds. *Public Opinion in Occupied Germany: The OMGUS Surveys, 1945–1949*. Urbana, 1970.
Merritt, Anna J., and Richard L. Merritt, eds. *Public Opinion in Semisovereign Germany: The HICOG Surveys, 1949–1955*. Urbana/Chicago, 1980.
Merritt, Richard L. *Democracy Imposed: U.S. Occupation Policy and the German Public, 1945–1949*. New Haven/London, 1995.
Meyer, Hildegard. *Nord-Amerika im Urteil des deutschen Schrifttums bis zur Mitte des 19. Jahrhunderts*. Hamburg, 1929.
Milich, Klaus, and Jeffrey Peck, eds. *Multiculturalism in Transit: A German-American Exchange*. New York, 1998.
Milton, Arthur. *Berlin in Seven Days: A Guide for People in a Hurry*. New York, 1935.
Molho, Anthony, and Gordon S. Wood, eds. *Imagined Histories: American Historians Interpret the Past*. Princeton, 1998.
Molnar, Thomas. *The Emerging Atlantic Culture*. New Brunswick, NJ/London, 1994.
Moore, R. Laurence. *European Socialists and the American Promised Land*. New York, 1970.
Morgan, Roger. *The United States and West Germany, 1945–1973: A Study in Alliance Politics*. London, 1974.
Mulder, John M., and John F. Wilson, eds. *Religion in American History: Interpretive Essays*. Englewood Cliffs, NJ, 1978.
Müller, Emil-Peter. *Antiamerikanismus in Deutschland: zwischen Care-Paket und Cruise Missile*. Cologne, 1986.
Mullin, Robert Bruce, and Russell E. Richey, eds. *Reimagining Denominationalism: Interpretive Essays*. New York/Oxford, 1994.
Nadel, Stanley. *Little Germany: Ethnicity, Religion and Class in New York City, 1845–80*. Urbana, 1990.

Natter, Wolfgang G. *Literature at War, 1914–1940: Representing the "Time of Greatness" in Germany*. New Haven/London, 1999.

Nelson, Bruce C. *Beyond the Martyrs: A Social History of Chicago's Anarchists, 1870–1900*. New Brunswick, NJ, 1988.

Nelson, Cary, and Dilip Parameshwar Gaonkar, eds. *Disciplinarity and Dissent in Cultural Studies*. New York/London, 1996.

Neuhaus, Richard John, and Michael Cromartie, eds. *Piety and Politics: Evangelicals and Fundamentalists Confront the World*. Washington, D.C., 1987.

Niebuhr, H. Richard, Wilhelm Pauck, and Francis Miller. *The Church against the World*. Chicago/New York, 1935.

Niedhart, Gottfried, Detlef Junker, and Michael W. Richter, eds. *Deutschland in Europa: Nationale Interessen und internationale Ordnung im 20. Jahrhundert*. Mannheim, 1997.

Niethammer, Lutz, ed. *"Hinterher merkt man, daß es richtig war, daß es schiefgegangen ist:" Nachkriegs-Erfahrungen im Ruhrgebiet*. Vol. 2 of *Lebensgeschichte und Sozialkultur im Ruhrgebiet 1930 bis 1960*. Bonn, 1983.

Niraumand, Mariam. *The Americanization of the Holocaust*. Berlin, 1995.

Noelle-Neumann, Elisabeth, and Renate Köcher. *Die verletzte Nation: Über den Versuch der Deutschen, ihren Charakter zu ändern*. Stuttgart, 1987.

Nolan, Mary. *Visions of Modernity: American Business and the Modernization of Germany*. Oxford/New York, 1994.

Noll, Mark. *History of Christianity in the United States and Canada*. Grand Rapids, MI, 1992.

Nordhoff, Charles. *The Communistic Societies of the United States from Personal Observations*. New York, 1966.

Novick, Peter. *The Holocaust in American Life*. Boston/New York, 1999.

Obermann, Karl. *Joseph Weydemeyer: Ein Lebensbild, 1818–1866*. Berlin, 1968.

Oestreicher, Richard. *Solidarity and Fragmentation: Working People and Class Consciousness in Detroit, 1875–1900*. Urbana, 1986.

Opitz, Reinhard, ed. *Europastrategien des deutschen Kapitals*. Cologne, 1977.

Organization for European Economic Co-operation, ed. *Tourism and European Recovery: An OEEC Report*. Paris, 1951.

Ostendorf, Berndt. *Multikulturelle Gesellschaft: Modell Amerika?* Munich, 1994.

_____. *Creolization and Creoles: The Concepts and their History with Special Attention to Louisiana*. Odense, 1997.

Otte, Max. *A Rising Middle Power? German Foreign Policy in Transformation, 1989–1999*. New York, 2000.

Padover, Saul K. *Experiment in Germany: The Story of an American Intelligence Officer*. New York, 1945.

Peabody, Elizabeth Palmer. *Letters of Elizabeth Palmer Peabody, American Renaissance Woman*. Edited by Bruce A. Ronda. Middletown, CT, 1984.

Pells, Richard. *Not Like Us: How Europeans Have Loved, Hated and Transformed American Culture Since World War II*. New York, 1997.

Peterson, Brent O. *Popular Narratives and Ethnic Identity: Literature and Community in Die Abendschule*. Ithaca, 1991.

Peterson, Edward N. *The American Occupation of Germany: Retreat to Victory*. Detroit, 1978.

Pickle, Linda S. *Contented among Strangers: Rural German-Speaking Women and their Families in the Nineteenth-Century Midwest*. Urbana, 1996.

Pierard, Richard V., ed. *The Revolution of the Candles: Christians in the Revolution of the German Democratic Republic*. Translated by Edwin P. Arnold. Macon, 1996.

Poiger, Uta G. *Jazz, Rock, and Rebels: Cold War Politics and American Culture in a Divided Germany*. Berkeley/Los Angeles, 2000.

Pommerin, Reiner, ed. *The American Impact on Postwar Germany*. Providence/Oxford, 1995.

Poore, Carol J. *German-American Socialist Literature, 1865–1900*. Bern, 1982.

_____. *Deutsch-amerikanische sozialistische Literatur, 1865–1900*. Berlin, 1987.

Pratt, Mary Louise. *Imperial Eyes: Travel Writing and Transculturation*. London/New York, 1992.

Prelinger, Catherine M. *Charity, Challenge, and Change: Religious Dimensions of the Mid-Nineteenth-Century Women's Movement in Germany*. Westport, CT, 1987.

Pruys, Guido Marc. *Die Rhetorik der Filmsynchronisation: Wie ausländische Spielfilme in Deutschland zensiert, verändert und gesehen werden.* (Medienbibliothek: Serie B, Studien; Bd. 14.) Tübingen, 1997.

Quill, Timothy. *The Impact of the Liturgical Movement on American Lutheranism.* Lanham, MD, 1997.

Reichmann, Eberhard, ed. *The Teaching of German: Problems and Methods.* Philadelphia, 1970.

Rentschler, Eric. *The Ministry of Illusion: Nazi Cinema and Its Afterlife.* Cambridge, 1996.

Resek, Carl, ed. *War and the Intellectuals: Essays by Randolph S. Bourne, 1915–1919.* New York/Evanston, 1964.

Ritter, Gerhard A. *Die Sozialdemokratie im Deutschen Kaiserreich in sozialgeschichtlicher Perspektive.* Munich, 1989.

_____. *Arbeiter, Arbeiterbewegung und soziale Ideen in Deutschland: Beiträge zur Geschichte des 19. und 20. Jahrhunderts.* Munich, 1996.

Ritter, Gerhard A., and Klaus Tenfelde. *Arbeiter im Deutschen Kaiserreich 1871–1914.* Bonn, 1992.

Robert, R. *Konzentrationspolitik in der Bundesrepublik.* Berlin, 1976.

Roeber, A. Gregg. *Palatines, Liberty, and Property: German Lutherans in Colonial British America.* Baltimore, 1993.

Roediger, David. *The Wages of Whiteness: Race and the Making of the American Working Class.* London, 1991.

_____. *Towards the Abolition of Whiteness: Essays on Race, Politics, and Working-Class History.* London, 1994.

Rollin, Roger, ed. *The Americanization of the Global Village: Essays in Contemporary Popular Culture.* Bowling Green, 1989.

Roof, Judith, and Robyn Wiegman, eds. *Who Can Speak? Authority and Critical Identity.* Urbana/Chicago, 1995.

Rosenbaum, Ron. *Explaining Hitler: The Search for the Origins of His Evil.* New York, 1998.

Ross, Steven J. *Workers on the Edge: Work, Leisure, and Politics in Industrializing Cincinnati, 1788–1890.* New York, 1985.

Roth, Guenther. *The Social Democrats in Imperial Germany: A Study in Working-Class Isolation and National Integration.* Totowa, NJ, 1963.

Rudolph, Frederick. *The American College and University: A History.* New York, 1962.

Rupieper, Hermann-Josef. *Der besetzte Verbündete: Die amerikanische Deutschlandpolitik 1949–1955.* Opladen, 1991.

Rupieper, Hermann-Josef et al., eds. *American Policy and the Reconstruction of West Germany.* Washington, D.C./New York, 1993.

Sachse, Julius Friedrich. *The German Pietists of Provincial Pennsylvania, 1694–1708.* Philadelphia, 1895.

Saldívar, José David. *The Dialectics of Our America: Genealogy, Cultural Critique, and Literary History.* Durham, NC, 1991.

_____. *Border Matters: Remapping American Cultural Studies.* Berkeley, 1997.

Schem, Alexander J. *Deutsch-amerikanisches Conversations-Lexicon.* New York, 1871.

Schirrmacher, Frank, ed. *Die Walser-Bubis-Debatte: Eine Dokumentation.* Frankfurt, 1999.

Schissler, Hanna, ed. *The Miracle Years: A Cultural History of West Germany, 1949–1968.* Princeton/Oxford, 2000.

Schlüter, Hermann. *Die Anfänge der deutschen Arbeiterbewegung in Amerika.* Stuttgart, 1907.

_____. *Die Internationale in Amerika: Ein Beitrag zur Geschichte der Arbeiterbewegung in den Vereinigten Staaten.* Chicago, 1918.

Schmidt, Alexander. *Reisen in die Moderne: Der Amerika-Diskurs des deutschen Bürgertums vor dem Ersten Weltkrieg im europäischen Vergleich.* Berlin, 1997.

Schmidt, Eberhart. *Die verhinderte Neuordnung.* Frankfurt, 1981.

Schmidtchen, Gerhard. *Was den Deutschen heilig ist: Religiöse und politische Strömungen in der Bundesrepublik Deutschland.* Munich, 1979.

Schnoor, Rainer, ed. *Amerikanistik in der DDR: Geschichte-Analysen-Zeitzeugenberichte.* Berlin, 1999.

Schoenbaum, David, and Elizabeth Pond. *Annäherung an Deutschland: Die Strapazen der Normalität.* Stuttgart, 1997.

Schulte-Sasse, Linda. *Entertaining the Third Reich: Illusions of Wholeness in Nazi Cinema*. Durham, NC, 1997.

Schurz, Carl. *Intimate Letters of Carl Schurz, 1841–1869*. Edited and translated by Joseph Schafer. Madison, 1928.

Schwarz, Angela. *Die Reise ins Dritte Reich: Britische Augenzeugen im nationalsozialistischen Deutschland (1933–1939)*. Göttingen/Zurich, 1993.

Senghaas, Dieter. *Abschreckung und Frieden: Studien zur Kritik organisierter Friedlosigkeit*. Frankfurt, 1969.

Shafir, Shlomo. *Ambiguous Relations: The American Jewish Community and Germany Since 1945*. Detroit, 1999.

Shirer, William L. *End of a Berlin Diary*. New York, 1947.

Shore, Elliott, Ken Fones-Wolf, and James P. Danky, eds. *The German-American Radical Press: The Shaping of a Left Political Culture, 1850–1940*. Urbana/Chicago, 1992.

Sklar, Kathryn Kish, Anja Schüler and Susan Strasser, eds. *Social Justice Feminists in the United States and Germany*. Ithaca, 1998.

Skocpol, Theda. *Protecting Soldiers and Mothers: The Political Origins of Social Policy in the United States*. Cambridge/London, 1992.

Sloterdijk, Peter. *Versprechen auf Deutsch*. Frankfurt, 1990.

Sollors, Werner, ed. *The Invention of Ethnicity*. New York, 1989.

Smith, Goldwin. *A Plea for the Abolition of Tests in the University of Oxford*. Oxford, 1864.

Stanton, Elizabeth Cady, Susan B. Anthony, and Mathila J. Gage, eds. *History of Woman Suffrage*. 3 vols. Rochester, NY, 1881.

Stern, Fritz. *Einstein's German World*. Princeton, 1999.

Stoeffler, F. Ernest. *The Rise of Evangelical Pietism*. Leiden, 1965.

_____. *German Pietism during the Eighteenth Century*. Leiden, 1973.

Stokes, Raymond G. *Divide and Prosper: The Heirs of I. G. Farben under Allied Authority, 1945–1951*. Berkeley, 1988.

Stölken-Fitschen, Ilona. *Atombombe und Geistesgeschichte: Eine Studie der fünfziger Jahre aus deutscher Sicht*. Baden-Baden, 1995.

Stuecher, Dorothea. *Twice Removed: The Experience of German-American Women Writers in the 19th Century*. New York, 1990.

Stummer, Peter O., and Christopher Balme, eds. *Fusion of Cultures?* Amsterdam/Atlanta, 1996.

Swoboda, Jörg. *Die Revolution der Kerzen: Christen in den Umwälzungen der DDR*. Wuppertal/Kassel, 1990.

Tatar, Maria M. *Lustmord: Sexual Murder in Weimar Germany*. Princeton, 1995.

Taylor, Jr., Henry Louis, ed. *Race and the City: Work, Community, and Protest in Cincinnati, 1820–1970*. Urbana, 1993.

Terrell, Mary Church. *A Colored Woman in a White World*. 1940 edition. New York, 1996.

Tent, James F. *Mission on the Rhine*. Chicago, 1982.

Teraoka, Arlene Akiko. *East, West, and Others: The Third World in Postwar German Literature*. Lincoln, 1996.

Tharp, Louise Hall. *The Peabody Sisters of Salem*. Boston, 1950.

Thernstrom, Stephan, ed. *Harvard Encyclopedia of American Ethnic Groups*. Cambridge, MA, 1980.

Thwing, Charles Franklin. *The American and the German University: One Hundred Years of History*. New York, 1928.

Timm, Angelika. *Jewish Claims Against East Germany: Moral Obligation and Pragmatic Policy*. Budapest, 1997.

Tolzmann, Don Heinrich. *The Cincinnati Germans after the Great War*. New York, 1987.

Trachtenberg, Marc. *A Constructed Peace: The Making of the European Settlement, 1945–1963*. Princeton, 1999.

Trefousse, Hans L. *Carl Schurz: A Biography*. Knoxville, 1982.

_____, ed. *Germany and America: Essays on Problems of International Relations and Immigration*. New York, 1980.

Trommler, Frank, and Joseph McVeigh, eds. *America and the Germans: An Assessment of a Three-Hundred-Year History*. 2 vols. Philadelphia, 1985.

Turner, James. *Without God, Without Creed: The Origins of Unbelief in America.* Baltimore/London, 1985.

Turner, Stephen. *The Social Theory of Practices: Tradition, Tacit Knowledge, and Presuppositions.* Chicago, 1994.

Tyler, Alice Felt. *Freedom's Ferment: Phases of American Social History from the Colonial Period to the Outbreak of the Civil War.* New York, 1962.

Urwin, Derek W. *The Community of Europe: A History of European Integration since 1945.* London, 1995.

Van Cleve, John, and A. Leslie Willson. *Remarks on the Needed Reform of German Studies in the United States.* Columbia, SC, 1993.

Vecoli, Rudolph J., and Suzanne M. Sinke, eds. *A Century of European Migrations, 1830–1930.* Urbana/Chicago, 1991.

Vogel, Rolf, ed. *The German Path to Israel.* London, 1969.

Wagner, Maria, ed. *Was die Deutschen aus Amerika berichteten, 1828–1865.* Stuttgart, 1985.

Wagnleitner, Reinhold. *Coca-Colonization and the Cold War: The Cultural Mission of the United States in Austria after the Second World War.* Chapel Hill, 1994.

Walker, Mack. *Germany and the Emigration, 1816–1885.* Cambridge, MA, 1964.

Walz, John Albrecht. *German Influence in American Education and Culture.* Philadelphia, 1936.

Weidenfeld, Werner. *America and Europe: Is the Break Inevitable?* Gütersloh, 1996.

Weigelt, Klaus, ed. *Das Deutschland- und Amerikabild: Beiträge zum gegenseitigen Verständnis beider Völker.* Melle, 1986.

Weiner, Marc A. *Richard Wagner and the Anti-Semitic Imagination.* Lincoln, 1995.

Wellbery, David E. *The Specular Moment: Goethe's Early Lyric and the Beginnings of Romanticism.* Stanford, 1996.

Wellenreuther, Hermann. *Glaube und Politik in Pennsylvania, 1681–1776: Die Wandlungen der Obrigkeitsdoktrin und des Peace Testimony der Quäker.* Cologne/Vienna, 1972.

White, Hayden. *Metahistory: The Historical Imagination in Nineteenth-Century Europe.* Baltimore/London, 1973.

Willett, Ralph. *The Americanization of Germany, 1945–1949.* London/New York, 1989.

Wilson, W. Daniel. *Das Goethe-Tabu: Protest und Menschenrechte im klassischen Weimar.* Munich, 1999.

Wittke, Carl. *The Utopian Communist: A Biography of Wilhelm Weitling, Nineteenth-Century Reformer.* Baton Rouge, 1950.

_____. *Refugees of Revolution: The German Forty-Eighters in America.* Philadelphia, 1952.

_____. *The German Language Press in America.* Lexington, KY, 1957.

Wokeck, Marianne S. *Trade in Strangers: The Beginnings of Mass Migration to North America.* University Park, 1999.

Woodward, C. Vann. *The Old World's New World.* New York/Oxford, 1991.

Wuthnow, Robert. *After Heaven: Spirituality in America Since the 1950s.* Berkeley, 1998.

Yoder, John H. *The Christian Witness to the State.* Newton, KS, 1964.

_____. *The Politics of Jesus.* Grand Rapids, 1972.

Zantop, Susanne. *Colonial Fantasies: Conquest, Family, and Nation in Precolonial Germany, 1770–1870.* Durham, NC, 1997.

Zentner, Kurt, ed. *Aufstieg aus dem Nichts: Deutschland von 1945 bis 1953. Eine Soziographie in zwei Bänden.* 2 vols. Cologne/Berlin, 1954.

Zucker, Adolf E., ed. *The Forty-Eighters: Political Refugees of the German Revolution of 1848.* New York, 1950.

Zuckermann, Moshe. *Zweierlei Holocaust: Der Holocaust in den politischen Kulturen Israels und Deutschlands.* Göttingen, 1998.

Zwahr, Hartmut. *Zur Konstituierung des Proletariats als Klasse: Strukturuntersuchungen über das Leipziger Proletariat während der industriellen Revolution.* Munich, 1981.

_____, ed. *Die Konstituierung der deutschen Arbeiterklasse von den dreißiger bis zu den siebziger Jahren des 19. Jahrhunderts.* Berlin, 1981.

INDEX

GERMAN MINORITIES IN EUROPE
Ethnic Identity and Cultural Belonging

Edited by **Stefan Wolff**

The study of ethnic minorities and their role in the domestic politics of their host states has long attracted scholars from a wide range of disciplines in the social sciences and humanities. By contrast, national (or external) minorities have been underrepresented in the literature on ethnic minorities, although interest has increased since the collapse of communism and, more recently, the eruption of violent conflict in Kosovo. Though numbering in the millions and spread over twenty countries in western, central, and eastern Europe, ethnic Germans in particular have attracted little attention.

This volume addresses the issue of Germany's external minorities, exploring the complex interrelationship between their ethnic identity and sense of cultural belonging on the one hand, and the political, economic, legal, and social situation in their respective societies on the other. Leading specialists, representing a wide spectrum of viewpoints on the social and political conditions under which German minorities live today, provide case studies of all the major individual minority groups. In this way, a comprehensive picture of Germans and German culture in Europe emerges that provides both historical and contemporary perspectives on a diaspora community with an uncertain future between assimilation, segregation, and emigration.

2001. 248 pages, 6 maps, 6 tables, bibliog., index
ISBN 1-57181-738-7 hardback **$45.00/£30.00**
ISBN 1-57181-342-X paperback **$22.50/£15.00**

CROSSING BOUNDARIES

*The Exclusion and Inclusion of Minorities
in Germany and the United States*

Edited by **Larry Eugene Jones**

"Crossing Boundaries"—these two words serve not only as the leitmotiv around which this collection of essays has been organized but also as a metaphor for the life and career of the person who inspired their composition—Georg G. Iggers, whose entire life has been one of crossing boundaries: geographical, racial, and professional. Just as Iggers has done his best as a historian to break down professional and disciplinary boundaries, this volume examines, from different angles, the ways in which Germany and the United States have dealt with the inclusion and exclusion of minorities.

Comparing the respective fates of the Jews in Germany and the African Americans in the United States, this collection offers new insight as to how and why the struggle for equality played out so differently in the two countries and in what ways the issues of migration, multiethnicity, discrimination, and integration have informed the historical discourse in the postmodern era. Larry Eugene Jones is Professor of History at Canisius College.

Summer 2001. 272 pages, bibliog.
ISBN 1-57181-285-7 hardback ca. **$69.95/£47.00**
ISBN 1-57181-306-3 paperback ca. **$25.00/£17.00**

CELEBRATING ETHNICITY AND NATION

*American Festive Culture from the Revolution
to the Early 20th Century*

Edited by **Jürgen Heideking, Geneviève Fabre,** and **Kai Dreisbach**

Arising out of the context of the reconfiguration of Europe, new perspectives are applied by the authors of this volume to the process of nation-building in the United States. By focusing on a variety of public celebrations and festivities from the Revolution to the early twentieth century—the formative period of American national identity—the authors reveal the complex inter-relationships among collective identities on the local, regional, and national level, which, over time, shaped the peculiar character of American national-ism. This volume combines vivid descriptions of various public celebrations with a sophisticated methodological and theoretical approach.

2001. 304 pages, bibliog., index
ISBN 1-57181-237-7 hardback **$69.95/£47.00**
ISBN 1-57181-243-1 paperback **$25.00/£17.00**

Volume 1 of European Studies in American History